MISSION TO LATIN AMERICA

*The Successes and Failures
of a Twentieth Century Crusade*

Gerald M. Costello

ORBIS BOOKS
Maryknoll, New York 10545

The Catholic Foreign Mission Society of America (Maryknoll) recruits and trains people for overseas missionary service. Through Orbis Books Maryknoll aims to foster the international dialogue that is essential to mission. The books published, however, reflect the opinions of their authors and are not meant to represent the official position of the Society.

Library of Congress Cataloging in Publication Data

Costello, Gerald M.
  Mission to Latin America.

  1. Missions—Latin America. 2. Catholic Church in Latin America. I. Title.
BV2831.C66   266'.2'8   78-12974
ISBN 0-88344-312-0

Gerald M. Costello has been a newspaperman since his graduation from the University of Notre Dame in 1952, working in the daily, weekly and religious journalism fields. He is the founding editor of the Paterson diocesan weekly, The Beacon, twice winner (1975 and 1977) of the Catholic Press Association's highest award for general excellence. He lives with his wife and six children in Pompton Plains, N.J.

To my family:
My wife, Jane;
my children, Nancy, Eileen,
Michael, Brian, John, and Robert;
my parents, Michael and Catherine Costello;
and to the memory of a great man:
the late Bishop Lawrence B. Casey of Paterson

Contents

Foreword

It has been called a modern crusade, a description not that far off the mark. There was, indeed, a crusading spirit in the hearts of the thousands of American men and women, lay and religious, who answered Pope John's plea to help the church in Latin America. But a crusade needs more than enthusiasm and good intentions in order to succeed, and this one, like those of long ago, showed early signs of faltering. By all accounts, it has fallen short of its original goals.

Mission to Latin America is the story of that crusade. I have followed the progress of the book closely, because its subject matter is one of deep personal concern to me. It was at Notre Dame, for example, at a meeting of religious superiors in 1961, that a representative of Pope John XXIII first delivered the Holy Father's ringing call for U.S. religious communities to "tithe" their priests and sisters for Latin America.

A good number of my fellow priests of the Congregation of the Holy Cross have served as missioners in Latin America. (Many of them are still there; others, regrettably, ran afoul of leaders of oppressive regimes and were forced to return to the United States.)

Notre Dame was the training center for the first group of volunteers in the Peace Corps, which was really an effort that paralleled, under government auspices, what the U.S. church was trying to do. That first class was being trained for an agricultural project in Chile, and I promised them that if they made it I'd visit them wherever they were working throughout the thousand-mile long central valley of Chile. It turned out to be a great opportunity to see the rural poor where they lived.

But my interest in Latin America goes far beyond the outward associations of university and religious community. I have made more than thirty trips to Latin America since my first visit in 1956, and I have seen what a life of poverty is like throughout the southern hemisphere.

No one who has witnessed the tragic effects of the migration of impoverished *campesinos* to the cities—the endless rings of slums around Lima or Rio or Mexico City—can forget the sight, or ignore the needs they represent. No one who has seen ramshackle one-room schoolhouses where planks double as chairs and desks—and who realizes that only half of Latin America's children will get even *that* far—can forget our obligation to teach. No one who has seen the enormous Amazon basin or the great arable plains beyond the mountains of Colombia and Venezuela can escape the realization that while it might be no better than a short-range solution, the land is there to provide better food for millions of poor people—if they can be given the means to improve their agriculture.

Thus my own concern for Latin America and its people. The concerns are some of the same ones, I believe, that impelled our priests, sisters, and lay people to answer Pope John's call.

How will the story of the United States' modern mission crusade end? It is too early to say, for it is still going on. Great people have been involved as the story has unfolded thus far: Pope John himself; the remarkable Monsignor Luigi Ligutti, whose interests and influence have been limited only by the size of the world and the work of Christ's church; Cardinal Richard Cushing, who made the needs of Latin America his own; Father John Considine, who climaxed his long Maryknoll mission career by directing this historic Latin American endeavor.

Their stories are here. So, too, are those of the missioners themselves, the men and women who have tried to be the "other Christs" that Latin America so desperately needs.

It is fitting that they should be at the heart of this book, for they and all the others living and working with Latin America's poor and oppressed are those who are the subject of this beautiful passage from "La pastoral en las misiones de América Latina," cited in Gustavo Gutiérrez's *Theology of Liberation:*

> All the dynamism of the cosmos, and of human history, the movements toward the creation of a more just and fraternal world, the overcoming of social inequities among men, the efforts, so urgently needed on our continent, to liberate man from all that depersonalizes him—physical and moral misery, ignorance and hunger, as well as the awareness of human dignity, all these originate, are transformed, and reach their perfection in the saving work of Christ. In Him and through Him, salvation is present at the heart of man's history.

—Theodore M. Hesburgh, C.S.C.

Acknowledgments

This book could not have been written without the thoughtful and considerate help of many people, especially the U.S. missioners in Latin America, men and women, who were interviewed or with whom I corresponded. Their experiences and insights are central to the judgments that the book reaches. I hope they will know how much I am indebted to them all.

Many others must be thanked:

Father John Reedy, C.S.C., director of Ave Maria Press, and James O'Gara, editor of *Commonweal*, for initial and sustaining encouragement.

Gary MacEoin, whose reporting and commentary on Latin America has enriched the English-speaking world for years, for advice and generously offered critical evaluations.

Father Louis M. Colonnese, former director of the Division for Latin America, U.S. Catholic Conference, for sharing a great volume of previously unpublished material related to the U.S. mission program.

Anne Buckley, managing editor of *The Advocate*, Newark, for many helpful editorial suggestions, and to others who read all or part of the manuscript and offered advice and/or corrections: Father Frederick McGuire, C.M., development director of the Center for Applied Research in the Apostolate (CARA); Father William McIntire, M.M., secretary general of Maryknoll; Frances L. Neason, executive director, Secretariat for Latin America, National Conference of Catholic Bishops; and Father Joseph O'Hare, S.J., editor of *America*.

Patricia McFaul, of the editorial staff of *The Long Island Catholic*, Rockville Centre, for compiling statistical information on the U.S. mission program in Latin America.

Those who shared previously unpublished material that has added greatly to the manuscript: Father George Mader of the Newark Archdiocese, former interim director of the Papal Volunteers for Latin America; Father Joseph Nangle, O.F.M., adviser for political issues in the Department of Social Development and World Peace, U.S. Catholic Conference; and Sister Mary O'Keefe, O.P., of Edgewood College, Madison, Wisconsin.

Missioners in Latin America whose hospitality was most welcome and is still appreciated: Fathers Leo Donnelly, S.S.C.; Elias Manning, O.F.M., Conv.; Gerard McCrane, M.M.; Fidelis McKee, O.F.M., Donald Steed, M.M.; and Frank Maurovich, former Maryknoll Associate.

Those whose assistance and friendship have been of inestimable value, in many ways: Richard W. Conklin, director of information services, University of Notre Dame; Bishop John Fitzpatrick of Brownsville, former chairman, Committee for the Church in Latin America, NCCB; Father Joseph Fitzpatrick, S.J., chairman, department of sociology, Fordham University; Monsignor Joseph Gremillion, Fellow in Theology, University of Notre Dame; Bishop Nevin Hayes, O. Carm., auxiliary bishop of Chicago and chairman, Committee for the Church in Latin America, NCCB; Father Theodore M. Hesburgh, C.S.C., president, University of Notre Dame; Thomas Quigley, head of the Latin America section of the Justice and Peace Division, U.S. Catholic Conference; Bishop James S. Rausch of Phoenix, former general secretary, USCC-NCCB.

Staff members of *The Beacon* for their patience and assistance, particularly my former secretary, Gail Greco Murphy; Leo P. Carroll, business and advertising manager; and Victor F. Winkler, assistant editor.

Those from other diocesan newspapers who assisted in making material available: Patricia Kern of the *Catholic Times*, Columbus; Thomas Kilbridge, *The Pilot*, Boston; William McShane of the *St. Louis Review;* and Father Gerald Shekleton of *The Witness*, Dubuque; and to various representatives of NC News Service, Washington, especially John Muthig, Rome bureau chief, and Jaime Fonseca, Latin America specialist.

Those at Orbis Books for their encouragement, especially Philip Scharper and John Eagleson.

And finally, an acknowledgment of the debt everyone interested in the mission role of the U.S. church owes to a great man of God, Father John J. Considine, M.M.

Introduction

In the early 1960s the Roman Catholic church in the United States undertook a collective mission effort unprecedented in its history. Urged on by pleas from Rome, alarmed by the spread of "godless" communism, encouraged by an increasingly international-minded hierarchy, and moved by a sincere desire to help others in Christ's name, the U.S. church sent thousands of its men and women—priests and brothers, sisters, lay people—to Latin America. This book is the story of that enterprise—why it came about, how it fared, where it stands today.

On the surface, many would judge it a failure. The missioners of the sixties have come home, most of them, and the problems of Latin America seem no less staggering than they did before the missioners arrived. But that is too flat a judgment, too quick a disposition of the effort involved: the spartan living, the sweat and tears, the loneliness and frustration—and the terribly small rewards. There were, and there continue to be, successes as well as failures. I will attempt to discuss them both. This book is a journalist's report on one phenomenon of U.S. church life—our mission experience in Latin America.

Historians, theologians, and social scientists have written in scholarly detail on many of the points with which this book deals. In preparing this work, I have benefited from their judgments and, where appropriate, I have attempted to acknowledge them by name. But as a reporter I have relied more on the experiences of the men and women who lived this mission undertaking. I have conducted more than one hundred interviews—in Latin America, the United States, Canada, and Rome—with missioners, former missioners, and those who are connected in some way with their work. In addition, I have corresponded with another 150 people who have had a mission interest in Latin America. I owe a special debt to all of them, for their accounts, based on personal experience, form the heart of this book.

One of those whom I interviewed—Cardinal Antonio Samore, the man Pius XII chose to direct Latin American activities, now librarian and archivist of the Holy Roman Church—objects to the term "missioner" in speaking of foreign religious personnel who go to work in Latin American countries. "This has been a Catholic continent for several centuries," he points out. "The word 'mission' carries with it a meaning of evangelization, which is not really appropriate."

There is no room for argument, of course, on technical grounds. Strictly

1

speaking, our people in Latin America are not "missionaries." However, I will make use of that commonly accepted term for ease of expression and understanding. And it should be remembered that while many of those to whom our U.S. men and women went to minister were Catholic in name, their faith experience had been almost nonexistent. In that sense, our priests and sisters were—and are—missioners in the finest tradition of the church, people who bring Christ's Word to those places where it is not known.

The years have brought troubling questions. Should we have gone at all? Should we be there now? Should we plan to go in the future? There are no simple answers; no easy yes, no outright no. There are qualifications without end, fine points for the historians and missiologists to debate for years to come. But the fact is that we *did* go, that we continue to be there. Despite the mistakes—and they have been many—what must be remembered is that thousands of U.S. Christians responded to a call for help, and answered it in good faith.

This book is written with them in mind—somewhat in awe of their sacrifices, and in appreciation for them. It is written as well with thoughts of all—North Americans, Latin Americans, and others throughout the world—who are trying to find the best way to translate Christ's eternal message of love into a better life for our millions of brothers and sisters in Latin America.

Pompton Plains, N.J.
January 1979

1

Caranavi

Caranavi, Bolivia. Regional market town, Nor Yungas section. Population, 4,000; elevation, about 2,000 feet.

Caranavi. It sits in a clearing in a jungle area northeast of La Paz. By air it is only eighty miles away from the capital, but most travelers journey by jeep, truck, or bus. It takes six hours to negotiate those eighty miles on a primitive switchback road that is terrifying to a first-time visitor.

It begins easily enough, a wide gray-dirt straight line slicing across a high plateau just east of La Paz. Herds of llama poke about the thin tufts of grass off to the side. The road lifts, then, and narrows, reaching the *cumbre*—the crest of this Andean ridge more than 16,000 feet high, usually hidden by thick, clinging mists—before it begins its dizzying plunge down and down into Caranavi.

The road becomes impossibly narrow, hugging the sides of steep Andean slopes where the dropoffs are measured in thousands of feet. In most places, two vehicles cannot pass; one must back up to the nearest cutout until the other goes by. Every so often the traveler sees tiny cross-topped shrines at the road's edge. Each marks the spot where someone has been killed in a plunge over the side.

Even veterans of the Bolivian jungle find the journey exhausting, and they are as relieved as the first-time traveler to round the final blind curve and see, stretched out below them, Caranavi.

There was no Caranavi until twenty years ago, when the government of President Víctor Paz Estenssoro launched a dramatic land distribution program to improve the life of the Aymara Indians. If Aymara families agreed to move from their barren altiplano homeland, they were given land around new central towns—such as Caranavi—which would be built in the heart of fertile areas.

The Caranavi soil was good, but the steep hillsides made crop production a challenge. That was one problem; the climate was another. Used to the cold thin air of the altiplano, many of the Aymaras found it difficult to adjust to Caranavi's steamy heat. The most pleasant months are July and August, the middle of Bolivia's winter. There is a long rainy season, and in summertime temperatures of 120 degrees are not unusual.

3

Still, many of the Aymara emigres found a better life in Caranavi than they had known on the altiplano. They settled not only in Caranavi, but in dozens of "colonies" on the thickly-vegetated hills around it, extending out some forty or fifty miles from the town. Caranavi became a combination frontier town and commercial center; today its weekend population might climb to nine or ten thousand.

There is a central plaza, a twenty-bed hospital, a school, a military base with several hundred soldiers. One long side street is reserved for the *mercado*, where derby-hatted Aymara women sit in individual family market stalls, selling batteries and threads and notions, vegetables, unrefrigerated meat, dried coca leaves. There is a gasoline station where the pump is literally that; customers hand-pump the fuel from a big barrel into their vehicles.

And there is more: fronting on the plaza, a Roman Catholic church and a rectory, the parish of Our Lady of Divine Love. Two blocks away is a convent. Both rectory and convent are staffed by North Americans, missionaries who responded to the same kind of call heard by thousands of their compatriots and who found themselves, improbably, doing the work of God in this clearing in the Bolivian jungle.

U.S. missioners have been here since 1960, their presence spanning a period of mission involvement unlike anything else in the history of the U.S. church. They came, these North Americans, not only from the traditional mission-sending societies, but from small religious communities and from dioceses all over the United States. They were moved by many things—a crusade against communism, an identification with a vigorous new president, and, perhaps most of all, a personal response to a request from one of history's most beloved popes. They came and they built, and for a while they appeared to prosper. No challenge seemed too much of a test for committed Christians—and committed U.S. Christians, at that.

But a time came when signs of progress leveled, and Caranavi's U.S. missioners began the same kind of self-questioning that was going on in hundreds of other U.S. missions in Latin America: Would this approach be better? Should we make an adjustment here?

Then, gradually, it developed that there were no signs of progress at all; the U.S.-style churches had been built but no more people came than had come before. The questions became doubts. One veteran Bolivian missioner recalled that period not long ago, and put the problem succinctly: the old razzmatazz was gone.

Some of the U.S. missioners went stale. Some men and women left the active ministry. Many went home to their dioceses. They had gone off with pictures and feature stories in diocesan newspapers that joked lightly about their clumsiness in the Spanish language; they came home quietly and took parish assignments and turned down requests to go out and give talks to rosary societies on "the missions." The original mission groups stayed on, and so did a stubborn few of those nonprofessionals who had found their calling in ministering to the tormented people of this vast land—people who had spent generations as victims of one oppressor or another.

Then a new mission approach began to emerge, radically new. It sprang, significantly, from Latin Americans themselves, and it was the haunting specter of oppression that had spawned it. Making people aware of the oppression was part of it; another part was in encouraging them to develop ideas on how to fight it. The missioners who remained began to learn instead of to teach, to serve instead of to lead. And, somehow, that became the operative mission approach, and it goes on—tested, hardened, imperfect, searching. Committed. It has been that way in hundreds of U.S.-staffed missions in Latin America. It has been that way in Caranavi.

A Mission Begins

For purposes of church administration, Caranavi is part of the prelacy of Coroico, a small town between Caranavi and La Paz. The prelacy is the responsibility of the Franciscans' Holy Name Province, headquartered in New York, for reasons that the friars recall today with matter-of-fact bemusement.

The late Father Celsus Wheeler was provincial in the mid-fifties, and in 1957 he accepted an invitation to visit the province's mission in Goiaz, Brazil. He traveled by way of Bolivia in order to visit a friend in Santa Cruz. When Archbishop Umberto Mozzoni, the papal nuncio to Bolivia, heard that Father Celsus would be in La Paz, he asked him to lunch. "And Celsus didn't just go to lunch," one long-time missioner said some years after the incident. "He was wined and dined."

What followed the luncheon, according to the story, was the result of either a classic breakdown in communication or a very fine Italian hand. Mozzoni wired the Franciscan minister general in Rome that Holy Name Province would be taking on a new mission responsibility in Bolivia, to go along with the one it already had in Brazil. Father Celsus, having gone on to Goiaz, returned to New York and professed to be flabbergasted to find the minister general's congratulations for his generous commitment. Father Celsus, the story goes, remembered making no such promise. But take over the prelacy is what Holy Name Province did, and it has been there ever since.

Its only bishop in that time has been Thomas Manning, a native of Baltimore who was thirty-nine years old at his consecration in 1959. The fact that the bishop would be a member of Holy Name Province was, apparently, one of the inducements for the original commitment.

Caranavi is one of a dozen major parishes in the prelacy, which has a population of 200,000. The first priest to serve there was Father Joseph Nangle, a Franciscan from Boston who later was pastor of a Lima parish for many years, spent two years with the U.S. Mission Council in Washington, and is now with the Department of Social Development and World Peace,

U.S. Catholic Conference. He had gone to Caranavi in January 1960, a year and a half after his ordination.

"I was sent to open up Caranavi," he recalled in 1976, "and I had no training at all. I went to Caranavi, and I couldn't even ask for a glass of water. Maybe no one would have had a glass of water to give me," he smiled.

> Conditions were primitive. The town was just opening up; there were maybe fifteen houses in all. I spent every weekend there for three years, until the Paterson diocesan priests came. By that time the population must have jumped 500 percent and Caranavi was beginning to take on the appearance of an organized town. I had even put up a rustic little church. But the Paterson priests didn't have much; they were starting from scratch.

Among the U.S. bishops who were attentive to early papal calls for assistance to Latin America—from both Pope Pius XII and Pope John XXIII—Cardinal Ritter of St. Louis and Boston's Cardinal Cushing are perhaps the best known. But a number of bishops from smaller dioceses were equally responsive. One of them was Bishop James A. McNulty of Paterson, New Jersey.

A courtly man who had been an auxiliary bishop of Newark before his appointment to Paterson in 1953, he credited Pope John's 1961 call for the U.S. church to send 10 percent of its personnel to Latin America as having a strong personal impact on him. Selection of a mission within the Holy Name Franciscans' area of responsibility was a natural next step; the ties between diocese and province ran long and deep. Bishop McNulty composed a brief but effective note to priests of the diocese, explaining the reasons why he had decided to take on a diocesan mission, and asking for volunteers to staff it. Some fifteen priests stepped forward for the job and three were accepted: Fathers Charles Cassidy, Armand Conte, and John Heusser.

The departure ceremony for the Paterson priests filled the Cathedral of St. John the Baptist; the homilist was Bishop Fulton J. Sheen. They underwent four months of training at the language school operated in Lima by the Society of St. James the Apostle, the mission organization founded by Cardinal Cushing, with headquarters in Boston. With that training behind them, and after long consultation sessions with Father Nangle, they began their mission work at Caranavi in late 1962.

"We were ill-matched," Father Heusser recalled more than a decade later, "and we knew it. I remember Joe Nangle telling us it was much easier to run a mission than a mission house. I found out what he meant." Father Cassidy stayed only a brief while before determining that he was not suited personally for mission duty; he returned to the diocese and has been a pastor for many years. Father Heusser and Father Conte stayed on, with Father Heusser as pastor.

"We weren't much different from the rest of the troops sent down here to stem communism," Father Heusser wrote from Bolivia years later. The communist problem was one which troubled Bishop McNulty, who was soon attempting to obtain sisters from the diocese to join the Paterson priests in Caranavi. After receiving a commitment from Mother Joanna Marie of the Sisters of Charity of St. Elizabeth, Convent Station, he wrote her early in 1963: "One matter which caused me some anxiety was the possibility of a communist takeover in Bolivia. I asked about this possibility of the ranking ecclesiastics and Catholic laymen in La Paz. The answer given me was that there is some communistic subversion but the situation, while critical, is not desperate. This is the psychological hour to send help."

There were practical suggestions as well: "It is important that the missionary sisters be generous, flexible, and of outgoing personality. One ought to be skilled in music. . . ."

Bishop McNulty was visiting the Caranavi mission in February 1963, when he learned of his appointment as bishop of Buffalo. His successor, appointed several months later, was Bishop James J. Navagh, who had been bishop of Ogdensburg, New York, and before that, auxiliary bishop of Raleigh.

"Our development as missioners suffered with the changeover," Father Heusser said recently. "There was a marked change in attitude, a different approach to the problem. Bishop McNulty's original thought was that we should rough it. He authorized a dollar a day for our expenses, and I can remember him telling us personally and directly not to get 'luxuries' like a generator." (Father Nangle, the Franciscan, recalled that Bishop McNulty wanted the missioners to have no more than the people themselves, only a few amenities in order to survive. "The Paterson men didn't overdo it, that's for sure," he said.)

But things began to change—even in the final weeks of the McNulty administration. Before leaving Paterson to take over the Buffalo diocese—and after seeing living conditions in Caranavi first-hand—Bishop McNulty upped the daily living allowance to five dollars and authorized purchase not only of a generator, but a refrigerator as well. That approach would grow under Bishop Navagh, who wanted to see signs of progress. "We were on our way," Father Heusser said, "to establishing a parish plant, U.S.A.-style, in the middle of a Bolivian jungle."

Despite some rectory tensions, and despite Father Heusser's misgivings about the scope of the building program, both priests thrust themselves into their assignment. Father Heusser concentrated on strengthening the network of colonies that were all part of the Caranavi parish, and Father Conte stayed closer to home base—acquiring land, building, dealing with the local authorities.

Bishop Navagh was pleased to find what appeared to be a thriving Latin American mission as part of his new diocese. It was a time to move forward, and Bishop Navagh had been in Paterson for only a few weeks when he announced the establishment of a second diocesan mission—this one for Ica, Peru, a coastal town on the Pan-American Highway, some four hours south of Lima. ("I know that we have other burdens and we already have a mission in Bolivia, but unless the diocese is generous and our priests are generous, God will not bless us.")

Meanwhile, he was specific in his directions to Fathers Heusser and Conte:

> Please do not think that material progress is progress, because it is not. There are certain things that we need such as churches and schools and convents and rectories, but these are merely instruments which are useful for the end, which is the sanctification of souls. . . . Your main task is to mix with the people, teach them the gospel, get them to mass and the sacraments, and put them on the road to heaven. I do appreciate that we have to do what we can to help in other respects, but this is the main task, and upon this I direct you to concentrate.

There were regular letters back to the new bishop, spiritual report cards on numbers at masses and confessions ("these are very rare"), and the low quality of a typical *campo* school: "The teacher is very religious, a member of our Legion of Mary, active, and yet her children could not all make the sign of the cross, much less say their Our Father and Hail Mary by memory."

> We had a mission in China when I first entered the community, and I thought of that. I remember my mother saying, "Oh, you wouldn't do that to me, would you?" But the idea stayed in my mind, and after I became a nurse and was still aware of the need in South America, I thought I could go there and cure everybody. Pope John's plea brought it to a head, I guess.

So said Sister Grace Lavina Reilly, interviewed on her golden jubilee as a Sister of Charity in 1976, recalling some of the circumstances that had brought her to Caranavi thirteen years earlier. She was one of the original group of four. She and Sister Mary Ellen were nurses; Sister Mary Frederick and Sister Ann James were teachers.

Sister Mary Frederick adapted to Caranavi particularly well. She was a happy woman who endeared herself to the youngsters of Caranavi as she had to the other Sisters of Charity. At the top of each page of her letters, she would write "God Alone"—as she did early in 1964 to Bishop Navagh: "Please God, we may be able to instruct these dear souls to know and love God and appreciate the sacraments He has given to aid us to salvation. . . . It will be a happy day when we have a church in which Our Lord can stay day and night."

Sister Mary Frederick, who loved Bolivia, was to remain there forever. One of the crosses at the side of the treacherous road from La Paz is there for her. "I was in the convent that day," Sister Grace Lavina recalls.

The other two sisters were working somewhere else and Mary Frederick was going to a colony where Father Heusser was working. There was to be a first communion program that day. A twelve-year-old girl was going with her.

We'll never know exactly what happened, but with a truck coming down the road she was trying to back up enough to give it room to pass by. One of her rear wheels went over, and then the car slipped right over the cliff. The girl had gotten out; she was all right. But Sister Mary Frederick was killed. Killed instantly, I'm sure. Father Armand came and got me and told me the news. He was very comforting, very helpful.

Armand Conte, by this time, had become pastor of the Caranavi parish. Bishop Navagh approved the change in October 1963, explaining in a letter to Father Heusser why Bishop Manning had made it: "You are a good missioner and he thinks that, relieved of the burden of direction, you can give all of your time to the wonderful work of leading God's children to Him."

The work continued. In the summer of 1964, Father Conte told Bishop Navagh that Caranavi's "most pressing need" was another priest. A few months later in the spring of 1965, the mission marked an important day, as Father Heusser wrote to Bishop Navagh: "It was a pleasure to celebrate Mass for the first time in the new church of Caranavi this past Monday. It was raining, and the rain made it a double blessing, for otherwise we would have been dodging the leaks in the old structure."

And yet, for the first time, there were growing signs of pessimism. In August of 1965, Father Conte gave voice to some of them. He wrote to Bishop Navagh:

The mission moves slowly. We have not made the impression desirable as yet. People are slow in reacting. Of course our mentalities and outlooks are so diverse. There is also a lack of communication with other priests to exchange and compare ideas. One can easily go stale. We don't have any information on the changes and directions from Vatican II.

Father Conte complained as well of the lack of timely reading material, difficulties in rectory living—classic mission complaints, to be sure—and concluded with wishes that Bishop Navagh be kept "healthy and strong for many years."

But Father Conte's next letter to the Paterson Chancery, several weeks later, was addressed to Msgr. William Louis, the administrator of the diocese. Bishop Navagh had died in Rome during the final session of the Vatican Council. "It was sudden," Father Conte said, "and hard for us to accept."

The new bishop, installed in May of 1966, was Lawrence B. Casey, sixty-year-old auxiliary of Rochester. Father Conte wrote to him of favorable developments in the mission—an effective convent staff, with the nursing sisters having taken over the responsibility for the hospital; the beginnings of a parochial school. Bishop Casey replied optimistically about restaffing both the Caranavi and Ica missions and about hopes for a personal visit to Caranavi (a hope which had also been expressed by Bishop Navagh, whose delicate health never made it possible). But while the surface might have been calm, the mission was churning within.

The end of the original five-year commitment was approaching, and Father Heusser, looking back ten years later, weighed the Caranavi years soberly:

> The general impression that Caranavi left me with was a deep hurt, a total lack of dialogue, a feeling that we had never really reached the people, money wasted. It was a time of learning, misdirection of efforts, and yet as so often we reminded ourselves, we were only sowing seed; others would reap the benefits. Since then, I've come to respect the refrain: where we labored most, we received the least. I can't explain the why of it, but it seems to be true.

Father Conte sounded a hesitant note before coming home for good:

> The two of us priests here in the mission also have catechists who help in the schools. The area is big, and the immigrant families multiply daily. But the day still has only twenty-four hours, and each priest is still only one man. Will we be able to build a Christian community here in Caranavi, or do we just hold on to what we have with the baptized superstition the "Catholics" profess here?

In Caranavi, in other places in Latin America, and in chanceries and provincial headquarters in the United States, it was a time of reassessment. From the mid-sixties on, talk turned from the question of how best to improve the mission to whether or not the mission should continue. Several factors were involved: discouragement over the lack of visible progress, a growing independence among Latin Americans and a questioning of the North American role, and, perhaps most significantly, an ominous thinning of the ranks in the American priesthood and among women religious.

"We discussed our plans for Bolivia and Peru during the personnel sessions," Bishop Casey wrote to Father Conte in June of 1966. "We decided we would not be able to send anyone down this year because we are so short-handed here." But a year later, when a decision had to be made, the diocese determined it would continue staffing the mission. The Conte-Heusser five-year commitment was up, and they were to be replaced by two other Paterson priests.

Father Heusser, the original pastor, was frank as he described in later years his disappointments in Caranavi. "We went down to set up a North American parish," he said, "and that's what we did. Caranavi is a North American plant, and we had it hung around our necks. I felt a constant tension, especially in the final years; I needed another diocese where I would have freer rein."

The other diocese he chose was not back in the United States, but in Bolivia—the Corocoro diocese, where thirteen priests are spread thin over a rugged land where living conditions are primitive. He is still there today. "After returning to the 'dollar-a-day' type of life that I've lived the past eight years here," he said, "I welcome a comparison in the results these two missions have accomplished. But if there has been success in working as a loner, much of the credit is due to a personality that shies away from crowds, loves the country, and can stand certain physical discomforts."

Armand Conte seemed to embody the qualities a superior might look for in selecting an effective missioner: personal strength, an ability to mix with new people, compassion. Pictures from his mission days show him leading a procession in an Indian fiesta, confetti in his hair; helping a workman at the construction site of a new chapel; tenderly lifting a dying, tubercular woman from her hovel of a home while her four-year-old daughter looks on.

His mission tour over, he came home to Paterson, visited his parents' mom-and-pop Italian grocery store on Summer Street, and reflected on Caranavi: "There's a sense of satisfaction in the priesthood there, more so than here. It's because there's been such a lack of attention to those people, because you feel that you're so much more needed." He admitted to "modest success" in the five years in Caranavi and predicted that the new men would do well as they carried on: "A change, you know, is good for a mission. They'll bring in new ideas, and they'll be good ones. But the work will continue."

Armand Conte became pastor of St. Michael's in Netcong, and, a few years later, of St. Gerard's, a busy parish in Paterson. In 1974 he startled the parish and the diocese by leaving the priesthood and getting married. His wife was from Caranavi.

The priests the diocese decided on to replace the original missioners were Father James Kielty, an Irish-born storyteller with a gift for languages who had served as a White Father missionary in Africa, and Father Daniel Mahoney, a lanky, handsome curate from a diocesan parish in Lincoln Park.

Bishop Casey's interest in keeping the Caranavi mission alive is evident in a letter he wrote to Father Mahoney's parents in October 1967—a note of appreciation for allowing their son to undertake "a very demanding and difficult assignment." He wrote:

The human viewpoint, with all the shortages we have here in the diocese, would be to keep all the priests we could get and not give any to dioceses which needed them more. But this is the Catholic church and our interests are universal, and I honestly believe that one of the reasons the vocations to the priesthood and the sisters are holding up so well in this diocese is due to the fact that we have six devoted priests working in South America, and also a good number of sisters.

At the same time, however, Bishop Casey was becoming aware of growing expressions of independence on the part of the Latin American church. As a member of the U.S. bishops' Latin America committee, he traveled to Chile in late 1967 to attend a meeting of the inter-American bishops. "The message I heard," he recalled years later, "was that they welcomed our presence, but looked forward to the day when they would be self-sufficient as far as the church is concerned. It's a good goal. But it's still a long way from fulfillment."

Father Kielty concentrated his initial efforts in two areas: expanding the catechist program that had been successfully developed by Sister Kathleen Rowe, one of the second group of Sisters of Charity to go to Caranavi, and learning the native Aymara language. He was soon able to offer Mass in Aymara. "It is very well attended," he wrote in April 1968, "and the opposition we expected from the Spanish-speaking did not materialize."

The catechist program covered the hundred colonies in the hills around Caranavi. Chosen by the people of their own villages, the catechists came to Caranavi for organized weekend training sessions and returned to the colonies to conduct religious meetings and serve as spiritual leaders. "You can be cynical about things down here," Father Mahoney said, "until you see something like the way the catechist program is going. That's something that's tremendously encouraging."

The easy-going humor of the two missioners leaned heavily on understatement and, for a time, seemed to buoy them for the more serious work at hand. When he gave up one of his duties—as part-time chaplain to the army base at Caranavi—Father Kielty wrote to Bishop Casey: "Your letter arrived just as I was resigning from the Bolivian Armed Forces. Nobody seemed to be too upset by this blow to the national security, and there already is a Franciscan dying to climb into my uniform."

In the summer of 1968, Father Mahoney joked with an interviewer about the one tennis game he'd managed to get in with Father Kielty: "Here I am, in the middle of Bolivia, with only one other guy around who plays tennis. I can beat him, really beat him—but there's no time to play. That's a crime."

And once, when the Franciscans' regional superior was speaking on a radio hookup to all the Coroico parishes, he reported that on a trip back to the States he had visited Father Celsus, the aging former provincial who had started it all. "Every time he thinks of Bolivia," the superior said, "he cries." Listening in Caranavi, Father Kielty turned to Father Mahoney and uttered a sardonic two-word comment: "He should."

What of the Future?

Underneath the laughter, Father Kielty and Father Mahoney soon were doing some hard thinking about the future of the mission. There had been financial problems; a bad check from a local businessman cost the mission several thousand dollars. But beyond that the missioners seemed confused about their role and their tenure in Caranavi. In September 1968, barely a year after arriving in Caranavi, Father Kielty told Bishop Casey that the mission's future was uncertain. He did not favor closing out Paterson's commitment at that time, but said it should end after five years—with any future priests from the diocese who wanted to volunteer for Latin American mission work joining the Maryknoll missionary society as associate members. He predicted—inaccurately to date, in both cases—that the Franciscans and the Sisters of Charity would be pulling out.

Father Mahoney followed up Father Kielty's visit home with one of his own a month later and pursued some of the same thoughts. He cited basic problems: the long preparation needed for genuinely effective mission work; the necessity (and extreme difficulty) of communicating in Aymara; the physical dangers to religious personnel. He also told Bishop Casey that since Caranavi is a key area in the Coroico prelacy, it needed long-term priests "who have a more professional outlook on the situation than diocesan priests." He also claimed that priests of the Paterson diocese in Caranavi failed to receive effective leadership from Coroico.

If the bishop decided to reconsider his involvement in Caranavi, Father Mahoney suggested, one priest should be withdrawn by the end of the year, and work already begun "as far as the physical structures in Caranavi are concerned" should be completed.

The next day, October 16, 1968, Bishop Casey had a telephone conversation with Bishop Manning, who was on a brief leave from Coroico and was staying in Massachusetts. Bishop Manning agreed that the mission could be run by one priest but thought that Father Mahoney's problems might be exaggerated because of his difficulties in Spanish. In the same conversation, Bishop Manning reported that a vote taken at the Franciscans' general chapter was unanimously in favor of maintaining existing mission commitments—and that therefore they would be staying in Coroico.

Bishop Casey was less sure of the ability of the mission to survive with one priest. Although lacking in mission experience, he was a veteran of church personnel work and felt that compounding normal problems of mission life by living alone would result in the closing of Caranavi. The bishop wanted to keep it going not only to honor the diocese's commitment, but to support the Sisters of Charity—who were firm in their decision to stay on.

Father Kielty had left, however—going to Ica to determine the possibility of signing on at the Peruvian mission—while Father Mahoney was convinced of his ability to handle Caranavi on his own. He bore no ill will toward Father Kielty; instead, he spoke of him eloquently to Bishop Casey: "He is a very deep, spiritual man who does not ask anything for himself, but rather cuts the cake as he sees it. The trouble with having men of integrity is that sometimes they create difficult times for their bishop. . . . We are sorry if we have put you in this situation."

What lay ahead for Caranavi? Father Mahoney considered that question at length in a rambling, unusually candid tape-recording mailed to Bishop Casey at the end of 1968, a month after Father Kielty had departed. "I see nothing now to think that a mistake has been made," he said. He went on for several minutes about the state of the mission: catechists, budget matters, the hiring of a general manager. Then he spoke unhappily of some of the Aymara customs and how they distorted Christian practices—and their effect on the U.S. missioner:

> It really is a terrible experience to come down to Bolivia and find that you are, in the eyes of these people, little more than a glorified witch doctor blessing all their *campos* and other things. There may be value to it. I'm not saying it's completely bad. But certainly we are continuing the thing that has been done for the past four hundred years, which resulted in what we see today in Bolivia in the *campos*—a Christianity of the pagan Inca religion mixed with the Christianity of today. . . . The priest running through the bush saying mass, pouring water, rubbing oil, gibbering in lingo Spanish will appeal to the superstitious and ignorant, but not to the thinker. We must offer these men an opportunity to join a Christian community and to stay Catholic. Like democracy, Catholicism really hasn't been tried in Bolivia.

Father Mahoney praised the effectiveness of the sisters' medical, food, and hygiene projects, and the strength of the catechetical program—relating each topic to the ability to get along with one priest in the mission. Another factor, he continued, was the financial one; the people of Caranavi simply refused even to make a show of supporting the missioners. "We are the gringos," he said. "We've got the money." He continued on that note:

> When they say they prefer American priests we may be very flattered—until we find out that it's basically an economic matter with them. If the priest is Bolivian, you have to support him; but if he's American, you don't have to. And what's even better, he gives *you* money. So as long as there's a strong American image of a take-charge church down here in Caranavi, the people in the *pueblo* will never consider their responsibility. With the presence of two priests, the people always felt superfluous and not needed.

Father Mahoney said the foundation work which Fathers Heusser and Conte had put into Caranavi had made the one-priest mission possible—"all I have to do is keep the top spinning." But his concluding thoughts went in another direction: "The burden and the concern that is put upon the diocese, the uncertain future of the prelature, . . . makes it very prudent and wise to consider our pulling out rather than to continue our work here in Caranavi. There are other ways of a diocese working and assisting in the missions. . . ."

Armand Conte, at that time pastor of the parish in Netcong, had mixed reactions to Father Mahoney's "state of the mission" tape. He implied that more personal visitations should be made and that budget allotments should be dealt with more carefully. On other points, he was understanding, if not in full agreement. As long as the diocese was going to send priests to strange areas (and prepare them in different language schools), and without strong local direction, the priests, he said, will apply their own methods.

"We were left free by Bishop Manning to proceed as we thought best," he wrote to Bishop Casey. "Now, though, with his years of experience in the zone, there should be a definite program established for his prelacy. If our diocesan men really want to go to the missions, it might be advisable to lease them out to one of the missionary orders such as Maryknoll for three or five years."

Looking back at his Caranavi experience nearly ten years later, Father Mahoney says he was poorly prepared—"but I don't know if there was any way in which we could have been prepared adequately." He cites his 1968 tape recording as evidence:

> It reflected my lack of preparation. I didn't know how to put those people into my culture; I was kind of absolute. But I came to recognize their customs, their superstitions, as evidence of their Catholicism, something we could build on. At first I hated all those fiestas as something that was taking advantage of the people; gradually I saw them as something, a tool we could work with.

The decision, inevitably, had been made; all that remained was the setting of a date. Early in 1971, the diocese of Paterson relinquished the parish of Our Lady of Divine Love, Caranavi, to the prelacy of Coroico.

Bishop Casey believed the diocese benefited from the experience. A few months before his death in 1977 he said:

> If we're strictly parochial and limit our interest to our own concerns, we're not a healthy diocese. We must be mission-minded. But what direction that interest should take is another matter. Certainly, sending untrained diocesan personnel to operate independently, far from home, wasn't the answer, as we've seen.
>
> We still contribute to the support of Caranavi and the other former mission in Ica, Peru, and to a parish in La Paz as well. We have many men and women from the diocese who are in the missions as part of the religious communities. And if a diocesan priest came to me today and said he'd like to be a missionary in Latin America, I'd make every effort

to see that he'd be able to go. But he'd have to be connected with an organization such as Maryknoll, and there'd have to be a lot more preparation.

The Sisters of Charity stayed on. Father Mahoney served out his commitment in the prelacy, staying for most of that time in Coroico before returning to Paterson for a series of diocesan assignments—most recently as a hospital chaplain. Father Kielty remained briefly in Ica, then returned to the Paterson diocese as a teacher and assistant pastor. Then, in 1974, he became a missioner again—in Africa, where his mission career had started out.

The mission went ahead under direct Franciscan control, but there was little continuity in the personnel assigned. It was a time of emerging Latin sensitivities. Archcritic of the mission effort Ivan Illich had made his mark; not only were the Latin Americans challenging the reasons for the U.S. presence; the North Americans were doing the same thing—as Father Mahoney had in his taped message to Bishop Casey. New phrases crept into common usage —*comunidades de base*, liberation theology, conscientization—even in Caranavi.

One veteran missioner returned to Caranavi. After five years back in the United States, Sister Grace Lavina rejoined the Caranavi sisters in 1974, two years short of her golden jubilee as a Sister of Charity. She later described some of the emotion she felt on her return:

Different little children would come up to me from time to time and tell me that their mothers had told them to come to talk to me. If it hadn't been for me, they said, they wouldn't be alive. I had taken care of them when they were little girls. Those are the things that make you think it was all worthwhile.

Sister Grace found the Caranavi people better off materially, but was surprised to see so little participation in church activities. "I think that one reason is that there were so many different priests there all the time," she said, "so many different approaches. They kept coming and going; there was no continuity."

Father Larry De Coste is one priest who hopes to change that. A twenty-nine-year-old Franciscan from East Providence, Rhode Island, he is part of the new generation of Caranavi missioners, one of a six-member team that has been in charge of the parish for two years. The team includes three priests, a brother, and two sisters. "There's resentment in the town over the fact that the priests haven't stayed longer," he said, but added that he thought the team might change that. "The team ministry really works here."

He and Sister Ceil McManus, another member of the team, reviewed their progress in August 1976 during a brief visit to La Paz. Sister Ceil, who is thirty and comes from Rochelle Park, New Jersey, conceded that there still are no final, definitive answers to the questions that constantly preoccupy them: What are we doing here; what *should* we be doing?

"There's an increasing sensitivity to the fact that we don't have all the answers," she said. "We're listening to these people, and then we try to make a blend of whatever good we have and what beauty they have, and make something good of it."

(Late in 1977, after serving in Caranavi for four years, Sister Ceil had to return to New Jersey for reasons of health. The Sisters of Charity continued to assign two people to Caranavi, however, with Sister Carol Williams joining Sister Anton: era, a Caranavi "veteran" of four years. And early in 1978, the community decided to try to expand, rather than simply maintain, its commitment to Bolivia. Said Sister Therese Dorothy, superior of the sisters' western province: "It's true that we are straining to meet the needs of our schools and hospitals here. But I wish every one of our sisters—and a lot of Americans—could visit Bolivia and see the poverty. Those people have no one else to turn to if the church isn't serving them.")

As the result of a team decision, all members are studying Aymara.

"We are trying to work through local *comunidades de base*," Father De Coste said, referring to the small neighborhood Christian communities which will be discussed in later chapters.

Once you have community, you can start to have people become independent. Being a priest in Caranavi, there's never been a lack of things to do. The people have always placed a big demand on us for masses, for example, but it's always attached to the idea of punishment. It's mismotivated, of course, but a priest who doesn't do much thinking about it can go out, say his mass, and feel fulfilled. I have a feeling we're doing something worthwhile in the other direction, helping people to realize the significance of the sacraments . . . and helping them to improve their lot at the same time. This doesn't mean a rejection of the old approach, throwing out the mass or anything like that. It's just that we're using it as instruction now.

Caranavi continues to grow. A genuine Caranavi community is forming; its people will now list Caranavi as their home town instead of the altiplano village that might have been the original family home.

There is a growing pride, as well, in what they have made of themselves. "The whole *comunidad de base* program is a way of helping people to see that their future is in their own hands," Father De Coste said, "and that they can't always depend on us."

There is a youthful enthusiasm to this parish team—a team that professes a desire to benefit from all that has happened in Caranavi in the past.

The Caranavi experience stretches back almost twenty years—a period on which Bishop Manning reflected, as he wrote in September 1976: "We have made mistakes, some big ones," he conceded. "We have put values on structures and other things not important to the Latin American, and not really necessary for the growth and strength of the church."

He would continue to send U.S. missioners, but require two full years for intensive training and orientation—in language, history, culture, sociology, and economics. He would have each U.S. bishop visit a Latin American mission for at least a month. Earlier he wrote:

> My greatest disappointment is the loss of priests and sisters to the Latin American mission. Many come for a time and do not return. I know that these are difficult times for the church in the United States and that thinking about Latin America has radically changed. . . . I wish I could give a solid opinion as to why so many priests and sisters do not return to Latin America. I can only guess that they lack spiritual and professional training for the job.

2

Why a Mission to Latin America?

A few years ago when annual meetings were being held by CICOP—the Catholic Inter-American Cooperation Program, which fostered discussion of church-related Latin American affairs—a priest showed up at the registration desk and asked if he might sit in on some of the sessions. Certainly, came the reply. Was Father a former missionary? No, he answered. Did he have a special connection with Latin America? No, not really. Well, then, was there some particular reason he wanted to attend the meeting? "There sure is," he said, identifying himself as pastor of a parish in the city where the conference was taking place:

> One of my curates is a fellow who came back from our South American mission about six months ago, and the other one just got back from the same mission last week. I thought they'd get along like long-lost brothers, but they won't even talk to each other. All I'm trying to do is find out what the hell's going on down there!

The pastor in the story—an apocryphal story, perhaps, but not far removed from reality—has a good deal of company in the U.S. church. Until recent years, the priests and people of the church in North America knew little and cared less about their brothers and sisters to the south. Pastoral practices in the Latin American church were faintly mysterious, and the lack of financial support was impossible to understand. No problem was more puzzling than the vocations shortage. With all of the Catholic countries down there, North Americans wondered, why should we have to send our missionaries? Why don't they have their own priests?

Based on what little North Americans knew, it was a logical question. And paradoxically, the problem is ultimately traceable to the colonization of Latin America ("inappropriately called its discovery," as Brazil's Dr. Luis A. Gomez de Souza has observed) by those most Catholic nations, Spain and Portugal. The characteristics of that colonization—the imposition of a dominant standard from outside and the exploitation of people and resources—set a tragic model for later centuries. The Counter-Reformation church of the time— rigid, jealous, inward-looking—was a powerful partner in the colonizing enterprise, with results that were, in the long view, disastrous. "It went in more for distributing the sacraments than for evangelizing," Chilean pastoral theologian Segundo Galilea has written. "The faith was imposed as part of a culture."

Rubem Alves, religion professor at São Paulo State University at Campinas, writing of a later wave of European Protestant missionaries to Latin America, speaks of an attitude which also characterized the Spanish and Portuguese priests of the sixteenth and seventeenth centuries: "The missionaries could not have any critical insights about what was taking place. They were totally dominated by the passion for extending to pagan countries the benefits of the Christian faith. And they were absolutely sure that their faith was superior and that their faith was the true faith."

Who were these early missionaries? Priests of religious orders, mostly —Jesuits, Franciscans, Mercedarians, Augustinians, Dominicans. It should be said that despite their active cooperation with the crown and their over-whelming preoccupation with spiritual matters, with eternal salvation, they did not entirely overlook the physical well-being of the native inhabitants whose land was being overrun. And there was some measure of competition between the missioners who wanted to Christianize the Indians (however imperfectly) and the adventurers who were anxious to exploit them.

The *encomienda* system developed from the priests' efforts. Social scientists of later generations would criticize it as paternalistic—again, setting an unfor-tunate pattern for the future—but it served a positive purpose at the time. The *encomienda* was a center at which the missioners would gather groups of Indians and teach them not only the faith but of other aspects of the civilized world. Significantly, they achieved their success in this direction through their own persuasive efforts rather than by force.

A parallel development was that of the *reducción*—particularly in what is now Paraguay, where the Jesuits were active in the seventeenth century. Gary MacEoin writes:

> They persuaded the Indians to come out of the forests and establish towns where they built magnificent churches, discovered and utilized unsuspected talents of the natives as masons, stoneworkers, wood-workers, sculptors, and painters. Education of the Indians progressed so rapidly that many of them acquired a sound classical training.

But the *encomiendas* and *reducciones* were all too atypical, and all too short-lived. Commercial interests among the colonizers succeeded in transforming the *encomiendas* into miniature feudal communities—forerunners of the hacienda system—with the Indians as serfs. This development was hastened by the expulsion of the Jesuits (in 1755 from Portuguese-held territory; in 1767 from land dominated by Spain) as the result of European power strug-gles.

Many of the missioners genuinely attempted to minister to the needs of the

Indians, building schools and hospitals and charitable institutions, but few went about their pastoral efforts with the enlightened approach of those who had developed the *encomiendas* and *reducciones.*

In a 1976 interview with Father John Gorski, a U.S. Maryknoll priest who is executive secretary of the mission department of CELAM, NC News Service's Agostino Bono recounted how the missioners who arrived with the conquistadores made a practice of building their churches atop the temples of the conquered people. Their aim, of course, was not only to suppress the native religion but to provide a lasting reminder of the superiority of their own.

The mission approach of their time was precisely the opposite of what Father Gorski urges for today, as quoted by Bono: "Missionaries have to avoid the thought that Christ comes down in their suitcases. If we really believe that Christ comes before us, then we must first discern how the Holy Spirit is already present among these people."

There was no room for that concept in the theology of the colonizing priests of Portugal and Spain. For almost all of them, Christ not only came in their suitcases; once having arrived, he was locked into their tabernacles of gold. The triumphal attitude they bore set patterns that persist to this day.

Many who have written of Latin America's colonial history speak of four distinct eras in Spain's occupation of the New World:

1. The initial "seeding" period, from 1492 to 1566.
2. The period of consolidation, from 1566 (the accession of Philip II) throughout the Hapsburg period to 1700.
3. "Relaxation and decline"—from 1700 (accession of Philip V, the first Bourbon) to 1815.
4. Contemporary republican history, from 1815 (beginning the period in which most Latin American countries gained their independence) to the present.

(Current events suggest that future historians will have marked off a new period, beginning with the end of World War II, when the new Latin America began to emerge. Indeed, perhaps the Latin America of the 1970s is so different from that of the 1930s that such a delineation should already have been made.)

Father Segundo Galilea, speaking at Mexico City in 1971 at the first Inter-American Conference of Major Superiors, pointed to the "Latin American 'Christendom' " which was shaped during those first two periods. He noted the style of spreading the faith: the importation of European church structures, the failure to require any true personal conversion, the preoccupation with form—European form, at that—rather than substance. Father Galilea said:

> The churchmen of that day did not have the vision to foresee the potential values of a church immersed in an American setting. The church came to America "made from the top down," and it never

developed from the bottom up. From the start it displayed feudal, monolithic, characteristics, often ill-fitted to the local realities. Very rapidly a Latin American "Christendom" was formed, and Catholicism was identified with society. . . . [This] forms the backdrop to Latin American Catholicism.

The pattern of development that followed was almost foreordained, given that beginning and in the absence of dramatic change over the years: a gradual identification of the church with the ruling (and, generally, the exploitative) class; a similarly gradual alienation of the poor from the church and the priests who represented it. The church never abandoned the poor; it maintained its charitable works and, for some, its schools. But it never became committed to forces working for social change; indeed, it stood as a symbol of reaction, of caution—of domination.

The chronic lack of vocations in the Latin American church goes back to those early attitudes, in the view of many observers. As it was expressed several years ago by Father Roger Vekemans, writing in *Ave Maria* magazine:

The lack of priests stems at least partly from a cultural problem (absolute or relative illiteracy), which in turn is rooted in the theological problem we started with: that Hispanic Catholicism was never sufficiently interested in humanizing conditions of life in this world.

A veneer of Catholicism stayed with the people. The late Bishop James A. McNulty of Buffalo, speaking on problems of the Latin American church in a talk in Florida in 1967, called the people "Catholic in heart." But sadly, he continued, "they treasure from achievements of two centuries ago only two souvenirs—the sacrament of baptism and a wonderful devotion to the Blessed Mother."

Rumblings of Freedom

The foundations of the Latin American church were poorly equipped to stand firm against the rumblings of freedom that moved from one province to another in the late 1700s, spurred by the success of the French Revolution and, to a lesser degree, that in the United States—and the chain-reaction explosions of independence that followed. The years following the wars of independence were even worse for the church than the unsettled period that had preceded them, resulting, once again, in long-term difficulties from which it has not yet recovered.

The "third period" of development of Latin American Catholicism—from 1700 to 1815—was the period in which the church's fortunes began to dissolve. Abroad, in Europe, Catholic thought declined and the new rationalism was in the ascendancy. Anticlericalism, a cornerstone of the philosophy of the European rationalists, was a particularly effective weapon for their Latin American confreres. They could point out to the masses that the clergy had never integrated itself with the natives, whom its members considered inferior, but instead was clearly an ally of the ruling forces across the sea.

The right of patronage, through which the rulers of Spain and Portugal continued to play a key role in the appointment of bishops, took on added significance. If the "right" bishops could be selected, obviously, the church would have fewer worries about the storms now sweeping the continent. Conservative to begin with, the church became more withdrawn and suspicious. As the people increasingly identified it with the ruling class, they were more easily persuaded that it was not serving their interests. The gulf between church and people, a wide gulf under any circumstances, grew wider.

The wars of independence, wars in which the antireligious spirit of European thought formed a philosophical backdrop, resulted in a strong outburst of laicism. The phenomenon was described by the late Bishop Manuel Larraín of Talca, Chile, and Dr. Joseph A. Gagliano of Loyola University, Chicago, at the first CICOP conference in 1964:

> Tolerance was [the laicist parties'] key doctrine, but their followers invented a civil religion characterized by an intolerance which preyed upon Latin American Catholicism. Laicism was a naturalistic religion, without dogmas, which assumed a different character in each one of its followers. All concurred, however, in their strong desire to snatch from the Catholic Church, one by one, the prerogatives which allowed her to bring religion into public life. The aim was to confine her to the sacristy.

When independence arrived, the church was in a terrible condition—pastorally, administratively, materially. Its open allegiance to royalty, no longer the ruling force, had alienated great masses of people. Many of its European priests—who had done remarkably little to foster the growth of a native clergy—simply packed up and went home, leaving a legacy of shutdown churches and the peoples' impression that they had been deserted. That idea was to remain for a long time. Finally, patronage, the *patronato*, opened even more doors of trouble.

Spain and Portugal wanted to retain the right to appoint bishops in Latin America. (Who knew, they wondered, how long the phenomenon of independence would be fashionable?) Failing that, they took every step possible to delay agreements between the new nations and the Holy See—agreements that would have led to different provisions for episcopal appointments. Rome was holding out for still another option: an end to the whole *patronato* business. This stalemate produced one vacant see after another—and the further weakening of the institutional church.

This was a dire problem for the church under any circumstances. The fact that it took place when new nations were being carved out from former colonial empires resulted in an administrative situation that was nothing less than chaotic.

In Colombia, six dioceses fell vacant, and by 1829 there was not a single bishop left in Mexico. In that same year, MacEoin writes, only ten of twenty-nine Latin American dioceses had bishops, and many seminaries closed:

> For a generation or more the confusion continued. Even after new arrangements, sometimes formal, sometimes informal, were made to regularize church-state relations and permit the appointment of bishops, the church never fully recovered, not even in the countries in which things worked out most favorably for it. . . . Church discipline became more relaxed. Vocations declined. State support of seminaries and other educational institutions was withdrawn or reduced. . . .

From there on, it seemed that the only direction in which the church could go was down.

That is just what happened. Pope Leo XII's action in restoring the Latin American hierarchy, beginning in 1827, went unaccompanied by formal concordats with the various nations, leading to further difficulties. Dictatorships emerged in many of the new countries, where rulers used the church to advance their ends—setting up their own bishops, expelling clergy who refused to cooperate with the regime in power, manipulating church leaders to strengthen their basic political conservatism.

The liberals' persistent anticlericalism left the church with no effective choice but to further its alliance with conservatives, Dr. Gagliano says, since it saw the liberalism of Latin America as a menace to its independence and economic security. While this development served to achieve the short-sighted goal of maintaining that security, it further widened the chasm which already separated it from the masses and, in fact, made it all but unbridgeable.

Not only were the masses alienated. The church's ties with an emerging Establishment of militarists and oligarchs repelled many of the intelligentsia, who, Bishop Larraín noted, looked instead to the material philosophies of Bentham and Comte for solutions to their countries' ills.

All of these things worked adversely on the interior life of the church. According to Dr. Gagliano:

> Preoccupied with political disputes, the hierarchy did not, and perhaps could not, often adequately concern itself with the problem of church reform. The need for reform preceded the independence period, but it became increasingly urgent following the turbulent and disruptive years of revolution.

Paramount among the problems was that of the clergy itself. The priests of post-independence Latin America were few in number; the exodus of European missionaries had not yet been fully reversed, and native vocations had never developed as fully as they should have. This was due to several factors: an educational system that was often inadequate, the physical isolation of many groups of people, the lingering prejudice toward Indians felt by many of the European-born and their descendants.

What resulted was an impoverished clergy that was often poorly educated and required to serve great numbers of people. It looked in vain for direction from a leadership that was occupied with more temporal concerns. It was hardly a situation to encourage new candidates for the priesthood.

"The shortage of priests in Latin America has a history as long as its struggle for independence," says Father Renato Poblete, S.J.

> The natural enthusiasm of the continent's youth was directed primarily toward participation in the forging of a nation while, on the other hand, the clergy was in great part in opposition to the movement. Rome's acknowledgement of the new republics was, due to European influence, neither prompt nor enthusiastic, and a portion of the Spanish clergy returned to the homeland after independence was secured. This attitude on the part of church authorities weakened considerably its image and that of the priest as its representative. In a new world of emerging concepts, the church seemed to have lost its relevance and the priesthood its appeal.

Father Poblete, who spoke on the vocations crisis at the third CICOP meeting in 1966, pointed to a more rapid population growth as a factor that worsened the problem. Chile had 770 priests in 1750 and the same number one century later—after independence—but by that time the population had doubled. In Mexico, there were nearly 7,500 priests in 1810, but that number had been cut by more than half forty years later—while the country's population grew by 1.5 million.

> The priest has been overwhelmed by numbers. But more important than this is the qualitative change that this demographic explosion has produced. This is seen in the rapid social and cultural changes that have modified the existing structures and influenced every aspect of social life, both at the group and institutional level. Religious vocations have not escaped the effects of these mutations.

Changes Were Slow

With the church of Latin America so encased in institutional rigidity during the 1800s, change was slow to come. This was particularly true of social change, which, as Bishop Larraín wrote, was often seen as part of a liberal plot to despoil the church. Even in countries where it was relatively secure, the church played no significant role in the quest for social reform.

"In view of the profound upheaval in Latin America during the present century," Bishop Larraín said, "the loss of its identity as the champion of social justice has been among the most unfortunate consequences for the church."

When did that begin to change?

It is impossible to pinpoint, of course, but perhaps the year 1899 might serve as a modern starting point. In that year Pope Leo XIII convoked the first general meeting of the Latin American hierarchy, in Rome. No single dramatic change resulted—as happened at the Rio de Janeiro general meeting in 1955, when CELAM was formed, or the historic Medellín conference of 1968, with its resolutions calling for a sweeping program of social and ecclesiastical reform.

But the meeting assisted the Latin American hierarchy to lay a foundation for its operations, over the next half century or so, along the lines of the enlightened type of traditionalism represented by Leo himself. It lent a new emphasis to the regional and international dimension of the church for its Latin American leaders, and—perhaps of greatest significance—gave them personal exposure to the pontiff whose startling social teachings clearly marked out a role for the church in the modern industrial world.

It was only in recent years—perhaps at mid-century—that the Latin American church began to search seriously for revolutionary new approaches to meet its vast pastoral problems, including its chronic shortage of priests. By that time spokesmen for social change had assumed roles of leadership and were calling on the church to take a direct role in dealing with poverty, injustice, and other social problems. Father Galilea notes that it was in this period that the same spokesmen began to realize the inadequacy of parish structures, of a ritualistic approach to religion, of a pastoral approach centered on the sacraments.

But it was at the same time that the church in other parts of the world, particularly in North America, was becoming aware of the staggering problems of the Latin American church—again, with emphasis on the need for priests. Urged on by the appeals of Rome and an evangelizing zeal, the new missioners of the twentieth century resolved to help. Sadly, perhaps tragically, the methods they brought with them, for the most part, were the same ones that the new wave of Latin American church leaders was struggling to throw off.

3

Awakening of Concern

"It all started with the land," Monsignor Luigi Ligutti recalled:

It's always been my feeling that throughout history, the problems of the world have been the problems of the land and the people. That was what I was interested in, and when Archbishop O'Hara pushed me to get into Latin American work, during the war—well, to tell the truth, he didn't have to push too hard.

I knew what possibilities the land in South America had if it were properly used and distributed. I had a soil specialist tell me that with just a portion of the Amazon Valley under cultivation by Chinese or Japanese farmers, we could close down all the rest of the farms in the world.

In a country setting near the Via Aurelia Antica just outside Rome—at the retirement cottage he calls Villa Stillman, after a friend and benefactor —Msgr. Ligutti thought back to the 1940s and 1950s, when the U.S. church's concern for Latin America was in its infancy. It was a period in which he had been a dominant influence, establishing contacts that were to lead to an era of intercontinental cooperation unlike anything the church had known. But he insisted on keeping the record straight. "Be sure that Archbishop O'Hara gets credit," he said. "He started it all. He was one of the greatest men I ever knew."

Edwin Vincent O'Hara, born in 1881, was a pastor in Oregon when he founded the National Catholic Rural Life Conference in 1923. He had already built a national reputation for his work in catechetics, applying the instructions of Pope Pius X in that field, and, not surprisingly, went on to become a bishop—first of Great Falls, Montana (from 1930 to 1939) and then of Kansas City, Missouri, from 1939 until his death in 1956. Two years before he died he received the personal title of archbishop (through Msgr. Ligutti's intervention, according to Ligutti biographer Msgr. Vincent Yzermans).

Archbishop O'Hara was convinced that the church in the United States, with its abundance of financial and personal resources, could aid its struggling sister church to the south. He interested others: Father Joseph Code, a distinguished church historian who prepared a pioneering survey on the use of

United States church personnel in Latin America, and a young Precious Blood priest named Joseph M. Marling. Father Marling became O'Hara's auxiliary bishop in Kansas City and in 1956 was named bishop of Jefferson City. The concern for Latin America that O'Hara helped to develop was to have a long-term effect for Bishop Marling: to this day, the proportion of Jefferson City priests serving in Latin America is higher than that of any other United States diocese.

But Archbishop O'Hara paid special attention to Ligutti, whom he had gotten to know through rural life work. Ligutti, born in Italy's Udine province in 1895, had already begun studies for the priesthood when he came to the United States, with other members of his family, in 1911. He continued his seminary training in Iowa, where the Liguttis had joined a growing Italian community in Des Moines. He was ordained for the Des Moines diocese in 1917, when he was only 22, becoming—and for some time remaining—the youngest priest in the United States. His assignment to the rural parish of Granger, where he developed an amazingly successful pastoral-social ministry, led first to regional and then national prominence in the Catholic rural life movement.

Ligutti never lost interest in that primary love, but by the time he began to get involved with Latin America, he had broadened his horizons. "The world has been his parish," wrote Msgr. George G. Higgins, and that hardly overstates the case. He became enormously influential in any area in which the servant church was called on to provide help: immigration, world peace and hunger, relief work. Many of those interests came together in his Latin American role.

"O'Hara kept after me to get involved," Ligutti said. "He was some salesman."

O'Hara and Ligutti's common rural life background was more than coincidental. The earliest figures in the United States' postwar move toward Latin America were almost exclusively connected in some way or other with rural life work. One of them was the late Bishop Joseph H. Schlarman of Peoria, with whom Ligutti made three trips to Latin America during the forties. Schlarman and others encouraged Ligutti to develop on an international basis the same kind of rural life congresses he had engineered at home, and so they came: 1953 in Manizales, Colombia, 1955 in Panama, 1957 in Venezuela, 1959 in Chile. They were the building blocks for more formal intercontinental ecclesial cooperation, still to come.

Ligutti was not without his critics. A few influential prelates provided encouragement for his Latin American ventures, Cardinal Spellman among them, but others were less cooperative. "People like Stritch and Mooney," he said, referring to the cardinal-archbishops of Chicago and Detroit, "couldn't have cared less."

He recalled inviting one of Cardinal Stritch's auxiliaries in Chicago—again, a companion from the Rural Life Conference—to attend an international congress in Buenos Aires. "He couldn't come and he had to plead sickness," Ligutti said, "but it was just that Stritch wouldn't let him go. He just couldn't figure out what business the U.S. church might have in Latin America."

Msgr. Joseph B. Gremillion, for many years secretary of the World Justice and Peace Commission at the Vatican, was himself influential in arousing United States concern for Latin America during the 1950s, principally through a series of articles written following a tour of twelve Latin American nations in 1957. But he feels that Ligutti was the prime mover in this direction, and, because of his evaluation of what the Latin American experience was to mean to the United States church, sees Ligutti's role as one of towering importance.

"Ligutti developed a triangle between Latin America, North America, and Rome," he said. "He knew Montini well, and Archbishop Samore, who was Pope Pius's Latin America specialist. He would mimeograph his reports on Latin America and send them to key bishops in that triangle. This not only built up North American concern for Latin America, but it opened Roman eyes to the non-relationship between the two."

How significant were these developments? Gremillion views the opening toward Latin America as beginning the process through which the U.S. church became aware of its ecclesial universality. "In all truth I regard this as the most significant effect of the Latin American apostolate on the North American church," he said, "and one which in itself justifies the effort."

Ligutti always saw the church as the one stable, continuing, and unifying institution in Latin America, and repeatedly pointed that out to anyone in the government who asked his advice—and, perhaps, to a few who didn't. "No matter what we try to do," he wrote to one American official in 1951, "if we don't take the Catholic church into account, we are just wasting our time, our efforts, and our money. The same can be said of most mission fields. And for heaven's sake"—this last sentence was underlined—"don't think you can make them think the way you think they ought to think!"

A Time of Gradual Growth

There was an increasing number of United States missioners in a position to benefit from Ligutti's advice by this time. It was not nearly the wave that was to come later, of course, but the growth, if slow, was steady.

U.S. priests and sisters from mission-sending societies had been at work in some Latin American areas before World War II. There were Conventual Franciscans in Costa Rica, Marianists in Peru, Capuchins in Nicaragua, Vincentians in Panama, Jesuits in Honduras, Oblates in Brazil, Redemptorists in Brazil and Paraguay, sisters of the Servants of the Immaculate Heart of Mary in Peru—the list goes on. But the war years brought in many others, most of them because the routes to their normal areas of mission service had been closed off. Holy Cross priests went to Chile; Franciscans of the Immaculate Conception province (of New York) went to Honduras, and those of Sacred Heart province (St. Louis) to Brazil.

And there was Maryknoll. Its reservoir of trained missioners was stymied; priests were unable to get to China, and those in enemy territory—thirteen in Japan, thirty in Manchuria—were interned. Maryknoll, which had been formed in 1911 as the Catholic Foreign Mission Society of America and had become the United States' best-known mission organization, opened missions in 1942 in Peru, Bolivia, and Chile, and a year later in Guatemala. Maryknoll Sisters were represented, too—in Chile, Bolivia, Peru, the Canal Zone, and Nicaragua.

In line with their tradition, they built. "We built parish plants and schools and other institutions the same way our counterparts were doing in the U.S.," said Father William J. McIntire, Maryknoll's secretary general. "So much so that in Peru, the bishop of Puno could joke that Maryknoll would leave more ruins in the Peruvian altiplano than the Incas."

Father Albert Nevins, the veteran Maryknoll journalist who is now executive editor of *Our Sunday Visitor*, wrote of the organization's early Latin American ventures in *The Meaning of Maryknoll*, published in 1954. In Peru, the accent was on building a native clergy, and Maryknollers there drew up a detailed game plan toward that end—including construction of a minor seminary, San Ambrosio, which was opened in 1944. Their counterparts in Chile concentrated on working with the urban poor and strengthening family life, creating a favorable impression on that nation's progressive hierarchy. In 1953, Bishop Larraín of Talca praised Maryknoll's work as "one of the best foundations for fraternal relations between our people and those of the United States."

But looking back, it was not all that smooth. "We emphasized," Father McIntire said in 1976, "the training of candidates for a celibate priesthood, although frankly with little success." Maryknoll mission magazines gave "a generally rather romantic view of our mission work, emphasizing the difficulties and joys the missioners experienced, and the poverty of the people —but with virtually no political or social analysis of the causes of the poverty."

Eventually Maryknoll came to realize that the seminary at Puno had an alienating effect. "Some of those who were ordained were ashamed to use the native language," Father McIntire says. "Over the years we had trained eight hundred boys, but only twelve were ordained. As of recently, only six or seven were still in the priesthood, and of those only three were working in the altiplano. The bishops of the area decided to close the Puno seminary in 1969. Since then, Maryknollers in the altiplano have emphasized lay leadership training and have had encouraging results."

Father Don Steed, a Maryknoller who has been in Bolivia since the early fifties, put the problem this way:

We never made headway because we didn't understand the people. All we were were diocesan priests. Could we operate the church here? Yes, we could, strictly speaking. But it's something like the pilot who's had experience with a Piper Cub trying to bring in a B-17. He might be able to do it, but he'll find out there's quite a difference.

The judgments of the seventies, though, bear the weight of thirty years of development of both social and theological thought. The small band of U.S. missioners in Latin America during the war and in the postwar years—the Maryknollers and the others—knew nothing of a Second Vatican Council, a liberation theology. God-fearing men and women, they offered extreme personal sacrifices to make Christ's words live for poor people of other lands, far from home.

Many members of the Latin American hierachy were becoming aware that the time of relative tranquility for the church establishment was coming to an end, that a period of great social change was on the horizon. The number of priests on hand to meet the challenge was woefully inadequate, and they looked to the outside for help. They were aware that the United States had a surfeit of priests, but sought them with some misgivings, uneasy as they contemplated what kind of people might come—from the country they still saw as the Protestant colossus of the north.

They were reassured on two levels. The three-way communication opened by Msgr. Ligutti led to personal friendships among bishops of both continents—not great in number, perhaps, but significant because of the importance of the bishops involved: people like Ritter and Cushing in the United States, and Larraín and Camara in Latin America. And on the other level, the bishops of Latin America began to see how well the new United States missionaries handled themselves. That assuaged their fears and paved the way for the experiment that was to follow.

It was a time in which seeds of change were being planted for the Latin American church. The church was still much more the partner of wealth and strength than the social conscience it would become in the sixties and seventies, but signs of future development began to appear.

Chile, which for some time had produced progressive spokesmen in the hierarchy, particularly in the Santiago archdiocese, could point to a Bishop Larraín, who was saying as early as 1944: "Social order requires a thorough-going reform, and it is the Catholic's duty to fight for it." In 1947, the bishops of Chile expanded that idea in a joint pastoral letter. "The supreme goal pointed out by the social encyclicals is the redemption of the proletariat and the reform of social life in accordance with the principles of the Gospel," it said. "To reach it, the Christian concepts of work, capital, and ownership must be re-established."

On the other side of the continent, in Brazil's teeming Northeast, Dom

Eugenio de Araujo Sales, the future cardinal-archbishop of Rio de Janeiro, led five other priests in forming the Movement of Natal in 1948. This forerunner of long-range pastoral plans—which later became common throughout Latin America—attracted worldwide attention. Abbé François Houtart, the renowned religious sociologist, called it the starting point of the pastoral renewal of Brazil, "perhaps the most successful pastoral experiment in underdeveloped areas in the world."

Father Tiago Cloin, a Dutch Redemptorist who began working in Brazil at the end of the war (and who later became a bishop), has observed that what developed from the pastoral plan approach was a realization that the main task of the church was not to multiply traditional works such as parishes, schools, and hospitals, but to provide creative pastoral activity "which follows new ways courageously and aims at the rapid transformation of society. . . . [It] requires theological reflection on the contents of revelation, on one hand, and continued analysis of socio-religious reality on the other."

Meanwhile, new U.S. and European missionary priests were appearing with what was amounting to some regularity and doing—as has been seen with the Maryknollers—what they had done at home: build and expand. In fairness, it should be pointed out that the advanced thinking of the Chilean bishops and individuals such as Dom Eugenio was hardly representative of the Latin American clerical mind. If the new postwar missioners didn't set out to abandon traditional building programs and to transform society instead, it was—at least in part—because no one even asked them to consider it. Most Latin American bishops of the time were only too glad for the help, and frequently left missioners to go about whatever work they wanted to do.

Were American priests welcome or simply tolerated during this period? The answer seems to vary from one region to another and to be influenced heavily by individual experiences. Father Harvey Steele, the Nova Scotia priest who pioneered the cooperative movement in Latin America, detected an early antipathy toward North America and its missioners when he began working in the Dominican Republic in 1946. "At that time I felt it was unjustified," he has recalled.

But Bishop Nevin W. Hayes, the Chicago auxiliary who was elected chairman of the U.S. bishops' Latin America committee in 1976, has another recollection. "Being American was a novelty," he said, looking back on his career as a Carmelite missioner in Peru which began in 1951.

> The pro-American feeling was tremendous. There was a fierce pride in our parish in Lima. The peoples' conditioning was different; they had been used to old-style, European-type priests. We had four young guys who got people involved in parish activities of all kinds. There was a sports club, where families would pay a dollar a month. For that their kids could take part in all kinds of sports, or just hang around. The priests would be there, as often as not, and that opened all kinds of doors.

Gary MacEoin believes that the initial response to the new U.S. missioners was warm, but that sentiment gave way quickly—especially among liberal, intellectual elements, who began to see the North Americans' presence and their work as a form of spiritual colonialism. MacEoin dates the emergence of the new era of the Latin American church from a seminar at the Colegio de Belén, Havana, which began December 31, 1945, and consisted of delegates chosen by the bishops of each country in the Americas.

"We had come," he later wrote, "to inform each other and be informed of the social problems of the Americas, as a prelude to developing common policies." He described Jesuit Father John La Farge, then editor of *America*, and Father Raymond McGowan, head of the Social Action Department of what was then the National Catholic Welfare Conference, as the "main architects" of the seminar.

In that spirit of cooperation, MacEoin says, most in the Latin American church welcomed the postwar mini-tide of Americans. In an optimism born of Marshall Plan–success thinking, he says, the newcomers from the North thought they had the knowhow to remake the church in Latin America in the image and likeness of the church at home. He writes:

Many Latin American seminarians and young priests were caught up in this movement, and it seemed for a short time to be accomplishing a basic transformation of the system. Before long, nevertheless, it became apparent that the successful but highly subsidized pilot programs were no more than tokenism. Like foreign aid in the civil sphere, what was being done was admirable, but each year the problem grew bigger and the possibility of solution dimmer. To provide more ample and efficient techniques for bringing the rites of religion to the people while leaving them in their present conditions would merely advance the cause of superstition. To make men religious, they first had to be made men.

Thanks in part to Ligutti's persistent prodding, Rome's interest in Latin America perked up. To some degree it was parochial; Protestant missioners —evangelical Protestants, at that—were making considerable headway. And to a degree there were political elements in Rome's concern; communism seemed on the verge of making great strides. But there were higher motives, too. Pope Pius was disturbed by the imbalance between priests and people in Latin America and with the failure of the church to be an effective force with the masses. Ligutti had succeeded in welding a network of realists within the Latin American hierarchy, but too many bishops remained isolated from their brothers. The Vatican determined to give high priority to exploring all of these concerns, and the man Pope Pius chose to coordinate that effort was Archbishop Antonio Samore.

Born in Bardi, Italy, in 1905, Samore was a veteran of the Vatican's diplomatic corps. He had served in Lithuania and Switzerland and within the

Vatican itself before being appointed to the apostolic delegation in Washington, where he spent a year. He was promoted to nuncio, serving from 1950 to 1953 in Colombia, before being summoned home. "When I returned to Rome," he recalled in 1976, "my superior—Monsignor Tardini, the secretary of state—told me to consider myself in charge of Latin America. My office was secretary of the Congregation of Extraordinary Ecclesiastical Affairs."

It was then that the idea of what was to become CELAM—Consejo Episcopal Latinoamericano, the Latin American Bishops' Conference—was first broached, Cardinal Samore said. In his quiet and comfortable office in the Vatican Secret Archives, where he is director, he recounted some of the details that went into its preparation:

> Today there is no equivalent to the post I held. Tardini simply said, "You were there; you know the situation. You're in charge." But he directed me.
>
> He told me that Pope Pius was interested in the prospects of formation of a conference of Latin American bishops. Under Tardini's direction, I studied the project, not of a council, which would have included all bishops, but of a conference, which would be an assembly of a large number of bishops, representing them all.
>
> We took the occasion of the 1955 Eucharistic Congress in Rio de Janeiro to convoke this. It was held following the congress, in July and August, with one hundred bishops—from Mexico to Argentina— representing all six hundred Latin American bishops.

Cardinal Adeodato Piazza, secretary of the Sacred Consistorial Congregation, was chairman, and Samore executive secretary of the conference. Its purpose, he said, was "to know the situation of the church in Latin America."

Years after the meeting, Mexico's Cardinal Miranda said Pope Pius's pastoral letter of invitation to the Rio conference was a "magnificent" document. "He didn't partake of any pessimism about the future of Latin America," the Mexican prelate said. "All those who were privileged to be present . . . recognized that memorable reunion of two weeks as the most significant gathering in the whole history of Latin America."

CELAM, the organization that was formed as a result of the Rio conference, was unique. National organizations of hierarchies had existed previously, but this was the first regional conference—a federation of seventeen national Latin American conferences plus a sectional conference representing the hierarchies of the five Central American countries.

Pius's invitation—dated June 29, 1955, and called *Ad Ecclesiam Christi*—was seen as the "magna carta of the current revival, the fundamental programmatic document touching the future of Catholicism in Latin America" by Dr. Aristide Calvani Silva of Caracas. At the first CICOP meeting, nine years later, he pointed to the significance of the pontiff's appeal that Latin America be considered a responsibility not only of the Latin Americans themselves. "With fatherly concern," Pope Pius had written, "we address ourselves not only to the prelates and people of Latin America, but to all other peoples, in order that in one way or another each may contribute its own concourse and aid."

"At Rio, the bishops were really united for the first time," Cardinal Samore recalled.

They spent the first two days there just assimilating the information I had put together. The general purpose of the meeting was to understand the situation of the church in Latin America, and it should be remembered that the decision to form a permanent organization—which, of course, became CELAM—was only one of the two major conclusions. The other was to realize the need to examine ways of revitalizing Latin American religious life. The bishops themselves saw the need to invite clergy from other countries in order to help with this; this was one of the most important outcomes of the meeting.

Many U.S. bishops had helped the Latin American mission effort at an early stage, some principally with financial assistance—such as New York's Cardinal Spellman—and others with personnel. The first archdiocese to respond on an organized basis was St. Louis, where Archbishop (later Cardinal) Joseph E. Ritter called for priest-volunteers in 1956 to open a mission in Bolivia. Cardinal Samore credited Msgr. (later Bishop) Paul F. Tanner of the bishops' conference—at that time the National Catholic Welfare Conference —with assisting in organization matters.

And there was the archbishop of Boston.

The Society of St. James

If Msgr. Ligutti was the technician behind the U.S. church's slowly-building concern for Latin America, its popularizer was Archbishop Richard J. Cushing, who moved strongly and even impetuously in whatever project in which he was involved. His identification with Latin American mission work—especially through the Society of St. James the Apostle, which he founded in 1958—helped to alert other U.S. dioceses and religious communities to the needs of Latin America, and he was a major contributor, for better or worse, to the flood of missioners who headed south in the 1960s.

His biographers trace his interest in Latin American mission work to his first official visit to Rome as archbishop, in 1948, when Pope Pius expressed interest in his "lend-lease" program for priests—through which vocation-rich Boston sent some volunteers to other dioceses short of priests—and suggested Latin America as an appropriate area for that kind of largesse.

But it was not until ten years later that the Society of St. James came into being, and it was only after an exchange of correspondence and several meetings with a relatively unknown U.S. missioner that Cardinal Cushing took the step. Cardinal Cushing was unquestionably the founder of the society, but it is difficult to say whether he would ever have done it had it not been for the determined—and largely unsung—efforts of Father Francis Kennard.

Frank Kennard had been a priest of the Portland (Oregon) archdiocese for five years in 1953 when he read of Pope Pius's concern over the state of the Latin American church and asked if he could go there to work. The thought of a U.S. diocesan priest becoming involved in such an undertaking was all but unknown; Archbishop Edward Howard told him to think it over for a year. When the year was up and Father Kennard hadn't changed his mind, the archbishop gave him his blessing.

"I wrote to various places in Latin America to see if they were interested," he said in 1977, "and the first one who answered was Archbishop Landazuri, the future cardinal who was coadjutor of Lima at the time. He said they'd be glad to have me, and that's how I ended up in Peru. I had no preparation at all, other than reading a lot and listening to a few Spanish records. And as I remember it, I never even finished them."

Kennard arrived in Peru in September 1954, one of the first—perhaps *the* first—U.S. diocesan priest-missioner to volunteer for Latin American work. (He declines to lay claim to the title himself, recalling that a diocesan priest from Columbus, Ohio, named Francis Hickey was already in Peru when he arrived. However, Father Hickey's original decision to go to Peru was based on his physical condition rather than missionary interests. Ordained in 1931, Hickey had been a college teacher, pastor, World War II chaplain in Europe, and campus chaplain at Ohio State University when he was forced to retire for health reasons in 1953. He went to live with his brother, an engineer at the Cerro de Pasco corporation's smelting facility in the Andean town of Oroya. As his health improved, he worked in the local parish. A prolonged bout of altitude sickness then sent him to the city of Trujillo, where he began to teach at a school operated by the Brothers of Mary. His most productive years in Latin America still lay ahead. In 1957, he opened a boarding house for students and called it Casa Rosa María. At first he took in twelve boys, then expanded facilities to make room for as many as thirty. He continued to operate the school—promoting exchange visits between his Peruvian students and those in Columbus—before his second, and final, retirement in 1969. He died in McAllen, Texas, his birthplace, at the age of sixty-nine in 1972.)

Archbishop Landazuri wanted to give Father Kennard a Lima assignment, but the U.S. priest requested something more remote. "I went down because of the priest shortage I'd heard about," he said. "I asked to be sent somewhere where there were no priests."

He ended up in an Andean provincial town called Huarachiri, a day's trip by truck from Lima for the six months of the year when the roads were open.

There had been no resident priest in Huarachiri since the turn of the century, and Father Kennard covered the fifty-two villages in the sprawling parish by foot or on horseback.

His work caught the eye of the apostolic nuncio, Archbishop Francesco Lardone, who thought Kennard's mission approach might set the style for others. He called Kennard in and requested him to write to several U.S. bishops, asking them to send more priests to work in Peru. "Cushing was one who wrote back," Father Kennard said. "He invited me to Boston to speak to his priests, and not long after that began mentioning the idea of diocesan priests working in Latin America, with an organization to support them, in his column in *The Pilot.*"

Father Kennard returned to Portland early in 1958 to spend a brief period in a hospital studying what he termed "basic medicine," enough to meet the emergency requirements of his mission parish, and then went on to accept the Cushing invitation to speak to priests in Boston. He stayed with Msgr. Edward Murray, a classmate (at the North American College in Rome) of a Portland priest with whom Kennard was friendly.

Kennard was encouraged by another (and quite coincidental) Boston visitor, Monsignor Ligutti, who met with him and Murray, and helped to pave the way for the meeting with Cushing. The cardinal was hesitant, Ligutti recalls; he feared that some of the Latin American hierarchy, working through Kennard, were simply looking for money.

The Cushing-Kennard meeting finally came off, with Msgr. Murray in attendance, and Cushing took advantage of a spring conference of priests which was going on at the time, priests who were marking the fifth anniversary of their ordination, to put Kennard's salesmanship to the test. "Talk to them," he told Father Kennard. "See how many of them you can convince." The missioner's appeal for diocesan priests to go to Latin America apparently had some effect; five members of the audience volunteered on the spot.

"At that point," says Bishop Thomas V. Daily, a former St. James missioner and now auxiliary of Boston, "Cushing sat up and took notice."

Thus the Society of St. James the Apostle was born, with Father Kennard staying on in Boston to help write the regula, the ground rules under which it would operate. It was set up as a clerical institute rather than a religious order, somewhat after the Sulpician system, enabling priests to sign on for a period of service, and then return to their home dioceses, with no administrative problems.

Cardinal Cushing was impressed with what Kennard had accomplished. "You might be just the man to get this off the ground for me," he told him. But Kennard returned to Peru without any firm commitment. He went to the new Abancay diocese as vicar general to help select the parishes in which the first St. James contingent would serve. They were rural and poor and without priests of their own. But the cardinal's representative, on an inspection tour, rejected them. "We don't want our men living in mud huts," said Msgr.

Edward Sweeney, the Propagation of the Faith director whom Cushing had chosen to go to Peru and scout the territory for the St. James Society.

Rejecting the poor parishes in favor of those which were already better off created problems within the diocese, Kennard recalls, and he dispatched a letter of protest to Boston. He explained that the native priests were counting on those parishes—"prosperous" parishes only in relative terms—since they would be their only means of support.

That was an early problem not only with St. James priests, Bishop Daily has said, but with other U.S. mission groups who went to Latin America in force. "I remember some Peruvian priests were upset," he said, "because we used to come in as a team and their territory would be cut in half. This meant they'd be losing money, and, as imperfectly as they might be ministering, this was something—the fiesta fees and other things—that they needed to survive." Kennard stated the problem bluntly. "I didn't pull any punches," he said, "and the cardinal was furious. That was the end of my game as far as St. James was concerned."

Sweeney was named the society's first director. One of the earliest St. James volunteers, still in Peru in the mid-seventies, said the choice wasn't surprising. "Cushing felt that the key to any organization was a good money raiser," he said. "He didn't need to know anything about Latin America."

Kennard received little public credit for his role in the formation of the St. James Society, although at a dinner some years ago in Lima for members of the organization—with Cardinal John Wright present, but not Cardinal Cushing—Msgr. Murray referred to him as "the real founder."

Kennard has no unpleasant memories of the experience. He stayed on in Peru, opening up a new mission on the Amazon before returning to the United States in 1971. He now works out of Dallas, Oregon, serving as vicar for the Spanish-speaking in the Portland archdiocese—more than 100,000 of them, half of whom are permanent residents. He is responsible for four parishes and a wide stretch of land covering most of western Oregon. "It's a big assignment," says the man who pioneered the Latin American missions for U.S. diocesan priests. "One of these days I'm going to have to slow down, but not now. There's too much to do."

There were heavy political overtones to mission duty in the early years of the St. James Society; saving Latin America from communism was, after all, one of the reasons it had come into being. Cardinal Cushing saw to it that volunteers (as well as other Latin American missioners of that day) received copies of J. Edgar Hoover's *Masters of Deceit*, as well as his own *Questions and Answers on Communism*.

It was part of a general pattern through which U.S. missionaries— sometimes by design, sometimes not—attempted to sell their country's vaunted knowhow as the best approach to solving problems of any sort, political or ecclesiastical. "The spirit of nationalism was such a vital factor then," Bishop Daily said. "Our original mistake—the St. James Society's, and the other missioners' at that time—was that we were trying to tell them how to run the church in Peru."

If that fault stands out in retrospect, it was no hindrance then to the society's rapid growth. By 1962, only three years after the first departure ceremony took place, the St. James Society had more than seventy priests at work in Latin America. Much of the successful growth rate had to be attributed to the salesmanship of Cushing, who plunged into the project with a missioner's zeal himself. Despite chronic poor health, he personalized his interest in the mission undertaking with visits of his own to Latin America, not only publicizing the venture and adding potential new recruits, but also enriching the already extensive lode of Cushing anecdotes.

In the society's formative days, he plugged it regularly on the radio. One story has it that a Boston priest who had written to the chancery merely to inquire about the new society was driving while listening to a Cushing broadcast—the one on which the cardinal was to announce the names of the first group selected for mission duty—and, to his amazement, heard his own name. He went.

The cardinal himself joked about a wedding he performed in Bolivia. As it was retold by John Henry Cutler in *Cardinal Cushing of Boston*, local priests had declined to marry the couple, who had twelve children born out of wedlock. "I got all dressed up like St. Patrick for them," Cushing said. "I wore everything. I waited twenty minutes at the altar, then they marched in—all the kids, followed by their mother and father. Outside, after the ceremony, the bridegroom said, 'I'm glad I waited twenty years. I got married by the pope!' "

Cushing's ability to handle benefactors, large and small, was legendary, and it was of great assistance in supporting mission operations. A typical sample, from the closing of a letter: "Begging God's choicest blessings upon you and yours, and asking you, please, if you will be good enough to advise me when the TV sets will be sent, I am, your devoted and grateful friend."

Pope John paid personal tribute to Cushing's Latin American efforts, and the cardinal responded with a sober assessment of the situation: "The people are very religious, but they are uninformed. There are hundreds of thousands who have no priests to guide them."

His words helped to attract more and more missioners, both in and out of the St. James Society. Where there had been 1,600 United States missionaries in Latin America in 1950, ten years later the number had risen by 50 percent to 2,400—priests, brothers, and sisters, almost all of them members of religious communities, as well as a small number of lay people.

Most who were there saw their work in a thoroughly positive light. Father John M. Maerz, a Redemptorist of the Baltimore Province who had spent many years in Brazil, wrote in 1960 of the contributions his community had made:

For thirty years 160 young American Redemptorists have been in the saddle and, more recently, in their jeeps, bringing into the lives of these abandoned souls the warming consolation of God's sacramental presence. . . . Surely the preaching of the Gospel is necessary and beneficial; in fact, it is the first duty of the missioner. But it is first merely in time, not in importance. The most important duty is to lay the foundation of a permanent indigenous church.

Sister Mary O'Keefe, a Dominican teacher whose doctoral dissertation examined the role of Maryknoll in Peru, described the pre-1960 Maryknollers in that country:

By and large, they were enthusiastic loyal Americans from middle-class backgrounds, predominantly from the northeastern United States. They can perhaps best be described as uncritically patriotic and political. . . . They were more or less alike in their common lack of knowledge concerning Peru, the Peruvian church, and U.S.-Peruvian relations. They were also relatively unconcerned about this lack of knowledge.

Their seminary training—pre-Vatican II and traditional—prepared them, really, for the typical religious-sacramental role of the average American priest. This was their basic orientation, except they were to serve in mission lands. The over-all goal as perceived by them was "to establish the local church" and to meet the need for priests. They were very North American in their mentality as well as very open, generous, and dedicated, and they took with them the American parish model they knew. Some few indicated an added interest in the social needs of those with whom they would work.

Many missioners who were just as "uncritical" as the Maryknollers described by Sister O'Keefe realized later how much their attitudes had changed. Father Joseph R. May, a Redemptorist who first went to Brazil in 1954, wrote twenty-two years later:

I came to Brazil in the days of pre-Vatican II, with very little knowledge of sociology and vague concepts of Latin American and North American politics. The experience of these years had undoubtedly awakened me to the problem of poverty, to a certain mistrust of the intentions of politicians in general, both North and South American, to a recognition of the need of building Latin American society from the base with education, formation of principles for thinking, and community consciousness.

Father Philip Casper, a Capuchin now in his sixties, first went to Nicaragua in 1944, and reflected on the experience in 1976: "My lack of good preparation gave me an erroneous notion that I was to force, or at least urge, my American culture on the Indians. What it amounted to was that I thought my culture was superior, and I had nothing to learn from other cultures." What about the "spiritual colonialism" often ascribed to U.S. missioners? Casper said that most are "still guilty" of the fault. "Some few of us have learned the hard way to avoid it," he said, "after years of guilt."

A Capuchin contemporary of Father Casper, Father Joseph Walsh, who went to Nicaragua, was asked why he volunteered for mission work. "I was sent with an obedience and had no Spanish training," he said. "Caps always do things the hard way!"

Still another Capuchin, a twenty-year veteran of Nicaraguan work, assessed mission attitudes from the vantage point of the seventies: "Unless a person wants to 'put on the mind of Christ,' he'd do better not to enter Latin American work," said Father Justinian Liebl. "Christ came as one of the oppressed with a message of life for the oppressors. We, the church today, tend to come as the oppressors to the oppressed, telling them *we* have a message of life—and they say, 'Oh, yeah? Show us!' "

Rome continued to maintain a watchful attitude in regard to the swelling number of missioners and to developments within the Latin American church itself.

Pope Pius XII had only a few months left in his reign when he established the Pontifical Commission for Latin America (CAL) in April 1958, a move generally regarded as a reaction to the sharply progressive turn taken by the early leaders of CELAM. Gary MacEoin writes:

> From the outset, [CELAM] was given its tone and direction by such progressives as the late Bishop Manuel Larraín of Chile, Archbishop Helder Camara of Brazil, and Bishop Sergio Méndez Arceo of Mexico. However, its early efforts to fulfill its stated function of 'adapting pastoral activity to contemporary needs' were effectively aborted by a parallel body set up in Rome—the Commission for Latin America (CAL)—staffed by reactionary members of the Roman Curia.

Cardinal Confalonieri was named president of CAL and then-Archbishop Samore its vice president and effective leader. Its functions were spelled out in the Annuario Pontificio, the Vatican yearbook, which said that CAL has "the duty to study in its entirety the fundamental problems of Catholic life in Latin America, encouraging close cooperation among the Roman congregations responsible for their solution. It should also follow and sustain CELAM and its general secretariat."

That kind of language wasn't good enough even for loyalists such as Maryknoll Father Vincent T. Mallon, a Latin America missioner-journalist who was to become chief aide to the Vatican's nuncio in Peru, the redoubtable

Archbishop Romolo Carboni. "The aims and scopes of CAL," he said in later years, "particularly in the minds of those living in Latin America, were never too carefully defined. It *was* in Rome, and Rome has a way of wanting the local church to handle things until there are signs of trouble."

Samore himself thought CAL could have been a coordinating agent for North American mission efforts in Latin America, the lack of which became distressingly evident as years went on. "We wanted the Latin American and United States bishops' conferences to go through Rome," he said, "not to dominate the activity, but simply to coordinate it. Maybe the enthusiasm was too great, maybe we did too much without good preparation. . . ."

CAL never achieved what it had set out to do, and today, its staff sharply reduced, it is all but inactive. But it did serve to point out the desirability of closer intercontinental cooperation within the church family, and that was not long in coming. The "first real and formal relationship" between the hierarchies of North America and Latin America, as Msgr. Gremillion describes it, was a meeting which took place at Georgetown University in Washington in November 1959.

"The U.S. bishops, as usual, were worried that it would be just another pitch for money," Gremillion said. "But it wasn't that at all." The Georgetown meeting was, indeed, the keystone for the years of joint inter-American church efforts that flowered in the sixties and continued into the seventies. Preparations for the meeting began a year in advance, when Samore wrote to Washington to inquire what the U.S. church was doing for Latin America.

Msgr. Paul F. Tanner, then general secretary of NCWC, asked Father Frederick McGuire, who was in charge of the U.S. Mission Secretariat, to draw up a reply. A Vincentian who had been a missionary in China, Father McGuire was to become associate director and then director of the U.S. Catholic Conference's Latin America division. Today he is development director for CARA, the Center for Applied Research in the Apostolate, and retains a lively interest in Latin American mission activities.

He compiled the information requested: a résumé of how many missioners were there, how many communities were involved, an estimate of how much money was being used to support the United States mission effort in Latin America. The administrative board put it together, and Archbishop Karl Alter of Cincinnati, the board's chairman, forwarded it to Rome. "He appended a note to it," McGuire said, "which said, in effect, if there's anything else you'd like us to do, let us know and we'll comply."

The Vatican's response was to request a meeting in Washington with six Latin American bishops, six from Canada, and six from the United States, who would be charged with formulating an inter-American church program. The meeting took place November 2–3, 1959, at Georgetown, and from it—in addition to the groundwork for future inter-American hierarchical cooperation—came a concrete plan of assistance. From existing funds, the U.S. church would send $1 million a year to the Pontifical Commission (CAL) to assist in meeting the needs of the church in Latin America. The six U.S. bishops who attended the meeting would constitute the committee to oversee the operation, and from their number Cardinal Cushing, who was at the helm of the already-existing St. James Society, was appointed committee chairman.

The meeting set in motion a direct involvement in Latin American affairs that the United States church, despite all its worthy motives, was not really ready to undertake. Years later one of Cushing's successors as chairman of the U.S. bishops' Latin America committee, Bishop John Fitzpatrick of Brownsville, would sum up the problem: "We should have cased the joint before opening up a franchise."

4

Years of Rapid Growth

A decade later he would be recognized in church circles all over the world as the pope's foreign minister, but on August 17, 1961, at the University of Notre Dame, Monsignor Agostino Casaroli was only a substitute speaker, and a late substitute at that. The Conference of Major Superiors for Men had organized the Second Religious Congress of the United States from August 16 to 19 at Notre Dame, and in view of its decision to consider the problems confronting the church in Latin America, the principal speaker was to be Archbishop Samore, vice president of the Pontifical Commission for Latin America and secretary of the Sacred Congregation for Extraordinary Ecclesiastical Affairs.

But a funeral intervened. Cardinal Domenico Tardini, Pope John XXIII's secretary of state and the man to whom the pontiff had first confided his idea for an ecumenical council, had died, and Archbishop Samore had to remain in Rome for the funeral. Msgr. Casaroli, minutante of the extraordinary ecclesiastical affairs congregation—a young Vatican diplomat who showed signs of promise—was chosen to substitute for Archbishop Samore at the Notre Dame meeting.

The speech he delivered that day would rank as one of the most significant in the history of the U.S. church. It served as a blueprint for the United States' full-scale mission involvement in Latin America; its words set in motion a series of events that were to alter thousands of lives and change the face of the church on two continents. There was a bit of gimmickry to it, and the charismatic appeal of Pope John was close by in the background. But few talks of its kind in the modern church have been as successful in dramatizing a need and drawing forth the desired response to meet it (for the text of the speech, see Appendix I).

Casaroli made it clear at the outset that his was not to be a pro forma pious message; Rome wanted action. The "compelling evidence" of the facts combined with "heart-rending" papal appeals for Latin America would, Casaroli predicted, "lead you to adopt positive resolutions such as the Holy See eagerly expects from this assembly and from the magnificent groups of thousands of men and women religious you represent."

He cited the duty of charity, the importance and the influence of Latin

44

America, and the weakness of the church structure there—the "well-known lack of clergy," the inroads of Protestantism, the menace of Marxism. Some people, Casaroli said, were fearful that Latin America would be lost to the church, but that was not the mood in the Holy See. He quoted optimistic comments about Latin America made by both Pope John and Pope Pius.

The Vatican diplomat concluded the first section of his brief talk with a two-point summary: the church family must collaborate so that none of its rich Latin American heritage would be lost; the church has a "sacred duty" to activate the mostly latent force of the Latin American church itself.

Continuing, Casaroli said the Latin American church was struggling against terrible odds, particularly in regard to the shortage of personnel, to "break the vicious circle in which it seems to be imprisoned." The Holy See was doing its best to aid the effort through its support for organizations such as CELAM and in other ways, and other countries—especially Spain and Belgium, as well as the North American nations—had been of great assistance.

Casaroli cited the Vatican's confidence in North American religious men and women in Latin America—some 2,700 of them at this point—but added: "The need is felt to request yet more from your generosity." He then quoted directly from Samore, the man originally scheduled to give the talk, who had considered possible objections to an expansion of Latin American mission work, and offered his response to them.

Those who were concerned with the needs of their own country, Samore said, should remember that the Lord rewards generosity with "ever more numerous" vocations: "Indeed, I know of particular cases in which, after the acceptance by a particular congregation, for a supernatural motive and at the cost of no little sacrifice, of new fields of apostolic endeavor, their vocations were actually multiplied in a geometrical progression. . . . " Samore's answer to those whose mission apostolate was in another section of the world: "I shall never say: Go to Latin America rather than to other countries; I should be guilty of a serious fault and would feel remorse for it. But I do venture to say: Go, even more than you do now, in even greater numbers, to Latin America, without diminishing your efforts and your contribution in favor of other parts of the earth."

Casaroli then proceeded to the heart of his message: announcement of a future plan and the need for coordination. On an intercontinental level, he said, that would be met by the Pontifical Commission for Latin America, which he described as the "high command" for the effort. There were other agencies—CELAM, and national-level groups such as the United States' Latin America Bureau—to assist in the operation.

On Samore's behalf, in the name of CAL, Casaroli presented the outline of a Ten-Year Plan of Aid to Latin America, calling for both personnel and financial help. "The decade of the 1960s," he said, "may be decisive for the destiny of Latin America even in religious matters, with all the consequences for the church either for good or evil. If an extraordinary generous and wise effort is made within those ten years, we have every reason to expect that, with God's help, the battle will be won."

The plan envisioned direct help in several areas: actual pastoral ministry; seminaries; educational, catechetical, and charitable activities (the latter linked with "health programs" and "social service").

The personnel who would be sent, Casaroli said, should be qualified; "in no case should personnel of what might be called inferior quality be set aside for this work." Then he led up to his main point—"Is it opportune for each community to determine now a certain percentage of its personnel which will be set aside for the service of the church in Latin America?"—and went on to deliver the request that would so profoundly affect the U.S. church:

> The judgment and the decision is left to you. However, interpreting the mind of the Pontifical Commission, I offer you an ideal toward which we request every religious province to strive. This ideal is the following, namely, that each religious province aim to contribute to Latin America in the next ten years a tithe—10 percent—of its present membership as of this current year. For example, if the present membership is five-hundred, the ideal would be to contribute by the end of this decade fifty members for Latin America.
>
> Naturally, all will not be able to achieve this ideal. But it may be possible to reach at least 90 or 80 percent of it.

And so the request was made. It was delivered by Casaroli, speaking for Samore, but the conclusion of the talk made it clear that a higher source was behind it. Said Casaroli:

> The saintly and fatherly Pastor, whom God has set over His Church in our day, when speaking to the superiors general of the institutes of perfection on March 25, 1960, said, "It is necessary that all those who wish to share in the apostolic anxiety of Our heart, should make every effort and every sacrifice to meet the expectations of that great Continent, Latin America."
>
> With that prayer, the Holy Father includes his gratitude and his benediction upon all those of his children who give a generous response.

Fifteen years later those words, that request, remained firmly fixed in the minds of many U.S. missioners. "I read about that speech," one sister said, "and I felt that Pope John was talking directly to me." Many others shared her sentiments, if not in those precise words, certainly in spirit. In view of the depth of the impression made by the papal request and its lasting effect, there is some irony in the fact that the idea—the call for 10 percent, a tithe—originated not with the pope, nor with Samore, nor with his substitute, Casaroli.

It came instead from a dynamic, imaginative U.S. Maryknoller who had as much to do with the U.S. mission effort in Latin America as Ligutti, Samore, or Cushing—perhaps even more. Of him Father Frederick McGuire said: "I don't think there's any one priest in the United States who's made a greater contribution to missionary work." His name is Father John J. Considine.

Maryknoll's Idea Man

John Considine, born in 1897 in New Bedford, Massachusetts, had had a career somewhat out of the Maryknoll mainstream. Ordained in 1923, he went to Rome the following year and remained for a decade, in charge of Fides, an information and research unit of the Holy See that dealt with world missions. The position gave him an opportunity to travel extensively and familiarize himself with the church's mission problems on a global level. Latin America was one area in which he was particularly interested, and his book credits—both before and after a three-year term as Maryknoll's vicar general in the forties—included works on Latin America.

He was a logical choice to head the new Latin America Bureau of NCWC, which came into being following the 1959 inter-American bishops' meeting at Georgetown, and when Cardinal Cushing asked Maryknoll for his services, on a one-year loan basis, the mission society readily complied. He signed on in June of 1960, and fulfilled a summer teaching commitment at Notre Dame before taking up full-time duties in Washington in the fall of that year.

"Father Considine is an idea man," Father McGuire said in a 1976 interview.

He felt that you had to have some goal to strike at, and that's where the 10 percent idea came in. He was convinced that the greatest need in Latin America was priests. There were very few ordinations, and great areas were completely neglected as far as the sacraments were concerned. And he believed that if you gave the religious communities something to strike at, it would be better than approaching them with something nebulous and uncertain.

It's the same thing when you're raising money for Latin America. If you can point to a specific need rather than just say the church is poor and needs your help, you're much better off.

The specific need that Father Considine saw was religious personnel, and the goal—10 percent for Latin America—had the kind of sales-quota approach that somehow seems to appeal in the United States. He took the suggestion to Samore, and it was not long before the Vatican began making plans in that direction. "Samore had absolute confidence in John Considine," Father McGuire recalled. "So did Cushing. As far as they were concerned, if Father Considine said it, it's okay."

The next question to be considered was the manner in which the request was to be presented. Coming from a Father Considine or even an Archbishop Samore, the impact might be—would be, probably—minimal. Coming, on the other hand, from a beloved pope, at a time when American interest in Latin America seemed to be surging—well, who knew how successful that might be?

Father Considine's role in the momentous papal call has remained unpublicized over the years. He would not comment on it when I discussed it with him early in 1977. A few months earlier, responding to a question in his Vatican Library office, Cardinal Samore hunched his shoulders a bit, and extended his hands outward, palms up. "The figure of 10 per cent? I don't remember who first thought of it." He smiled. "But it could have been Father Considine."

Even if he had not originated the idea, it was reasonable to assume that Pope John would have been interested in attracting more mission personnel to Latin America. This was not only a natural progression from the policies and programs of his predecessor, but also a reflection of his personal background. Early in his church career he had taken interest in the missions, and at one point was responsible for a major exhibit in Rome on Latin American (and African) mission work in conjunction with the 1925 Holy Year. Named archbishop and apostolic visitor to Bulgaria in the same year, he had been told he would be there only a short time before being appointed nuncio to an unidentified South American country. His biographers have not explained why that never came about; at any rate, he stayed on in the Balkans for two decades.

In the last months of his life, Pope John made it clear that he regarded his Latin American efforts as one of the major accomplishments of his pontificate, along with the convocation of the Second Vatican Council and his historic encyclicals. One of his first official acts, thirty days after his coronation, was to welcome the Latin American bishops who were in Rome and express his special concern for their problems. In a talk in March 1960, a talk Msgr. Casaroli referred to in his Notre Dame speech, he told a gathering of men and women general superiors of his preoccupation with the mission needs of Latin America. "Personnel must be sent there," he said, "in the greatest numbers possible."

The United States was not the only country to which Pope John made personal (if sometimes indirect) appeals for Latin American mission personnel. After delivering his talk on behalf of the pope at Notre Dame, Monsignor Casaroli went on to Canada where he made the same appeal, on August 22, 1961, to a joint session of the men's and women's sections of the Canadian Religious Conference. There were special papal calls for assistance as well to various European countries. In France, for example, the pope asked the bishops for Latin American volunteers in July 1962. In the next several years there were to be some 350 French diocesan priests at work in Latin America, representing eighty-three dioceses.

Pope John, then, looked on the 10 percent call to the United States as his own, and so did most North Americans who heard it. "It was a magic number that Americans latched on to," said Father Vincent Mallon, the Maryknoll priest who, at the time, was working in Peru. "The times were ripe for just that kind of call."

Cardinal Humberto Medeiros of Boston, then a priest in the Fall River diocese (and later an active member of the bishops' Latin America committee), recalled a similar response. "At the time of Pope John's call there was enthusiasm being generated for volunteer work of all sorts," he said, "a wave of altruism which touched many. The feeling was that this may not last, but here was something good. There was an aura of romance about it, a romance of Christian challenge."

Sister Marlene De Nardo, who entered the Sisters of Notre Dame in California in the fifties, spent more than a decade in Brazil, and is now a lecturer and writer specializing in Latin American affairs, expressed her thoughts about that era in personal terms:

> I remember reading about Latin America when I was in the novitiate. I had the kind of idealism you have when you're very young. I began reading about Latin America, about the most needy nations. I wanted to go because it seemed to be an ideal way of doing what was the most radical, far-out thing that someone could do for Christ. And there's no doubt about it: My community's commitment was a direct response to the plea of the Holy Father.

The timing of the papal call was tailor-made for the young and adventurous in the vibrant U.S. Catholic community, brimming with pride at the election of the United States' first Catholic president, a man who—surely some must have seen this as more than human coincidence—shared Pope John's intense preoccupation with Latin America.

John, the pope, and John Kennedy, the president. Here were two men destined, it seemed, to lead everyone—but especially Catholic America—to a new golden age of peace and prosperity. What better way was there to show thanks for our good fortune than to share it with others? Why not those in Latin America—so dear to the leaders we loved, so short on the blessings we enjoyed, so threatened by godless communism?

As critics were to point out—almost without exception, critics who spoke with the wisdom of hindsight—the patriotic zeal of the U.S. missioners colored their entire mission approach. They were, as more than one commentator has observed, bringing their Americanism with them as much as—perhaps more than—their Christianity. It was a "can-do" kind of Americanism, a style that, eventually, simply did not play in Peru—or Bolivia, or Brazil, or the other Latin American nations into which the United States began pouring personnel.

Father Isaac J. Calicchio, a forty-five-year-old Franciscan who has spent seven years in Honduras and four in El Salvador, pinpointed the problem. Speaking in 1976, he said:

> Americans brought American knowhow with them, but they didn't take into account the systems already in use here. They had the idea that every parish had to have a rectory, a convent for sisters, a school, and a church. Then they began to build dispensaries, clinics, basketball courts, hospitals, roads, cooperatives—all necessary, but all American style. Very few took into account the native customs, systems, attitudes, management. The staff had to be U.S. if it were to succeed.

Father Eugene Culhane, the former managing editor of *America*, later with LADOC, the bishops' Latin American Documentation service, and now working at the Jesuits' central headquarters in Rome, wonders if we read too much into Pope John's appeal:

> Did Rome really mean for us to become so deeply involved in Latin America in 1961? Did they want us to do that as much as they seemed to indicate at the time? I have the feeling that so much of it was political—a reaction to Castro, a desire to keep communism away from the rest of Latin America. Many people in Latin America feel that instead of making a contribution, we were the cause of many of the problems they have today—just as we were the cause of problems in Vietnam by trying to help there.

Others would point to the shortcomings of the 1961 mission push as years went on: "Originally our mission of the sixties was an act of imperialism," said Thomas Quigley, the Latin America specialist in the USCC's Justice and Peace Division. "There's no doubt about that. The bishops down there just watched us come—and watched to see what we'd do wrong."

One of those bishops, Germán Schmitz, an auxiliary of Lima, said priests and bishops in Peru were happy to have the U.S. missioners coming in the early sixties, and recognized their missionary zeal and high ideals. "It wasn't their fault or ours that problems arose," Bishop Schmitz said. "It just happened."

Father Joseph Nangle, the Franciscan who would later go on to a Lima parish but was still in Bolivia at this point, was blunter in his 1976 evaluation of the papal plan: "The problem was the idea itself," he said. "Pope John was off the wall when he asked for 10 percent of the American priests and sisters. It was an impossible idea. A Peruvian priest years later told me that when he heard that, he and his companions were ready to call a panic meeting. They knew there wouldn't be enough planning to carry it off."

Dan C. McCurry, writing on church-financed missions in Peru for a larger study on U.S. relations with that country, is even more blistering in his critique. Citing an earlier study by Father David Farrell, C.S.C. ("The North American Missionary in Peru," prepared for the Peru Policy Project, Adlai Stevenson Institute), he says of the influx of U.S. personnel:

> Conceived in surprise, executed in haste, and now abandoned in frustration, this missionary invasion (in Farrell's words) "was governed more by strategy and tactics than by anything resembling policy criteria. . . . The most glaring error was that it took place with the Peruvian laity and clergy as passive bystanders."

An Early Critic

As noted, most of the criticism about the papal 10 percent plan and the eager U.S. response to it came years after the fact. But one contemporary critic—who was later to have an enormous impact on the U.S. mission experience in Latin America—was Ivan Illich, the New York priest who had been responsible for the archdiocese's impressively successful Puerto Rican program. In 1961, Illich was opening his Center of Intercultural Formation in Cuernavaca, Mexico, as a training ground for U.S. personnel who were being assigned to Latin America.

Monsignor Illich had no taste for the 10 percent plan; the thought of sending waves of untested U.S. missioners to Latin America appalled him. Similarly, he had no use for the new lay mission organization—PAVLA, the Papal Volunteers for Latin America—which was part of Father Considine's comprehensive program of assistance. "Latin America," he would write, "can no longer tolerate being a haven for U.S. liberals who cannot make their point at home, an outlet for apostles too 'apostolic' to find their vocation as competent professionals within their own community."

Despite such strong words and the policy differences that they reflected, Illich was—thanks to an accident of timing and the highly-placed connections he enjoyed in the persons of Cardinals Spellman and Cushing—in charge of what was to become the major training center for U.S. missioners.

It is one of the supreme ironies of the United States mission involvement in Latin America that, in large measure, its missionary personnel were either entirely lacking in Latin American cultural formation, or were sent to be trained by a man who would boast in later years that his efforts were consciously directed against the implementation of Pope John's call. Had the program been coordinated from the beginning, of course, it would not have worked out that way. But coordination was a luxury the Latin American mission program would never enjoy.

There were several factors that led to that absence of coordination, a condition that most of the involved parties have long since conceded. The distances were formidable, for one thing, and communication was often an added problem. The veteran mission groups had learned to cope with this, but bishops and other religious superiors who were used to steady contact with all of their people found it an intolerable burden.

Even more pressing was the problem of time. Clearly there was a hurry-up tone to Pope John's plea; it was as if troops were being rushed to the front to contain an enemy breakthrough. The idea seemed to be that trained personnel were desirable, but if there weren't any to be had, others would do.

Finally, there was the age-old ecclesiastical problem of jurisdiction. There was no central agency that could say that a certain number of priests was needed at a specific location to perform a specific task, and then would be in charge of their recruitment, their training, and their placement. Too many people from both North and South America were making these decisions without regard to an overall order of battle, to a great extent because there were—and are—so many independent jurisdictions in the church. According to Father McGuire:

> John Considine had hoped to be able to do something like this, to have an office which would allocate people where they were needed most. But it just couldn't work; he had no authority over the religious communities.
>
> Dealing with people in Latin America presented a similar problem. They were supposed to put their requests in through our office, but some of them bypassed that. A bishop would come up from Latin America who might have an entré—a religious community, for example—and he would just bypass Father Considine. Then he'd get a commitment from the religious community, without any relationship to Father Considine's office at all. Much of this was done without Father Considine's knowledge. It was a fait accompli by the time he heard about it.

Cardinal Samore referred regretfully to the same lack of coordination. As noted previously, he had originally wanted both Latin American and North American bishops to go through Rome—"not to dominate, but to coordinate"—perhaps through the Pontifical Commission for Latin America. But even if all parties concerned had agreed to such an arrangement, the three-way traffic pattern—South America-Rome-North America—would certainly have proved unmanageable. And not many would have wanted Rome that closely involved.

Added to all these problems was the fact that the United States was developing an unusual mission mix in Latin America. There were, on the one hand, the mission veterans, those religious-community men and women who had been in Latin America previously, often for many years. On the other hand there were the newcomers, those responding to the urgent papal appeal, who were often pitifully untrained. An effective central agency could not only have coordinated their assignments, but also would have insured that the new groups would have avoided typical mistakes of new missioners by benefiting from the experience of their predecessors.

But it didn't happen that way, and what emerged was a pattern in which a few aggressive Latin American personalities were able to induce United States missioners to work in their particular dioceses, or countries, resulting in imbalances that have persisted, in some cases, to this day.

Peru, for example, received a disproportionately large number of missioners in the sixties. Its success in attracting so many men and women is directly traceable to the efforts of the man to whom one U.S. bishop referred smilingly as "a supersalesman in every sense of the word": the apostolic nuncio to Peru, Archbishop Romolo Carboni.

"There's only one reason our diocese opened up a mission in Peru in 1963," a U.S. chancery official said in a conversation a dozen years later, "and that reason was Carboni. The bishop was convinced, absolutely convinced, that Carboni was going to be the next pope, and he wanted to be sure he was on his right side."

It's easy to see how Carboni might impress a North American that way. Affable, genial, outgoing, he quickly puts a guest at ease, giving full attention to whatever the caller might want to discuss. Since 1970 he has been the papal nuncio to Italy, a diplomatic post long on protocol and formality. He presides over a splendid mansion on five lovingly-kept acres in central Rome, a ten-minute walk from the Via Veneto.

"The Peruvian bishops needed priests," Archbishop Carboni said in a relaxed interview.

This was one of the first things they told me when I arrived in Peru in 1959. Soon we worked up a plan. I asked each of the bishops to write to me, giving every essential fact they could about their diocese: its location, population, temperature, altitude; what kind of communications and roads they had; how many churches and chapels—and how many people they needed. We translated this into English, and on one page we had all the essentials. We printed them up, and sent them to bishops and religious superiors in the United States and Canada. It was very practical. . . .

Carboni's resident expert on appealing to North America was Father Mallon, the Maryknoller, who had been working in Lima and responded in 1960 to the nuncio's call for a U.S. priest who could speak Spanish to be his secretary.

"I spent five years with him," Father Mallon said.

He was a remarkable man. I traveled all over Peru with him, and I mean all over Peru. He knew the country inside out. There was a running joke at the time, a Kilroy-was-here kind of thing, because there seemed to be a contest in every out-of-the-way corner of Peru as to who would get there first—the president, Belaúnde, or the nuncio. I think that Carboni won more than he lost.

Mallon played a key role in marshaling forces to attract the coming wave of United States missioners:

We realized that American bishops were coming down who knew nothing about the problems. Where would they start? CELAM was still in its infancy. Americans wanted to know where to send people, how many were needed. . . .

Our questionnaires with the data from the Peruvian bishops went all over North America. We knew that, say, the bishop of Ica had been in a few days before and told us he needed two priests; that Chimbote needed sisters. . . . It was just a matter of putting the information together in a way that North Americans could understand, and getting it to them. Many of them came down to Peru because they weren't getting this kind of help anywhere else.

Not all the U.S. missioners ended up being pleased with the situation. Father George Dudak, a Paterson priest who was cofounder of the diocesan mission in Ica, recalls that Carboni glossed over some of the practical problems in managing to obtain a commitment from the New Jersey diocese:

The Sisters of St. Joseph of Carondelet had opened a school in Ica, patterned after Villa María in Lima, which was very successful. They had committed themselves to a school primarily for middle-class people, but when they got to Ica they ran up against economic problems, and an awfully small number of students. The superior said they would pull out unless they got some American priests to help them, and Carboni went into action. He talked to Maryknoll, to the St. James Society—to no avail. Then he met Bishop Navagh—the bishop of Ogdensburg at the time, and soon to become bishop of Paterson—at the opening session of the Vatican Council. And that's how we got involved in Ica.

The problem was that we were never told the truth of the situation. We thought we were going there to start a parish, to work with the poor, the people in the hospital—all the things that were really worthwhile. We got there and found out that the people expected us to build a school for boys from middle-class families.

The bishop there never knew what to do with us. And we certainly weren't popular with the priests who were already there—mostly

Spanish, and a few native Peruvians. "Here come the hotshot Americans," they were saying. "Let's see what they can do."

Bishop Schmitz recalls that the Peruvian bishops were thinking almost entirely in terms of numbers. "What Carboni did," said the Lima auxiliary, "he did without quarrel from the Peruvian hierarchy. The local bishops acquiesced in Carboni's role; they were just happy to get the priests."

Whatever questions the Carboni tactics might occasion today, they were successful beyond a doubt at the time. According to Father Mallon:

> I wrote an article then on the need for coordinating the requirements of Latin America and the resources of the American church. It was an effort to urge CELAM to take a hand in coordinating the whole thing. But there was no information on a national level except in Peru, and it showed. When I left in 1965, the number of priests and brothers who had come to Peru equaled all those who had gone to the rest of the South American countries.

Carboni notes that in his ten-year tenure in Peru (a term that ended in some difficulty, with Lima's Cardinal Landazuri Ricketts politely but firmly telling the nuncio not to concern himself with internal problems among the Peruvian clergy), 150 religious congregations from other countries—mainly the United States and Canada—went to Peru. In that same period, 68 percent of all diocesan priests from the United States who went to Latin America went to Peru. "Peru had the lion's share of foreign priests and sisters, no doubt about it," the archbishop said. "The need was there; it was simply a matter of presenting it to people in the right way."

"Don't Plan Too Much. Send Men."

However mixed the results might have been, Peru did manage to develop some coordination to its mission requests. Not many countries would match that achievement. Not only were there not enough Carbonis to go around; some of his counterparts wanted nothing of his approach. One of them was Archbishop Mozzoni, the former nuncio in Bolivia who had attracted U.S. Franciscans a few years earlier, and who held a similar position in Argentina when the United States mission buildup began in earnest. Xaverian Brother Thomas More Page, now executive director of the Conference of Major Superiors of Men, was part of a U.S. fact-finding group that visited Latin America in 1963. Part of his journal entry for February 24, when the visitors were in Buenos Aires, reads:

> Later on in the morning we were the guests of the apostolic nuncio, Archbishop Umberto Mozzoni. He told us we were rushing too much

and that the bishops were tired of making plans. His bishops are preoccupied with their immediate problems that were demanding a solution. . . . After inviting us to be his guests for dinner at El Cabinero, he said, "Don't plan too much. Send men."

Send men. In the early sixties, that was the bottom line on the success or failure of any U.S. mission endeavor in Latin America. But just how were they to be sent?

"If I could have advised Pope John based on what I know now," Bishop John Fitzpatrick of Brownsville said in 1976, "I would have suggested that he establish a commission to study the needs of the church in Latin America, to set up criteria for help—and not only in personnel."

As chairman of the U.S. bishops' Latin America committee, he had had extensive opportunities to see at first hand the results, the fruits of the mission invasion of the sixties.

There should have been complete understanding on the part of the American bishops as to what kind of people would be needed, and that the Latin American bishops would take and use them as well as could have been possible. I wouldn't have opted for the situation where one diocese sends its own men down, puts up its buildings, and forms its own little island.

In a talk he gave in October 1976 to officials of the Society of the Propagation of the Faith, Bishop Fitzpatrick expanded on that theme:

Are we Americans really being missionary when we commit ourselves to Latin America for only three years or five years, leaving ourselves a back door through which to escape? It seems to me that it's part and parcel of a missionary's commitment that he is willing and really wants to stay where he's going forever, and not just for a time.

CELAM addressed itself to the problem of coordinating mission efforts, as Brother Thomas More noted in the diary of his 1963 trip:

Msgr. Guerrero Julián Mendoza, secretary general of CELAM, . . . explained how this organization works with and through CAL, the Pontifical Latin American Commission in Rome headed by Archbishop Samore. . . . In November of this year all the bishops of Latin America will present their needs to CAL, which will list the priority of these needs and then present them to the Latin America Bureau of NCWC, whose chairman is Father John Considine, M.M. Father Considine will then distribute this list to the American bishops. . . .

On paper, for a visiting group of U.S. mission observers, it sounded perfect. But it was a game plan that never went into effect.

As far as numbers were concerned, the United States response to Pope John's call was good, but not exceptional. In the two-year period beginning in January 1962, 761 missioners from the United States entered Latin American church service. There were 335 sisters, 244 priests, 182 lay missioners. The diocesan clergy, up until that point all but unrepresented in Latin America, accounted for 10 percent of the total number of priests in that period. Almost 50 of the 140 ordinaries had responded to the papal call. It was, reported Father Considine in *The Church in the New Latin America*, a "phenomenon never before recorded in United States ecclesiastical annals."

A few months earlier, there had been an optimistic report for Pope John to contemplate. Writing to the Holy Father on March 19, 1963, Archbishop Joseph T. McGucken of San Francisco, chairman of the subcommittee for recruitment of the United States bishops' Latin America committee, reported "substantial progress."

Eighty-eight percent of the dioceses and 85 percent of the "generalates and provincialates" had indicated "active interest" in the request for personnel, Archbishop McGucken said, and among the communities of sisters, interest was only slightly less, at 79 per cent.

The San Francisco archbishop noted special projects within United States borders directed at the Spanish-speaking, and quoted various religious superiors as they indicated their desire to comply with the Holy Father's wishes: "Each year the community will strive to send additional personnel in compliance with the wishes of the Holy Father," wrote Mother Kathryn Marie, C.S.C., of the Sisters of the Holy Cross at Notre Dame. The School Sisters of St. Francis, Milwaukee, said: "In accordance with the directives of the Holy See we plan to send additional sisters regularly so as to reach the 10 percent of our membership as suggested by His Holiness."

Archbishop McGucken concluded:

This spirit of zealous generosity is reflected within the rank and file of the clerical and religious forces in the United States. Hundreds of our clergy and thousands of our religious sisters have expressed an apostolic desire to serve the church in Latin America.

It is notable in the United States at the present moment that this growing movement to serve the church in Latin America does not represent the assignment of superfluous personnel. No such superfluity exists. It represents, rather, an admirable readiness on the part of ordinaries and superiors to sacrifice great needs in the homeland to serve the far larger needs of the church in a neighboring region which throughout great areas suffers grave jeopardy through a shortage of personnel.

The actual contribution to date is modest but the preparations for more substantial assignments of personnel are clearly evident.

Pope John's reply—addressed to the U.S. bishops through Cardinal Cushing, as head of the Latin America committee—was a touching testimony of faith. Dated March 21, 1963, less than three months before his death, it expressed in intensely personal language the Holy Father's "profound joy" on receiving the U.S. report (a report widely circulated in reproduced handscript form throughout the United States). The ailing pontiff wrote:

> Nor is this response surprising, since We are well aware of the eager cooperation which the American bishops and religious have always given to every praiseworthy undertaking. . . . We realize that it is not superfluous personnel that is sent to these countries, but that grave domestic needs are curtailed in order to grant laudable aid to the Church in Latin America, which you regard as a wider field of action to which the active concern of Catholics must be channeled, in order to assist a so important and imperiled member of the Mystical Body of Christ.

The pope paid tribute to U.S. bishops for encouraging religious personnel as well as their own priests to go to Latin America (". . . among all these initiatives special recognition is due to the Pious Society of St. James the Apostle, founded by you, beloved Son, which has already furnished 78 priests, half of them from your own diocese . . . ").

It was natural, Pope John continued, that religious congregations would make the most impact: "We are pleased to note that Our expectations have been satisfied and will be even more completely fulfilled, We feel confident, in the near future. . . . "

Confident, perhaps. But the long-range outlook was clearly in doubt.

> We are prompted to express once more Our sincere thankfulness to you, Beloved Son, to the other U.S.A. Cardinals and Bishops, and Major Religious Superiors of Men and Women and also to send Our words of encouragement to persevere fervently therein. The most serious problem to be worked on in Latin America, namely, the shortage of clergy, is still far from its hoped-for solution. We obtained authoritative and sorrowful confirmation of this from the Latin American Archbishops and Bishops who came to Rome for the Ecumenical Council, and who described the shortage to Us in all its extent as their urgent need and their preoccupying trouble.

Pope John expressed optimism—regrettably unfounded, as it turned out—on one point:

We are certain that by means of efficacious collaboration between your various organizms [sic] set up by the Hierarchy and Religious, and Our Pontifical Commission for Latin America, so providently instituted exactly five years ago by Our Predecessor Pius XII of venerated memory, all activities will be fruitfully coordinated.

There would be changes, deep changes, as the result of the United States mission adventure into Latin America. But ironically, they were not to be the changes Pope John longed for.

At a policy-making level, the experience reversed the thinking of much of the U.S. hierarchy, preparing it for a global involvement it could never otherwise have envisioned. According to Msgr. Joseph Gremillion:

Until 1960 and into the years of Vatican II, the bishops of North America didn't know anything about the Latin American church. The U.S. church had been very nationalistic, inward-looking. It regarded foreign lands as lands for "missionaries," for mission orders. There was no sense of brotherhood. There weren't ten bishops in the United States who knew the names of five of their brother-bishops in Latin America.

That would all soon change. So would the lives of hundreds of U.S. Catholics who took part in that mission wave, and it was on that level that the impact of the Latin American mission experience was to be driven home. One of those missioners was Brother Julian Riley, C.F.X., who was forty-three years old when he went off to teach in a Bolivian school in 1962. "It changed my views forever," he said, "chiefly by my being able to see the God-given individuality, the unique personality in even the most wretched child. To paraphrase Will Rogers, I never met a poor Bolivian I didn't like. I can't say the same for the wealthy and powerful."

How would he feel about the 10 percent call, looking back on it years later? How would he advise a new Pope John in 1977, a pope considering the same kind of appeal? His answer was flatly practical:

The ten percent idea is a gimmick; don't take it too seriously. Don't send anyone down to Latin America to solve his personal problems; they tend to aggravate in the loneliness and strangeness of a different *ambiente*. Be willing to invest your money moderately. But don't expect to "get your money's worth."

Father Conall McHugh, a Conventual Franciscan who went to Costa Rica to do parish work in 1959 at the age of thirty, underwent the same kind of changes in his eleven-year tour of duty. "When I first went to Costa Rica," he said, "I thought we had all the answers. Then I saw first-hand the big companies' policies, their treatment of people, and our government putting dollars first. I see our economic life as too high for some and too low for others. Capitalism should have some kind of a ceiling on how much an individual and a company can own."

But the people who should have been changed—the faceless, numberless Latin Americans who should have been enriched, being exposed to the love of Christ through these friendly visitors from the North—were strangely untouched.

"I'll always remember what one old Peruvian told me," Father Leo Donnelly, a Columban priest in Lima, recalled. " 'You came down here,' he said—he meant mostly the Americans, but all the rest of us, the Australians like myself, were also included—'You came down here with a full chalice, overflowing. Instead you should have come with an empty cup. We would have filled it for you.' "

5

A Response to Pope John:
The Religious Communities

Mrs. Charles Mitchell of Marshfield, Massachusetts, looks back now in bemusement and some disbelief to that day in September 1962, when, improbably, she found herself flying to Peru. The trip in itself was more or less incredible, she remembers; what made it more so was the fact that she spent most of the time on the flight conjugating Spanish verbs in her mind.

She was Sister Richard Clare then, a member of the Sisters of St. Joseph of Carondelet. The Sisters of St. Joseph of Carondelet were one of more than a hundred U.S. religious communities, of both men and women, that responded to Pope John's call for personnel to be sent to Latin America. Sister Richard Clare, who had been Peggy O'Brien of St. Louis, was one of three sisters—all now out of religious life—who formed the community's first contingent of volunteers. One of her companions was from California, the other from St. Paul. She recalled:

> We had all kinds of great ideas as to what was going to happen. We expected a military escort at the airport. We heard that the papal nuncio wanted us so bad that we really expected him to be there. We pulled into the airport on a foggy, dreary day, and there was no military escort, no archbishop. Just a couple of American nuns, who were very friendly, but that was all. Eighteen members of my family saw us off; it was a traumatic departure. What a contrast to the landing! And all I could think of was that all I knew in Spanish were the different endings of the verbs.

There were hundreds of U.S. priests and sisters in 1962 and 1963 who could identify with Sister Richard Clare, who knew exactly how she felt. Their communities, moved by Pope John's wishes as formulated by Father John Considine and relayed by Monsignor Casaroli, were sending the troops into the Latin American mission field. They were recruits, true, unused to mission duties and mostly unprepared for what lay ahead. The superiors wished for better training, for more time. But the call had gone out; the need existed now. And the priests and brothers and sisters went into the campaign.

Archbishop Joseph McGucken's 1963 report to Pope John spelled out the details enthusiastically. There were 81 U.S. religious communities of priests at work in Latin America, about 35 percent of the national total of 231. Of those, thirteen had begun their involvement since the 1961 papal appeal, and another 44 were getting ready to move into Latin American assignments. The increase of United States religious priests at work in Latin America since the papal call stood at 279, a rise of 23 percent over the previous figure. The new total was 1,478.

The totals for women's religious communities were even more impressive. There were 529 separate communities in the United States at the time, and 119 of them were at work in Latin America. Thirty-five had begun their missions since the 1961 appeal, and an additional 97—a remarkable figure—had made specific commitments to go to Latin America in the near future.

Archbishop McGucken's report included excerpts from responses to his questionnaires: "We shall continue to increase our personnel," wrote Mother M. Lorenza, C.PP.S., of the Sisters of the Most Precious Blood, O'Fallon, Missouri, "until we have complied with the wishes of the Holy Father—and more than that if possible." Reverend Mother M. Cyril, R.S.M., of the Sisters of Mercy of Burlingame, California, said: "We propose to send four sisters in 1964 and to continue to send sisters until our quota of 10 percent of our membership (427) is fulfilled."

That kind of optimism was not unusual at the time. Vocations were at a peak; people were available for the kind of Latin American duties the pope so clearly wanted. That was the situation, certainly, in the community of the Sisters of St. Joseph of Carondelet, who had sent a team of superiors to Peru to check out details once their commitment was made. They had been asked to set up schools, one in Ica, and another, in cooperation with a community of Marist priests, in Arequipa. And while they were there, on their preliminary trip, the apostolic nuncio—Archbishop Carboni—had another thought: Could the sisters also staff the Military Hospital in Lima?

It seemed an insignificant enough request at the time, but it was to have long-range effects on the sisters' preparation. Because the Sisters of St. Joseph of Carondelet were to work at the Peruvian Military Hospital, they were denied training at Monsignor Illich's Cuernavaca center. Illich wanted no connection with the South American military, not even at the hospital level. As a result, Sister Richard Clare's preparation for her Latin American assignment consisted of a four-week course in the Spanish language in St. Louis, and she flew to Peru reciting the endings of Spanish verbs.

The nuns who met her and her companions at the Lima airport were IHM sisters from Villa María, who proved to be the welcoming committee for hundreds of U.S. sisters answering the papal call in the early sixties. (If they made their fellow U.S. missioners feel at home, they also gave them a touch of the local ambience, particularly the relative degree of independence that would be theirs in Peru. There were Pisco Sours for the new arrivals, who agreed that home was never like this.)

"Four or five days later we went to see the hospital," recalled Mrs. Mitchell, a nurse. "It had previously been staffed by nuns from Europe. The convent was absolutely filthy, which discouraged us no end. And we knew nothing, not even how to get something to eat."

The IHMs in Lima weren't the only congregation that took the trouble to welcome the new wave of nonprofessional missionary sisters; they had an assist from the Maryknoll sisters. One who took part in that project was Sister Bernadette Desmond, who arrived to work in the "model parish" of Santa Rosa in 1960 and later was the coordinator—the equivalent of regional superior—for Maryknoll sisters in Peru. "We had all been made to feel very welcome ourselves," she said of her own arrival. "We were the great white mothers and fathers—which, when you look back on it, almost forced you into a paternalistic role."

In addition to providing "a good English education" for middle-class Peruvians, the Maryknoll sisters of that time felt a responsibility to share with the growing number of incoming missioners their own Peruvian experience. The group from Maryknoll had absorbed a good deal in their formation as far as mission work was concerned. There was contact with returning missioner-lecturers, part of the Maryknoll community tradition. They had a background that simply had not been available to the others, who had been exposed to a crash-program approach that left many questions unanswered.

Many of the newcomers had come to Latin America from provincial U.S. settings, Sister Bernadette remembers:

> Some of us and some of them were very young; some had held top professional jobs. We all faced a lack of organization. And we had all just started to be aware of the fact that although you tend to come into a situation like this with your own cultural values dominating, you soon begin to understand more clearly that there are basic Gospel values common to all cultures and that no culture has all the answers.

A Case of Cultural Shock

For most American religious—both men and women—the shock of coming up against Latin American realities in the early sixties was a memorable experience. "My education as a priest started the day I hit Peru," said Maryknoll Father James Madden.

"I was twenty-four when I arrived in Brazil," recalled Father Elias Manning, a Conventual Franciscan from Troy, New York.

> We used to joke about the primitive conditions we expected to find, the old romantic idea about the missioner going out on horseback to say Mass for the peasants. And then we saw downtown Rio!

The paternal approach was as much a problem for the Conventual Franciscans in those days as it was for anybody else. We moved in with the idea that we had plenty of money, plenty of people backing us in the States. All we had to do, we felt, was to get things moving. We operated for a long time that way. The people just stood back, feeling that the way we operated we didn't need their help. Then the change in thinking came about . . . and some of those who couldn't go along with the changes in attitude it required were the ones who left.

Father John J. Burkhart was one of the original members of a mission to Peru established by the Augustinians' midwest province in direct response to Pope John's call ("Volunteers weren't forthcoming, and I was asked to go"). He described the difficulties of the early years:

There was a continual adjustment problem: first, adjustment to a new language, customs, and culture; then adjustment to physical hardships—roads, no water and no sewerage, no electricity; adjustment to different ways of doing things, to the local religious practices of a non-American church organization; and finally, adjustment to loneliness.

(Father Burkhart, who has been in mission promotion and development work since returning from Peru in 1971, found an unexpected benefit, however, in his assignment: "Since I went to the mission right before the Vatican Council's changes were effected and confusion reigned in the States, my personal feeling is that at least indirectly my presence in the missions probably saved my priestly vocation. Had I been in the States I would have been part and parcel of the movement for some radical change. In South America, the change was more gradual, more meaningful, and hopefully more lasting. My faith was definitely buoyed up and strengthened by my mission experience.")

Missioners from religious communities whose Latin American assignments began in the early sixties recall a variety of problems that impressed them at the time. For Franciscan Father Isaac Calicchio, who went to Honduras, it was the strong traditional ties of the Indians to magic, spiritism, and witchcraft, which deeply affected the practice of their nominal Catholic religion. Father John F. Henry, a Jesuit who was assigned to Chile, was moved by a feeling of helplessness to meet the poverty he saw. In Mexico, Dominican Sister Katherine Wejrowski (of the Congregation of Holy Cross, Edmonds, Washington) had a complaint about the orphanages at which she worked: "I always found plenty to do, but some left in discouragement with a feeling they were not needed." In Bolivia, where he taught for ten years, Christian Brother Regis Moynihan developed a similar impression. "I experienced a growing feeling that I was wasting my time," he said, "a feeling that the people there really didn't need our help based on their way of thinking. . . . I enjoyed the experience, felt I had made my best efforts, and yet made very little impact."

While most missioners of the time were dissatisfied with the preparation they had received for their assignments, particularly in conditioning them for the realities they were to encounter, the feeling was by no means universal. Many who went through the Illich method of orientation—either at Cuernavaca or at a companion training center at Petropolis, Brazil, near Rio de Janeiro—felt a good deal more ready for the work they were about to undertake. (And other Illich students, it must be noted, felt just the opposite. A future chapter will discuss this in more detail.)

Sister Marlene De Nardo was sent to Petropolis along with four other sisters of Notre Dame when she volunteered to work in Brazil in 1962. Most of the fifty people there were U.S. missioners, almost all of them priests.

Illich used a shock-treatment approach, Sister Marlene recalls. He challenged the group, asking if the Americans were coming to take the God of the people, or if they were bringing a God of their own. "What was so positive about the school," she said, "was not so much that it prepared us for what we'd find; I don't know that anything could have done that. But it opened us up to possibilities. This was important to us, coming from the U.S. situation. Illich made it clear to us that we didn't have all the answers."

There were three general categories of U.S. religious communities that were involved in the Latin America "boom" of the time: first, the large orders with congregations and provinces in many countries—Franciscans, Jesuits, Redemptorists, and the like—which had previously had a Latin American mission involvement; second, other U.S. congregations without previous experience that undertook Latin American commitments in direct response to the 1961 papal call; and finally, the organizations—actually, only two, the Maryknoll priests and sisters—whose sole purpose was the training and assignment of U.S. men and women for mission duty. (The Society of St. James the Apostle, as noted previously, consists entirely of diocesan personnel who volunteer for Latin American duty, for a specific period. The St. James Society will be discussed further in the following chapter, which considers the role of U.S. dioceses in responding to the call of Pope John.)

Almost all of the communities in the first category—those which had previously-existing Latin American missions—saw an increase in the number of volunteers for those assignments. Latin America was receiving an unusually high amount of attention in the North American church at the time; religious personnel were constantly being reminded of the plight of their brothers and sisters to the south. And many communities were making a conscious effort to meet the suggested 10 percent commitment, actively recruiting Latin America volunteers as a result.

Those who had been there, the pioneers, eased the way. Father James Sullivan of the Oblates of Mary Immaculate had been in Brazil since 1953 and helped to welcome an influx of new personnel in the sixties. There was a close

OMI tradition in Brazil on which to build. "From the very beginning, we were a close group," Father Sullivan said. "The first guys, for example. . . . We were spread pretty thin, and one man would wait four and five hours just to make a phone call to another one. They'd make a seven-hour drive just for another guy's birthday."

Some of the established mission groups had difficulties as the years went on, and it became apparent that new methods of preparation, of involvement in the lives of the people, were called for.

Father Joseph Nangle made this criticism of his own Franciscan mission organization:

> As Franciscans we're not trained for pastoral work as diocesan men are; our first allegiance is to the Franciscan community. So we go into a mission field, and the tendency is never to break into the local reality. Too, the areas themselves where we're working are so remote that they're almost inaccessible; there's no chance to plug in. We were trained that the more sacraments we dispensed, the better.

A Franciscan who followed him to Bolivia years later had the same reaction: "The original idea here was that you walk into Latin America, put up schools, convents, churches, and you have New Jersey revisited," said Father Fidelis McKee, elected superior of North American Franciscans in Bolivia in 1974. He also noted that poor preparation of missioners remained a problem for a long time: "When I came I was only the second of the Franciscans to have studied Spanish beforehand, and that was in 1971."

Father James B. Malley joined the Jesuits' long-time mission in northeast Brazil in 1965 and, looking back at it later, said "the fundamental assumptions seem wrong." He continued:

> The pastoral ministry was directed toward maintaining (by outside resources, human and material) an obsolete parish structure. We arrived equating Christianity with North American Catholicism and culture. We did try to learn and adjust, but I came to feel that the foreign presence—just by being there and letting the old structures survive —was holding back the painful birth of a bright new life.

The second category of U.S. religious personnel who were in Latin America at the time were those whose communities had established their missions at the urging of Rome, and some missioners feel now there was a distinct advantage to being in that situation. "The mission groups who were there before the sixties tended to be so established in their ways that later they couldn't do anything about it," said Sister Marlene De Nardo. "In our case we were freer, and we were able to do things differently."

In a talk given at Maryknoll's 1976 convocation on the theme of global justice, she discussed the growth of the Notre Dame sisters' experience in Brazil:

> Gradually during the years we learned to take on the joys and the sorrows of the peasant farmers, students and urban workers, but not without difficulty. Our American perspective was simply "American" and that made it hard for us to even conceive another posture in life. Nonetheless, eventually by some grace, we began experiencing events as the people did. With them we became enthused during the years of new political and social freedom in the early sixties, and with them we were angry and discouraged during the repressive years of torture and totalitarianism after the military coup in 1964.

Political events of that same year were also a strong formative force in the eventful mission career of Holy Cross Father Daniel Panchot, who studied theology in Chile from 1962 to 1965 and later returned there as a missioner, following another assignment in Peru. In November 1975, he was arrested and imprisoned for two weeks before being expelled "from what had come to be my second home," as he told the global justice convocation in 1976.

Father Panchot recalled that the principal influences on his priesthood had been Vatican II, the renewal of the Chilean church, and the 1964 election between Christian Democrat Eduardo Frei and Salvador Allende, the Marxist candidate:

> The campaign brought out all of the traditional fears and prejudices between Christians and Marxists. The whole future of Christianity in Chile seemed to be conditioned on a Frei victory. The church had to go out and show itself, especially to the masses. . . . And the church wanted to make a good impression, show a smiling face. Frei won a 56 percent majority. In Chilean politics this was a landslide. This experience had a powerful effect on our formation as seminarians. It showed us a lot about the church, and it showed us a lot about the people, too.

If the newer mission-sending organizations were able to be more flexible than were their pioneering predecessors, there were particular sets of problems to be faced as well. More often than not, the volunteers came from a background that included no mission formation, or a very limited exposure to it. Even those who benefited from the Illich style of orientation were coming to their assignments with no deep appreciation of the church's historic mission role. Another problem dealt with the most familiar identifying feature of religious orders: community life. In many cases it was sorely affected by the small size of individual mission communities.

"Community life with only one, two, or three other brothers, at times the same ones for several years running," presented a serious problem, said

Christian Brother Julian Riley. (Brother Julian, whose twelve-year teaching career in Bolivia began in 1962, has strong positive feelings about the overall mission experience, particularly in "teaching the students to respect themselves and their neighbors by showing them respect myself.")

Father Gerard Theis, a member of the midwest Augustinian community that began its Peru mission in 1964, saw the need for the missioners' spiritual formation as one area that was frequently overlooked. There were those who had been apparently well-prepared as far as language and culture were concerned, but had not readied themselves spiritually and evangelically. "The church developed," he commented, "built on prayer and the Scriptures, not dependent on either the political situation or the number of clerical-religious pastoral agents available."

There was a different aspect to the problems faced by the third category of U.S. religious communities in Latin America, the Maryknollers. They did not have to stumble through the unfamiliarity of mission life, as did the new volunteers, and they weren't there with an eye toward expanding their community—as, perhaps, the Marianists or Carmelites or Redemptorists might be—but simply to fulfill their basic mission assignment.

Maryknoll's growth in the period was not tied directly to the papal appeal; vocations in general were numerous and anyone who chose Maryknoll had known that a mission assignment somewhere—anywhere—was likely. Maryknoll's interest in Latin America was genuine, but it was part of a wider, global concern.

As the most identifiable U.S. mission organization, Maryknoll found itself in something of an awkward situation regarding the new missioners of the sixties. If the local Maryknoll community worked too hard at welcoming the newly-arrived religious mission from the States, it might be accused of elbowing in, showing it had all the answers. If it hesitated, its members could be accused of being aloof and standoffish. For the most part, Maryknoll priests and sisters in Latin America took a middle course, making assistance available to other U.S. missioners if it was needed—and wanted.

The theory behind that kind of assistance was that Maryknoll had already been through the course and could pass along the benefits of its experience, sometimes painfully gained, to those who were arriving. It was an assumption that was to be challenged in later years by some commentators. A critic of U.S. church policies in Peru during the 1960s places much of the blame on Maryknoll. He is himself a former Maryknoll priest, Joseph Michenfelder, who believes that U.S. missioners evolved an expedient "un-policy" during the period, marked by attitudes of triumphalism, paternalism, and "ecclesiastical interventionism"—in which U.S. mission interests were combined with those of the papal nuncio, at the expense of the Peruvian church and, ultimately, the Peruvian people.

In "The Policies of the U.S. Catholic Church in Peru—1960–68," Michenfelder asserted:

The Maryknoll fathers and sisters, by way of their numerical strength, diversity of "apostolic works," twenty years experience in Peru, and remarkable prestige among Latin and North Americans alike, tended quite naturally to be pacesetters for the smaller, less experienced communities of religious. The latter were not, in point of fact, "professional missioners." . . . Without implying that Maryknollers consciously promoted the body of un-policy outlined above, much of the onus rests with them. Indeed, their recent impressive internal reform, based on the documents of their 1966 general chapter, is a kind of admission that their modus operandi in Peru and elsewhere was thoroughly incompatible with the signs of the times, and that authentic mission policy is indispensable to their own future and the future of the people they hope to serve as instruments of liberation.

Those early years were, by and large, uncritical times for missionaries sent to Latin America by their religious communities. Latin American bishops were too pleased with the numbers to be overly concerned with the level of performance; for the missioners themselves, it was still a time of excitement and adventure. And for everyone connected with the mission enterprise, it was a period in which the church had not had to face the challenges, the examinations of conscience and purpose, which would be demanded by Vatican II.

As years went on and success seemed to become more elusive, critical commentaries—much as Michenfelder's above, or such as Ivan Illich's famous *America* magazine article, "The Seamy Side of Charity," of which much more will be said in a later chapter—began to appear.

For U.S. religious communities, though, the definitive critique of their effort appeared a decade after the big mission push from the north began, and it came from a panel of experts in the field: the First Inter-American Conference of Religious, meeting in Mexico City from February 8 through 12, 1971. The findings were heavily negative.

While the response to Pope John's call had been generous, the conference found, the personnel selected were not always the best, and choices were made according to norms unacceptable in the seventies. There was a lack of planning and coordinating, both in sending and receiving churches, and the preparation of personnel was often inadequate. Language and acculturation centers "had many shortcomings and did not always live up to expectations."

Many of those religious who were sent, continued the unrelievedly harsh evaluation, had no appreciation of the needs of the local churches, a fault not entirely their own, since Latin American bishops who were pleased with the numerical response simply asked for more and more people. "Specific tasks were seldom indicated by the hierarchy," the report said, "with the result that many North American religious were asking themselves what they were really doing in Latin America."

The conference found that no solid criteria had ever been established, on a large scale, for either sending or receiving missioners. Instead, it said, "personnel were sent to help the congregation's efforts rather than the church of Latin America. The new views in the theology of the mission and the importance of local churches even were not yet properly understood." Some North American congregations developed triumphalistic attitudes; they made a point of calling attention to their members working in other parts of the world.

The gloomy critique seemed to have no end of unfavorable comments: North American religious personnel had not been inserted in a definite pastoral plan; the concentration of North American missioners led to two problems: the establishment of ghettos and the phenomenon of dependency, in which Latin American bishops came to rely more and more on personnel from the north. Far from inspiring the Latin American church to a time of greatness through its example, the North American mission was doing just the opposite.

The Canadian church was very much a part of the picture, the conference noted; the United States was not alone in the situation. Canada's response had been as generous as the United States': from 1,000 Latin America missioners in 1960, to more than 2,000 in 1971, including almost 1,000 sisters and nearly 500 religious-order priests and 278 brothers. But the errors were the same as well. "We were answering an urgent call from the Holy See," said Bishop Albert Sanschagrin of St. Hyacinthe, Quebec, a one-time missionary in Chile and, at the time of the Mexico City conference, president of the Office for Latin America of the Canadian Catholic Conference. "Very often, we were not prepared to fulfill completely and effectively what was expected of us. Hence the mistakes were made. We admit this. Our errors were mostly due to inexperience and lack of planning."

The pessimistic conclusions of the conference were that the North American presence in Latin America, particularly its concentration in limited areas, had slowed the entire process of liberation. In addition to the attitudes of superiority and the ghetto mentality it fostered, it led also to an aura of fear. Because North American religious missioners are insecure and uncertain, the report said, they "are reluctant to integrate fully into the Latin American situation."

The conference report noted, ultimately, that the church of Latin America had been built on foreign values and structures, from Europe, initially, and then from North America, and that both "are now irrelevant to the new man in Latin America, the Christian of Vatican II and Medellín."

Success—in Self-Fulfillment

It was the kind of critical assessment which would have touched off a furor in the early sixties. The North American religious who had responded to the call for Latin American volunteers would have angrily dismissed it as an ungrateful outburst. But it attracted little attention, let alone complaint, when it was delivered in the seventies. The overwhelming majority of North American missioners, past and present, could recognize the truth it contained.

It was not that the experience of the religious personnel who had taken part in the enterprise of the sixties was all that negative; far from it. But most of the positive results they reported, rather than benefiting the Latin American church or its people, were those involving self-fulfillment in one way or another. The mission experience had enriched the missioners more than it had helped Latin Americans. It was Illich who said that North America would receive more from the Latin American church than it would ever give; the judgments of individual missioners tend to bear him out.

Jesuit Father James Malley, for example, looks back on the satisfaction of his years in South America. He speaks of "the wonderful Brazilian people who began the process of teaching me to be human; living in the slums, and being authentically poor in many (but not all) dimensions."

Augustinian Father John Burkhart: "Being accepted by the people not because I was a foreigner but despite that fact, and being wanted, not tolerated, as their pastor."

Another Augustinian priest, Father Gerard Theis: "My Peruvian brothers taught me how to be human . . . open, warm, trusting and self-giving."

Father Elias Manning, who now heads the Conventual Franciscans' U.S. custody in Brazil, saw that kind of personal growth at the heart of the development of those U.S. mission communities that have kept pace with developments in the Latin American church:

> We came with the idea that we only have something to give—a real intellectual and cultural paternalism—and nothing to learn. Over the past few years we've really changed. For one thing, there's the length of time we've been there, and the type of men who are staying. The uncommitted left long ago. Two, we've gotten to be fluent in the language; that used to be a real barrier. Third, many people took courses on their own, learned about all the beauties and the strengths of local cultural values. Finally, we've changed our thinking about what constitutes a mission and what constitutes the missioner's job. What does he do? Everything you read today knocks the old ideas, the old approaches. Missioners have absorbed this new mentality. And once you receive something like this, it opens up your mind even more.

Sister Richard Clare, who was so disappointed in her airport welcome to Peru, went through the same kind of personal growth in her seven years there. She stayed on at the military hospital for most of that time, even though she wasn't convinced it was a good idea. "There were other apostolates," she said, "where we were so much more needed." But still she feels that she made an impact:

I felt I did that personally, in the lives of the people I touched. They saw nursing in a new light. I felt I had an impact on the doctors, how they treated patients. I pushed hard, and I found myself speaking up. I remember one woman patient whose doctors wanted to tie her tubes, over her objections. She had no voice in the decision, but her husband did—and I was able to influence him. A year later I found she had a healthy boy and named him Richard, after my religious name. And I was able to stop an abortion planned on a mother who was stricken with cancer. Her condition was incurable, and she was to die later on—but she did give birth to a healthy baby.

How many lives I affected, I don't know. But I know I affected some.

One of the most appealing elements of Latin America missionary life, she recalls, was the inter-community cooperation she found—a condition she had not experienced in the United States.

Her personal development was influenced immeasurably by her years in Peru, she feels. They were years which did not weaken her faith, she says, but rather led her to new areas of service and a different approach to her life. She went into the public health field after leaving the Sisters of St. Joseph of Carondelet and today, married to a teacher (and former priest), heads a municipal health program that operates out of a Boston hospital. "There was a great initial appeal to Latin American work," she said, "in terms of excitement and challenge. But the long-range values were something else. It was an eye-opener. It simply opens people up to a different way of life."

Personal growth, and the lessons of time. They are the two lingering impressions of Latin American mission duty a reporter has after writing and talking to hundreds of religious people who have gone through it.

None expressed it better than Father Matthias R. Mueller, a Dominican who has been in Bolivia since 1958 and feels that perhaps his work hasn't borne all the fruit it should have in that time. There were the old problems, he said, of entering mission work with preconceived ideas and a lack of orientation. "Maybe it takes ten or twelve years to wake up," he reflected. "At least it did for me. But, thank God—I think I've grown!"

6

A Response to Pope John:
The Dioceses

Father Considine, in the introduction to *The Church in the New Latin America* (which he edited in connection with the first CICOP meeting, held in 1964), related the story of a pastor from St. Cloud, Minnesota, who had been given $125 by a high school boy in his parish. The youth had earned the money over a period of more than a year, raising pigs and a couple of cows, and had plans for spending every penny of it—until he heard that the St. Cloud diocese was making arrangements to open a mission in South America. "I think it's so fine to help the people in Latin America who need priests," he told the pastor, and asked that the money be given to one of the new diocesan missioners.

"It is astonishing," the unnamed pastor said, "what a flurry of excitement passed over the diocese of St. Cloud when Bishop Bartholome announced that he was sending several of his priests to help the people in one of the dioceses in Venezuela. Everybody wanted to have a part in it."

It happened in St. Cloud, and it happened all over the United States. Ogdensburg, Dubuque, Newark, LaCrosse, Manchester, Buffalo, Yakima, Erie. . . . In the early sixties dioceses by the dozens were packing off priests to remote areas of Central and South America to open their own diocesan missions.

At the beginning of 1960, there were only 14 United States diocesan priests serving in overseas missions, but the number was to spiral upward in geometric fashion: in 1962, it was 31; 1964, 80; 1966, 215. (The figure peaked in 1970 at 373; by 1977 it was down to 182.) All but a handful of the diocesan missioners were working in Latin America, living testimony to the growing realization on the part of the United States bishops that mission activity had become the responsibility of the whole church, and not only its religious communities. It was testimony as well to the personal affection many of them felt for Pope John.

There had been no formal call as such for dioceses to send personnel to Latin America. Monsignor Casaroli's 1961 appeal at Notre Dame had been addressed specifically to religious men and women, and there was no corresponding bid to the diocesan clergy. Nevertheless, such a request had been implicit

73

in all the appeals for assistance to Latin America, from both Pope Pius XII and Pope John, which had been issued since the mid-fifties. Occasional diocesan priest-missioners such as Oregon's Father Kennard could be found from time to time, and the St. James Society, founded in 1958, provided an organizational shelter for a few other diocesan priests who wished to serve in Latin America. But in 1960 there was nothing, as yet, like a formal diocesan mission—with one major, remarkable exception.

It was early in 1956 when Archbishop Joseph E. Ritter of St. Louis, sitting at lunch with priests from his chancery staff, mentioned having received a letter from the nuncio in Bolivia, Archbishop Mozzoni, asking for priests to work there. It was an unusual request at the time, but one made on solid footing: Pope Pius had said that diocesan priests should be sent into foreign mission fields and would underscore the point in his encyclical *Fidei Donum*.

Dissuaded by his lunch companions from rejecting the suggestion outright, Archbishop Ritter agreed to search out volunteers. He limited his request to those priests who had been ordained for between five and ten years, and asked them to consider a five-year tour of duty—two of orientation, three of active service—which would be renewable.

The response was somewhat overwhelming. Of sixty-two priests who were eligible under those conditions, a full forty volunteered. Three men were ultimately accepted, and they left St. Louis in May 1956 to open Cristo Rey parish in La Paz. The United States' first diocesan mission in Latin America, and its only one for many years, was under way.

"St. Louis was the most successful diocesan mission organization I know," Father Gerard McCrane said years later. The Maryknoll regional superior in Peru, who has come in contact with many diocesan priests in his years in Latin America, singled out the selection of personnel as the key factor. "They maintained their own identity, but plugged in with other groups too," he said. "That first group contained exceptional men. That was a quality that wasn't always true of other diocesan efforts."

The first three volunteers, Fathers Andrew A. Kennedy, David A. Ratermann, and Andrew B. Schierhoff, were still in Bolivia twenty years later, with Schierhoff by that time an auxiliary bishop of La Paz and Ratermann back after having spent three years, in the late sixties, in St. Louis.

Monsignor Ratermann is one of three members of his family to serve in Latin America. (A brother, George, is a Maryknoll priest who worked in Guatemala, and his sister Joan, also a member of Maryknoll, has been in Chile for twenty-five years.) For a story on the twentieth anniversary of the mission that appeared in the *St. Louis Review*, the archdiocesan newspaper, he told staff writer William McShane what led him to undertake the mission assignment, and how his attitudes had changed over the years.

"I thought it was a good challenge," he said, adding that his brother and sister had been an influence as well.

Naturally, I've always had an interest in it. Even as little kids we prayed the family rosary, and at the end we'd always add prayers for the missionary activities of the church. When I was a little boy my mother had me pray at her knees, and the last thing was a prayer to St. Therese of Lisieux, patroness of the missions. My mother had a great devotion to her. I can still hear the prayer I had to say: "O little St. Therese, sweet flower of Jesus, make Davey a good boy all the time."

How did his mission work go at first?

My ideas were very haughty, very proud. I thought of the church in the States as being a pretty darn good church, vigorous, flourishing. I thought of the church in Latin America as being impoverished and weak in many ways. My initial sense of direction, priority, was that I thought the church should develop and become like the church in the United States. I thought of all those things back home I had benefited from as terribly important things we should promote.

Very honestly I have gone 180 degrees on this. It is a basic fallacy to think of the church as having to be born and develop in one area by a plan that has been the history of development in another. Rather the church in any one area has to develop with the climate, resources, culture, needs, and social situation. Vatican II confirms this. I think now it sounds awful to say, but I think we were trying to make North American Catholics out of these people.

The St. Louis Bolivian mission provides one of the few continuing success stories in regard to United States diocesan missions in Latin America. The original parish remained, and four others were added, three in Bolivia and one in Chile. At one point fourteen archdiocesan priests were assigned to Latin America, a figure second only to the number provided by Boston. As recently as 1976 the number of Latin American missioners from St. Louis was eleven, an indication of the continuing interest of Ritter's successor, Cardinal John Carberry.

On the twentieth anniversary of the mission, Carberry described it as an enterprise in which the full archdiocesan community—priests, religious, and laity—had a share. "Cooperating with the grace of God we have indeed become the instruments of a labor to bring God's redeeming love to more people," he said.

There have been indications, however, that the same ailments that afflicted many other diocesan missions have begun to catch up with St. Louis. "The cardinal has been supportive and wants to continue the mission," said Father Robert Leibrecht during a 1976 interview in La Paz. He is a two-term volunteer, having served in Bolivia from 1962 to 1972, then returning in 1974 for three more years. "Nobody wants to close any of the parishes founded over the years unless it's a matter of absolute necessity. But most people have been here ten years or more; there's only one new man. We may have to do some closing because there's a tremendous lack of interest on the part of the priests in St. Louis."

Of the twenty-three St. Louis priests who have served in the archdiocesan mission, eleven—including the original three—remained on active duty there in 1976, an unusually high figure. "The men who go to the mission field have the complete support of the cardinal, and believe me, it's appreciated," Monsignor Ratermann said. "We have a high percentage of men who have stayed in the missions, and that's no accident."

Cardinal Ritter—he was elevated to that office in 1961, six years before his death—had a strong influence on the U.S. church (more so, certainly, than he did on his fellow bishops). He was one of the first border state bishops to order his Catholic school system desegregated (in 1957), became a leading progressive voice during the Vatican Council, saw to it that the first vernacular mass in the United States was offered in his diocese. But his institution of a diocesan mission for Latin America, while perhaps not as widely recognized as being among his major accomplishments, would prove to be of extreme significance, serving as a model when other dioceses joined the Latin America boom in the early sixties.

Indeed, Ritter had only one serious rival in the U.S. hierarchy when it came to demonstrating a visible and continuing interest in Latin America. In the amount of recognition each would receive for that interest, the rival would win hands down.

Cushing, the Legend

"Cardinal Cushing was superb in his approach to Latin America," said Father Frederick McGuire, the long-time director of the Mission Secretariat and later director of the bishops' Latin America Division. "I give him credit for the fact that the Latin America Bureau ever got off the ground. There was opposition. But because of his backing, we got things done. The heart was always there for Latin America."

The often-controversial Father Louis Colonnese, who joined the Latin America Bureau in 1963 and became its director in 1968, recalled the storm of protests which followed the first CICOP session in 1964, adding: "Were it not for the insistence, protection, interest, and involvement of Richard Cardinal Cushing, Archbishop of Boston, we would have been immediately closed down by the hierarchy."

Cushing was the cliché come to life, a legend in his own time. As he did with other projects in which he became personally involved, he threw all his energy into the success of the Missionary Society of St. James the Apostle. No matter how much the society's founding might have been influenced by Father Kennard, as noted earlier, and whether or not there was any substance to one observer's mischievous contention that Cushing started the society simply because he wanted to go Ritter one better, the fact remains: The priests of St. James quickly established themselves as a key element in the U.S. missionary movement, and have stayed in that position since.

"Cushing's whole priesthood had been spent with the Propagation of the Faith," noted the society's current superior, Father Dennis Dever. "Prior to Pope John's appeal he was ordaining a great number of priests, and encouraging them to go to other dioceses in a kind of lend-lease arrangement. The mission direction was almost an outgrowth of this, spurred by his outlook of the church as universal. We still try to be faithful to his ideal," he continued. "We give of ourselves in order to awaken in other people the need to give of themselves."

Cushing's (and Kennard's) plan resulted in an organization that accepted already-ordained priests from English-speaking dioceses who volunteered to spend a minimum of five years in Latin America. The St. James Society is not a religious order; its members remain priests of their home dioceses and return there, if they choose, after five years. "We exist," a fact sheet from the society says, "because diocesan priests constitute the largest untapped resource in the church to respond to the urgent requests for priests in the critical area of Latin America."

The society grew steadily in its early years, particularly after the 1961 papal call drew special attention to the need for help in Latin America. There were many volunteers from the Boston archdiocese itself, and they were quickly joined by individual priests from other dioceses whose bishops were willing to cooperate but wanted to avoid the problems involved in setting up a separate mission.

Still, the growth, while healthy enough, failed to match the optimistic expectations of its leaders. Monsignor Edward Sweeney, the first superior, envisioned the St. James Society staffing all the countries of South America, one by one. The first three to be designated—Peru, Ecuador, and Bolivia —were the only three in which mission stations were actually set up, and remain the only three areas of operation for the society today.

There were other plans for expansion. Father Jerome Pashby, a Boston priest ordained in 1960 who joined the society three years later, recalls that there was dissatisfaction with the Maryknoll language school program in Cochabamba, Bolivia, where St. James volunteers were being prepared at the time, to the extent that the society decided to launch its own course. It operated its own language/cultural preparation school until March 1977, when declining enrollment forced its shutdown.

"We started this place with visions of hundreds of diocesan priests coming down," Pashby said in an interview at the school, several months before the closing was announced. (He had been its rector, and now serves as a missioner in another section of Peru.) "There was simply no thought of a vocations drop at the time."

Membership in the St. James Society reached over one hundred in the late sixties, dropped sharply to the seventy-eighty level around 1970, and has remained more or less firm since that time. The roster in January 1978 showed seventy-two active priest-volunteers (twenty-six from Boston, a total of fifty-four from all U.S. dioceses, and eighteen from other countries, including six from England and five from Scotland).

Some members believe that factors other than the overall drop in vocations play a role in the decline. Father Dever said:

> When I was in the seminary, we were always being visited by men home from the missions. We had a mission club, and there was an effort made to give us a broader outlook on the church. I was in the seminary when the society was founded; locally we were very much in touch with the spirit of missions through Cushing.
>
> But I think that in the late sixties there was a change in emphasis in the seminaries, to social involvement at home. "Why go all the way to Latin America," people were asking, "when there's a need for us right in our own back yard?"

Cardinal Humberto Medeiros, "protector" of the society today as archbishop of Boston, has a long record of involvement in Latin American activities. A ten-year member of the bishops' committee for Latin America, he has traveled there many times and has made visits to most of the St. James missions. But he is troubled by the picture of diminishing vocations. "I'm very much in contact with the society," he said. "As far as new members from Boston are concerned, I let them go if they ask. But I really can't encourage them. Our own needs here at home are too pressing."

A bronze bust of Cushing stood on a pedestal in a sunny corner of the courtyard of the Lima language school, which was located on a breezy bluff overlooking the Pacific. Cushing's spirit seems rarely far from St. James. "I was influenced by Pope John's call," Pashby said, "but it was Cushing who really oriented me toward mission work. Did I know him well? Not well, really; I met him." He laughed affectionately. "He growled at me once or twice, that's all."

Pashby noted that over half of the first group of St. James volunteers remain in Latin America today ("I couldn't be pried out of here now myself"), but he offered one intriguing possible reason for the proliferation of diocesan missions early in the 1960s: "Some of it could have been due to a negative public relations effect on Cushing's part," he said. "The cardinal would say things like 'I've got a hundred men down there in Latin America,' and other U.S. bishops would say 'Who needs that?' Then they'd start their own missions."

Archbishop McGucken had the pertinent statistics in his 1963 report to Pope John. "Of the 146 Most Reverend Diocesan Ordinaries queried by the survey," he wrote, "88 percent replied as actively concerned."

Spelled out, the McGucken report indicated that forty dioceses had at least one diocesan priest working in Latin America, and that fifty-two more had plans for such activity. He singled out for special mention Cushing (the committee chairman), whose St. James Society had seventy-eight priests on the job at that point (thirty-nine from Boston, and thirty-nine from other dioceses, U.S. and foreign), and Ritter, plus two others:

His Excellency Bishop John P. Treacy of La Crosse, Wisconsin, has priests also in Bolivia, while his Excellency Bishop Bernard J. Topel of Spokane has a diocesan band in Guatemala. A total of eight other archdioceses or dioceses have accepted responsibility for parishes in Latin America since the papal appeal of 1961, while some twenty-eight other Ordinaries have granted permission to clergy under their jurisdiction to take up work in other Latin American dioceses.

Pope John replied:

It is with edification and consolation that We recall the priceless work of Our Venerable Brothers the Bishops of the United States, who not only encourage Men and Women Religious to undertake new foundations in the South (i.e., Latin America), thus depriving themselves of such services, but have, with their diocesan clergy, assumed the direction of numerous parishes.

The U.S. bishop interested in providing priests for Latin America at the time had to determine which route he would take: to join forces with the St. James Society, or to go it on his own. (There was a Maryknoll Associate program as well, but in those formative years it was not much of a factor. Maryknoll veterans were not enthused at the thought of outside priests coming in to claim the Maryknoll banner. "Somebody said it was like Army men calling themselves Marines," one observer said years later. "The feeling was that they were getting the title without the training." Those attitudes largely changed as years went by, but one missioner said flatly that Maryknoll "missed the boat" in not being farsighted enough to build up its associate program earlier.)

One of the chief benefits the St. James Society offered was its flexibility. It combined the strengths of a large organization, an important factor for a mission operation, with the independence associated with separate diocesan ventures. That combination was to prove to be of great significance in the late sixties and early seventies, when differences over the conduct of operations were to tear some mission stations apart—both those run by dioceses and by religious communities. "We avoided most of the problems of that period of polarization," said Father Pashby. "We had made a deliberate decision not to adopt a strict pastoral plan. That way, people could serve according to the ways in which they could function best."

Still, many bishops decided to set up their own diocesan missions. The prestige value of such an undertaking was unquestionably a factor, but there were others: the clear intention of both Pope Pius and Pope John that each diocese should consider itself part of the missionary program, the availability of personnel, the ease of setting up operations in those areas (such as Peru, under Carboni's influence) that were making the heaviest pitches.

Father Frederick McGuire recalls that many priests came to Washington to see Father Considine during this period, asking his advice about areas to cover and people to see. (Their inquiries led him to begin searching for a proper training center, a search that would culminate in Ivan Illich's Cuernavaca program.) But for each diocesan priest who came to Washington for consultation, there were many more who did not, stymieing Considine's plans for an effective program of coordination. Diocesan missions were growing, and they were growing on their own.

The Ritter Influence

Ritter, who had started it all, remained in St. Louis, but his influence continued to be felt. In Kansas City, Missouri, a new bishop launched a mission in Coripata, Bolivia, with two diocesan priests. The bishop was Charles Helmsing, who had served as Ritter's auxiliary when the St. Louis mission was begun six years earlier. "It was started out like any other Little America," a Kansas City priest named Chuck Tobin recounted years later in La Paz. "There was a parish house, a guest house, a garage for the jeeps. . . ."

From Rockford, Illinois, Father J. Philip Reilly went off to Peru: "We felt our diocese should answer the plea of the Holy Father, and therefore the we became I." Summing it up in 1976, he said: "We accepted a parish as a diocesan mission offering, and for ten years have staffed it with two diocesan priests and two religious. Five diocesan men have served or are serving here. There's been frustration with difficulties in communication, both language and cultural. It takes time not only to recognize cultural difference, but to respect and value it."

Another small midwestern diocese established a reputation for Latin American missionary involvement that grew to near-legend status. The diocese was Jefferson City, Missouri, and its bishop was Joseph M. Marling, appointed to the post in 1956 after serving, as noted earlier, as auxiliary in Kansas City under Archbishop O'Hara. He strongly encouraged a vital mission commitment, and soon the diocese had a half-dozen men serving in Peru. That policy continues today under his successor, Bishop Michael F.

McAuliffe, who has seven priests (of a total of 115 in the diocese) serving in two Peruvian dioceses.

According to Bishop McAuliffe:

> When I came to the Diocese of Jefferson City, I indicated in my first address to my people that I certainly wanted us to continue our mission work in Peru, but they had to show that they wanted it too, by their interest and support. I learned that Bishop Marling, my predecessor, had made many trips to Peru. His reasons weren't apparent until I made my first trip. It became evident that there were many problems to be solved. As intricate as they were, it was also clear they couldn't be solved in Jefferson City. An added factor was the support that could be shown to our missionaries by my visits. Other bishops and religious superiors realize very quickly the meaning of their visits and the real necessity for doing so if the work is to succeed. . . .
>
> We do intend to continue our mission efforts in Peru. From our experience the path that we follow is the one I would recommend to my brother bishops. If they really want their people to be mission-minded, this is the way to get them turned on.

Bridgeport, Camden, Paterson, Milwaukee . . . The list went on.

Chicago ("flowering with talent under Cardinal Meyer's direction," Father McGuire remembers) established the pace-setting San Miguelito parish in Panama, with Father Leo Mahon in charge. A paper Mahon presented at the first CICOP meeting (1964) hints at his far-sighted vision. He listed a series of requirements for the effective missioner, among them "creating family (community) rather than organization"; "focusing the sacraments as encounters with Christ rather than statistical receptions"; "striving for fulfillment of the law and not mere observance."

The ideal Latin America missioner, Mahon said, should be:

> (1) a catalyst—not the substance of change; (2) a co-creator—not a functionary; (3) a thought-provoker rather than a mere teacher; (4) a revolutionary—not a modernizer; (5) a discoverer rather than an administrator; (6) a brother rather than a father in the Christian family; (7) a man of divine rather than of ecclesiastical faith; (8) a creator of liturgy rather than a mere performer.

Heady stuff in 1964—and thoroughly up-to-date in the mid-seventies.

Some dioceses made significant contributions to Latin America and the United States mission consciousness apart from, or in addition to, the actual sending of priests. The McGucken report to Pope John mentioned Archbishop Robert Lucey's promotion of CCD in Latin America from the San

Antonio archdiocese; the New York program for Puerto Ricans and other Spanish-speaking (which Illich, several years earlier, had developed for Cardinal Spellman); the contribution of Miami and other dioceses in caring for Cuban refugees.

And there was Davenport, Iowa, which did as much as any other diocese to raise Latin American awareness on the part of United States Catholics, largely because of the efforts of an indefatigable young priest named Louis Michael Colonnese.

Blessed with a wise bishop, the late Ralph L. Hayes, whom he loved and respected (and who, not coincidentally, gave him a remarkably free hand), Colonnese conducted a series of seminars—diocesan, regional, and, ultimately, on a national scale—which called attention to the problems of Latin America and suggested ways in which United States Catholics might respond. By the standards of that period, Colonnese's subject material, not to mention his solutions to the problems he described, bordered on the revolutionary, if not heretical. The conservative element in the diocese branded his tactics as "rabble-rousing," but then—as later in his career, when he became director of the bishops' Latin America Bureau—Colonnese was hardly one to be deterred by words.

Colonnese wrote years later:

> It can't be denied that the program initiated tensions, but that had to come. Remember that all of this was prior to the Vatican Council. One religious said we left a trail of divisions wherever we went. And there was no small amount of truth in this. It got so bad that some bishops forbade me from entering their dioceses . . . but all of this only served to make us grow more and more.

As was the case with the religious-order priests and sisters who joined the Latin American mission crusade in the early sixties, the diocesan priest-missioners encountered a largely uncritical response to their efforts.

Writing in 1963 in *Latin America—The Eleventh Hour*, Gary MacEoin quoted Chile's Bishop Larraín as minimizing fears that the incoming U.S. missioners would be unable to make the necessary cultural adjustments that effective mission work required. "There is a great and growing awareness among the missionary priests . . . from the United States . . . who are devoting their lives to helping in Latin America, of the need for cultural accommodation to make their sacrifice fruitful. We recognize this and are grateful for it."

An even stronger endorsement came (in the same book) from Peruvian Bishop Alcides Mendoza Castro ("a young, dynamic, churchman from the highlands"), who heaped praise on the St. James Society:

> I had only 11 priests in a diocese that needs 120. Then Cardinal Cushing sent me twelve of his, and already they have worked a transformation

which they themselves do not realize, in that they have introduced the possibility of a progress and a rebirth where none existed. I'm no longer afraid of Khrushchev. I'm no longer afraid of Castro. Their agitators succeeded because they filled a vacuum. The vacuum doesn't exist any more. These priests have filled it. They are God's blessing on my diocese.

MacEoin himself was hardly less enthusiastic as he described the work of the diocesan priests of the St. James Society:

The apostolate of these priests is based on the belief that the parish in Latin America must be built on a middle-class community capable of providing the economic basis for the functioning of schools and other community services, and engaged actively in the work of the parish through a sense of common effort and participation. This is very much the type of parish which exists in the United States, and very often in Latin America the work must begin entirely from scratch.

He likened the parishes to those begun by Maryknoll missioners, adding:

The impact such a parish makes in as little as 10 or 12 years has to be seen to be believed, with benefits visible at all levels. There is a vast improvement in attendance at church. The children who graduate from the school have better economic opportunities because of the level of their education. Vocations become more numerous. Community organizations, including credit unions and cooperatives, spring up and flourish. People gain a sense of self-confidence. No other United States aid to Latin America produces such rapid and dramatic results.

(MacEoin's views were to change drastically, as did those of others who witnessed the long-range effects of the mission style of the early sixties. In *Revolution Next Door*, written in 1971, he spoke of missioners having recognized their spiritual colonialism in "trying to impose structures and attitudes from their home churches," and in correspondence in 1977 confirmed the switch: "Yes, I have changed radically since I wrote *The Eleventh Hour*. The U.S.-style parish was a disaster, an extension of American imperialism.")

They Could See for Themselves

The missioners in the field didn't have to be told whether they were doing the job or not; they could see the problems as they unfolded.

Father George Dudak, who went to Ica, Peru, to staff the Paterson diocesan mission in 1964 (and who has been pastor in a rural parish in North Jersey for the past several years), quickly picked up an appreciation for those who had already been through the grind. "The Maryknollers were the pros," he said. "The fellows from St. James were good, too, but they were still learning. Maryknoll knew the ropes; St. James was still making mistakes, . . . and the diocesan priests who were on their own, as we were, were making twice as many mistakes."

The problem of available personnel was critical. "There were only two of us," Dudak said. "We had no reserves. This was the type of mistake Maryknoll had learned to avoid. Also, there was no master plan for assignment of U.S. mission personnel. It was strictly haphazard, as far as I could see."

The feeling that the Paterson priests had been sold short—that they had been given a relatively easy assignment to help set up a school for the middle class in Ica, when there was so much more to be done—was to cut even deeper, Father Dudak said:

> One story helps to illustrate my feeling about the mission to Peru. It's true, and it's very symbolic. There was a girl who was burned very badly, a beautiful girl of about ten who was in our parish. It had taken two days to get her into a hospital, and her burns became badly infected. I visited her in the hospital. Her family wasn't there to buy the medicine she needed, and the sisters who ran the hospital couldn't afford it. So the girl died. I paid twenty dollars or whatever it was for the medicine, but it was too late. She died. That cracked me up. What are we doing working with the rich, I kept asking myself. We're barking up the wrong tree. There's so much to be done for the poor. . . .

Father Gerard T. McCrane, former Maryknoll superior in Peru and now head of the Maryknoll language school in Cochabamba, Bolivia, could understand Dudak's reaction to the personnel situation:

> One thing to remember about a diocese with a handful of men down here is that it's severely limited in how it can move its personnel. If you've got two guys and they can't get along with one another, you're locked in to that situation. A larger organization such as ours can move people around.
>
> Also, with a diocesan mission, a new bishop can come in and decide on a drastic change in policies as far as Latin American mission work is concerned. That happened with one man here in Peru, who was called home by a new bishop, against his wishes, after being here for ten years. He finally went, but it left a bad taste all around.
>
> I've been very impressed with the quality of diocesan missioners I've met in Peru over the years. I'm sure of their commitment. But I always had the impression they were too isolated, not integrated with each other or with the local church. They were sort of parachuted into wherever they were going.

Father Charles Davignon of Burlington, Vermont, who is critical of the early Latin American effort of the U.S. church, has seen the missionary picture from different perspectives. Ordained in 1956, he volunteered for work with the St. James Society in 1963 but couldn't get a release at the time from his diocese. Three years later he was able to go to South America, but because St. James was parish-oriented and because he wanted to put his educational background to use (he had been a high school principal in Montpelier), he joined Maryknoll as an associate. He was involved in radio school and communications work in Peru until 1972, when he returned to Burlington as director of communications. Then he rejoined Maryknoll in 1974 as coordinator of the new justice and peace office, and in June 1976, was appointed Latin America adviser for the International Justice and Peace Office of the U.S. Catholic Conference. Now he holds two offices at Maryknoll: vice president for development of the Graduate School of Theology and coordinator, Center for Mission Studies.

"We should have unified our whole mission approach and not allowed its splintering into diocesan groups," he said. "It was a mistake to bite off such a vast mission endeavor. If the bishops had gotten together and beefed up the Latin America Bureau at the time, things would have been different."

How deeply were the U.S. bishops committed, truly committed, to the Latin America mission undertaking? The soundings differ widely. Archbishop McGucken's 1963 summary for Pope John, of course, painted a picture of thoroughgoing cooperation. Two years later Bishop James McNulty of Buffalo, drawing up a report at the authorization of the U.S. hierarchy itself, presented a concise summary of the involvement of the United States church in Latin America which indicated a similar degree of commitment.

Of McNulty's personal concern there was no doubt; he had abundant evidence to support him. As bishop of Paterson he had launched the diocesan mission in Bolivia and had made the rigorous journey to Caranavi as a personal expression of support. He provided headquarters in Paterson for AID, the Association for International Development (not to be confused with the governmental organization, a subsequently-formed body with identical initials and an almost-identical name). The Paterson-based AID was a lay-run church organization aimed at spurring enlightened economic development in Third World settings. And once he got to Buffalo in 1963, the bishop committed his new diocese to mission undertakings in Peru and Bolivia.

The letter Bishop McNulty wrote in December 1965 was drawn up at the direction of the U.S. bishops, who held their annual meeting that year in Rome, during the Vatican Council. The bishops called for the establishment of the first Latin American Cooperation Week (January 23–30, 1966) to be culminated by the first special collection for that purpose, and asked Bishop McNulty, vice chairman of the committee for Latin America, to prepare the necessary background information. He wrote:

As to the United States diocesan clergy pledged to Latin America, it seems safe to say that at no time in the history of the Church in the United States have so many bishops on their own initiative undertaken to place such a substantial number of their diocesan personnel at the disposal of bishops in other nations to meet a crisis.

As of January, 1965, clergy belonging to 49 archdioceses and dioceses were on short-term service in Latin American countries, many of them members of the Missionary Society of St. James the Apostle. "We send our affectionate paternal greetings to those numerous dioceses," declared Pope Paul VI (in an apostolic letter to the bishops of the United States January 6, 1965) "which have spontaneously placed at the disposal of the Latin American dioceses a total of 179 priests, mostly dedicated to pastoral ministry in 59 parishes entrusted to them in 11 nations of that continent."

The McNulty letter said the right things:

On the needs of Latin America's Church and people, it is the voice of the Latin American bishops themselves which should be heard, not ours. The plight of their people is driven home to us by the series of dramatic pastorals issued during recent years by the various episcopal conferences of the Latin American nations. . . .

And then came the direct appeal:

Aware of the fact that Catholics of the United States have heretofore known little about the Church and its 200,000,000 members who are their brothers in the Latin American orbit, the bishops of the United States strongly encourage the establishment of a Latin American cooperation week, to be observed for the primary purpose of building greater understanding and friendly concern for our fellow Christians of Latin America. To this end each diocese is urged to encourage a program embracing spiritual, cultural, educational and financial activities touching Latin America.

That reading of the situation contrasted sharply with that of Father Colonnese, although Bishop McNulty was a man whom he personally liked, and of whom he would speak affectionately years later. Colonnese by this time was administrative director of the Latin America Bureau, and had been dispatched to Rome (as had Monsignor William Quinn of Chicago, the bureau's associate director) to lobby among the bishops on behalf of the Latin America collection.

"The work was depressing," he said. "McNulty tried to arrange gettogethers with the Latin bishops during the council, but not too successfully. It was frustrating for the Latins. They weren't flattered by being invited out to dinner by the American bishops; what they were looking for was commitment."

Bishop McNulty was "morally encouraging," Colonnese said, but failed to project his interest in Latin America to other bishops. "American bishops seem to always respect the thinking of their brother bishops, even when it's erroneous. Fraternal correction and admonition is sadly lacking."

In trying to sell the bishops on the Latin America collection, Colonnese carried a letter of introduction, signed by Ritter and Cushing. Some bishops were courteous, he said; some were cold. And some were "outright hostile." He concluded glumly: "The discussions I had with bishops during those personal meetings revealed to me that there was almost total ignorance among the United States hierarchy concerning the condition of things in Latin America."

Still, the figures show that a substantial number of those bishops sent their priests to Latin America. Some of those who went were fulfilling long-ago dreams of "going to the missions"; others were pressured into it when a bishop's public commitment to a diocesan mission came up against a marked shortage of volunteers. Some succeeded despite their lack of formal mission training; others failed spectacularly. Some went to Latin America to solve their own problems in the priesthood, found no answer, and entered a new kind of life. Many went and served and returned to their home dioceses; a small percentage found that mission work was their genuine calling, and are still working at it.

And some—Father Raymond Herman was one, but there are others like him—became so involved in their work, in their people, that they will never come back. Raymond Herman came from Dubuque, Iowa, answering a call for mission volunteers that went out in 1962, and went to Bolivia. He took to the work. He threw himself into the operation of two slum parishes in Cochabamba: Cala Cala and Cristo Rey. He mastered the difficult Quechua language. He was the driving force behind a string of schools, clinics, cooperatives, sports fields, and nursing centers.

He moved onward from Cochabamba, deeper into the country, to the village of Morochata, a base of operations for the dozens of hamlets out in the *campo* which he served. "Ever since college," he told one visitor, "I have wanted to give everything to our Lord, and only since I have come to Morochata do I feel that I am really happy, and to some degree at least, successful in giving all to Christ."

Father Raymond Herman was not a political activist; his only politics was poverty. He worked with the poor. One project in which he became personally involved was the renovation of a government building, which had been planned as a tourist hotel, and its conversion into a clinic-hospital. He was on his way home from its dedication ceremony when he was robbed and beaten. His assailants also shot him, putting two .22-calibre bullets into his right temple; he was pronounced dead in the little ten-bed hospital which he had helped build and which he had blessed earlier that evening, Monday, October 20, 1975.

At a memorial mass concelebrated with forty-three priests in the cathedral at Cochabamba, Archbishop Armando Gutiérrez spoke about the priest from Dubuque, Iowa, who had given twelve years of his life to the Bolivian people. "The virtues his parents imbued in him fructified in his love for Christ, the church, and the poor," the archbishop said. "He knew how to communicate with people's hearts to bring them the word of God."

Father Leon Connolly, one of three remaining Dubuque priests in Bolivia, accompanied the body home and spoke at the funeral mass in St. John's Church, Independence, Iowa, the town where Father Herman was born in 1930. "I personally am convinced," he said, "that Father Ray Herman is one of those symbolic persons who from time to time God sends into our lives and the life of the church. And so as spokesman for our archdiocesan community, I express for all of us our tremendous debt of gratitude to Father Herman for his eighteen years of priestly service, which gave life to silent words, and which serve as a symbolic and prophetic guide to each of us."

The record of the Latin America years shows that some diocesan priest-missioners never should have gone. And some, some like Father Ray Herman, went and were crowned in glory.

"Who knows the answers?" reflected Boston's Bishop Thomas Daily. Ordained for the archdiocese, a five-year veteran of service with the St. James Society, he came to terms with his own missionhood—his capabilities, his limitations—one day in Peru:

I came across an Indian lying on the ground outside his hut, wrapped in a dirty poncho. His wife was there and his kids were running around, and he was dying. This man doesn't have time for the whole world to change, I realized; he's going to be dead in five minutes. He had no time for a social revolution; he only had time for what I could give him—food for his journey.

I thought about this, and how it related to everything I did as a missioner. No matter how immense the problems were, I felt, the people I worked with needed the sacraments and the Gospel. That same day people were born and people were dying, and I was a priest. I realized that I may not be able to change the world. But I can give what I can.

7

A Response to Pope John: The Laity

It is of paramount importance that laymen be made to understand the necessities of the Church in Latin America and the many problems involved. For the Latin American countries, when restored to the ancient vigour of their Catholic life, will become a reservoir of spiritual energy that will meet not only their own needs but those of many other parts of the world.

There is a well-founded hope that selected teams of generous laymen in various countries, in response to the appeal of their bishops, can be organized to volunteer for the service of the Church in Latin America for a given period of years. These laymen, convinced that "the great hour of Christian conscience has struck" (Pope Pius XII, Easter, 1948), ready to leave their fatherland and prepared to suffer and toil for the cause of Christ, deserve the title of "Papal Volunteers for Latin America," and are worthy of association in an organization bearing that title.

The Papal Volunteers. That was from their charter, and that was how the Pontifical Commission for Latin America felt about their potential when it created the organization in May 1960.

There were other U.S. lay mission organizations: the Grail, of Loveland, Ohio; Catholics for Latin America; AID (the Association for International Development), based in Paterson, New Jersey; International Catholic Auxiliaries of Evanston, Illinois, among them. But PAVLA—the Papal Volunteers for Latin America—with its specific Vatican commission, its national organization, and the high visibility it achieved during its lifetime, is the lay organization most readily identified with Latin America mission efforts of recent years.

Few organizations began with higher hopes, or ended as unhappily, with criticism from almost everyone concerned with it. The critics seem to vie with each other, in fact, when it comes to pointing out the problems with the PAVLA program as it developed, and as it finally ground to a halt, during the sixties.

But there was unbounded optimism at the outset. "The Pontifical Commission," the founding document concluded, "which has carefully studied this project, has approved it unanimously, aware that the organization of the Papal Volunteers can prove a powerful instrument of apostolate in Latin America. His Holiness Pope John XXIII has deigned to grant his blessing to the undertaking."

Not unexpectedly, the idea for PAVLA sprang originally from Father John Considine, soon after the first inter-American bishops' meeting at Georgetown in 1959. Considine had not yet formally assumed the title of director of the new Latin America Bureau when the Pontifical Commission for Latin America put the PAVLA program into effect May 19, 1960.

One of Father Considine's long-time associates felt there was an initial problem which was never overcome. "It was the name itself," said Msgr. William Quinn, co-director of the Latin America Bureau for many years. "Papal Volunteers for Latin America. It was just a bad name to begin with."

Volunteers in the field came to know what he was talking about. Many said that because of the connection with the Vatican implied in the title, they were incorrectly identified as religious, leading to a permanent state of confusion about their purpose and their presence.

Another close aid of Father Considine, and later his successor, has more substantive criticism. "If PAVLA had gone the way John Considine had envisioned it," Father Frederick McGuire reflected, "it would have been a different story."

> The idea was for requests to come from Latin America for a specific person to do a specific job. Then that person would be recruited and trained, and sent down with the proper culture background, language training, and so on.
>
> But it got out of hand. The recruiting system developed so well that people were coming in without places to be sent to. We ended up saying, "Can't you use this person, or that one?" As a result, more than 50 percent never fulfilled their two-year promise. The bishops of Latin America finally suggested that the expenditure of money wasn't merited by the results that were being attained, and the whole thing was finally phased out.

Who were the Papal Volunteers? Most of them were relatively young men and women, quite well educated, whose active participation in church life was considerably higher than average. Between 1960 and 1970 nearly one thousand of them accepted the call that had gone forth from the Pontifical Commission in its 1960 document, "Papal Volunteers for Apostolic Collaboration in Latin America."

The commission listed six requirements for those laypeople who would be Papal Volunteers: "probity of life"; teaching knowledge of Catholic doctrine;

technical knowledge in order to train leaders; an acquaintance with Latin American culture; speaking knowledge of either Spanish or Portuguese; and knowledge of a special activity to which his or her work team would be dedicated.

They would make themselves available for work in Latin America for a fixed period (two years, as it turned out, for most U.S. volunteers) in teams of from three to ten members, under the direction of local bishops. They would also work in collaboration with Latin American lay people. Their vaguely-defined goal was "to help in training excellent and qualified leaders," and they were strictly enjoined not to take the place of local leaders.

At the outset, the need for Papal Volunteers was pegged squarely on the absence of priests. "All those who experience concern for the difficulties which the Church is facing in Latin American countries are quite aware that the greatest single obstacle is the distressing shortage of priests and religious," the commission said. "Hence the continuous preoccupation of the Pontifical Commission, of CELAM, and of all those concerned with the future of the Catholic religion in Latin America to encourage the inflow of many apostolic workers into those countries." In later years, especially in a postconciliar setting, that rationale would come back to disturb many volunteers, adding to their confusion over the nature of their mission and the future of their work.

The commission called for lay people from various countries to volunteer for work in Latin America, but it was the United States that provided the quickest and, numerically, the most convincing response. An obvious influencing factor in the early 1960s was the appeal of the new Kennedy administration and its call to U.S. citizens, particularly the young and idealistic, to "ask what you can do for your country." For many Catholics, PAVLA was the answer. It clearly paralleled the administration's Peace Corps, but it had the added benefit of a spiritual dimension. This gave U.S. Catholics an opportunity to serve not only their country and its popular young president, but also their church and its equally idolized leader, Pope John.

With Latin American activities of the U.S. church still dispersed and only loosely organized, U.S. headquarters for PAVLA was established not in Washington but in Chicago, since that was home base for its early coordinators, Msgr. Quinn and David O'Shea, a layman who served as national executive secretary. Chicago remained the center of PAVLA operations throughout most of the administration of Father Raymond A. Kevane, a priest of the Sioux City Diocese who became national director in July 1964, succeeding Jesuit Father Victor Fernandez, and who, for the next five years, was the man most closely identified with the program.

The key to the recruitment program developed by Kevane and his associates was a network of diocesan PAVLA directors. Not all dioceses were supportive enough to appoint a director, and some others were given a director in name only, but about fifty dioceses, large and small, had active coordinators who helped to give PAVLA an initial look of success.

Homily outlines sent across the country from the national office explained PAVLA's purpose (". . . U.S. Catholic lay people serve as catalysts, forming leaders, stimulating in Latin Americans a deep commitment to the Christian development of their own society") and its method of operation:

1. The volunteer agrees to serve for two years or more in a project in Latin America where his talents and experience are asked for and needed.
2. The volunteer's parish and diocese agree to provide him with language and cultural training, travel, insurance and regular support expenses.
3. The Latin American project agrees to provide the project setting, living quarters and some incidental expenses.

The training program was organized into five stages: the initial orientation; a formal orientation course (eventually handled at PAVLA's National Training Center in Washington); advanced language and culture study in Latin America, at Ponce (Puerto Rico), Cuernavaca (Mexico), or Petropolis (Brazil); continued in-service formation once a volunteer had been assigned to his or her project; and reorientation when the Latin America commitment was completed.

As it developed, the first stage of the program, the initial orientation, varied markedly from diocese to diocese, just as the in-service formation, stage four, depended on the interest of the regional director. The final "reorientation" never assumed much importance; whatever effect it might have had was often blunted by the unhappy circumstances under which many volunteers would leave PAVLA.

But stages two and three, the National Training Center and the Latin America study programs, achieved notable results. The Washington center was located at 3719 12th Street, N.E., a place known as Oak Terrace, where classes of some thirty to forty volunteers would study for six-week periods. The trainees had four courses, offered through the Catholic University School of Education: the church in the modern world; principles of the spiritual life and the lay apostolate; Christian social doctrine; and comparative analysis of North American and Latin American cultures. The fee, to be paid by the volunteer's diocese or other sponsoring agency, was $375 for room, board, and tuition. Those who were able to do so received college credits for their work, while those whose academic background was more limited simply audited the courses.

Continuing on to Cuernavaca or Petropolis, volunteers sat side by side with priests, sisters, and other mission-bound compatriots, and, along with them, were exposed to the shock-treatment techniques of Ivan Illich. For the most part, it seemed to work. "If the success of PAVLA had been dependent just on the background and training—at least in our experience—there would have been no trouble," one former volunteer said some years later. "Ours was fine."

Ann Held Griffin and her husband Dan were in one of the early PAVLA waves. With their daughter, Georgia, a toddler at the time, they went off to Brazil, imbued with the volunteer spirit that was a hallmark of the period. (Now divorced, a situation they agree was not related to their Latin American experience, the couple works in Washington. A one-time managing editor of *Ave Maria* magazine, he is on the foreign desk of the *Washington Post*; she is on the staff of *Americas*, the magazine of the Organization of American States.)

Their early orientation took place at Seton Hall College in South Orange, New Jersey, in a program developed by AID of Paterson. It covered the philosophy of missions and Latin American sociology and cultures, and planted what Mrs. Griffin describes as "one good idea after another." Then it was on to Petropolis, a pleasant town less than an hour from Rio, for a rugged five months of intensive language and culture training.

> We studied five hours a day, five days a week. There were four students to a teacher. It was so intensive that you'd have people almost breaking down. This was Illich's approach, of course. If you cracked, fine; he'd either build you back up or he'd lose you. One man in his forties had been a prisoner of war in World War II; it had been rough on him.
>
> We studied the history of Brazil, the philosophy of aid, evangelization. It was a fantastic time. The Vatican Council was going on; there were so many ideas that were up for grabs.
>
> And so we finished, and we were ready to go to work. We were so marvelously prepared. . . .
>
> But we had nothing to do.

What to Do?

Nothing to do. It was a complaint which, in one form or another, would dog PAVLA throughout most of its decade of existence. At times there were problems of communication, of financial snafus, of an inability to get along with co-workers, either Latin or North American. But most of PAVLA's serious difficulties were traceable to what its volunteers were doing—or not doing—in the field. In some cases, there were simply no jobs; in others, it was a matter of not having work for enough people. Volunteers, many times, did not know what they were supposed to do. There were identity problems connected with the work: Are we religious missioners, the volunteers kept asking themselves, or are we social developers?

All of these forces combined to produce a negative image that the Papal Volunteers never lived down. And the problem was far deeper than one of image; PAVLA simply did not get the job done. Critics and observers—those writing at the time and those reflecting on the PAVLA experience some years later, in the mid-seventies—cite a variety of reasons. One of the most articulate critics is the man who was PAVLA's final director, Thomas Quigley, now head of the Latin America section of the U.S. Catholic Conference International Justice and Peace Division.

"The program went from god-awful to horrible," he said in an interview, "and many fine people went as well."

> Why? Well, basically there was an inadequate concept of what it was all about. We had the Peace Corps mentality, that what we're doing has to be good, because we're here out of the generosity of our hearts as Americans. Implicitly this was some form of paternalism; there was never a question that it might be counterproductive.
>
> The impression was widespread that the people down there included a lot of basket cases. They were looking for something and what they found, instead, was themselves. The structure was so loose that it failed to provide normal checks and balances, or any sense of support. Some people in the States now look back on their mission years in Latin America with fondness. It was their Camelot; a good time.

Father Theodore M. Hesburgh, president of the University of Notre Dame, noted that his experience with PAVLA was "all bad." A close friend of Sargent Shriver, the first director of the Peace Corps, Hesburgh made Notre Dame available as the site of the first Peace Corps training project and had opportunity over the years to contrast its operation with that of PAVLA. He recalled one experience in Chile where Peace Corps members had convinced local people to complete a road to an isolated village, in return for which they were to receive a food supply. Papal Volunteers came on the scene with food to give away, he said, and the road was never built.

"PAVLA didn't get to set up projects properly," Hesburgh said. "Most of the volunteers were wandering around. I admired their spirit, but they were poorly programmed. I would have preferred seeing young Catholic people going into the Peace Corps. Its members were better prepared, and there were more definite assignments."

Frances Neason had an opportunity to see PAVLA's problems from an administrative level. Secretary during that period to both Fathers Considine and McGuire, and now executive director of NCCB's Secretariat for Latin America, she noted that the short period of service, two years, had built-in problems, and said that while training and preparation of volunteers was good, initial screening was something else. "If there was a good local office at the diocesan level, as there was, for example, with Father George Mader in Newark, there wasn't so much of a problem," she said. "But that wasn't always the case. And the biggest problem of all was that there was poor communication between parties, between the dioceses and the volunteers in the field; between the dioceses and the national office."

Father Edmund Leising, an Oblate missionary in Brazil since the 1940s, was blunter in his criticism, pointing out that while many missioners of the period were guilty of the same improper attitudes—"We Americans had it, and they didn't"—the Papal Volunteers were much worse prepared for their jobs. "The Papal Volunteers left the States with the idea that they had to *do something* and then take a picture of it," he said. "Their impact was almost zero."

One of PAVLA's severest critics was the man who eventually oversaw its disbanding: Father Colonnese, who succeeded Father Considine as head of the Latin America Bureau in 1968. On one hand, he was dissatisfied with the volunteers' performance: "Their training was deficient. The mistakes they committed were numerous. Complaints were reaching my office from all parts of Latin America. The incidence of mental problems among Papal Volunteers was staggering."

From another standpoint, Colonnese was disenchanted with what he felt was happening to the program:

> There were bishops and local officials who saw PAVLA as a one-way street to financial aid from the U.S. The number of requests from areas where PAVLA volunteers were stationed was much higher than from those areas where there was no PAVLA presence. PAVLA volunteers were displacing Latins from jobs. . . . They were not the "technicians" sent to help the Latins where qualified local people could not be found. They were being sent (although not in every case) as "priest-helpers" and were happily accepted because it meant no expense to the local ordinary.

Colonnese consolidated all the Latin American Bureau offices in Washington in 1968, including, to Kevane's displeasure, that of PAVLA. It was at best an uncomfortable situation. The two priests disagreed politically, and they disagreed personally. Certainly they disagreed about PAVLA. How long the relationship could exist was uncertain, but one thing was clear: Colonnese and Kevane were on a collision course.

If Kevane disagreed with Colonnese about PAVLA, it did not mean he could not be critical of the organization. In 1967 he spoke of the need for PAVLA's renewal, for its re-formation more along Latin than North American lines. Others connected with PAVLA were concerned about program failures, the dwindling number of volunteers, the persistent "negative image" problem, so much so that a major meeting was called, in Chicago, in September of that year, to chart a course for PAVLA's future.

Many of the answers might have been more readily available had Kevane and other PAVLA officials paid more attention to the volunteers themselves, both those in the field and those who had returned. A common complaint on the part of the volunteers was that they felt abandoned while they were in their mission posts and ignored after they came home. In Newark, for example, Father George Mader's correspondence was filled with comments along those lines.

Gilda Martoglio, a nurse from Lyndhurst, New Jersey, who was working as a PAVLA nurse in Brazil, wrote: "I'm envied by most of the other volunteers I've met. . . . The vast majority of them never hear from their directors after they leave the U.S. I don't think I could ever tell you how much it means to me to know that you're there and interested in me and my welfare. . . ."

Rosemary Warren, another Newark archdiocesan Papal Volunteer, had repeated problems with the national office both while she was in Ponce, where she studied, and in Lima, where she was assigned. "I am arriving at the point where I must reassess my entire outlook on PAVLA," she wrote in one letter. "I fear too much red tape is involved and, as a consequence, vital personal contact is lacking along the line."

A second letter, written in that same month: "Lately I have been hard pressed to give one good reason for being a Papal Volunteer. . . . Since I have been in Ponce, I have had no correspondence from the national office with the exception of my monthly statement from Central Funding."

A third letter, from Lima: "I have heard that there may be a reorganization of the Papal Volunteers, but know little of the plans. . . . We have no field representative here since John Keenan left, and get our news from rather unofficial sources these days."

Ann Held Griffin made many of the same critical points in a 1967 article in *Ave Maria* timed to coincide with the opening of the Chicago meeting, contending that the reasons volunteers were being ignored or given only condescending treatment was that they were, after all, lay people:

> Unfortunately, the organization is still haunted by the implications of the reason given for the original appeal to the laity in 1960 (the shortage of priests in Latin America). . . . Therefore, the aura of the sacristy hangs on, even though the overwhelming majority of volunteers are engaged in work that does not by any stretch of the imagination call for a priest or a religious. . . . The program's national directors and more than 95 percent of its diocesan directors are all priests.

The organization, she continued, had left it to the volunteers to try to determine whether their witness should be "lay" or "religious." "To date," she concluded, "neither the PAVLA administration nor—with few exceptions—the volunteers themselves have decided which they want to be."

It was hardly a triumphal mood that greeted diocesan PAVLA directors and other delegates to the Chicago meeting in September 1967, even though, as the first national conference of the Papal Volunteers, it had drawn a personal letter of greeting from Pope Paul VI. The pontiff wrote:

Our pastoral heart looks upon the needs of the Church in Latin America and, realizing the weighty responsibility entrusted to the Volunteers, We augur that their organization will be able to recruit numerous workers of high professional competence, deep apostolic dedication and extraordinary generosity who, upon request and with the approval of the Bishops of Latin Amerca, will labor for development in that great continent with their counterparts there.

The pope's augury was unrealistic. One speaker noted that the current number of Papal Volunteers then in the field was 278, a decrease of 75 in two years.

Numbers were not the principal concern of Father Kevane, whose keynote address candidly explored PAVLA's "past errors." He listed problems in personnel placement first. From the outset, he said, there had been a lack of finances and experienced personnel. He continued:

For this reason individual dioceses were invited in 1961 to develop their own personnel in projects in Latin America. Many of the projects so chosen were the result simply of contact by correspondence, or of personal contacts made by Latin American authorities traveling in the United States, or by diocesan officials traveling in Latin America looking for places to assign the lay personnel they had recruited.

It was a frank, even startling admission of failure, but there was more to come. The lack of a clear knowledge of PAVLA's purpose, Kevane said, had resulted in confusion about the volunteers' role: Were they quasi-religious or professional? He cited other problems. There had been poor contact with local authorities in regard to priorities. There were cases of unequal salaries, and there were other professional considerations to be studied. The quality of diocesan programs was uneven, depending in a large measure on the interest and ability of the local directors. The bishops had not been fully supportive of PAVLA, but that was partly due to PAVLA itself and its lack of self-promotion.

Nor had Kevane, when he finished, exhausted the litany of PAVLA's faults. Too often, said Colombian priest-sociologist Gustavo Pérez Ramírez, volunteers had allowed themselves to be used for cheap labor. "Papal Volunteers," he said, "cannot be conceived of as simply a ready supply of manpower to fill unoccupied jobs and opportunities in the dioceses of Latin America, no matter how urgently their collaboration is needed."

Another speaker was then-Bishop Marcos McGrath, who said that while the response to Latin America's call for volunteers had been good from a numerical standpoint, the relatively short period of service was a drawback. In two years, he said, volunteers were just beginning to know their way around. And he pointed to another fact that would become clearer as the years went on:

"In these programs, it is quite obvious to us all now—and to the volunteers themselves—that they are the prime beneficiaries of the program."

Nearly 150 people attended the meeting, including 39 returned and 7 active volunteers and 54 diocesan directors of PAVLA.

Also on hand were the six people who comprised the "National Lay Advisory Committee," which Kevane had formed a year earlier. (All were men, and all were from Chicago.) Their final recommendation called for dioceses to turn over the responsibility for volunteers to the national office, for the national office to have a flat rate to cover each volunteer (variations in pay continued to be a problem for volunteers in the field), and in general for a strengthening of the role of the national office. It would have final authority on assigning volunteers, for example, and on the adoption of specific projects. The proposal made eminently good sense, but after seven years of getting things done with its own free-style system, PAVLA was simply not equipped for such a radical change.

If it did not succeed in reversing PAVLA's downturn, the Chicago meeting at least gave delegates a sense of encouragement that problems were being recognized and admitted rather than hidden, that new direction seemed a possibility, however slim. The bishops were trying to drum up more interest than they had shown in the past, too; a new three-member subcommittee for PAVLA (Bishop Joseph Hodges of Wheeling; Bishop Glennon Flavin, then auxiliary of St. Louis and about to be installed as bishop of Lincoln; and then-Bishop Humberto Medeiros of Brownsville) promised to work for the appointment of full-time diocesan directors wherever possible and the formation of diocesan PAVLA committees.

Problems in the Field

But in the field PAVLA was doing little better than stumbling along; its volunteers faced a wide range of problems that left many of them discouraged and discontent. Gilda Martoglio, the New Jersey nurse stationed in Brazil, came up against a typical set of problems, and wrote about them regularly to Father Mader, her diocesan director. In addition to experiencing some confusion about her own role, she had been critical of the local bishop, Dom Avelar Brandão of Teresina. At that time president of CELAM, he would go on to become cardinal-archbishop of São Salvador da Bahia. While his international reputation as a liberal leader was well-established, Miss Martoglio and other volunteers found him to be highly authoritarian on his home territory. Her moves to criticize what she felt was the bishop's unwarranted interference with PAVLA activities brought a rebuke from the national PAVLA office—and added to her concern. Excerpts from her exchange of correspondence with Father Mader hint at the frustration in the field and illustrate the priest's patient but ultimately unsuccessful approach in attempting to deal with it.

Some of her complaints dealt with practical, everyday matters, with mixups on salary checks taking place repeatedly (an experience shared by many volunteers). A typical note when a check failed to arrive:

If PAVLA doesn't have adequate personnel to handle even the mechanical details with some degree of efficiency, then I suggest they hire more. If the budget won't permit it then I think PAVLA should give serious consideration to limiting the number of volunteers it accepts and only accept that number to which they can provide adequate and conscientious service.

But most of Miss Martoglio's complaints were more reflective, and touched on deeper issues. She wrote from Teresina:

The more I see, hear, and experience about PAVLA, the more I question the validity of its programs and projects. It sure sounds great on paper, but the realities of it are an entirely different matter. It seems to me that they violate the very principles and concepts which they say they foster, . . . the prime one being the intrinsic worth and dignity of the human. Right now, there are nurses here who, as a result of their PAVLA projects, are doubting their own work and usefulness and have even lost confidence in their professional capabilities! I'm not saying that PAVLA is all wrong, because any relatively new organization is bound to make some good bloopers. But they don't seem to have profited from their past mistakes, and they don't *really* listen to what the volunteers are saying.

Several weeks later she wrote:

We have been told by PAVLA that our actual "work accomplishments" may not have as far-reaching an effect as our "good examples" of Christian living and all that this encompasses. From my point of view, this does not mean just being seen going to mass, being kind and friendly to our neighbors, receiving communion, respecting our co-workers, etc. To me it means being involved—and I do mean involved—in the totality and autonomy of man. I cannot see how this can be done, or is even plausible, if we divorce ourselves from the reality of the situation here in Teresina, . . . and the reality of the situation here in Teresina is that there are criticisms to be made, criticisms (from where I sit) which have to be made.

Father Mader's response to this and similar complaints was measured in tone:

Please recall that this is all so new. PAVLA is inserting itself into a culture which fears and hates the gringo for the most part, . . . a culture in which the church has been used for superstition as well as meaningful spirituality. . . . It is a culture where the bishops, on the whole, are products of the conquistador mentality, . . . but it is, it really is, changing. How is it changing? By your presence, for one thing.

When Miss Martoglio wrote a long and discouraged letter questioning the value of her own work in view of the monumental problems of disease and poverty she had all around her, Father Mader tried to reassure her:

If you consider this from the viewpoint of your absence on the scene you may see that there has been a real value in your presence. . . . You have already touched the lives of many of the innocent, the silent participators in this entire affair, the sick and needy. . . . I would hate to see you leave there.

But two months later, after a visit from a U.S. PAVLA official, Miss Martoglio's disenchantment with the organization had, if anything, deepened. Again she wrote Father Mader:

To me, PAVLA is a political administrative machine of the church (and at this point I find it hard to believe that this is the church that Christ founded). . . . It is financially able to put up a good front. It is all caught up in business-administrative busyness, while the basic reason for its very inception has gotten lost in a mound of paperwork. . . .

She wrote on for two pages, and then added:

I just glanced back over what I have written so far and couldn't help but note the words I've used in relation to myself—frustration, sarcasm, bitterness, anger, empty vacuum, want to cry, lack understanding, a political pawn, completely and utterly drained, closed mentality, lack of respect, negative, uncharitable. . . . Quite a list, no? And in relatively only a few pages, too. . . . Is this the lay spirituality that PAVLA and Dom Avelar talk about promoting?

Role confusion to begin with, frustrations in trying to carry out a job—they were experiences all too common to volunteers, to those who stayed, at any rate. Volunteer Robert Winslow wrote in 1969 of problems with his ordinary in Brazil:

It is unthinkable for foreigners, particularly Americans, to attempt to modify the bishop's methods. The problems this situation creates for PAVLA are patently monumental. On the one hand the joy of serving the People of God is completely frustrated in the volunteers since the People of God cannot be truly served under the circumstances.

Ann Held Griffin told a story to illustrate one volunteer's impatience with the endless rounds of discussion with his companions about PAVLA—its role, its methods of operation, its goals. He jumped up from one such session and stormed out of the room, saying "The hell with PAVLA! I've got work to do!"

In Washington, Father Ray Kevane had work to do too. Unhappy over the move from Chicago, and unhappier still over the long-range prospects of PAVLA now that Father Colonnese was in charge of the Latin America Bureau, the Sioux City priest tried to rally diocesan directors and friendly bishops to his corner for the anticipated battle for survival.

Reports from the field could not have been encouraging, particularly reports such as the letter he received in September 1968 from Gilda Martoglio and another volunteer, Janice Smrekar. They had checked up on the whereabouts of the thirty or forty people who had been their classmates in the 1967 PAVLA training course they attended, and their report was a damning indictment of the entire PAVLA program.

Nine classmates had already left PAVLA, they wrote, and, using only first names or nicknames, they spelled out the unhappy situation of eight others:

A. Ed—No project, but making a name for himself as a singer in a choir in Lima (and still hoping for a project).

B. Gladys—Teaching English, religion, and writing in the most modern school in the area to boys from middle- and upper-class families, but feeling the need to be involved.

C. Kelly and Scally—"Making rounds" looking for sick people to whom medicine could be doled out.

D. Jackie—Making a "home" out of the PV house in Lima, and presently in Bogota with the Lima choir to sing for the pope.

E. Ruth and Sue—Sent to open and administer a maternity hospital and neither with the background to do so.

F. Pat—Sent to a project where all she was able to develop, unfortunately, was a case of hepatitis.

They are fine Christian people who want to change mentalities, but because of poor project selection or poor orientation on the project they have not been given opportunity to do so.

The volunteers continued, widening their sights:

By not properly advising project directors of its objectives PAVLA exposes volunteers to a sense of loss of personal value, demoralization, and a deterioration of the image of PAVLA.

We know that no organization can have 100 percent effectiveness, and we don't expect it of PAVLA. But does the proportion of PAVLA projects which are effective, when compared to the proportion which are ineffective (according to PAVLA's stated philosophy), validate the entire program? . . . We feel that the administration of PAVLA, as a structure within the American Church, is fostering the same type of conservatism that exists in the North American and Latin American Churches—a conservatism in which there is a sharp dichotomy between philosophy and action.

The lay mission movement to Latin America, launched at the beginning of the decade with such bright promise, was under fire from all sides. Was it worth saving? Despite its problems, Kevane thought so; he was convinced of it. To complaints such as those from Gilda Martoglio and Janice Smrekar he had an answer: the size and scope of the operation and its necessarily bureaucratic structures invariably would result in "misunderstandings." "Let us proceed," he told his diocesan directors after admitting that PAVLA had faults and offering hope for improvements. "We have a program approved by our bishops, one in which we all have a stake, one in which we all can work together in a spirit of brotherly love." Colonnese had other ideas. "PAVLA was in a shambles," he wrote, "and I knew there was only one way to resolve the problem: destroy it." The adversaries staked out their positions for the showdown that each knew would be coming soon.

8

Coordination at Home

The struggle between Father Colonnese and Father Kevane over the future of the Papal Volunteers was only part of a larger, ongoing battle to determine the overall course of U.S. church efforts toward Latin America. To one degree or another, it had been going on almost from the outset of the full-scale mission involvement that began in 1960. As the sixties progressed, the struggle increased in intensity and battle lines became more clearly drawn, reflecting the explosive changes set off by Vatican II as well as revolutionary developments in theological thought emanating from Latin America itself. Basically, the struggle was between those who wanted to conduct mission operations along traditional lines and those who saw a radically new approach as the only hope of confronting Latin America's massive problems of poverty and social injustice.

In that context, Father John Considine was something of a traditionalist (although he had always been too much of an innovator not to see the strength of the more radical point of view). So were most of the leaders of religious communities that were sending missioners to Latin America, and so were most of the U.S. bishops. People such as Colonnese and Monsignor Ivan Illich emerged as leading spokesmen for the radical approach, Illich assuming that role at an especially early point. Still others—Father Frederick McGuire, for one—kept open the lines of communication between the opposing factions and tried as best they could to reconcile the points of view.

When that proved impossible, when the unavoidable split came about irrevocably at the end of the decade, those who had been in the battle realized how much it had sapped their strength. "Nobody really won," a survivor of the period recalled, "and a lot of people lost. The biggest losers, I guess, were the people in Latin America who thought we could do something for them."

Whatever quarrels would develop later on, there was none at all in 1960 over the selection of Father Considine to head the bishops' new Latin America program. Father McGuire, as head of the Mission Secretariat of the National Catholic Welfare Conference, helped to bring about the appointment when he went to Rome in December 1959, less than a month after the first historic meeting of a committee of United States, Canadian, and Latin American bishops at Georgetown University. McGuire reported to Cardinal Samore, the Vatican's Latin America specialist, that one of the recommendations of the meeting called for a yearly U.S. contribution of $1 million to the Vatican, to be earmarked for Latin America activities. "I expressed the idea that a million dollars a year wasn't the only answer," McGuire said in an interview. "In order to spur some real interest within the United States church, I felt it would be necessary to have some sort of a secretariat established for Latin America."

That suggestion began an exchange of correspondence between Samore and then-Monsignor Paul F. Tanner, at the time NCWC's general secretary, eventually resulting in the creation of a Latin America Bureau within the conference, and the appointment of Considine to be its director. Knowledgeable, articulate, thoroughly familiar with all aspects of mission work, the one-time Maryknoll vicar general had innumerable personal contacts in Latin America as well as in the rest of the mission world. Latins as well as his own compatriots were pleased with the appointment, as was Rome, and once he concluded a prior summer teaching commitment, Considine prepared to assume the new post on a full-time basis in September 1960. "It was a very popular choice," McGuire recalled. "In a sense, John Considine was the only man for the job."

The budget was a small one, only $25,000 a year initially, matching the scope of the operation. But before long Considine began to see it would have to grow, and grow rapidly, if it were to attempt to do all the things that should be done. Even before going on full-time duty, he realized that the proper training of personnel would have to be one of his first priorities, and he settled on the man he wanted to oversee that task: a fiery, brilliant young priest of the New York archdiocese named Ivan Illich. He was familiar with Illich's success in New York's Puerto Rican apostolate and was impressed with him after a personal meeting. But before he could sign him on, some roadblocks had to be hurdled. Illich was so well-known, even at an early age, that he had made enemies as well as friends.

Ivan Illich's sudden rise to prominence was no less intriguing than his international, almost exotic background, or his brooding, compelling dark countenance. Born in Vienna in 1926, he was fluent in several languages, including Yiddish, thanks to a childhood in which he had lived in several European countries and the attentive instruction given by a series of tutors and governesses. His father was a comfortably well-off Yugoslavian who came from a titled Catholic family in Dalmatia, and his mother was a Spanish Jew. Illich's academic achievements were notable: master's degrees in theology and philosophy from the Gregorian University in Rome; a doctorate in the philosophy of history, from the University of Salzburg; the completion of doctoral studies in natural science at the University of Florence, where his special field of study was crystallography.

His church connections, within the Vatican and without, were no less impressive. Jacques Maritain, the best-known Catholic philosopher of the day, was a family friend, one whom Illich would refer to as a central influence on his life. In Rome, his instructors hoped he would prepare for a career in the Vatican diplomatic service after ordination, but in a surprise move, one which later would be recognized as typical, Illich decided he would apply instead for service in the archdiocese of New York. He arrived in 1951. "I came here," he once told a fellow New York priest, "because my friends in Rome ribbed me about not being able to make it in an American parish."

New York had few priests quite like him. Assigned to a parish with a sizeable Puerto Rican population, located in Washington Heights, he quickly became involved with the concerns of its families. He immersed himself in developing an understanding of Puerto Rican problems, making several trips to the island, and soon had established himself as the archdiocese's "Puerto Rican man" on two counts: He knew more about the situation than anyone else, and he was becoming idolized by the members of the Puerto Rican community.

Illich's performance had already caught the eye of Cardinal Francis Spellman, who was pleased with what he saw. The attachment became a permanent one on a hot summer day in 1955. The cardinal had been concerned about poor attendance at St. Patrick's Cathedral for the archdiocese's yearly ceremony honoring San Juan, Puerto Rico's patron saint, and mentioned the problem to Illich.

"Illich had a ready answer for him," recalled Father Joseph P. Fitzpatrick, head of Fordham University's sociology department and a long-time associate of Illich:

> "If you're going to have a fiesta," he told the cardinal, "you've got to have it outside." The cardinal agreed, and Illich went to work. He arranged to have the fiesta at Fordham on the parade ground in front of Keating Hall, and promoted it every chance he had. Everyone else was frightened that it would simply bomb out, and their apprehension must have gotten to Ivan. On the day before the fiesta, he asked the maintenance people to have three thousand chairs ready, but to spread them around a little so the crowd would look bigger.
>
> Well, the following day they started coming early, and they kept coming. We ended up with thirty or thirty-five thousand people, swarming all over the place, mobbing Spellman and Mayor Wagner. All the papers gave it headline treatment on the front page the next day—"Puerto Ricans Mob Cardinal," things like that—with pictures of the cardinal being engulfed by this huge throng of people. He loved it. And he gave Illich credit for it.

He credited Illich not only for the success of the fiesta, but, more significantly, for the long-range effects it promised. The cardinal had previously designated Illich as coordinator of Spanish-American affairs for the archdiocese; now he appointed him vice-rector of the Catholic University at Ponce, Puerto Rico, with the responsibility of starting and heading a program in which U.S. priests would be trained in understanding Latin American culture.

Once cemented, the Spellman-Illich relationship would not be broken. When Illich was twenty-nine the cardinal had him named a monsignor, by far the youngest in the country. In later years, when the controversies surrounding Illich crossed international lines and reached to Rome itself, Spellman stood by him without question, staving off the priest's ultimate downfall simply by casting his personal vote of confidence. (One observer believes that Spellman's admiration for Illich went beyond his recognition of Illich's ability to deal with Puerto Ricans and his understanding of the Latin mentality. According to this theory, Spellman became impressed early in Illich's career because the young priest was able to make use of his Vatican connections to quash problems which could have been embarrassing to the cardinal and the archdiocese. Friends in Rome and clout as well—the combination could not have failed to impress the New York cardinal.)

The program at Ponce went well. More than a simple preparatory course for those priests involved in "Puerto Rican work," it aimed at a deeper understanding of Latin American-North American relationships. "We all thought that Puerto Rico would be the ideal midpoint, the bridge that would link the two," said Father Fitzpatrick, who would remain a close adviser and confidant of Illich. "We planned a library and documentation center to spread information to the non-Latin world about Latins, and vice-versa. We wanted to create a center where significant people from Latin America, Europe, and the United States would gather for dialogue and discussion, leading, we hoped, to mutual understanding."

One of the guest lecturers Illich brought in was John Considine, whose initial favorable impression of the New York priest would remain fixed in his mind, especially after the Latin America Bureau became a reality in 1960. By chance, it was the same year that Illich's Puerto Rican experiment would end, the result of his opposition to a Catholic political party that had been formed to combat the government of President Muñoz Marín. Illich's campaign against the Catholic party, and particularly its use of the birth control issue, infuriated Bishop James McManus, a U.S. Redemptorist who headed the Ponce diocese and who had founded the Catholic University there. McManus ordered Illich back to New York, where a sympathetic Cardinal Spellman helped him get a place on the Fordham political science faculty.

It was then that Considine decided to ask Illich to form a training institute for the new wave of missioners to Latin America, but that decision ran into head-on opposition from Monsignor Tanner, who was sensitive to the reasons behind Illich's hasty departure from Puerto Rico. Rather than risk an all-out battle with NCWC over the issue that early in the life of the Latin America

Bureau, Considine went another route, through Fordham's president, Father Laurence McGinley, with the same suggestion. Illich and his adviser Fitzpatrick were receptive to the idea, having already decided that Puerto Rico was not, after all, the ideal "bridge" between North and Latin American cultures. The concept had McGinley's backing as well.

An institute for training mission personnel, with the blessing of the new Latin America Bureau but away from direct control by NCWC, at a site that Illich would be able to choose—the ingredients seemed to be there for a successful undertaking, and Illich decided to go ahead.

The Cuernavaca School

In October 1960, Father McGinley formally approved the establishment of the Center of Intercultural Formation (CIF) as a parent organization for the operation. Traveling with funds obtained from Considine, Illich located an abandoned resort hotel named Chula Vista in the Mexican town of Cuernavaca and decided he had found the location for his institute.

Considine journeyed to the site the following month, concurred in the selection, and the famous Cuernavaca school, first known as CIF and later as CIDOC, the Center of Intercultural Documentation, was born. It was given formal status when the Center of Intercultural Formation was established as a New York corporation March 3, 1961, with Father McGinley as president, and, as board members, Considine, McGuire, Father Celsus Wheeler, head of the Franciscans' Holy Name province, and Porter Chandler, a New York attorney. The NCWC administrative board, headed by Archbishop Karl Alter of Cincinnati, approved Considine's request for funds to launch the project. Considine and Illich agreed that all training plans and operations were to be handled by CIF, with its base at Fordham and the training institute at Cuernavaca.

The first class met in June 1961, and the uproar that followed barely hinted at the trouble that was to come.

Convinced that too many U.S. missioners went to Latin America with prejudicial attitudes and a sense of superiority, Illich opted for the shock-treatment approach in preparing his students for what lay ahead. There was a high mortality rate. Only thirty-nine of the sixty-eight students (about half lay people and half priests and nuns) survived the rigors of the course. A contemporary newsmagazine story commented:

> The attrition due to five and one-half hours daily of language drill, plus lectures and discussions that may last as late as 2 A.M., was only partly responsible; Illich and his staff deliberately make the students angry, start arguments, challenge cherished beliefs. "I hate Yankees!" Illich may yell at a mild-mannered nun from New Jersey.

The dropouts lost little time in bringing Illich's unorthodox, Yankee-baiting methods to the attention of the U.S. Catholic public. Illich was unmoved by the resulting complaints and defended his approach without apology. "Those of good will alone," he said, "need not apply."

Fitzpatrick expressed the position more diplomatically in an article on CIF in *America* magazine the following February. Describing the difficulty of the course and the necessity of making students aware of cultural differences, more important than mere fluency of language, and stressing the need for spiritual formation, he said the experience "can serve as a testing period." If prospective missioners will not be able to cope with the difficulties they will encounter, Fitzpatrick implied, the time to find it out is before they begin their assignments:

> A person from outside Latin America will find himself facing a way of life there that is vastly different from his own, that is strange to him, often bewildering and provoking. Unless he understands the problems of communicating with people of another culture, he may quickly find his life frustrating. He may become critical, and his bewilderment may express itself in a hostility of which he is unaware but which will make his efforts useless.

The summer of 1961 marked the end of the Considine-Illich honeymoon, for reasons not entirely agreed upon by three who were close to the scene. Fitzpatrick recalls that the trouble began with that first training course, and particularly with the Papal Volunteers who formed a large percentage of those who attended:

> From the beginning, Illich felt that the concept of the Papal Volunteers was unsound. He saw no value at all in sending young people to Latin America for a year or two. That first course had a one-week break after seven weeks, and Illich told half of the PAVLA trainees not to come back. Considine immediately questioned the way Illich was running the program, and that began a whole series of tensions between them.

McGuire sees it another way:

> There were sparks between Illich and Considine right from the start. John got approval for $75,000 to get Cuernavaca going. Illich produced two budgets—one for show, with the $75,000 figure, the second considerably above that. Considine didn't like it at all. He had to fight to get the money to begin with and swore up and down he'd been stabbed in the back. Considine was strongly conservative on this; he wouldn't spend money he didn't have. Illich was the opposite. Considine recognized his ability, but he just couldn't work with him.

Colonnese, a third observer, agreed that relations between Illich and Considine "began to disintegrate" shortly after Cuernavaca opened, but had a different slant on the reasons behind it:

> The principal weakness of the operation was Illich's own stance on control. He gave every indication that he was responsible to nobody. He wanted to exercise total control of the center, but at the same time he denied any responsibility for fund-raising. This was one of the major sources of contention between CIF and the Latin America Bureau. Considine consistently declined to ask for any new funding from the bishops' committee because of Illich's refusal to recognize any control over his financial-administrative situation. Slowly but surely CIF drew farther away from those—primarily the Latin America Bureau—who had desired its formation.

Whatever the real reason, or whether it was a combination of all three, the distance widened noticeably between Considine and Illich. Before long, Illich began to express his challenging ideas in a more public fashion, and with more effect. It was an effect that, eventually, would be explosive as far as the Latin America program was concerned.

Considine had a happier experience with the second man to whom he turned for top-level assistance. Monsignor William Quinn was a priest of the Chicago archdiocese, already nationally known for his work with the Christian Family Movement—a haven, in that period, for Catholics, both religious and lay, who were known as "progressive"—and in his role as executive secretary of the Bishops' Committee for Migrant Workers. "I became involved in Latin American activities primarily because of my association with the migrant workers' field," he said in 1977. "John Considine asked me to work with him in large measure because of the contacts I had built up both with the migrants and the CFM people. The bureau had other avenues to approach the bishops, but they needed grassroots contacts. That's where I came in."

Quinn agreed to serve as codirector of the bureau provided he could remain in Chicago and continue at least part-time attention to his other interests. More concerned with the man than with his day-to-day whereabouts, Considine approved the arrangement. He asked Quinn to oversee the PAVLA office, which would be located in Chicago as a result of the agreement. (As national secretary, David O'Shea handled most of PAVLA's administrative work for two early priest-directors, Fathers James Clark of Fall River, Massachusetts, and Victor Fernandez, the Jesuit from California. The operation remained somewhat loosely-knit until Father Raymond Kevane became PAVLA's director in 1964.)

"The physical separation between my office and John's might have been a problem from time to time," conceded Quinn, today the pastor of a parish in

Maywood, Illinois. "But I don't think it was major. My work had nothing to do with the administrative load; I'm not an administrator and I never was."

One activity that occupied much of Quinn's and Considine's time, even before the Latin America Bureau formally came into being, was speaking about the problems of the church in Latin America. They turned up at one conference after another, sometimes singly, sometimes together, to talk about a topic that had become, in a relatively short time, a major concern of U.S. Catholics.

Both were at such a conference in Chicago in the summer of 1959 when their attention was drawn to an intense young priest who dominated one of the discussion periods with his probing questions and perceptive observations. Along with a third participant—Cardinal Cushing—they called him aside after the session to carry on the dialogue. For all three, it was the first meeting they had with Louis Michael Colonnese, a talented, impatient, single-minded priest whose future activities would have a profound effect on the course of the United States mission to Latin America.

"I knew from the very beginning," Colonnese wrote in the early seventies, "that my priesthood was going to provide me with a very lonely, and some-times sad, life." How much of that observation was actual prophecy and how much was reflective insight is difficult to tell, but the fact is that Mike Colonnese's priesthood has often been just that—sad and lonely. His rise to prominence, like that of Illich's, came early. But when he fell from official grace he chose, unlike Illich, to vanish from public view. Also, unlike Illich, he continued to exercise his priestly ministry, working for several years in Latin America, his whereabouts known only to a handful of people.

There has always been something of that quality about his priesthood, in fact: a tendency to stand apart, to challenge, to follow an outbound path. And with it all has been an intensity of purpose, an intolerance for those less dedicated, particularly if they mask their shortcoming behind the trappings of the institutional church. Colonnese was strangely unmoved by the pageantry of Vatican II, despite his youthful love for the church's rites and traditional pomp. As he wrote after attending two council sessions and coming in personal contact with most of the U.S. council fathers:

> After dealing with so many bishops for so long a period, I saw through the veneer. . . . Now it remained for me to depend upon shared faith, belief in the truth of the church. . . . I saw people who apparently believed strongly in the church. But those same people lacked commit-ment. The infallibility of the Pope was unquestionable. But the desti-tution of one's neighbor could be ignored. The dogmas of the Assump-tion and the Immaculate Conception, the celibacy of the priesthood, and others . . . these were held as inviolable. But the Sermon on the Mount was relegated to one sermon each year, and that without much effect.

The only son born to a closely-knit Italian-American family in Connecticut, Mike Colonnese studied at private secondary schools, at Belmont Abbey (one year), and Mount St. Mary's College in Maryland. He delighted his parents when he announced he would study for the priesthood as a member of the Paulists, but left after a year at the novitiate in Oak Ridge, New Jersey, dissatisfied with the Paulists' formation methods (the strong discipline affected his health, he said). He eventually completed his ordination studies in the diocese of Davenport, Iowa, where he had been attracted by reports of progressive policies and, as mentioned earlier, by a farsighted bishop in the person of the late Ralph Hayes.

From the start (in another similarity to Illich's career) Colonnese's early record in the priesthood drew attention his way. No assignment was so menial that it could not be turned into a challenge. Relegated to hot-lunch planning in his first parish, he gave it his full effort—and won an award from the state of Iowa for "variety in meals, excellence in preparation and serving, and cost reduction." Bored enough by summer inactivity to launch a grade-school-level athletic program, he put so much enthusiasm into it that he was swamped with youngsters from the beginning. Parents and other parishioners, and those from neighboring parishes as well, were impressed with this young priest's dedication, and the contacts he made with them led to a wide range of out-of-parish activities: the Christian Family Movement, Young Catholic Workers, Young Christian Students, the burgeoning liturgy movement.

Other priests in Davenport recognized Mike Colonnese as a doer, someone who made things happen, but all of his activities were somehow suspect, a bit too progressive. Their reserve, even their hostility, kept pace with the accolades Colonnese was beginning to receive from the outside. "I have never recovered from that rejection," he said, "because it continued for years."

More far-ranging success—and more bitterness—was still to come. Transferred to a Davenport high school to teach Spanish (although to that point he knew nothing of the language), he developed an interest in Latin American activities and attended a number of national meetings on that subject, including the one in Chicago where he met Considine and Quinn, while maintaining his CFM-YCS-YCW ties. Protests from parents, priests, and other faculty members greeted his introduction of "Latin American realities" into his high school Spanish classes, the "realities" including problems of race, exploitation, and social injustice, but Colonnese stormed ahead.

He opened the diocesan Office of the Lay Apostolate and eventually became its full-time director. He organized study weeks that grew in reputation until they were attracting crowds of up to 1,500 from several states, drawn, in part, by speakers such as Ivan Illich, Bill Quinn, and John Considine. Colonnese was out on the speaking trail, too, at least in those dioceses where his presence hadn't been barred by bishops, and religious superiors who were upset by his themes of religious involvement in the lay apostolate, the rights of workers, and the plight of Latin America's masses. "Superiors, bishops, and other clergy were disturbed by what they thought was a rabble-rousing kind of program," he said. But he was convinced that the tensions it created were not only healthy, but inevitable as well.

Considine had watched Colonnese's ascending star. Convinced of the young priest's genuine concern for Latin America, he asked Cushing in 1963 to request Colonnese's services through Bishop Hayes. Just as Quinn had done, Colonnese accepted with the proviso that he be allowed to remain in his own diocese, a request to which Considine agreed ("somewhat reluctantly," Colonnese said). This left the Latin America Bureau with a Washington-Chicago-Davenport base, which the principal parties, surprisingly, found not unwieldy at all. Colonnese was given the title of administrative director and placed in charge of the Davenport "administrative office" and the Chicago branch office which handled the PAVLA program.

"Considine was running pretty much of a one-man show," Colonnese recalled. "He was a great planner and was constantly fighting against the ignorance of and lack of interest in Latin America in the United States, especially among churchmen." A modest fund-raising program had been established, almost tentatively; there were limited efforts as well in the field of public relations. "For a lone individual, Considine had attacked a tremendously difficult job, and with success," Colonnese said. The Davenport priest was to expand the public information aspect of the Latin America Bureau, among other duties. He also determined to expand the fund-raising and educational activities of the bureau.

And so, by 1963, the triumvirate which would guide the Latin America Bureau for most of the sixties had formed, working out of its unlikely Washington-to-Chicago-to-Davenport triangle. One reason that it succeeded as long as it did was the regular schedule of planning meetings that its officials maintained. The sessions were held in Chicago, every six weeks or two months. The bureau's full-time people did not meet alone; they were joined by an informal advisory committee, more of a kitchen cabinet, really, and from the group as a whole emerged specific programs and proposals.

The regulars included Considine, Quinn, Colonnese, Monsignor James P. Shannon, the articulate young president of St. Thomas College who would become auxiliary bishop of St. Paul-Minneapolis in 1965 (and who would leave the episcopacy and the priesthood in 1970, a result of postconciliar turmoil and ill-treatment by some fellow bishops); Monsignor Joseph Gremillion, then with Catholic Relief Services and later secretary of the Vatican's Justice and Peace Commission. Others would take part on a less regular basis: Bishop McGrath, if he were in the United States; Fathers Clark or Fernandez, whose primary interest was PAVLA. Sessions would usually be held on a Saturday, starting early in the morning and winding up by late afternoon. Colonnese was the secretary ("a good administrative man," Quinn remembers).

It was at one of those early sessions that the planners developed a concept for a series of major gatherings to be held in the United States each year, at which time North Americans interested in Latin America would hear about Latin American problems from the Latin Americans themselves. The kernel of the idea came from Quinn, and the annual meetings—one of the major programs of the Latin America Bureau, and one which would cause stormy protests before it came to an eventual halt—would be known as the Catholic Inter-American Cooperation Program.

That was its formal title; everybody connected with it simply used the handier modified acronym: CICOP.

The Idea Behind CICOP

"CICOP was constructed to make people aware, to make them want to act, and to point ways toward effective action," Colonnese wrote several years later. "Its ultimate aim was nothing less than a personal commitment, great or small—not paternalistic—by every U.S. Catholic to some form of cooperation with the church and people of Latin America."

The idea for what eventually became CICOP first began to take shape when Quinn toured Latin America shortly after his appointment as codirector of the Latin America Bureau. Illich and Fitzpatrick provided him with the names of people he should see to familiarize himself with local problems, many of them well-known progressives: Fathers Jorge and José Calderón and Gustavo Gutiérrez, in Peru; Renato Poblete, at the Jesuits' social action headquarters, the Bellarmine Center, in Santiago, Chile. Bishop Larraín was at the center on the day Quinn arrived and was delighted to meet him. "I did the whole circuit," Quinn said, "and it was an eye-opener."

What many of his hosts told him, in one way or the other, was that North Americans were totally unfamiliar with the real problems of Latin America, and that some forum was needed, a forum in which Latin Americans themselves could communicate directly with North Americans and tell them their story. Back in Chicago, the Latin America Bureau's kitchen cabinet liked the idea and turned it into a formal proposal for what would become CICOP. "The idea from the start was that they would tell us, and we would listen," Quinn said. "I went to see Cushing about it, and there was no problem selling it. Our first money came from Boston."

"CICOP was designed to penetrate the mind and stir the heart of each American Catholic," Colonnese wrote in later years. "The purse and the hand would come into play following deep convictions about Latin America and its needs. And the purse and the hand would be extended, we had hoped, in a truly enlightened manner."

As Colonnese reconstructed CICOP's earliest stages, there were hints of problems to come right from the start:

The idea behind CICOP was to provide Latin American leaders with a platform where they could uninhibitedly express their own views to the

American public without being threatened by reprisals, denials of aid, and the like. We knew it was going to be a painful experience for us because much of what they would tell us would be quite distasteful.

Colonnese was right. CICOP would draw protests in years to come from bishops, from the State Department, from U.S. business people with interests in Latin America. Eventually it would be killed off. But in 1963 it was new and exciting. And it was an idea that almost bubbled over with promise.

With financial support for the first CICOP meeting assured, thanks to Cardinal Cushing's lead, the Latin America Bureau put together a planning committee that guaranteed a prominent role for Latin Americans from the outset. There were to be other aspects of CICOP's operations—the development of local and regional conferences; promotion of Latin America studies in U.S. educational institutions; the dissemination of information about Latin America through the mass media—but it was the annual meeting which was to be the keystone of the program. Its developers wanted to insure that it got off to a good start.

Bishop McGrath, then an auxiliary of Panama, was among the planners, as was Dom Helder Camara; Father Tiago Cloin, the Redemptorist from Brazil; Father Poblete from Santiago; Mexican Father Hector Samperio; and Marina Bandeira, head of the Movimento de Educação de Base (MEB), Brazil's basic education movement.

"It would be difficult to exaggerate the importance of this contingent of Latin American participants," John Considine said after the historic meeting had taken place. "Their role was indispensable for the success of the conference. At every session, in every gathering throughout the day and evening, it was their contribution which provided the essential conclusions, the requisite explanations and interpretations."

The U.S. planners included representatives of the Latin America Bureau, as well as Monsignor Gremillion; Monsignor Theodore McGarrick, then of Catholic University of Ponce (now an auxiliary bishop in New York City); Martin Work of the National Council of Catholic Men; Sister M. Josetta of the Sisters of Mercy in Washington; Fathers Boniface Wittenbrink and James Darby, representing the Conference of Major Superiors of Men; and Sister Mary Luke Tobin and Rose Emanuella, representing the Conference of Major Superiors of Women. San Francisco's Archbishop McGucken and then-Bishop Carroll of Miami were appointed to the planning committee, but did not attend any sessions.

The North Americans on the committee were dedicated, but not all of them were familiar with the Latin American problems they had to deal with. They repeatedly tried to head off Latin American suggestions in regard to controversial subjects to be covered, warning of problems with the U.S. bishops and of future difficulties in fund-raising if they were pursued. "It was this kind of 'lock-in' which would be a barrier to real progress and development within

CICOP and the Latin America Bureau in general in subsequent years," Colonnese later observed. Still, the Latins held their ground for the most part, and the agenda for the meeting, built around the theme "The Church in the New Latin America," contained much of the provocative material Quinn and Colonnese hoped it would.

Some 1,500 participants were on hand when the two-day meeting opened January 20, 1964, at the Edgewater Beach Hotel in Chicago. They were treated to an impressive sight: the grand entrance, in full ecclesiastical regalia, of CICOP's six "cardinal-presidents": Cushing of Boston, Meyer of Chicago, Ritter of St. Louis, Quintero of Caracas, Landazuri of Lima, and Silva of Santiago. The display smacked of the old triumphalism, which was still very much in style, but it served another purpose: assuring those who were hesitant about the orthodoxy of the unusual gathering that in the eyes of Holy Mother Church it all bore the stamp of approval.

McGrath's keynote address, tracing the development of the modern Latin American church, was well received, as was a talk by Bishop Larraín, then the president of CELAM. The list of well-known speakers went on: Father Poblete, analyzing the religious action of the church in Latin America; Illich, despite his personal difficulties with Considine; Abbé François Houtart, the specialist in pastoral planning; Dr. Aristide Calvani, a Christian Democrat from Venezuela; Archbishop Paul J. Hallinan of Atlanta, chairman of the bishops' subcommittee for inter-American cooperation; and Senator Hubert Humphrey, who invoked the memories of Pope John ("that great and good man") and John F. Kennedy, both dead only a few months. (Kennedy was named North American recipient of the first CICOP award; the Latin American winner was Alberto Lleras Camargo, who had been president of Colombia.)

Monsignor Shannon, the future bishop, was an introductory chairman; so was a long-time hero of many of the CICOP planners and participants —sixty-eight-year-old Monsignor Luigi Ligutti. "I love Latin America," he said in his brief talk. "The human resources of Latin America—and they come first—contain in themselves the greatest possibilities. There is the greatest potential, from a biological viewpoint, from a material viewpoint, from the viewpoint of Christian culture, that no other part of the world has possessed in like fashion thus far. In these possibilities, there is no limit."

(Several years later Colonnese offered a reflection on Ligutti—"this outstanding man"—and Latin America: "He was indefatigable in trying to arouse interest. He was relentless in his criticism of what was happening in the church in Latin America—the abuses and lack of commitment to the impoverished. I have always considered Luigi Ligutti as the man primarily responsible for programs such as CICOP and other organizations dedicated to a renewal of interest in Latin America. He has never received the honors appropriate to his labors on behalf of Latin America.")

There were workshops, small group sessions, major addresses—all built around the dual concepts behind the planners' theme: that North Americans would not be able to understand the real problems affecting the church in Latin America without a clear understanding of their historical origins, and that in Latin America's period of change the church should act with courage, in a spirit of hope and opportunity.

Its organizers termed the first CICOP conference a clear-cut success, despite a few organizational problems, the type expected with any new venture involving so many people. It had attracted huge crowds—upward of 2,300 heard the major addresses by Senator Humphrey and others—and drew widespread attention in the press.

The next few weeks brought an upsurge of mail to CICOP's Chicago office. Teachers and school officials wanted instructional materials; Catholic organizations wanted to know how they could help. "CICOP had struck a note which was heard throughout the United States and in many places in Latin America as well," Colonnese said.

And there were critics as well. Some State Department people grumbled about unfavorable references to United States policies in Latin America, and U.S. businessmen involved with Latin America were less than enthused about what they'd read of the conference. But the complaints were minimal, and most of them reached CICOP and the Latin America Bureau indirectly.

Thus CICOP became an established fixture of the Latin America Bureau program; for many U.S. Catholics it was the most readily recognized activity the bureau carried out. The controversies that would envelop CICOP in its later years had not surfaced, at least not to any significant degree.

Having tilled the soil, CICOP's planners concentrated on sowing seeds at the next few meetings. The second CICOP conference, also held in Chicago, was based on the theme of "The Church and Social Revolution in Latin America," and made the point that a radical change was required in Latin America—a revolution, hopefully peaceful—in which the church's role would be vital. There was a heavy concentration of Latin American speakers—including many Chileans, a fact which disturbed Colonnese ("While it was true that the church in Chile was probably the most progressive in Latin America, it was also true that it was heavily influenced by Christian Democrats and much involved in the latter's political activity"). The number of Protestant observers shot up markedly from the first conference, as did the number of Catholic religious participants, so much so that the committee took steps to see that CICOP did not become a forum in which Latin American mission activity would be the only area of discussion.

Talk of revolution, however peaceful, at the second conference led to uneasiness in the ranks of the bishops, who also heard from some businessmen about the dangers connected with CICOP. Some bishops wanted Archbishop Hallinan's subcommittee to be more vigilant about the CICOP program, Colonnese said, but no drastic moves were made against it. The large number of Latin American prelates connected with the CICOP meetings helped to guarantee the planners a relatively free hand in organizing the third conference.

"Religious Values in a Changing Latin America" was the theme of CICOP's third meeting, held in January 1966, at the Chicago Hilton. The ultimate goal of the meeting, Colonnese later said, was to attempt to get U.S. missioners to break with traditional pastoral ideas and theology, adapting their work to the signs and the needs of the times. That goal was reached in some measure, particularly in regard to U.S. women religious, but there were questionable side effects from the conference. Not only did criticism increase from within the United States; there were rumblings of discontent from conservative Latin American bishops as well. They found it impossible to understand how Latin America's controversial and threatening "new theology" (to be discussed in a later chapter) found such a favorable hearing, before such a distinguished audience, in the United States.

There were other memorable aspects of the third CICOP conference. Tragically, it was the last for Bishop Larraín; he was killed in an automobile accident in Chile the following June. With his death CICOP and the Latin America Bureau lost a powerful and articulate friend. But there were happier memories, too: The third CICOP international award went to Monsignor Ligutti, a unanimous choice for the honor.

Most of the controversy that would swirl about CICOP in its later years was only beginning to be felt. For the most part, with the exceptions noted above, there was general agreement in the church community both in North and Latin America that the CICOP conferences were doing what they had set out to do: informing North Americans, primarily through Latin Americans, about what was really happening south of the border. "This is the first time Latin Americans such as myself have been invited to discuss these problems as equals," Marina Bandeira had said after the first CICOP meeting. Most of her fellow Latin American CICOP participants shared a feeling of satisfaction that their day had come.

It was, in the mid-sixties, an era of good feeling as far as the Latin America Bureau was concerned. There were signs, to be sure, of the trouble that lay ahead: concern about inadequate preparation of Latin America missioners, an awareness of the weaknesses resulting from the lack of overall coordination of mission efforts, a realization that traditional-minded bishops both in North and Latin America were becoming disenchanted with the bureau's styles. (There was a nagging uncertainty, too, about Illich, whose unpredictable style was a continual source of concern.) But in terms of the whole North American church, interest in Latin America was at a peak, a result, in many ways, of the bureau's efforts. The number of volunteers for Latin America was at an all-time high; awareness of Latin American problems and of North American responsibilities in meeting them were constantly growing, thanks mainly to the successful CICOP program. And despite the distances over the Washington-Chicago-Davenport triangle, the bureau's people seemed to work well together.

"Considine and Colonnese were a good pair," Father Eugene Culhane recalled in later years. "When Colonnese began he was a young priest, very outgoing, very decisive. Considine was good at the gentlemanly level, but he didn't have the brashness you need to ask for money. Mike wasn't bashful at all; he was good at getting people to get things done. They were a good pair."

Finances were no problem at the outset. Father McGuire recalls that "people were generous" in sending money in; when one million dollars was being sent to the Pontifical Commission for Latin America in the early stages, it was raised through a variety of sources—including the Society for the Propagation of the Faith, the Holy Childhood Association, the Catholic Near East Welfare Association, and direct contributions. As the scope of the Latin America Bureau operations increased, with the all-important backing of Cardinal Cushing, more money was needed. Considine thought the best way to raise it would be through a once-a-year national collection, but that kind of move required the approval of the full bishops' meeting. He dispatched Colonnese to Rome in the Fall of 1965 (the U.S. bishops were holding their annual meeting there in conjunction with their attendance at the final session of the Second Vatican Council) to do some spadework.

Quinn had been in Rome during the second and third sessions of the Council, attempting to get Latin American bishops together with their North American counterparts. Despite help from Ligutti and others, it was no easy task. The North Americans were guarded in responding to the contacts he was trying to arrange, he recalls, simply because "they feared the money angle."

Colonnese came up against the same kind of unenthusiastic reception, but his salesmanship, combined with the support of prelates such as Cardinal Cushing and Bishop McNulty, assured a favorable decision when the Latin America collection came up for a vote. The bishops approved the collection, by a comfortable margin, in November 1965.

The formal announcement came in a statement the following month from Bishop McNulty, the vice chairman of the bishops' Latin America committee. The collection would climax the first Latin American Cooperation Week (to be held January 23–30, 1966, coinciding with the third CICOP conference) "as symbols of the fraternal ties between United States and Latin American Catholics."

McNulty reviewed the developments that had led to the involvement of the U.S. church in Latin America: "The Latin America Bureau was established by the United States bishops in response to an invitation of the Holy See for various nations to cooperate in Christian solidarity to aid the church in Latin America." He outlined its five-fold program: assistance to United States priests, brothers, and sisters in taking up service in Latin America; recruitment of lay personnel as Papal Volunteers; conducting the CICOP program;

forwarding gifts from private donors to Latin America; and providing special service to church institutions in Latin America. Bishop McNulty continued:

> Aware of the fact that Catholics of the United States have heretofore known little about the Church and its 200 million members who are their brothers in the Latin American orbit, the bishops of the United States strongly encourage the establishment of a Latin American Cooperation Week, to be observed for the primary purpose of building greater understanding and friendly concern for our fellow Christians of Latin America. To this end each diocese is urged to encourage a program embracing spiritual, cultural, educational, and financial activities touching Latin America. It is proposed that the observance be held during the last week of January, Sunday through Sunday. Further, in keeping with the widespread desire among us to join in friendly cooperation with our fellow Christians of Latin America, the bishops of the United States propose that a national collection for the Church in Latin America be taken up on the last Sunday of January.

The system under which the collection was set up—making it optional rather than mandatory for each diocese, a situation which continues today —resulted in totals which were, to some, surprisingly low.

"I was severely disappointed," said Colonnese of the first collection, which brought in $1,172,870—or, as he pointed out, two and half cents for each U.S. Catholic. "It was an incredibly shameful response on the part of the bishops (and I place the blame on them because had they cooperated, American lay Catholics would have generously responded)."

Colonnese Takes Charge

That kind of impatience came to be recognized as typical of Colonnese, whose unwavering determination to restructure U.S. church attitudes toward Latin America grew each year he spent in the bureau. He recalled that when he first signed on there were predictions that he wouldn't last in the job; he was "too progressive," "too leftist." And there were private predictions, by people who knew them both, that he wouldn't last long with Considine. The predictions turned out to be wrong. The two men frequently disagreed, but respected each other's abilities and got along on relatively good terms. "Considine was an intellectual who didn't play games with the truth," Colonnese said. "Even more important, he was an extremely just and fair man." Their conflicts were always resolved in a gentlemanly fashion, Colonnese said, and despite differences of opinion, "we worked well together until he retired from the bureau."

One area of Colonnese's operations that left Considine uneasy was his dealing with subordinates, and specifically the amount of freedom he gave them. A case in point was that of Jim Cotter, the Marquette journalism graduate hired by Colonnese to produce *Latin America Calls*, a tabloid designed to aid in fund-raising and in keeping U.S. Catholics informed about Latin America. Colonnese recalled:

> He would constantly remind me that I had to watch carefully over Jim's work, that he could create problems for us with the bishops. However, it was my contention that Jim was well-read on Latin America, on inter-American economic and political policies, and so forth. The bishops would simply have to learn that there was more than just a hierarchical point of view, that they were not the only men entrusted with the truth, and that laymen also shared in the inspiration of the Holy Spirit.

That kind of attitude, not unexpectedly, wore thin with some bishop-members of the Latin America committee, none more so than Coleman Carroll. The feeling was mutual; Colonnese was rarely able to agree with the Miami prelate on anything. A typical encounter would have Carroll telling Colonnese to remember his place, and Colonnese shooting back that if Carroll wanted a lackey, he'd have to look elsewhere. More than once Colonnese stormed out of meetings of the Latin America Committee, only to be calmed by others and, eventually, to return.

Such a shouting match occurred at a committee meeting prior to the CICOP meeting in St. Louis in 1968, when Cardinal John Dearden of Detroit, then president of the National Conference of Catholic Bishops, stepped in to remind Colonnese of Carroll's position—and of Colonnese's own. Colonnese left abruptly, vowing never to return. It took the urgings of Bishop Joseph Green, then bishop of Reno, and Bishop Joseph Breitenbeck, then a Detroit auxiliary, to get Colonnese back—and a petition from a delegation of Latin American bishops to get the committee to have him.

That was Colonnese. He saw the Latin American reality from one point of view—informed, certainly, and sympathetic as well. Few North Americans had a clearer grasp of Latin American needs as they were articulated by the moderate and progressive voices of Latin America. No one in the States understands us the way you do, he was told by one bishop or theologian after another, and that was probably true. But seeing the problems as he did, so clearly and with such a sense of urgency, he had no use for those who didn't, or for those who interpreted them differently.

It was a problem he came up against in Rome, when he was attempting to convince U.S. bishops, in no-nonsense terms, of the need for a Latin America collection:

> Some of my friends, my more sedate friends, tried to convince me that I should be less frank and more diplomatic. Diplomacy for them was what

it had always been in the church; lack of character, lack of honesty, deception, flattery. I couldn't be convinced. And so my attitude was looked upon as juvenile. Why should I, I asked myself, and I asked others, have to persuade the bishops to fulfill their own obligations? If they want to fulfill their commitment, fine, but I'll be damned if I'm going to play games with them.

He was impatient as well with the bureauracy of the bishops' conference. It was fine for a business corporation, he thought, but made no allowance for the movement of the Spirit.

From his earliest days in the Latin America Bureau, working with Considine and Quinn, Colonnese saw the problems that loomed ahead: the "over-eager response to the call for help," the inadequate formation of U.S. missioners (particularly, he felt, as far as PAVLA was concerned). He stopped short of going on record against the further presence of U.S. mission personnel, but that kind of drastic possibility was in his mind. For Colonnese, seeing the traps that lay in the future direction of U.S. mission policy was one thing. Getting others to see them his way was something else.

Considine had presided over a period of growth and the development of a genuine U.S. interest in Latin America, but it was a demanding job, and when he turned seventy in October 1967 a successor had to be found. And it was Colonnese—despite his youth, despite his reputation for bishop-baiting, despite his own reservations about the wisdom of all that the bureau was doing—to whom the bishops turned.

His appointment as director in April 1968 came at roughly the same time as the implementation of a reorganization of the old National Catholic Welfare Conference into the National Conference of Catholic Bishops and its corporate, legal arm, the U.S. Catholic Conference, and that brought a new set of challenges. It was an appointment that would touch off a stormy two-year period for the bureau, and that came as no surprise to Colonnese himself. "I was well aware," he wrote years later, "of the harm which was (wittingly or otherwise) resulting from conscious or subconscious exploitation of culture, moral predispositions, irrelevant historical attitudes, non-responsive theology, and general non-adaptability. I also knew what was surely to happen on the American scene once I brought these matters out into public view."

9

The Beginning of Disenchantment

Boston, Massachusetts; January, 1967. The fourth conference of the Catholic Inter-American Cooperation Program was about to get under way at the Statler Hilton. It was the first CICOP meeting to be held outside Chicago, and was built around the theme "The Integration of Man and Society in Latin America: A Christian View." There were more people on the planning committee, more speakers, more bishops in attendance than there had been at any of the three previous CICOP conferences in Chicago. And yet nothing would make the 1967 meeting more memorable than a magazine article which would appear, by elaborate design, at the same time the conference opened, and which was distributed to the three thousand people who were there.

The article was Ivan Illich's "The Seamy Side of Charity," a blistering indictment of every imaginable aspect of the Latin America mission program of the North American church. The featured piece in the January 21 issue of *America,* the respected Jesuit-edited journal of opinion, it used harsh and demeaning language to describe the concept behind the U.S. mission program ("an outburst of charitable frenzy" which "masks a universal and unconscious fear of a new Church") and the missioners themselves (people who tend "to fill the role of a colonial power's lackey chaplain" and who "must humbly accept the possibility that they are useless or even harmful").

"The Seamy Side of Charity" stood the U.S. church on its ear. The first reaction, of course, was that at the conference itself: stunned disbelief at first, then a roar of protest, angry disagreement with Illich's thesis and outrage that he (and *America)* would use the conference to get his message across. "Colossal lies," thundered CICOP's embittered host, Cardinal Richard Cushing, and privately the CICOP delegates were saying much worse than that. Illich had touched an open nerve.

How far from the target was he? What kind of shape was the U.S. mission program really in? According to official sources, it couldn't be better. Bishop McNulty, speaking to a Catholic women's group in Florida that spring, said that U.S. response to Latin America's call for help had been remarkable. He hinted that the number of U.S. volunteers would be even higher unless potential missioners could somehow be restrained: "We all need priests. Yet out of our needs we have very gladly sent our gifted priests to those in need. If we sent all our volunteers, we would have hardly anyone at home, such is the interest of the United States priesthood in Latin America."

Less than a year before, Father Raymond Kevane, director of the Papal Volunteers for Latin America, wrote of that organization's success in overcoming earlier faults. A new program with full-time field representatives "will insure not only that we are in tune with another culture, but that we shall constantly adapt to the myriad changes that go along with its progress." He said: "Scores of volunteers have come to know and love the people of Latin America and their culture. Once they have returned to their homeland, they will never forget their enriching experience."

It was a glowing picture, but for all too many of the troops in the field, it was something else again. The middle sixties, and beyond, was a time when frustrations began to surface. It was a time when there were no results to be shown, no changes to be seen, and when getting discouraged was easier to do because the troops were so far from home.

They realized it in different ways. For Father George Dudak, the Paterson diocesan priest who covered a dozen rural outposts outside of Ica, Peru, it all came home one memorable night:

> I had gotten some filmstrips on the Vatican Council and took them to one of the churches, a dirt-floor building without any electricity. I hooked up the machine to the portable generator in the truck, and inside I tacked up a sheet to show the slides on. The people stood in that dirt chapel watching the pageantry, the colors, the vestments. . . . They were simply in another world. It was like watching people from Mars.

It hit harder and was more discouraging to Gilda Martoglio, the PAVLA nurse from New Jersey who was stationed in Brazil. She wrote home: "Is the value of our work here—which only touches so few of the people—of any real worth when in reality it is helping to foster and sustain existing structures (ecclesiastical, political, or otherwise) which are in direct conflict with our objectives and our purposes for being here? Our very presence seems to contribute to the great social unrest which is sweeping the country." In a despairing moment, she thought that even the vaccination program in which she took part seemed pointless: "Have I helped save them from dying of typhoid so that they can now die from malnutrition and dehydration instead?"

Sister Bernadette Desmond recalls Maryknoll's situation in Lima at the time: "It was the beginning of a lot of unrest. So many religious were working in cities with middle- and upper-class people. We began going through the process of asking ourselves what are we doing, why are we here? That's when people began to do things like going to work in the barriadas with the poor."

"A lot of people got hurt," said Franciscan Father Joseph Nangle, who had moved from Bolivia to Peru at that time. "It was a painful process. Some people came up against such a stone wall that they lost everything."

Ellen Mary Conroy, a Papal Volunteer from Ohio working in a medical lab in Lima, complained that one day out of five she had nothing at all to do, and the rest of the time worked no more than four hours a day. "There's a great need to define the role of the Papal Volunteers," she wrote. "I wouldn't have come as a catechist or missionary; I came as a professional to share my professional skills." In any event, she said, she felt as if she were adding to Peru's unemployment problem and wondered why the United States should send technicians at all, when the same kind of people were sitting around in Lima, available but out of work. "The whole situation just doesn't make sense."

The feeling was far short of unanimous, but a new generation of Latin America missioners was asking, as Sister Bernadette Desmond did, why they were there, and concluding, with Ellen Mary Conroy, that the whole situation made no sense at all. They were the people caught up in the tumult and change and hope that marked the years immediately after the Vatican Council. They were in the middle of the explosion of challenging new theologies being ignited in Latin America itself. They were the people, too, trapped in the day-to-day reality of dealing with hopeless poverty, frustrated with the evil and injustice and cruelty that were all parts of the pattern. And when they finally cried out, in utter frustration, what the hell *are* we doing here, along came Ivan Illich to tell them: in all honesty, you're probably making things worse. And after that, the Latin America mission movement was never quite the same.

The Latin America Bureau had an advance copy of "The Seamy Side of Charity," but the people there weren't too concerned about its impact. Father Colonnese recalls that a member of Serra International provided the bureau with its copy, having pirated it from the *National Catholic Reporter*—which had had first crack at the article two months earlier.

(Donald Thorman, the late publisher of the *National Catholic Reporter*, and Robert Hoyt, who had been its editor, both recalled that Illich submitted the manuscript, and that it was sent back, not with a rejection slip, but with a suggestion that it be reworked. "We felt it was needlessly polemical," Hoyt said in a conversation in 1977. "That was the last we heard of it until it appeared in *America*, and that amused us a little. At the time we were taking a shellacking from *America* and everybody else for being too abrasive, and they came out with Illich's piece just as it was. Maybe it was all for the best. If it *had* run in *NCR*, it might have been dismissed as one more attack on the organized church—and not received the attention that it did.")

The lack of alarm within the bureau, Colonnese said, stemmed from the fact that the issues raised in the article were the same ones often discussed by bureau people themselves, although in somewhat more restrained terms. "I agreed with Illich," he wrote, "but I was opposed to the tactics he employed."

The bureau's advance assessment, that "The Seamy Side of Charity" wouldn't cause too much of a stir, was dead wrong. No single document since

Monsignor Casaroli's appeal at Notre Dame in 1961 on behalf of Pope John XXIII had as much impact on the future course of U.S. mission work in Latin America. A few would agree totally with Illich, others would see some elements of truth in what he had to say, and still others, perhaps most, rejected his arguments, sometimes bitterly. But after the article appeared, few people involved in the Latin America mission enterprise, if any, could carry out their assignments without re-examining what they were doing, without asking themselves if, perhaps, there *was* something after all to what Illich was saying.

"Yes, we were hit by the Illich article," said Father William McIntire, Maryknoll's secretary general. "It was a challenge to the United States mission effort."

"It created so much disturbance," said Colonnese, "that no one was any longer sure of himself or herself except the very, very conservative, who really never reflected on the article even though they had read it."

Father Charles Davignon, at the time a Maryknoll associate working in Peru, said a pattern of self-questioning spread throughout the mission communities. "A lot of it came from Illich," he said. "He made them look at themselves more critically."

The managing editor and Latin America specialist for *America*, Father Eugene Culhane, saw the article a week before its publication and thought it "something hot but not unreasonable." Illich had asked to have the article come out the week of the CICOP meeting, Culhane said, and brought copies of the magazine with him to Boston. "That really steamed Cushing," Culhane said, "and it also upset Colonnese—primarily for the reason that he didn't want to have to contend with anything that would break his stride."

Culhane recalls that the original title was "The Shady Side of Charity"—a phrase that appears verbatim in the article—but because that didn't convey its abrasive quality the adjective was changed to "seamy." "Over the years," Culhane added, "Illich had reached the conclusion that the United States was having a steamroller effect on Latin America. This article was simply the culmination of his thinking. It was a big flash in the pan, in a way. But people extracted the truths that it did contain. Illich was a great overstater, but there was always a grain of truth in what he had to say."

What Illich Said

What *did* Illich have to say? As Culhane pointed out, the same things he had been saying for some time. But the manner in which he said them this time, and the place and context in which he presented them, gave them a bold-face, exclamation-point quality that no one could ignore. ("One might regret that the monsignor included so much in his article," Father Joseph Fitzpatrick, Illich's friend, would write a few weeks later. "It binds together into one small package all the ideological missiles he has been launching for the past decade.

These ideas, spread thinly over the years, are a difficult enough dose to swallow; but crowded into four pages of a periodical, they produce indigestion in the strongest stomach.")

Since it was halfway through the decade, Illich reasoned at the outset of "The Seamy Side of Charity," it was time to reassess the U.S. church's Latin American endeavor, the "so-called papal plan" which was "part of the many-faceted effort to keep Latin America within the ideologies of the West." Numerically, he wrote, the effort was a flop. He invited readers to reflect on the burdens that foreign help imposes on the Latin American church: "Why not, for once, consider the shady side of charity?"

Promising that his article would consider "only the negative results," Illich turned first to finances. The outpouring of money from the United States had made the Latin American church a satellite and trapped its bishops into needing more and more cash, he charged. Accepting government or private money "for the poor" turns the church into a political power, but one with marked limitations: "It is committed enough to produce some results, but when it is threatened by real change, it withdraws rather than permit social awareness to spread like wildfire."

Picking up on what would become a familiar theme for him in the next few years, Illich linked the church's presence in Latin America with U.S. military presence in Vietnam and the Johnson administration's mammoth spending for the "war on poverty." He wrote: "We have not yet begun to face the seamy side of clerical manpower involvement and the Church's complicity in stifling universal awakening too revolutionary to lie quietly within the 'Great Society.' "

He conceded that every U.S. missioner had enriched some life and had taken some values back home. But the facts must be faced, he continued: Missioners sent to Latin America can "make an alien Church more foreign, an over-staffed Church priest-ridden, and bishops into abject beggars." The promise of more clergy is like a "bewitching siren," he contended, one that "keeps the local bureaucracy going."

One painful charge followed another:

> Exporting Church employees to Latin America masks a universal and unconscious fear of a new Church. North and South American authorities, differently motivated but equally fearful, become accomplices in maintaining a clerical and irrelevant Church.
>
> The United States Church must face the painful side of generosity: the burden that a life gratuitously offered imposes on the recipient. The men who go to Latin America must humbly accept the possibility that they are useless or even harmful, although they give all they have. . . .
>
> The [Alliance for Progress] program is too small to permit even the achievement of a threshold of sustained growth. It is a bone thrown to the dog, that he remain quiet in the backyard of the Americas.

The North American missioner, Illich said, arriving in Latin America along with the Alliance for Progress, the Central Intelligence Agency, the Peace Corps, and other "Camelot projects," is seen as a baptism of them all and thus "tends to fill the role of a colonial power's lackey chaplain."

If Illich had some missionaries agreeing with him up until that point, he probably lost them with his next salvo. Latin America can no longer be a haven, he said,

> for United States liberals who cannot make their point at home, an outlet for apostles too "apostolic" to find their vocation as competent professionals within their own community. The hardware salesman threatens to dump second-rate imitations of parishes, schools and catechisms —outmoded even in the United States—all around the continent. The traveling escapist threatens to further confuse a foreign world with his superficial protests, which were not viable even at home.

The U.S. church shouldn't be involved in political-social development according to anyone's doctrine, Illich concluded—even that of the pope. "The heart of the discussion," he said, "is therefore not how to send more men and money, but rather why they should be sent at all." Sending more people, he said, would only be a futile attempt to shore up a crumbling structure. "Instead of believing in the Church, we frantically attempt to construct it according to our own cloudy cultural image. We want to build community, relying on techniques, and are blind to the latent desire for unity that is striving to express itself among men."

The article threw the CICOP conferees into an uproar, with Cushing, predictably, leading the charge. He felt personally wounded by the scorching attack, having aided Illich both financially and by means of his considerable influence. (The financial aid would be cut off immediately; the cardinal canceled a $40,000 gift he had promised Illich to aid in a move from Chula Vista, the original Cuernavaca school building, to new quarters, a villa called Casa Blanca.)

Cushing addressed a full assembly at the CICOP conference, reading a letter from Archbishop Egidio Vagnozzi, the apostolic delegate in the United States, which called Illich's article "an attack on the papal program for Latin America"—hardly news to anyone who had read it. "That's the Holy See's answer," Cushing said, "to an article now being distributed by Jesuits around the hall." The cardinal described two of Illich's claims as "colossal lies"—one that the U.S. church had diverted home mission funds for Latin American use, the other that the U.S. response to Latin America's call for priestly aid was poor numerically. "That's a grave injustice to the bishops and the religious congregations," he roared.

Colonnese was particularly disturbed by the affront to Cushing caused by distribution of the offending article at the conference, which, ironically,

Father John Considine had decided to hold in Boston out of respect for the cardinal. He was, Colonnese said, "probably the most faithful and trusting friend of the Latin America Bureau among the American bishops." Colonnese found much in Illich's article with which he could agree, but faulted him for his "total lack of discretion." "I would have deferred to the cardinal out of respect for his generosity," Colonnese said, "despite whatever errors he might have made in terms of his work in Latin America (and they were numerous)."

Conceding that Illich was right on many points—"my own dismissal from the Latin America Bureau can be traced to my thinking on the same matters"—Colonnese nevertheless kept a comfortable distance from Cuernavaca over the years. He considered himself something of a revolutionary in the Illich style, but "nonetheless I resented the use of tactless cruelty which seemed to emanate from CIF." Illich failed to recognize, Colonnese continued, that many Latin America Bureau programs and CICOP projects reflected the philosophy which was being advanced at CIF. "The impression from them," Colonnese said, "was that no one ever had an original idea about Latin America outside of Cuernavaca."

Father Frederick McGuire has the same kind of mixed feeling about Illich: respect for his genius, his spirituality, his prophetic warnings, and at the same time an acknowledgement that he was "very difficult to keep under control." Illich would make agreements at Cuernavaca, he said, and let the Latin America Bureau worry about paying the bills.

Illich did much, he said, to focus the frustrations of newer missionaries who were discouraged by their lack of visible progress. "There was a tremendous growth in the concept of justice for the people, a lot of it because the missionaries were seeing for the first time the desperate situation in which people lived. They had a tendency, too, to be stronger in their denunciation of it than the local priests, who had seen it and lived with it all their lives."

Father Theodore Hesburgh, recalling his reaction to the Illich controversy during a 1976 interview, was more of an outright critic.

"The Illich syndrome concerns me," he said. "Illich said the United States church had nothing to offer to Latin America. Well, if he meant that we were going down there and saying, 'Look, you develop the way we do or else,' I agree. But simply to say that the United States has nothing to offer is not only wrong, but silly. . . despite all the wrong things that were done."

It was that type of criticism, albeit somewhat more exercised, to which Father Joseph Fitzpatrick attempted to reply in 1967, a few weeks after "The Seamy Side of Charity" had appeared, with the controversy still at a low boil. (Fitzpatrick cheerfully accepted one author's description of him as "a friend who has continually attempted to explain Ivan Illich to the world.")

Fitzpatrick's article, titled "What Is He Getting At?", also appeared in *America* (which, in the intervening weeks, had devoted many columns to letters, most of them from irate critics, in response to Illich). It would be unfortunate, Fitzpatrick said, if the controversy obscured the serious issues

Illich had raised, and conceded that part of the controversy was Illich himself—a brilliant man who "can turn on irresistible charm, or show brutal ridicule and disdain."

"He has a vision of the radical changes the Church must undergo if it is to be Christ present to the men of the 21st century," Fitzpatrick said. "And he is convinced that these changes cannot be achieved without violence to self—and sometimes to others." Then Fitzpatrick amplified Illich's main points:

> However convinced American business and government people may be that the United States model offers the brightest hope to Latin America, this is by no means a universally accepted position. If the impression is given that the advancement of Christ's work depends on the establishment of the American model, the Church is in grave danger.
>
> The Church has suffered over and over again because of its identification with social and economic structures. It must assert its freedom to form the People of God independently of contending economic and political interests.

No Second Thoughts

Interviewed in 1977, Fitzpatrick said Illich, with whom he has remained in close contact over the years, had no second thoughts about the abrasive style of "The Seamy Side of Charity." "His feeling about the article," Fitzpatrick said, "was 'if I hadn't done it that way, no one would have paid any attention.'"

Illich confirmed his views in a number of public statements over the years. He expressed pride in the fact that Cuernavaca had helped to reduce the number of United States missioners going to Latin America: "Our aim was to diminish as much as possible the damage these missionaries could do to themselves and to the people in those countries." In 1969, after leaving the active ministry, he said there is "nothing" that U.S. missioners can do to solve the problems of the poor in Latin America. "They promise things that cannot be furnished," he said. "No one is saved by the good intentions of these missionaries, but many are destroyed by someone telling them just how much they are lacking."

Nineteen sixty-seven, which began with the CICOP controversy, would turn out to be an event-filled year for Illich. Another of his articles that year ("The Vanishing Clergyman," which appeared in the June-July issue of *The Critic*) caused almost as much of an uproar as "The Seamy Side of Charity," particularly in his adopted land of Mexico. His position was that the church has worked itself into a corner where it cannot attract vocations or hold present clergy. Even Bishop Sergio Mendez Arceo of Cuernavaca, a long-time personal friend, said Illich's article "misses the whole spiritual factor in the priesthood, in its traditions and its human values."

After a summer of contestation, which included a physical attack on Illich by some rightist students, the Mexican bishops petitioned Cardinal Spellman to recall him to New York. Loyal as ever, the cardinal—in one of his final letters, dated November 10, 1967—declined: "Illich is a priest of excellent standing in my diocese, in every way obedient." But within days of Spellman's death, the New York chancery received more mail, from Mexico and from the Vatican, making the same request. Spellman's temporary successor, Coadjutor Archbishop John Maguire, was as faithful to Illich as the cardinal had been. To Maguire's pro forma invitation that he return home, Illich replied that he had too many pressing commitments, and Maguire accepted the excuse.

The harassment was beginning to get to Illich, who wrote a subservient letter directly to Pope Paul VI ("I humbly kiss your ring and submit myself to your kindness . . . ") asking for a bill of particulars in regard to the complaints about him. There was no reply, but in June of 1968 he was summoned to Rome for interrogation by the Congregation for the Doctrine of the Faith. Employing tactics more reminiscent of the Inquisition than the postconciliar age, the congregation thrust a document with eighty-five direct questions at Illich. They ranged from inquiries about his family background to his theological and political views. And, by the way, had there been a lot of partying at Cuernavaca? Parties with women in the room?

Illich kept the messy business to himself for several months, but in January 1969, after the Vatican had formally forbidden priests and nuns from studying with Illich at Cuernavaca, he made public the summons to Rome and offered his version of what had taken place. Because the charges against him were "designed to wreck any hope of a human and Christian dialogue," he determined that he would not respond to them. With an eight-page letter to that effect in hand, he called on Cardinal Franjo Seper, the head of the congregation, who greeted him warmly in Croatian, the native tongue of both their families. As Illich told it, Seper was still speaking in Croatian when the interview had been concluded, when he heard what Illich had to say and understood that he was telling the congregation that he couldn't be bothered with its questions, but his words had a different ring: "Hadjite, hadjite, nemojete se vratti!" was what he said, according to Illich. "Get going, get going, and never come back!"

The ban on clerical attendance at Cuernavaca—there were "many complaints" and "unfortunate effects," the Vatican said, all unspecified—was observed for the most part, and the school's classrooms filled up instead with business people, scholars, and others seriously interested in Latin America. But the enterprise seemed to have lost its basic appeal for Illich, who resigned from the active ministry in March 1969 (still observing, he announced, the rules of celibacy and the daily office) and turned his iconoclastic talents to other fields, notably education and medicine. As CIDOC, Cuernavaca closed out its operation in February 1976, although a language school was continued on the site.

The later years of the mid-sixties—that unsettled period when United States missionaries were reassessing their presence as they had never done before—was marked by a series of developments in Latin America itself and within the U.S. mission structure that, increasingly, were reflecting the problems Illich was talking about.

To begin with, the Latin American church was asserting itself more and more in its dealings with the United States. The Latin American bishops seemed anxious to declare their own independence from the North, Illich's conclusions notwithstanding. There were a few tentative contacts between the bishops of both regions, one in Miami in June 1967, and a second in Santiago, Chile, that November. Bishop Carroll took a leading role at both meetings, at which the primary topic was the coordination of the program of United States assistance to the Latin church.

A more conclusive meeting of the inter-American bishops took place in June 1968 at Sacred Heart Seminary in Detroit. Coleman Carroll was still the acting chairman of the Latin America committee, but then-Archbishop Dearden, the NCCB-USCC president, played a more active part than he had previously. It was a nuts-and-bolts conference, dealing with the practical aspects of mission assistance, at which the Latins spoke up about the inadequacy of the training being provided to missioners. Their delegates, particularly Cardinal Silva, set down standards that they wanted the United States to follow in the future: first, preliminary training in language and culture; second, an intensive language course for full fluency; third, pastoral training in the Latin American country to which the missioner would be assigned. The suggestions were well received by the smaller mission-sending societies, Bishop Joseph Breitenbeck told an NC News Service reporter. However, he continued, "those orders that already have their own training programs were not as receptive, on the whole."

The Latin Position

Two spokesmen who repeatedly articulated the Latin position on U.S. assistance with special effectivness were Bishop Eduardo Pironio, the CELAM secretary-general, and Bishop Mark McGrath, the Notre-Dame-educated Holy Cross priest. McGrath had been an auxiliary bishop of Panama from 1961 until 1964, when he became bishop of Santiago de Veraguas. He preceded Pironio for a term as CELAM secretary-general in 1967 and was appointed archbishop of Panama in 1969—when he was still only forty-five.

"It is not as simple as coming down to help us," Pironio wrote in 1969. "Volunteers should go to the needy areas. For this reason the selection process should demand from the candidates a great human, Christian, and apostolic maturity." U.S. volunteers, he said, should "help reveal the vital energies of our church and facilitate the creation of authentically Latin American pastoral programs."

In a major address at St. Joseph's College in Philadelphia in February 1968,

McGrath dwelt on the pitfalls of inter-American efforts, making the point that a gap in understanding between North and South could offset the effects of the limited aid granted. "We should be working together on a theology of revolution," he said, telling his U.S. audience that only a radical change in the social and economic structure could bring about some measure of adequate human conditions for Latin America's poverty-stricken millions.

The religious relationship between North America and Latin America had been thwarted first by the superiority feeling of Protestant missioners "who came to save us," the bishop said, and then by a Catholic mentality that has signs printed with such slogans as "Send $10 to save Latin America for the faith." "The key to a working understanding," he said, "is the mutual recognition of each others' values and cultures. Despite our great Christian heritage in the United States and Latin America, Catholics have done very little to tackle the problems we have in common, to enhance and make work the values we share."

As leading prelates such as Pironio and McGrath spoke up, voicing with rising regularity their reservations about past patterns of U.S. mission assistance, individual bishops in Latin America were having the same second thoughts. "I underwent a change of thinking myself," Bishop Gennaro Prata recalled in a 1976 interview. An Italian Salesian with close personal ties to the United States, he taught for many years in La Paz before becoming an auxiliary bishop (and for several months administrator) of that archdiocese. He taught Spanish to the first group of St. Louis archdiocesan missioners in the late fifties, and in later years built up and maintained close contacts with other diocesan missioners, from Kansas City, Buffalo, Rochester, Paterson, and with men from the St. James Society.

"I started to realize the difficulties they were undergoing," he said:

They felt, many of them, that they didn't belong, that they were foreigners. Then I started thinking that the United States missionary effort needed some changes, above all a longer period of preparation, to include customs as well as language. At the beginning, they thought they could bring everything with them, and we admired it—the American parish with its nice rectory and the parish hall. Now we look for missioners who know more about dealing with the people.

With missionaries expressing reservations about their effectiveness in Latin America (increasingly so for public consumption) and Latin American prelates doing the same thing, the mission interest of U.S. Catholics began to slacken. Bishop Prata commented on it during a visit to the United States in 1970:

I'm planning on a drop of 50 percent as far as financial help from American dioceses is concerned. I say this not so much in a spirit of complaint as that of recognition of things as they are. And the overall problem isn't just financial. There are less priests volunteering for duty in Latin America. It's becoming difficult to replace those American priests in Latin America whose tours are up and who should be coming home. A bishop might have five priests to replace in the mission and be able to come up with only three.

That recognition was shared by the missioners themselves. Father Daniel Mahoney, one of the Paterson priests then in Caranavi, Bolivia, reflected on it that same year after watching, with a Bolivian audience, the stirring U.S. Information Agency film on John F. Kennedy, *Years of Lightning, Day of Drums*, and accepting the people's condolences as if the former president had just been killed. Writing in *The Beacon*, Paterson's diocesan newspaper, he said:

> I am sad, too, because standing here in Bolivia, it seems not only Kennedy but North America has been killed. What was true of America in 1963 is not true of us in 1970. In 1963, we had a mission to the world. In 1970 our mission is to survive! What can we think of a nation where $70 billion is spent for war and $1 billion for foreign aid?
>
> There will be no used clothing this year. Medicines will be hard to get. There is no money to ship them to those nations in need. The subsidies have been withdrawn. Missionaries must bring these in at their own cost. They look to the laity for additional help. But those collections are down.
>
> It would seem that survival is also the order of the age for the Catholic church in America. It too is losing its sense of mission.

Not all U.S. missioners were as pessimistic as Mahoney, but many knew the kind of unease he sensed, or they saw it in their fellow North Americans, and tried to express what was happening in a variety of ways. Father James Madden, a Maryknoll priest in Peru, recalled in 1976:

> I began to see myself as a foreigner in the eyes of the people here. I was on the streets all the time, and despite that, and despite the number of programs we had, there were few of those thousands of people in the parish that I had any contact with. I came to the conclusion that the parish just didn't mean that much in the lives of the people. I knew I didn't have all the answers, and it bothered me a little that priests who spent all their time in offices seemed to think that they did.

"A lot of fellows in the sixties expected a great response," said Boston Auxiliary Bishop Thomas V. Daily, a one-time St. James volunteer. "Because they didn't get it, a lot of them experienced what they saw as failure. Some of them couldn't handle it. The ones who could stayed on."

"We went through hell," conceded Conventual Franciscan Father Elias

Manning in Rio. "Some just packed up and went home; some left the priesthood altogether. Some of the seed has to die in order to produce."

"It was a painful process," said Father Joseph Nangle: "A lot of people got hurt—some maybe completely. I get an empty feeling when I think of that whole numbers business, the emphasis on 'how many?' Some people in the missions came up against such a stone wall that they lost everything."

"There was confusion, new ideas, political changes," recalled Jesuit Father John F. Henry, who spent thirteen years (1959–72) in Chile. "Our mission assignment was successful until 1967; then everybody started questioning his role."

Father James B. Malley encountered the same situation in his years as a Jesuit missioner in Brazil's Northeast from 1965 to 1971:

> The fundamental assumptions seemed wrong. The pastoral ministry was directed toward maintaining (by outside resources, human and material) an obsolete parish structure. The civil regime became more and more totalitarian and the church was (and allowed itself to be) used, except for some prophetic voices such as Dom Helder Camara.

Father Terence Pescatore, a Conventual Franciscan who was in Costa Rica from 1963 to 1974, said it became increasingly difficult for a U.S. missioner to be effective with the people: "Despite personal efforts at poverty, you were a member of a gringo order. It was difficult to destroy the image of wealth."

The phenomenon of mass frustration wasn't limited to religious missioners. Peace Corpsman Patrick J. McCann wrote to a Catholic magazine in 1967:

> Why is it that, with one exception, all the [Peace Corps] volunteers I've met who were just about ready to go home, and were practicing Catholics when they arrived, have left Brazil as non-practicing Catholics? I asked one of these volunteers and he told me it was because God doesn't exist in the Brazilian Church. I told myself it would never happen to me. And now I find that it *is* happening to me, if it hasn't happened already.

In PAVLA, more or less a Peace Corps counterpart within the church structure, many volunteers were experiencing the same kind of self-doubts, as noted earlier, leading some observers to wonder about the future of lay mission work entirely.

"Someone has described the lay volunteer or lay missionary movement as an evanescent phenomenon," Thomas Quigley (at the time PAVLA's executive secretary) wrote to a Maryknoll friend in 1970. "Certainly anyone who has been around the field for the last ten years would tend to agree. Whether it 'should' be in this state or whether it will see a resurgence a few years hence are separate questions."

In an interview some years later, Quigley saw one positive factor, more for the clergy than lay missioners, at that point in the United States mission experience:

It was a turning point in their lives. There was a new realization of what it meant to be a priest, and also of what it meant to be an American. They saw the United States in a new light. They had a renewed concept of mission in that sense.

The mission-sending organizations of the time might not have quarreled with Quigley's conclusion, but it was difficult for them to see what was happening in a positive light. Most of them were being torn by internal debate on their proper mission role, and nearly all of them were losing missioners. "We were jolted in any complacency we might have had by articles such as Illich's," said Maryknoll Father William McIntire. "And we were challenged by the thought of the Vatican Council on mission and the church. In the critical years, men on both ends of the spectrum dropped out. In the altiplano alone, there were about forty men and women who left after 1965." Maryknoll's membership reached a peak of 1,350 priests, brothers, and students in 1967, McIntire said, and stood at slightly under 1,000 by the mid-seventies. There are some 250 Maryknollers now in Latin America, down from a high of 325:

In the early sixties, we had a positive, even triumphalistic attitude about the church internationally and, specifically, about the American presence overseas. We were uncritical and didn't reflect on what the overseas presence was really doing. We weren't too concerned with the local church. In fact, we felt somewhat superior. Despite all these things, remarkable mission work was achieved. But a crisis in mission roles came toward the end of the sixties, due to a combination of factors—Vatican II, political developments, and United States foreign policy.

The Maryknoll organization was quick to respond to the Vatican Council's mission challenge. Its 1966 general chapter produced a dramatically new mission rationale, stressing a community's faith life rather than the sacraments themselves, calling for a deeper involvement of the laity and closer cooperation with non-Christians, and introducing a different concept of initial activity for the individual missioner: "His concern is not so much to bring every individual into the Church as to bring the Church to all men."

The chapter also took note of the problems that might be caused by official United States policy or actions and said: "When the sign [of missionary love and concern] is blemished or absent in the Christian community of the homeland, it hinders and often contradicts the work of the missioners on foreign soil." Maryknollers were urged to avoid on the one hand being politicians, or on the other hand being politically or socially naive, "for the force which the Church can inject into the modern society of man consists in that faith and charity put into vital practice, not in any external domination exercised by purely human needs."

There were some voices, in Maryknoll and outside it, who thought the "new mission" concept was being overemphasized, that mission work was being negatively influenced more by global developments than by the much-discussed "cultural shock."

"In general, the Latin America program would have been more successful if the church hadn't gone through the post-Vatican II crisis," Father Vincent Mallon said in 1976:

> It was unfortunate that the initial massive mission effort of the U.S. church ran into the unsettled times of Vatican II. That had more to do with the problems that developed than cultural shock or anything like it. The same kind of problems affected the church in other parts of the world, too.
>
> Before 1965, I never ran into laymen who were critical of American mission efforts. The criticism came mostly from American missioners themselves, to start with, then from local priests—but not from local bishops. Illich was a perfect example. A lot of our own people followed his lead and said, yes, let's get out of parishes, out of schools and everything else. But did the people who were directly affected ever say that? I don't think so.

The Illich role would be debated for years to come not only in the missions but also at home, where bishops, religious community leaders, and conference officials were charged with the responsibility of planning long-range mission strategy. Many planks in the Illich platform would eventually become articles of faith at the conferences of CICOP, which, after the one he dominated so completely in 1967, grew increasingly forceful in tone.

At the Boston meeting, almost lost in the wake of the Illich furor, there was a strong emphasis on the revolutionary development of Latin American nations, with Belgium's Cardinal Suenens stirring the audience with his assertion that Karl Marx was ahead of the Christians of his time. "We carry the torch of the gospel," he said, "yet sometimes others see better its light." Even Cardinal Cushing had some tough words: However disturbing and disconcerting it may be, he said, the current phase of development in Latin America "makes it clear that destiny is calling us to a rendezvous with revolution."

A "dollars si, yanquis no" theme developed at the 1968 CICOP meeting in St. Louis, where Senator Eugene McCarthy of Minnesota, then seeking the Democratic presidential nomination as an anti-Vietnam War candidate, was the featured speaker. He called on the United States to withdraw voluntarily from its dominant role in the Organization of American States, warning that unless the country changed its Latin American policy the continent would be lost to the free world. McCarthy blamed U.S. preoccupation with Vietnam for its failure to respond to the real needs of Latin America, adding that United States policy "must not betray our heritage, nor forsake our belief in ourselves as the true radicals and the true revolutionaries."

The fact that each succeeding conference seemed to strengthen CICOP's left-leaning reputation failed to bother Colonnese or Monsignor Bill Quinn, who were still the principal planners: "If CICOP leaned left," Quinn said in 1977, "it was largely because of my pressure. That's what needed to be done."

With each passing year Colonnese's role in the Latin America Bureau was becoming more important, a fact that left the bishops in something of a quandary when it came time to name John Considine's successor as director. Should it be Colonnese? Not only was he identified with a radical position on Latin America activities—radical, certainly, by then-current standards in the U.S. church community—but he had a way of offending those who questioned his judgments or failed to share his views. "Mike was thoroughly dedicated," said Father Frederick McGuire, a good friend, "but he was lacking in tact." (McGuire made an additional point: "He was right about most things.")

The bishops knew Colonnese could produce some major headaches for them in Washington; he was fiery, and his stands were strong ones. But he was the clear favorite to succeed Considine. He knew the territory, and he knew the people. Perhaps most important, he was the personal choice of most of the influential Latin Americans who dealt with the bureau; they were sure that in Colonnese they had an understanding friend. Lima's Cardinal Landazuri Ricketts told that to Colonnese one day, adding: "We consider you one of our own and are prepared to assist you whenever you call upon us." The U.S. bishops knew the extent of Colonnese's support in Latin America, and they knew that he would be the choice. John Considine, seventy years old, stepped down, and Mike Colonnese became director in the spring of 1968.

Under the reshuffling of the bishops' organization into the National Conference of Catholic Bishops and the United States Catholic Conference, the Latin America Bureau would become the Latin America Division (of the USCC Department of International Affairs) and, under Colonnese's guidance, consolidated all its operations in Washington. This was distressing news to Father Kevane, the PAVLA director, whose differences with Colonnese were personal as well as philosophical, and who wanted no part of the move from Chicago to Washington.

But move he did, along with everyone else in the Latin America Division, to the second floor of the Tower Building, over a drug store, at 14th and K Streets, two-and-a-half blocks from conference headquarters. Here Colonnese quickly took a firm grip on the controls. He instituted the Latin American Documentary Service (LADOC), which translated into English important documents from Latin America, and hired a first-rate editor-linguist, Father

Gene Culhane, to coordinate its activities. He gave a new direction to the distribution of funds raised by the national collection for Latin America, away from traditional bricks-and-mortar projects, and toward research and study programs that he saw as desperately needed. He signed on Father Fred McGuire as associate director, giving the division full-time access to the years of expertise McGuire gained with the old Mission Secretariat. He reviewed the direction the division had taken, and was unhappy with his conclusions:

> We were not helping to bring about the needed changes in the Latin American church. We were, in fact, helping to keep in existence outmoded and ineffective traditional institutional forms. . . . There was excessive and growing dependency on foreign assistance by the institutional church in Latin America. Such dependency could only end in tragedy because the assistance would one day have to come to an end.

And, finally, he turned his attention to the Papal Volunteers for Latin America.

PAVLA: Organization in Trouble

Kevane could issue reports on PAVLA that glowed with optimism, but the fact was that the organization was in serious trouble. Although few of its critics would be as unbending as was Colonnese, the truth was that in PAVLA there was much to be unhappy about. Not only had the number of volunteers slipped, but many of those who were in the field continued to be confused about their jobs. They complained about not having enough to do, about a lack of leadership, about misdirection of effort—all results of the problem cited by McGuire: instead of going to Latin America only to fill specific assignments, volunteers were frequently shipped off with nothing to do and had to shop around in order to look busy. Many Latin American bishops were trying to suggest, as diplomatically as possible, that the expenditure of money on PAVLA was not merited by the results that were being obtained.

There were some diocesan directors who insisted, along with Kevane, that things weren't really that bad. Father George Mader, the Newark director, had an effective program going. Other dioceses with productive PAVLA ventures, he said in a 1977 interview, included Manchester, Madison, St. Louis, and Worcester. According to Mader:

> The main problem was that PAVLA was clergy-dominated; it seemed that the laity weren't trusted. Originally it was true, as our critics claimed: We were just doing works of mercy. Later we learned, along with everyone else, and began to ask why these conditions of poverty and injustice prevailed. This is the direction that all mission groups started to take later on; PAVLA was heading in that direction too. Our feeling was

that PAVLA might not have been perfect, but it was doing something good; why take it away? But at the same time we knew it was a losing fight. PAVLA was always shunted aside at the CICOP meetings, something like a ne'er-do-well brother. I knew that as far as PAVLA was concerned, Colonnese had his foot on the oxygen hose.

The Kevane-Colonnese showdown had been building. Colonnese chafed over the fact that PAVLA had never been the integral part of the Latin America Bureau it should have been and felt that Kevane's "extreme conservatism" and coterie of friendly diocesan PAVLA directors kept policies of the bureau from being implemented in the lay volunteer organization. He disliked what he saw as a proliferation of Latin America "experts" in the PAVLA family and their unwillingness to use the bureau's experience and data. The results, he said, bore out his conclusions that PAVLA was in "a shambles."

The battle was joined when word got out that as new director of the Latin America Division, Colonnese was determined to do away with PAVLA entirely. Kevane made no secret of his dislike for Colonnese and asked pointed questions about the "leftist" direction the church's Latin America program was taking. Others took up the chorus. "The reaction was furious," Colonnese said. "Bishops, priests, and laymen all over the country began to attack me."

But it was Colonnese who held the day when the dispute formally reached the conference for adjudication. (The bishops could not help but have been mindful of the strong network of Colonnese supporters in Latin America, as well as the generally negative reports about PAVLA's condition under Kevane's leadership.) PAVLA would have its own budget under the new ground rules, but it was subject to the direction of the Latin America Division. PAVLA's policy had to be in line with that of the division, and Colonnese, as division director, would have the final word in administrative matters. Kevane, deeply disturbed, continued to wage the fight, but it served no purpose other than irritating Colonnese. "Kevane had become a yoke around the necks of progressive Latin American bishops, priests, and lay people," he said.

Finally, a year later, Kevane threw in the towel. He sent out a "Dear Friends" mimeographed letter August 4, 1969, announcing his resignation as director of PAVLA. It said, in part:

I am resigning simply because the Papal Volunteer program and Latin America mean so much to me. The current orientation of the program for Latin America—with which PAVLA is affiliated—is one with which I do not agree. My petition to higher authority that PAVLA be provided freedom from the administrative problems of the past year and be given a means of disassociation from that orientation will not be granted. This decision was made known to me a few days ago. Since any efforts of mine to keep PAVLA from that orientation will now quite clearly be unsuccessful, I feel I have no other option but to resign.

Kevane promptly returned to Sioux City, his home diocese (where he became chancellor, and, a little more than two years later, surprised fellow priests by leaving the active ministry and then marrying) without a replacement being named. Colonnese turned to Father Mader in Newark, who wanted no part of the PAVLA directorship on a permanent basis, but agreed to serve as an interim leader.

Actually Mader, a long-time advocate of increased responsibilities for lay volunteers, hoped that the Association for International Development—still based in Paterson, where Bishop McNulty had provided its home—could take over the assignment. He brought two AID people, Fritz Hofmeister and George Metcalfe, when he went to Washington for his interview, but Colonnese had other plans for PAVLA—none of which foresaw its continued existence for any length of time. (McGuire rattled Colonnese with still another proposal—that PAVLA headquarters be moved to Newark, with Mader running it from there. The idea never proceeded beyond that point.)

"When Ray resigned all hell broke loose," Mader said. "The diocesan directors wanted to know what was going on." Coleman Carroll (by this time an archbishop, with Miami having been elevated to archdiocesan status a year earlier) tried to reassure them. "In view of Father Kevane's resignation," he wrote on August 13, "you may have some questions about PAVLA's future." He told them that the bishops' conference and its Latin America subcommittee "will continue to do everything possible to support PAVLA and help it achieve its purpose in Latin America." He thanked them for their efforts, said the bishops would review the program in conjunction with CELAM, and promised that in the meantime the Latin America Division and Father Louis Colonnese and his staff would continue "all the service you have received in the past" and "full cooperation."

Mader knew differently. He agreed to be acting director for an extremely limited period—no more than three weeks, he said—and then only if a layman were named to the top post. (It would be three months before Colonnese appointed Tom Quigley, the man who would ultimately announce PAVLA's disbandment.) Mader did his best to defend the PAVLA program and its personnel in his dealing with Colonnese, and to defend Colonnese against the bitter charges being made by the diocesan directors who wanted PAVLA to keep going. But Mader had no illusions. "Colonnese considered PAVLA an albatross around his neck," he said. "I knew that I was nothing more than midwife at a wake."

The September issue of *The Papal Volunteer*, PAVLA's digest-sized house organ, featured a brief article in which Colonnese paid passing tribute to Kevane ("a debt of gratitude for tireless dedication . . . ") and then went on: "The fact that I am now advocating sweeping changes in the PAVLA program does not imply any disparagement of the high degree of apostolic zeal possessed by Father Kevane and his national office staff." It was simply that "changes are required to make PAVLA truly responsive to Latin America's needs, as correctly perceived by Latin Americans. Every effort will be made to adapt the PAVLA program to the point where it conforms to the will of the Latin American church." The "sweeping changes" meant, finally, the end of PAVLA. "It was a sad day when the PAVLA staff left the office," Colonnese wrote years later. "Victories are always sad. But I knew there was no other way."

Father Vince Mallon had a point when he remarked that the U.S. mission program to Latin America, beset with many difficulties toward the end of the sixties, was only going through what the rest of the universal church was experiencing in those postconciliar years. But there *was* an added note of sadness to it all: this was the first time the U.S. church had undertaken such a full-scale, totally committed mission effort, and now it seemed to be coming apart, a victim of its own Yankee overenthusiasm and a cruel combination of outside forces.

And in the background of it all, overseeing the imminent collapse of a mission dream with what must have been grim satisfaction, loomed Ivan Illich, the cadaverous prophet of doom who had seen it all coming. For all of those connected with the U.S. mission to Latin America, he dominated the last half of the decade, a focal point for all the discouragement, the frustration, the bitterness that marked the day. As each new year came and went, more and more of what Illich had predicted seemed to be coming true: a widening gap between rich and poor, the emergence of new repressive governments to stifle long-overdue expectations, a growing despair on the part of the masses—and the inability of the U.S. mission army to do much about it.

Sometimes grudgingly, sometimes not, U.S. missioners of the seventies would look back and realize that while his tactics might have been needlessly provocative and his powers of prophecy sometimes off the mark, there was much to what Ivan Illich had said.

Father Bernard Survil, a Greensburg (Pennsylvania) priest working as a Maryknoll associate in El Salvador until his expulsion from that country in 1977, said he still looks forward to a new surge of U.S. mission interest in Latin America—"this time with Ivan Illich's warnings well-heeded."

"Illich said over ten years ago that the church in Latin America will save the church in North America," said Conventual Franciscan Father Conall McHugh, who came home from Costa Rica in 1970 after eleven years as a missioner there. "I thought he was crazy at the time. Now I believe it."

But perhaps the final word on Ivan Illich rests in a story relayed by a Jesuit priest who was close to the Latin America mission program almost from the outset. It happened four or five years ago when the Jesuit visited a fellow U.S. priest, a missioner, in a Latin American capital where he had a high-level mission assignment. The missioner had been a long-time critic—more than that, an enemy—of Illich. Infuriated by the course at Cuernavaca, where he had planned to study, he had stormed out of the school years before—denouncing Illich's views, his anti-Americanism, his cruelty, and hinted darkly at the possibility of diabolical possession.

Now the missioner was going through trying days. Every conceivable aspect of his mission assignment was going wrong; the overall operation was in a shambles. The visiting Jesuit had known his friend had problems, but he had no idea they were this bad. He was shaken by the missioner's haggard appearance when he called on him. What's wrong, he wanted to know. What happened? The missioner didn't answer until he had poured a tumbler of scotch for each of them, and then he sat down and wearily raised his glass. "Joe," he told the Jesuit, "that sonovabitch Illich was right."

10

Developments in the Latin American Church

Jim Cotter, the editor of *Latin America Calls*, was in Colombia in August of 1968, covering the historic Medellín conference of Latin American bishops and the eucharistic congress that immediately preceded it. Pope Paul VI was present for the event, and Cotter wrote movingly of one incident at the community of San José de Mosquera, a few miles outside Bogotá, where the pontiff traveled to deliver a personal message to the *campesinos* who lived and worked there. After the ceremony, Cotter watched them returning to their homes, cheered despite the rain and the mud, and reflected on the scene: "The pope had come expressly to them and he had said he loves them and worries about them. It is no small thing to be loved and worried about, and these people felt they were returning home with a precious new possession."

What Pope Paul did on that rainy day in Colombia was, in a sense, what the entire Latin American church was attempting to do throughout the sixties. In a tumultuous, challenging, revolutionary *aggiornamento* that captivated the rest of the Catholic world, it tried to reach out to all the forgotten people of Latin America, to tell them they were loved and worried about too. Names would be remembered because of what had happened in the sixties: Pironio and Camara, Gutiérrez and Freire. Once-unfamiliar communities would become known, recognized for their role in the movement: Medellín, Golconda, Cineguilla. And a new terminology came into use—phrases which, if not quite household words, were at least identifiable to all who shared a concern for the Latin American church: conscientization, theology of liberation, *comunidades de base*.

This new Latin American church addressed itself to the once-forgotten masses, allying itself with them, calling on them to liberate themselves. It spoke out with clarity against oppression by unjust governments, against mistreatment by the moneyed and landed elite, and against dependence upon the outside, on foreign capital and goods—and on foreign priests. It stepped on the stage of world history, not fully sure of itself, but filled with a sense of its prophetic mission.

To be sure, it has not succeeded in transforming Latin America. The rigid class structures remain, the old lines between the haves and have-nots, and with them remain the cardboard shelters in the cities and the hovels in the fields. The new Latin American church is burdened with accusations of Marxism from the right and of tokenism from the left. It faces hostility not only from the outside, but also from within, from powerful ecclesiastical interests which want no part of its radical message. Not only has it failed to make things generally better; in some respects it has made them worse. And yet the leaders of this church go forward with confidence, encouraged in the sure conviction that its role is staked out by the Holy Spirit, that in being not only a church to help the poor but a church of the poor themselves, it will free them from sin and lead them toward a new Pentecost.

The fabric of the new Latin American church was spun from twin developments in twentieth-century social and theological teaching. The social teaching was not new. The idea that the church should be involved in the material concerns of people, especially of poor people—a concept central to the church of Latin America as it developed in the sixties—traces its modern origin to papal teachings going back to Leo XIII. The idea had been expanded significantly in more recent years. Pope John XXIII paid special attention to development in *Mater et Magistra* and *Pacem in Terris*, his two monumental encyclicals; the Second Vatican Council dedicated a section to it in the document *Gaudium et Spes*, and finally Pope Paul took it as his central theme in the 1967 encyclical, *Populorum Progressio*. (If the Latin American church made special use of *Populorum Progressio*, it is more than fitting. Some years ago Archbishop Mark McGrath told a group that he had been at a papal audience when a fellow Latin American bishop complimented the pope on the message of *Populorum Progressio*. "You know," the pope replied, according to McGrath, "we wrote that encyclical for Latin America.")

The new Latin American bishops took these cumulative teachings and applied them to the local circumstances with which they were familiar. Not only must the church teach people that Christ saves them from eternal damnation, they were saying, but from temporal oppression as well.

Nor were the theologians inattentive to this expanding social awareness. A number of Latin American priests influenced by European thought (notably French and Belgian) as well as by European missioner-theologians succeeded in linking the social gospel with a new approach to theology. Father Ernest Ranly, a U.S. missioner in Peru (of the Precious Blood Fathers), has cited the 1940s work of Father Louis Joseph Lebret, a French priest who studied the relationship between human beings and the economy, and the later efforts of Father José Comblin, the noted Belgian theologian who was concerned with development and revolution, as charting the course for what would be known as liberation theology. The action of Bishop Larraín in turning over church lands to agricultural workers in Chile and Dom Helder Camara's tireless efforts for the poor and oppressed in Brazil continued the process, he said: "What emerged was a new consciousness by the Latin Americans of themselves as poor, economically dominated Christians and Catholics, set apart from the socio-political power structures of the world."

Father Gustavo Gutiérrez, the Peruvian who would emerge as one of Latin America's best-known theologians, José Míguez Bonino, Hugo Assmann, Enrique Dussel, Juan Luis Segundo, and many other theologians and grassroots collaborators developed this consciousness into a dynamic new approach to theology. As Franciscan Father Joseph Nangle explained it: "Instead of applying the Scriptures and theological principles to existing situations, they turned the method around and sought out the personal and social life dimensions first, and only then applied Scripture and theology." What the daring new social theologians were saying, in effect, was that theology would have to get out of the academy and into the marketplace if it were to have any effect at all on the staggering problems of poverty and injustice in Latin America.

The internal problems faced by the church were no less staggering, problems of such dimension that the average North American Catholic finds it difficult to make sense of them. The clergy ratio alone hints at their scope: In the United States, there is one priest for every 900 Catholics, but in the "Catholic" country of Brazil, the ratio is one to almost 7,000. That is for the country as a whole; in the Northeast, where poverty is at its most unrelenting, the ratio is one to 12,000 or 13,000. No one is sure. Bishop Jude T. Prost, auxiliary of Belem, told an audience of U.S. Serra Club members in 1976 that there are some parishes in his diocese with 35,000 to 40,000 members. St. Peter and Paul parish, he said, has 55,000 Catholics—and one priest.

The statistics are similar for most of the rest of Latin America. It was the type of situation which seemed near hopeless—under traditional church guidelines—to Gary MacEoin, the author. "What can one man do who is charged with the spiritual care of ten, twenty, or thirty thousand illiterates?" he asked. "How can he even face up emotionally to the fact that his predecessors and he have done no more than establish a meaningless conformity?"

Chilean pastoral theologian Father Segundo Galilea pointed to a number of unfavorable factors that had brought the Latin American church to its unhappy state: socio-cultural, in which class lines always were clearly marked out; religious (with an accent on ritualism and superstition); historical (with a Spanish emphasis on the sacramental approach); political (the church-state concept of "Christendom"); pastoral (a lack of interest toward the Indian, and a resultant low vocation rate). "All of this," he said in 1971, "resulted in an increasing de-Christianization and an anemic faith that is grossly irrelevant for the present historical moment."

The priests and bishops of Latin America could hardly ignore problems of such a dimension, but they could, and they did, determine not to be dominated by them. A number of church leaders challenged their associates: Larraín, Camara, McGrath, Dom Eugenio Sales of Natal and Antonio Fragoso of Crateus, both in Brazil, Ramon Bogarín of Paraguay, Sergio Mendez Arceo, Ivan Illich's friend in Cuernavaca, Mexico, and others, used their considerable influence at home and in the deliberations of the Vatican Council to set pastoral and social standards by which the bishops of the region would be judged. Many of those standards would be set down formally at Medellín.

Meeting at Medellín

It was the Vatican Council that provided the proximate reason for convocation of the meeting at Medellín. It was expected that bishops of various ecclesiastical regions in the world would meet within a reasonable time after the council, and thus it was that the Latin American hierarchy held its second general meeting—the first had been at Rio de Janeiro in 1955, when CELAM was born—at Medellín in August 1968: to have the council's findings adapted to Latin America by Latin Americans.

That Medellín would achieve the benchmark status it did could not have come as a surprise to the Vatican, according to the long-time Rome correspondent for Religious News Service, Jesuit Father Robert Graham. Writing two months before the meeting took place, he had stated the matter simply, and, as it turned out, correctly: "The Vatican is now confident that the groundwork laid at this meeting will make of the [bishops'] conference the beginning of a new phase in the life of the Catholic church." César Aguiar, the Uruguayan sociologist, writing after the fact, put the measure of Medellín into even sharper focus: "It was the most important event of the century for the Latin American church."

CELAM set up committees that did the detailed agenda planning and preparation of documents for Medellín, continuing its record of guiding what Jaime Fonseca, NC News Service's Latin America specialist, called the "Latin-Americanization" of the church. Within that process, CELAM had fostered a critical look at ideas and practices inherited from European and U.S. missioners. It encouraged the establishment of institutions engaged in pastoral, liturgical, catechetical, and social planning. It had been responsible for this kind of work long before Medellín—its labors, in fact, produced some of the new ideas that influenced the thinking of Vatican II—but it was at Medellín that CELAM's efforts reached a fullness. The Medellín guidelines, Fonseca says, were a direct result of CELAM's efforts to come up with a realistic picture of the church and its weaknesses.

Coordinating its work with the Vatican, the Medellín planning committee decided to hold the meeting in August 1968, immediately after the conclusion of the Bogotá eucharistic congress. Planning hit a minor snag in the spring of that year with signs of unrest in which the church seemed to be the special target—including the kidnapping of Archbishop Mario Casariego in Guatemala—leading in turn to reservations in Rome about the pope's planned but as yet unannounced attendance. But in May the pontiff gave final approval for the trip, his first visit to Latin America, and his only journey to the western hemisphere, except for his United Nations appearance in 1965, since becoming pope. "It is a startlingly impressive sign," Graham wrote at the time, "of the pope's personal interest in the crisis through which the church in Latin America is now passing."

Cotter, the other RNS correspondent, admitted that the level of papal interest seemed to be high, but wrote of the impatience of Latin American progressives with what he said they called the Vatican Tango—two steps forward and two steps backward—when the times demanded a more forthright approach. "They charge," he said, "that the pope is an advocate of creeping gradualism at a time when the problems are running at full pace and dwarfing social action programs."

Crowds at the Bogotá eucharistic congress were somewhat smaller than expected, but those who were there were enthusiastic in their greeting to the Holy Father. Throughout his three-day stay, he made it clear that his heart was with the masses of Latin America, and that the eucharist which was the center of the meeting was symbolic of the church's answer to their material and spiritual hunger. The bishops, too, greeted the pope with fervent admiration when he formally convened their meeting Saturday, August 24, in the Bogotá cathedral. (It had been decided to hold the opening session in Bogotá to spare the pope a journey to Medellín, some 160 miles distant.)

The pope's measured words matched the momentous occasion. Reflecting on his "exact awareness of this blessed hour" and its historic nature, he said the church's previous efforts in Latin America now "demand something new and something great." He continued:

The future calls for effort, daring, and sacrifice, which introduce a deep anxiety into the church. We are in a moment of total deliberation. There enters into us, like an overwhelming wave, the restlessness characteristic of our time, and particularly in these countries, straining toward their complete development, and troubled by the awareness of their economic, social, political, and moral disequilibrium.

Pope Paul gave the bishops a threefold direction, spiritual, pastoral, and social, in which he counseled against violence: "Let us distinguish our responsibility from that of one who instead makes violence a noble ideal, a glorious heroism, an obliging theology." He spoke in favor of poverty:

The poverty of the church, in its decorous simplicity of form, is a testimony of fidelity to the Gospel. It is the condition, at times indispensable, for giving credit to her particular mission. It is an exercise, superhuman on occasions, of that liberty of spirit, with respect to the bonds of riches, which adds strength to the apostle's mission.

He concluded with a call to the Latin American bishops to chart a new civilization, both modern and Christian, in a spirit of truth and love. Two days later the bishops convened at Medellín and got down to business.

CELAM's preparation for the meeting had been thorough; the Medellín conference set out to cover an incredible variety of topics in a brief period. The Vatican II experience was still fresh in the bishops' minds, and that helped them to avoid the time-wasting procedural wrangling that often goes with international meetings. But the ambitious program of action they had set for themselves was still challenging. They wanted to establish pastoral guidelines, re-evaluate all facets of Christian life and practice, discuss the evangelization of both the elite and the mass membership of the church, sacramental usage, social justice, family life . . . the list seemed endless.

"They clearly wanted to bring the church into tune with the modern world," wrote Father Frederick McGuire, "but also to preserve the timeless message that Christ had bade it pass on unchanged to generations till the end of time." In a word, society's archaic structures had to be modernized, and the church, keeping its eternal mission in mind, could offer guidance in bringing that difficult task about.

The bishops' opening statement made that point; it spoke of Latin America as "a promising reality brimming with hope," but also of its "agonizing problems . . . that wound the Christian conscience." The bishops said:

> In spite of the efforts being made, there is the compounding of hunger and misery, of illness of a massive nature and infant mortality, of illiteracy and marginality, of profound inequality of income and tensions between the social classes, of outbreaks of violence and rare participation of the people in decisions affecting the common good.

Yet, in the face of that dark litany of problems, there was also hope:

> In the light of the faith that we profess as believers, we have undertaken to discover a plan of God in the "signs of the times." We interpret the aspirations and clamors of Latin America as signs that reveal the direction of the divine plan operating in the redeeming love of Christ which bases these aspirations on an awareness of fraternal solidarity.

The 130 bishops at Medellín spent a week in deliberations on sixteen major subject areas: justice, peace, family and demography, education, youth, pastoral care of the masses, pastoral concern for the elite, catechesis, liturgy, lay movements, priests, religious, formation of the clergy, poverty of the church, joint pastoral planning, and mass media. Each section was considered at two levels—factually, first, and then reflectively—before a set of conclusions was agreed upon.

The conclusions had a startlingly liberal tone, particularly in social and economic areas. The bishops recommended a crash program of church renewal and social justice; they condemned violence, both overt and in the passive form of violation of human rights. They called for increased production from both the government and the private sector, and urged more equitable distribution of the wealth. Education, they said, must deal with social justice, and seminary training must be corrected to bring students into contact with the realities of the modern world. Lay people must be integrated into pastoral work, and there must be collegiality in all church dealings. The church must identify with the poor and witness for simplicity in daily living.

Latin Americans must decide their own course, the bishops said: "The imposition of foreign values and criteria would constitute a new and grave alienation." That led directly to thoughts of liberation, an area in which the Medellín bishops grew increasingly forceful and increasingly eloquent:

> In these signs we perceive the first indications of the painful birth of a new civilization. And we cannot fail to see in this gigantic effort toward a rapid transformation and development an obvious sign of the Spirit who leads the history of man and of peoples toward their vocation.

A profound conversion was required for authentic liberation, the bishops declared. They said their call was not so much for structural change, but "in the insistence on the conversion of men which will in turn bring about this change."

Medellín spoke in negative terms of both capitalism and Marxism: "Both militate against the dignity of the human person." One makes capital and profit its primary concern, the other deals with collective man above all else. "We must denounce the fact that Latin America sees itself caught between these two options and remains dependent on one or the other of the centers of power which control its economy."

Institutionalized violence is a reality that demands urgent transformation, the bishops said, and the temptation to turn to violence as a means of achieving that transformation should not be surprising. "One should not abuse the patience of a people that for years has borne a situation that would not be acceptable to anyone with a degree of awareness of human rights."

The bishops gave formal endorsement to the concept of conscientization, the process by which people analyze their own situations reflectively, and to the formation of basic Christian communities, *comunidades de base*, in which small groups apply the conscientization approach to community problems.

And they spoke of the depth of their conviction of the need for liberation:

Because all liberation is an anticipation of the complete redemption of Christ, the church in Latin America is particularly in favor of all education efforts which tend to free our people. . . . A deafening cry pours from the throats of millions of men, asking their pastors for a liberation that reaches them from nowhere else.

The words were strong because the emotions were profound, and the rest of the Catholic world—and much of the Latin American world—was surprised. Father McGuire attempted to explain it to U.S. readers: "We North Americans have never had to face so many and such acute problems all at once. The solutions proposed by Medellín may therefore seem radical to us."

A radical element had, indeed, assumed the role of intellectual leadership in the Latin American church, and its philosophical base won all-important backing at the highest levels of CELAM. The influence of Gutiérrez and Freire, those most readily identified with liberation theology and conscientization, was unquestionably pervasive at Medellín, but much of the credit for what happened must also go to the man who was CELAM's secretary general at the time: Eduardo Pironio, a future cardinal, then bishop-administrator of the Avellaneda diocese in Argentina.

"He coined the idea of liberation instead of development at Medellín," McGuire said of Pironio in an interview in 1976. "He sees it in a framework of total liberation, with spiritual as well as material overtones. His influence was unmatchable. He's just a beautiful character in every way."

Born in Argentina in 1920, Eduardo Pironio was ordained at the age of twenty-three and went on to become a seminary professor of theology. At thirty-eight he became vicar general of the Mercedes diocese. He attended the first two sessions of the Vatican Council as a peritus, and in 1964, when he was forty-three, he was named a bishop.

Pironio exercised strong leadership first as secretary general and then president of CELAM, attempting to translate the thinking of liberation theology into programs of social action. In doing that, both at the Medellín conference and in other activities outside it, he learned how to resist pressure from extremists of both right and left. He was to go through that and more as bishop of Mar del Plata, when his outspoken stands against violence during the turbulent Perón administration brought him death threats. The threats were more than idle; many friends and associates were among the 1,300 people who died in the ongoing wave of political violence.

The bishop was active on the world church scene as well, taking an active role in the 1974 Synod of Bishops and the following year—after having served three years in Mar del Plata—earning appointment as pro-prefect of the Sacred Congregation for Religious and Secular Institutes. Pope Paul named him to the College of Cardinals in 1976.

In a 1970 interview, Pironio was asked about the Medellín conference, and he spoke of the pressures that were brought to bear: "Some voices from the right and from the left try to brand the Medellín guidelines either as a capitulation of the church to exploitation, or as an invitation to violence." There was no thought of condoning violence, he said—"that would be unchristian and contrary to the Gospel." In regard to liberation, he continued, it would be wrong to think of it in terms of temporal liberation only:

> We spoke at Medellín of total liberation as taken within the context of the Bible when describing the history of salvation which finds its crown in the mystery of Christ, who was crucified and resurrected for us. He is essentially the savior and liberator, but never a political restorer, for he said his kingdom is not of this world.
>
> Medellín is indeed a Pentecost for Latin America, inasmuch as it infused in our church a new spirit of conversion: the need of radically transforming Christians in order to commit them to the daily call of man and history, including liberation from all servitude—oppression of man by man, yes, but also oppression of man by sin.

The Theology of Liberation

The theologian most closely associated with what would be known as liberation theology—the touchstone for so much of what happened at Medellín and beyond—was a brilliant Peruvian, Father Gustavo Gutiérrez, professor of theology at the Catholic University of Peru. He would accept the Pironio interpretation of the modern meaning of liberation, but would also carry it further, challenging any deviation from its principles, questioning any vestige of dependency or subservience. That would prove to have a hard-hitting effect on U.S. mission work, as Father Nangle observed: "The local church, as in Peru, was forced to stand on its own hind legs. Actually, it seized the leadership of its own church. We could have swamped them with buildings and money and cars, but in the long run it didn't happen that way. And that was due to people like Gutiérrez who had the intellectual capacity to put us in our place."

Gutiérrez has written and spoken extensively in expounding his theories (although not always to friendly audiences; a group of U.S. bishops whom he addressed "looked at me as though I were a heretic," he once told Father Colonnese). Theology's function, Gutiérrez believes, is "a critical reflection on the church's presence and activity in the world, in the light of revelation." First comes the commitment to charity; theology comes later.

Why liberation; why not development? Development has been used to express the aspirations of poor nations, but it seems weak and pejorative, is Gutiérrez's reply—especially in Latin America: "Development should attack the cause of our plight, and among the central ones is the economic, social, political, and cultural dependence of some peoples on others. The word 'liberation' therefore is more accurate and conveys better the human side of the problem."

The stress in the fifties had been on development, but a new attitude emerged in the sixties, as Latin America got to understand its situation better and to examine the reasons for it. Underdevelopment was seen as the historical subproduct of the development of Latin America by other countries; the natural process of capitalism and its results leads to the conclusion that Latin America cannot develop within a capitalistic system. "Today the most conscientized groups agree that there will be a true development for Latin America only through liberation from domination by capitalist countries." This implies a showdown, Gutiérrez concedes, and he is less sure than other Latin American church leaders that it will come peacefully: "For many in our continent, this liberation will have to pass, sooner or later, through paths of violence."

The new church in Latin America, Gutiérrez says, acknowledges its solidarity with the plight of the individual nations, and admits its responsibility to help correct the evils of "institutionalized violence," those factors of poverty, exploitation, and injustice that are all part of neocolonial patterns under which decisions about Latin America historically have been made on the outside. Gutiérrez is uncompromising in his insistence that commitment to the necessary change must be complete. He deplores the fact that most of the church is still with the established order ("Some Christians are among the oppressed and others among the persecutors, and some among the tortured and others among those who torture") and that as a weapon, statements go only so far ("Can ecclesiastical authority stay on the level of generalized declarations?").

To do nothing in favor of the oppressed of Latin America is to act against them, Gutiérrez declares: "The church has no alternative. Only a total break with the unjust order to which it is bound, in a thousand conscious or unconscious ways, and a forthright commitment to a new society, will make people in Latin America believe in the message of love it bears."

The church is called on to "rethink" the wisdom of accepting aid from churches of wealthy nations; it can be self-defeating and lead to an attitude that settles for reformist solutions and superficial social changes. That would only prolong the misery and injustice, Gutiérrez contends, at the same time salving the consciences of Catholics in the rich countries. He concludes his *A Theology of Liberation* (originally published in Spanish in Lima in 1971): "To paraphrase a well-known text of Pascal, we can say that all the political theologies, the theologies of hope, of revolution, and of liberation, are not worth one act of genuine solidarity with exploited social classes. They are not worth one act of faith, love, and hope, committed—in one way or another—in active participation to liberate man from everything that dehumanizes him and prevents him from living according to the will of the Father."

Much, but admittedly not all, of that philosophy would form the backdrop for what emerged at Medellín. Gutiérrez wrote in 1971, with pardonable satisfaction: "The product of a profound historical movement, this aspiration to liberation is beginning to be accepted by the Christian community as a sign of the time, as a call to commitment and to implementation."

Equally a part of the Medellín background was the concept of conscientization, the act of becoming aware of one's self, one's problems, one's aspirations. "We wish to affirm," the Medellín bishops said, "that it is indispensable to form a social conscience and a realistic perception of the problems of the community and of social structures." The concept is no easier to define than it is (for most North Americans, at any rate) to spell or pronounce. The influential Bishop Leonidas Proaño of Riobamba, Ecuador, had a lyric but wordy try at it in a 1975 U.S. newspaper interview: Conscientization, he said, is

> the process by which man situates himself in relation to God and the call he makes; in relation to the world along with which he has to proceed, perfecting it and perfecting himself; in relation or in community with other men with whom and for whom as he perfects the world and perfects society he perfects himself, which means that he heads toward God, thus bringing about human history by means of his relationship with time.

Development of the idea of conscientization is generally associated with Paulo Freire, a Brazilian teacher born in Recife in 1921. He was a member of a middle-class family that was severely affected by the Depression, and in his dissertation for a doctorate at the University of Recife in 1959 he proposed a way to help the poor break away from the vicious cycle of oppression. He called it, in his native Portuguese, *conscientização*, the process of developing an awareness of one's existential situation. Employing it, people will reflect on what they are, where they are, and why. They will realize that their situation is not a result of blind fate, but of a humanly devised system maintained for the benefit of a few. "Development of an awareness of a situation of injustice and of a realization that the unjust situation is not inevitable quickly arouses the desire for action for change," Freire wrote.

His system was put to the test with impressive results in adult literacy programs sponsored by the Brazilian bishops' Movement for Basic Education, but Freire was to become a victim of the 1964 military takeover in his native land. The new government denounced his methods as communistic and finally saw to his deportation.

He has achieved world renown in the years since his exile and has seen his approach adopted and endorsed far beyond Brazil, or Latin America. The impact of his achievement at the most personal level was effectively recounted some years ago by Ivan Illich, who visited Freire's peasant pupils in a small Brazilian farm community before Freire had been deported. "I will never forget that evening," Illich wrote. "One man got up, struggled for words and finally put into one utterance the argument I want to make: 'I could not sleep last night . . . because last evening I wrote my name, . . . and I understand that I am I. This means that we are responsible.'"

Is conscientization, the product of an underdeveloped society, effective only in that kind of framework? Not at all, according to commentators such as Colonnese, who sees not only a use for it, but an actual need in wealthier nations such as the United States:

> We feel no guilt, and we weave endless rationalizations for our inequitable domestic and international policies and the structures they reinforce. We must bring ourselves to the point where we can see ourselves as we are seen in the Third World. Perhaps then we can begin to understand the overwhelming hypocrisy of claiming to be a Christian nation, motivated by love for mankind, while simultaneously sustaining unjust socio-economic structures that propagate misery.

Another phenomenon of the new Latin American church that came in for special attention at Medellín was the incredible growth of what were called basic Christian communities (*comunidades de base*), which had begun a few years earlier in Brazil and by the late sixties had reached every corner of Latin America. "It is necessary," the bishops said at Medellín, "that small basic communities be developed in order to establish a balance with minority groups, which are the groups in power."

The *comunidades de base* were, simply, small groups of people who had some common denominator—people from the same neighborhood, most frequently—who would meet informally with a discussion leader to reflect on their lives, their problems, within the context of Christian principles. It was a logical means of developing the conscientization concept at the most fundamental level, and its rapid growth attested to the need it filled. "It is the first and fundamental ecclesiastical nucleus," the Medellín bishops concluded, "which down on the grassroots level brings richness and expansion to the faith—and to religious worship, which is its expression. This community, which is the initial cell of the church and the radiating center for its evangelizing efforts, is today a most potent factor for human advancement and development."

Sister Marlene De Nardo looked at the basic Christian community from a long-range viewpoint: "It is a movement that has begun to change the masses into a 'people,' awakening in them a new consciousness of their own value and dignity as human persons called to be a free people of God." The communities, she said, called people from their own selfishness, individualism, and a desire for security and fostered instead a commitment to others. "It is a Christian message of freedom experienced not as an individual disposition or a private salvation, but as a covenant of a people with each other, and with their God."

Brazilian pastoral theologian Father José Marins traces the origins of the *comunidades de base* to the late fifties, where they emerged in three widely separated areas—Brazil, Chile, and Panama. (In Panama the communities were particularly associated with the innovative San Miguelito parish, where, Chicago's Father Leo Mahon recalled: "We took what would be known as the Freire approach of getting people to examine themselves, determine their own problems and their priorities in solving them. Community came out of that. Much of the church in Latin America advocates a strong social position but retains old theological positions. We felt, to be consistent and integrated, that social consciousness ought to come out of the word of God that people have.")

But generally the development of the *comunidades* is associated first with Brazil, where a combination of three factors helped to bring it about. The first was a campaign launched in the diocese of Barra do Pirai by Dom Agnelo Rossi (a future Vatican cardinal). To help in offsetting a chronic clergy shortage, he took selected worker-catechists and trained them to be community coordinators. The second was the effectiveness of the basic education movement centered at Natal, which used radio schools—reaching small, organized groups—for religious instruction. Third was the bishops' national pastoral plan, which seized on the success of a few experimental groups and called for the community approach to be multiplied.

The *comunidades* spread as rapidly as they did, Father Marins says, "because Christians suddenly realized that they had to evangelize the people of their continent who had been baptized but had no real contact with sacramental life or the word of God, no community oneness." It was a concept that spread on the initiative of the laity, as Phillip Berryman has pointed out:

The interesting feature is that the clergy has not initiated nor led this movement. The evangelization that takes place in these base communities involves a growing, critical consciousness in regard to traditional religiosity and a confrontation with the Christian Gospel. It implies liberation from the force of traditional religion.

The *comunidad de base* phenomenon continued its growth into the seventies. "I sense they will be the guarantee for Christianity's future," Father Segundo Galilea said in 1971, "and they may well be all we can count on in the secularized society that is now taking shape."

By the mid-seventies, many dioceses could point to scores or more of basic Christian communities, as did Bishop Proaño in Riobamba, Ecuador, where over one hundred *comunidades de base* were active. The purpose of individual meetings, he told an interviewer, depends on local needs, from sacramental and liturgical life to organizing in order to obtain potable water. Groups meet to study the Bible, to discover their problems, to question social structures, with an emphasis on organizing for community action for what needs to be done: to get water, to acquire land, to improve health care or education or farming methods, to rebuild a chapel.

Why are the people there in the *comunidades?* he asked himself:

To know the community, to seek a remedy for their ills, to have a church with vitality, to be free, to have justice, to be a person. We learn to think instead of acting on impulse. We learn to ask questions: With what intention (perhaps hidden) do others come to us? Who is behind the commerce that works to a *campesino*'s disadvantage? We don't need to be a ball, kicked back and forth.

And in two simple sentences he summed up what the basic Christian community has meant, what kind of attitude has spurred its unparalleled growth. "Let us not be dismayed by difficulties," he said. "They are like a trampoline, a springboard to get us over the obstacles and advance our progress."

New theologies, an intellectual vitality, grassroots enthusiasm for a different kind of Christianity filled with meaning for everyday life, and finally Medellín, a flowering of all that was new and challenging and hope-filled in the exciting climate of the church of Latin America—with all this happening, surely a new day for Latin America's masses could not be far off. Or could it?

The sad truth was that this new church did not stand alone. Not only was there still an old church, but it was an old church that maintained all the old connections: to governments, to an elite class, to money, to power. A Bishop Larraín could challenge his fellow prelates to new visions by word and example, a man of practical bent such as Pironio could bring them together to get a job done, a Dom Helder Camara could inspire the world as a man of Christian peace—but the fact was that there were not enough Larraíns and Pironios and Camaras, and there were too many others whom time had passed by. In the sixties, and into the seventies, the New Church of Latin America was receiving all the attention. But the Old Church (unavoidable exceptions such as Medellín notwithstanding) was still able to call many, if not most, of the shots.

These two faces of the church became infinitely clearer during the sixties, especially to U.S. missioners who had been challenged by the new theologians and the prophetic bishops and who were trying to put their messages into practice in the field.

"Among these Brazilian people—the mestizos, the blacks, the Indians—I found a new Christianity," said Sister Marlene De Nardo:

Not a Christianity based on doctrinally perfect concepts, nor one rooted in nonhistorical or theoretical understandings of faith, but rather a Christianity steeped in our rich biblical tradition and in the religiosity of the suffering friends of Yahweh.

Among these people I also discovered the two faces of the church:

a fearful but prophetic church situated among the poor masses, "voice of the voiceless," and a triumphant, established church self-conscious-ly standing at the side of the new leaders of the national security system. . . . Among the upper classes and educated elites, Christianity is mostly a cultural symbol, cherished and retained. Among the poor and humble, Christianity is a hope for freedom and a belief in a loving Father who can give some meaning to an otherwise inexplicable form of human existence.

Maryknoll Father James Madden, in Peru, not only saw the two churches but adapted his mission work because of what he learned from them. There was the official church, he said, and "what I call the real church, the People-of-God church." The only way to get in touch with the real church, he reasoned, was to get in contact with the *campesinos*, by living with them no matter how rugged their existence, how remote their homes: "My idea is that that's where reality is."

In Bolivia, Monsignor David Ratermann of St. Louis carried the idea a step further: "In the minds of our people there exist three different concepts or images of what the church is, and also of what is its mission among people." First, he said, is the traditional church among Spanish-speaking people, strong in faith and a sense of community (if somewhat exclusive), but marked by a lack of awareness of the social dimension of the gospel. The second church, he said, is the traditional Indian (Aymara and Quechua) church, serving the Indians' strong religious sense but resisting any element of change. "The fundamental attitude toward God is one of fear," he said, adding that this church fosters the idea of many lesser "gods" that must be placated—paid—to avoid their vengeance.

The third church, finally, is the renewed church springing up mainly (although not exclusively) among the Indian peasant classes. Although it suffers from a lack of confidence and the opposition of some priests, Rater-mann said, it is notable for its authentic communities of faith, hope, love, and prayer:

A renewed church is being born, one which is more authentically People of God. We understand more clearly now that the church is born and renewed constantly by the Word of God. What's all important is that the Word be heard, believed, meditated upon, and interiorized constantly in little groups of believers. This phenomenon is observable mainly in small groups who come together with their catechists and other pastoral servants who have a deep faith and also a strong desire to share this faith with others. It's quite evident that the Spirit of the Lord is working to renew the face of the earth. These groups are the microstructure of a renewed and more authentic church.

Mixed Notices at Home

The existence of the "two churches" (or, in Ratermann's example, three) was an inescapable reality for those who, first, had planned Medellín, and, later, those who were anxious to implement its conclusions. It was one thing for a liberal-radical element to have seized the intellectual initiative in the Latin American church, but quite another to see all its ideas materialize throughout the continent. The old church would have a great deal to say about putting Medellín into effect—or putting it on the shelf.

The significance of the Medellín documents is profound, without question; even had all its conclusions been abandoned by the church, their Christian eloquence would still serve to inspire others, to give hope to generations yet to come. At Medellín, Sister Marlene De Nardo said, "The church discovered itself as part of history and committed itself to the oppressed." Medellín's impact, said Father Galilea, was even greater than that of Vatican II: "For the first time, the church of Latin America gained a collective sense of its own unique identity and vocation."

Bishop Pironio, as we have seen, referred to Medellín as "a new Pentecost," and Aguiar called it "the most important event of the century" for the Latin American church. But despite all that happened at Medellín, there have been disappointments as well. Medellín was a critical success in the eyes of the world; at home, its notices were mixed at best. Father McGuire and Father Daniel Panchot took understanding approaches as to why that might be. McGuire wrote in 1973:

> Even though all 130 of the bishops who met at Medellín signed the conclusions and Pope Paul has given the document his approval, certain bishops inevitably had reservations on particular points—or indeed on the tenor of the whole document. Not all the bishops have demonstrated, in the five years that have elapsed since 1968, the same alacrity and conviction in applying these conclusions (but then, hasn't that been true of Vatican II, also?). There were both traditionalists and reformers among the bishops who went to Medellín, and since their return home, they have been, if anything, even further polarized, which was perhaps inevitable in a church whose members are only human. Nonetheless, the very fact that these guidelines were agreed on is a tremendous pressure for renewal. And inexorably the desired "updating" is taking place.

Panchot, the Holy Cross priest exiled from Chile, cited the tension at Medellín: "Some wanted to go faster; others wanted to go slower; some wanted to go more to the left; others more to the right. What was certain was that the church and the message of Christ were important for the new society Latin Americans were trying to construct."

Some commentators noted that talk of post-Medellín ferment applied only to the intelligentsia, that it had never reached the level of the people, thus leaving Medellín ineffective as far as practical results were concerned. Many have cited the failure of individual bishops to put Medellín's conclusions into effect. Father Ernest Ranly wrote:

> After the strong, stirring tones of Medellín the bishops went to their home dioceses and discovered there were the same problems of massive poverty, along with the vested interest of the elites. Neither the oppressors nor the oppressed were quick to rally to the new cry for freedom. In many countries, the political climate became precarious, if not hostile. If some of the hierarchy did not renege on their commitments in Medellín, they certainly began to play their cards very cautiously.

Said Mexico's Bishop Samuel Ruiz García, speaking of the Latin American church in the years after Medellín: "We can speak persuasively and precisely and can move our audiences to enthusiastic hope, but our great weakness is our frequent inability to put our plans into action. This general weakness . . . is being compounded . . . by the vastness of the problems we face."

The changes at Medellín were more apparent than real, Gary MacEoin glumly concluded in *Revolution Next Door*. The bishop-delegates might have debated documents drawn up by a handful of European-influenced theologians, and even signed some fairly revolutionary statements. But more than five hundred other Latin American bishops weren't even at Medellín, and in the long run the conservative absentees felt they could count on Vatican support—"old church support"—when the chips were down.

MacEoin, in fact, is the one of the few liberal commentators whose assessment of the Medellín documents themselves is less than enthusiastic. The direction was correct, he says, but at key points the Medellín authors seemed to have suffered a loss of nerve. The Medellín analysis of the political, social, and economic situation was clearly Marxist, MacEoin believes, "but the solution proposed by the bishops returns to the previous official position of the church." The documents use Marxian language in denouncing oppressive forces, but when they turn to solutions reject both capitalism and Marxism in favor of a restructuring of the economy along the lines suggested by the social magisterium of the church:

> The common explanation offered for the decision of the bishops was that they were simply following the long-standing tradition in church circles never to reject publicly a position that had been formulated by church authority. For that reason, they felt they still had to give lip service to what had so long been called the official position of the church.
>
> Outside the ranks of the bishops, I found nobody in Latin America who subscribed to this solution.

The radical priesthood in Latin America, as noted, had been developing for some time before Medellín, and in fact had been instrumental in formulating the Medellín documents. Buoyed by their success to that point, and then frustrated by the shortcomings of the followup to Medellín, they assumed an even stronger posture in the next few years. Challenging authority both in the church and the state, where they felt it necessary, they became ever more visible and began winning new converts, including, significantly, an increasingly large number of U.S. missioners. Medellín gave their cause some legitimacy, MacEoin points out, by taking the heat off them. Radical ideas? Nonsense, they told officials who raised complaints. We're only saying the same things the bishops said at Medellín.

Philip Wheaton, an Episcopalian missioner in the Dominican Republic for many years and then director of the Ecumenical Program for Inter-American Communication and Action, Washington, D.C., says the militancy of priests' organizations that emerged after Medellín was one of the conference's most important residual products. That kind of hard-line organization came about in Peru and Colombia, he said, in the Dominican Republic and Paraguay, in the Priests for the Third World movement in Argentina. "By far the most important contribution of Medellín," Wheaton suggests, "is that it began to challenge the church's practice of automatically equating authority with divine sanction."

MacEoin offered some insights into the philosophy and style of operation of the radicalized priests in *Revolution Next Door:* those of their number who stay within the church structures,

> like the radical intellectuals and students, are placing all their bets on the peasants and the urban slum dwellers. Most of those who have committed themselves to this new approach continue to offer the traditional church services to any who seek them, but without stressing that aspect of their ministry. . . . These priests do not see themselves as conduits of grace to tens of thousands of people. They are satisfied if they can create a few small islands of Christian life, leaving the future radiation to the Holy Spirit.

There were different levels of organization within this new approach to ministry. One of the best-known groups, in Peru, was ONIS, the National Office of Social Information, which not only attracted many U.S. missioners, but numbered some of them among its founders. The priests of ONIS—which was founded in March 1968 at Cineguilla, a village near Lima—were interested in getting the church to identify with workers and with the poor and to rid the Peruvian church of its foreign influence and color. ONIS's strong "Declaration of Cineguilla" documented and condemned social injustices in Peru (drawing faint but nevertheless encouraging support from Lima's Cardinal Landazuri Ricketts). "Never before in recent memory had priests spoken out so clearly and so radically on the human and structural problems confronting their country," said Father Nangle, an ONIS member (as were his associates at Santísimo Nombre parish in Lima), of the Cineguilla statement. Maryknoll Father William McIntire says that being a founding member of ONIS "nearly got me declared persona non grata."

ONIS was as concerned with divesting the Peruvian church of its traditional reliance on foreign elements as it was with the social question, and it was an ONIS-inspired demonstration in the city of Trujillo that eventually led to the recall of Archbishop Carboni, the nuncio. Carboni was irate over the protests that greeted the appointment of an Italian as new auxiliary of Trujillo, and wrote to Landazuri demanding that action be taken against the "rebel priests." Landazuri defended the priests, if not their specific protest, and the resultant uproar ended with Carboni being shifted back to Rome.

McIntire was a first-hand participant in another major meeting that year, the Golconda, Colombia, conference that resulted in a declaration attacking injustices similar to those cited at Cineguilla. The statement, issued in December, called in effect for a socialistic government in Colombia, a call which polarized the church community and upset most of the nation's solidly conservative hierarchy. Father Comblin had issued a cautionary note on the organization of radical priests' groups and the issuance of inflammatory statements on political matters, McIntire recalled. "He told me the work was premature and even dangerous, and might have the result of encouraging a strong right-wing reaction and repression in those countries."

There was even stronger criticism from Bishop Nevin Hayes, the Chicago Carmelite who headed the Sicuani diocese in Peru at the time (and who, in 1976, became chairman of the U.S. bishops' committee on Latin America). During a 1977 interview he spoke unhappily of "liberation theology as expounded by ONIS" and detailed his objection: "I say that's politics more than theology. All it does is create hatred. The worst thing to teach an oppressed people is violence; it hurts them terribly."

If the countries involved were being polarized by the new groups of radical priests, so was the U.S. mission community. It was one more burden for the missioners to carry, one more pressure point for a faltering mission corps to face.

The Latin American church that emerged during the sixties dealt heavily in terms that were difficult to define, words open to a wide range of subjective interpretations. People could talk about liberation, or, specifically, about liberation theology, and have two entirely different things in mind. "Revolution" might connote violence to one person and the peaceful establishment of a new order to another. Calls for church involvement in socialism or socialization carried subtle distinctions that often lent themselves more to division than to understanding. Much of the confusion was due to the dynamic nature of the church in the sixties, to be sure, but its effect on old church and new, on the old mission hand and the new-breed mission-servant, was unsettling.

It was a stimulating time intellectually and an exciting period politically for the church, no question about it. There was a pride and a thrill in seeing the Roman Catholic church in this troubled land declare itself the servant of the poor, pledging its commitment to find new roads to reach God's poor, even if some of its own members seemed to be looking for new roadblocks at the same time.

There was pride in the presence of a Dom Helder Camara, who could mesmerize a visiting group of North Americans as effectively as he could inspire people throughout the world. A member of one such group wrote:

> We realized we were in the presence of a man who was deeply aware of the problems facing the church in Latin America and who had his finger on the pulse of a nation. He sees in each person of his country and of the continent a brother, not a stranger; a fellow human being who must be made aware of his dignity as a man. One sensed in him the same spirit that moved Pope John. "I am speaking," he said, "not as a Brazilian who speaks to North Americans, but as a man who speaks to other men, a brother who speaks at home."

There was pride in all the new structures and the new theologies, the new confidence, the unbounded optimism that could lead a Latin American bishop to proclaim:

> Medellín was a point of arrival and a point of departure. But it was also a summons to all churches, a call for commitment to the oppressed of all the world, to let the People of Yahweh go forward freely to the Promised Land under the banner of God's words: "Let my people go!" forward toward the Incarnation, toward Calvary, toward the Resurrection!

And still. . . . How vast the troubles, how many the poor. How haunting the doubts. . . .

"For years," Gary MacEoin wrote in an article about Paulo Freire, about all that conscientization has accomplished, "I have been searching for an instance in which peasants have broken out of their oppression, even at the local level, but have found none. When I asked Freire, he admitted that neither has he."

11

The Downhill Turn

It was a peak year, a watershed year. It was 1968. There were more U.S. Catholic missioners—diocesan and religious priests, brothers, sisters, seminarians, and lay persons—than ever before, or since, at work in Latin America: 3,391, compared to 3,225 two years earlier, and 2,818 in 1970. And after that the numbers went down sharply. "Confusion, new ideas, political changes—up until that point our mission assignment was very, very success-ful," recalls Father John F. Henry, the Jesuit who was in Chile from 1959 until 1972. "After that, the changes made all the missioners start to question their role, and then nothing was the same."

Father Chuck Tobin, the Kansas City priest just beginning a mission tour in La Paz, recalls it as a time when building proposals were scrapped. "There had been plans for a new church here," he said of his hillside parish of San Antonio, "but they were put off. And anyway, the plans were drawn by an architect in Kansas City who'd never been here, which probably says something about the whole mission approach at the time."

It was a period of tension in Santísimo Nombre parish, Father Joseph Nangle's upper-middle-class enclave in Lima, where parishoners had been gradually introduced to the new theology, the "ONIS priests," and the teachings of Medellín, all of which had come to the fore in 1968. Most of Nangle's people found the new approach difficult to accept; parish discussions on the controversial matters were frequently heated. When Cardinal Lan-dazuri Ricketts asked him why the parish was divided, the Franciscan priest replied, in a gently kidding fashion, "because of the documents you came up with at Medellín." It was a healthy sign, Nangle thought: having well-to-do *limeños* confronted with social teachings of the church controversial enough to cause parish squabbles, and even some defections. Less assuring to Nangle was the difficulty that arose from another quarter, from the radical Peruvian priests who were no longer friendly to him and his mission, who had become so committed to their cause that they saw spending any time at all in apostolic work among the middle or upper class as a waste, if not a sin. "After much discussion and reflection in the parish council," Nangle said, "Santísimo

Nombre decided that it mattered not so much where you preached the gospel, as it did how the gospel was preached."

But exposure to that kind of confrontation had its effect on all U.S. missioners, he said, and 1968—the year of Medellín, of liberation theology, of new directions in the Latin American thrust of the U.S. church—was to be a critical year. "Those U.S. missioners who came back to the States before 1968 had little problem settling back down," he said. "But that hasn't been the case for those who came back since."

The fortunes of the U.S. mission involvement in Latin America were taking a downhill turn, from a numerical standpoint, at least, from which there would be no visible recovery. There was no single reason behind it; many forces were at work to bring it about. Father Colonnese pointed out that the two or three years after 1968 were times of "growing mistrust" among U.S. missioners serving the church in Latin America—an important factor in the decline:

Priests of the same community were mistrustful of one another. Religious sisters were mistrustful of priests, and laymen mistrustful of both of the former. There was a lack of confidence affecting work. Factions were developing. Some were deeply involved in revolutionary activity. Others were becoming more conservative in their reaction to the reality. Some were speaking out too freely and others were not saying enough.

The most obvious reasons for the drop in personnel was the fact that back home, in the United States, the church was beginning to feel the first effects of the vocations crunch. If there were to be fewer priests to serve the church in the United States, it followed that there would be fewer priests to meet the church's mission commitment. The Latin America Division laid its cards on the table early in the game, warning, in a 1969 news release, that the United States might not be able to continue supplying "any substantial number of personnel for work in Latin America" because of the pinch resulting from decreases in the rolls of the U.S. priesthood.

Not all in the release was pessimistic: "Sixty-three percent of the men's communities and 52 percent of the communities of women expect to remain in Latin America for the next five years," the division's article continued. But then, it admitted frankly: "This again is a hope which may not come to fruition due to the decrease in vocations."

But the constant tension and sparring among missioners and the vocations situation were only part of the picture. The period was one of unparalleled social unrest in the church, the philosophical changes wrought by the Vatican Council only now beginning to be felt in the front lines. There was an unprecedented freedom to question, to challenge, to be daring, to be different—all taking place in an atmosphere which, situated so far from home and traditional supervision, gave U.S. missioners a heady taste of freedom.

"The life here is very free," admitted Father Elias Manning, superior of an Oblate province in Brazil. "In one sense, you can abuse it . . . or you can really grow as a religious. Some men don't know what to do with the liberty; they can't handle it. You're forced to walk, to start walking out on a limb. It can help you to grow a lot more personally, but you can also fall off the limb."

As the end of the sixties approached, too many U.S. missioners were falling off the limb. Many of those who left the priesthood were married, apparently in greater numbers than for non-mission priests at home (although as of 1977, no large-scale study had been developed to contrast the two groups).

Father McGuire commented:

Father Considine used to say that a community without too much experience shouldn't go into a rural, lonely area—because they can't take it; they don't have that support which a missionary community gets. He would always recommend that they take something easier. Lonesomeness brings on tendencies . . . and so many times it was the priest and sister who married each other. They worked together in an isolated situation, and before long they were leaning on each other for support.

It was a critical period, recalls Maryknoll Father Tom Burns, a Long Islander who was ordained in 1969 and has been in Peru almost ever since:

My class seemed to be the breaking point of that whole period when priests were leaving in large numbers. We had twenty ordained in 1969, and for four years we lost no one at all, while the class ahead of us lost ten. Sixteen of our group are still priests, and of the four who left, two are working as lay missionaries. But we were prepared for the worst. I remember the first day we arrived in the language school at Cochabamba, and the leader talking to us in the orientation period. He said, "Shake hands with the guy next to you. He won't be here a year from now."

At the same time, a revolution of sorts was taking place in the U.S. seminaries. Students there were experiencing a new wave of freedom, coming in on the wings of Vatican II, which exposed them, as they had rarely been exposed before, to the outside world. They fell somewhere between two particularly restless groups of the period—the college students, whose protests centered on civil rights and the Vietnam war, and the young priests, impatient with the sluggish pace at which the church was adapting to the spirit of the Council—and the seminarians were quick to adopt the activism common to both. (Burns himself knew the situation; he headed, before his ordination, the Northeast Seminarians' organization that called for reform in especially strident fashion.)

"I found it hard to relate to our students when I came back from Peru in 1971," Father William McIntire said of his experience at Maryknoll. "They were angry, and I could understand that in the light of political developments. But it was still hard to relate to them."

Newly-ordained priests brought this attitude of unaccustomed activism with them, in many cases, to mission assignments, stretching already polarized communities almost to the breaking point. The veterans were frequently defensive, as had been evidenced a few years earlier in the response to Ivan Illich's challenging article in *America*.

Father Charles D. Gorman, a Washington, D.C., priest writing to the magazine from Santa Cruz, Bolivia, was fairly restrained in his response to Illich. He spoke, in effect, for hundreds of U.S. missioners of the period. Missioners were constantly restudying their policies, he argued; the overall picture was quite encouraging. There were other foreign missioners besides those from the United States; surely their work was no "extension of American foreign policy." All the foreign priests, he said—including the U.S. missioners —"have helped very definitely to change the dying church into one that has promise for the future."

The tone of Father Joseph Heim's letter (from Caracas) was more bitter:

> With one stroke of the pen, Monsignor Illich overrides a plea of the Holy Father, criticizes the North American bishops, insults the South American bishops, declares useless the efforts of missionary priests, nuns and laymen in South America, and—to insure a hearing from the "in-group" —takes a few swipes at United States intervention in Vietnam.
>
> Thank God that Monsignor Illich wasn't on hand to counsel St. Paul, or the apostle would have been dissuaded from ever leaving Palestine! If what is "foreign" is good, why shouldn't it be offered: If North America has personnel and material assistance to offer, by what incredible reversal of Christian thinking shouldn't it share its gifts with its neighbors?

Gorman and Heim were writing as individuals, but their comments were typical of those who had been through the mission mill, and resented Johnny-come-latelies telling them it had all been a waste.

However, another mission group, younger, for the most part, and with less time in the field, responded differently. The Illich thesis was making its mark. By the end of the decade more and more people, if not agreeing with him, were at least asking themselves the questions he had posed. Are we doing more harm than good? Is the whole effort going for naught? Do the Latin Americans even want us?

Listening to the Latins

They were asking the same questions in Washington, too, so much so that the Division for Latin America ultimately decided to look for the answers at the source: from the Latin Americans themselves. With the cooperation of the

Confederation of Latin American Religious (CLAR), the division convoked a meeting at which representatives of religious communities in the United States and Canada would go to listen to Latin American leaders in an effort to determine what works their missioners should undertake, if any, and what ones they shouldn't.

The conference opened February 8, 1971, at Casa Javier, a Jesuit retreat house outside Mexico City, and the keynoter was Mike Colonnese. He acknowledged that the U.S. mission effort in Latin America was at a crossroads, referring to calls for the endeavor to be downgraded if not abandoned. "They believe," he said, speaking of the program's critics, "that the presence of North American mission personnel artificially sustains non-responsive Latin American church structures that would otherwise collapse. This allegedly results in the indefinite postponement of long-delayed church renewal and realignment of pastoral priorities."

Colonnese referred to the unhappiness of many U.S. missioners. They were upset by the critics who lumped them all together when they complained about the ineffectiveness of U.S. mission people, he said, and they were conversely embarrassed by the praise lavished on them by Latin American bishops, fearful of losing the foreign personnel they felt they needed. U.S. missioners throughout Latin America were questioning their role, Colonnese said: "They live with the disquieting awareness of being simultaneously invited guests and interlopers."

Even at this late date, more than a decade after the Latin American mission program had begun in earnest, there was yet another reference to the inadequacy of preparation for the assignment. Colonnese quoted one especially candid admission from Bishop Thomas Manning, the Franciscan bishop of Coroico, Bolivia:

The biggest problem I had was not knowing Bolivia, its history, culture, people, and church. I suppose when I came, our superiors did not think this important. I tried to solve my problems by being with the people, using the language in conversation and reading everything I could get my hands on, especially newspapers. I certainly don't recommend this for anyone.

The Casa Javier meeting went on for four days, its final recommendations emerging as something of a set of standards, accepted by common consent, for United States mission operations in Latin America, for diocesan and lay missioners as well as those from religious communities.

As the meeting concluded, Father Renato Poblete, the Chilean Jesuit, and Bishop Eduardo Pironio, the CELAM president, stressed the points involved in the agreement. Even though "no urgent call has been heard similar to the one in the 1960s," Poblete said, Latin America still needed North American missioners, but it was interested more in quality than in quantity. "With a better screening process," he said, "fewer people will be chosen; North American superiors will not just send anybody who is available. It is felt that small numbers of religious will be able to accomplish more, because they will be better selected and prepared."

Said Pironio:

> Aid makes sense only when the receiving church decides to ask for it and use it. Methods must not be imposed, nor should patterns from elsewhere, however effective they may have proved there, be imported unchanged. . . . Anyone who comes to Latin America should arrive aware that God has special designs for this continent.

The old-line U.S. missioners were confused, and so were some of the more recent arrivals whose preparation had never caught up with the demands of the times. They wanted assurance that yes, indeed, their presence was welcome—no, more than that, *needed*. What they were getting, instead, was talk of quality rather than quantity and warnings about imposing methods from the outside. This, on top of the Illiches, the radical priests, and the liberation theologians—people who barely tolerated the U.S. presence in Latin America—was, simply, too much to take. The frustrations of the job, the loneliness, the failure to see any change for the better, the unrelenting poverty and oppression—all of these might be borne, many missioners reasoned, if they knew they were wanted. Without that, why bother? There was work to be done at home, for some; for others, there was a new life outside the church, or at least outside the active ministry.

They were, many of them, the brightest hopes of the U.S. church of the sixties. Their special crusade began in the clear, hopeful days of John F. Kennedy, of armies for peace and alliances for progress, of a church that stood rock-firm, of a pope whose heart seemed big enough to hold the world. It ended, quietly, in the gathering darkness of a fortress presidency and a troubled pope, a church that was offering options instead of answers, and a war in Vietnam that was tearing the United States apart.

Those who came home found that the crusading spirit toward Latin America inspired by Pope John had vanished; in its place was a grim determination to meet commitments and to avoid, at all costs, the embarrassment of a pullout. The parallels between the church's involvement in Latin America and the national involvement in Vietnam were all too obvious, except that, in 1970, there were still many people who thought the war in Vietnam could be won. Few U.S. church leaders familiar with our problems in Latin America harbored any delusions in that direction. Just as U.S. enthusiasm for the Vietnam endeavor was flagging, so was the U.S. church's zeal to "save" Latin America. It showed up at all levels of the U.S. church, including the structures that had been set up to give the Latin American program its base of support.

None of those structures was in more trouble than the Papal Volunteers for Latin America, and no one realized it more than the organization's new director. Tom Quigley knew what kind of shape PAVLA was in even before he took over the reigns from Father George Mader, the Newarker who had been the temporary successor to Father Kevane. The program was critically ill; all that remained to be done was to deliver the coup de grace, and Quigley set the stage for that in a lengthy memo to diocesan PAVLA directors dated April 8, 1970:

> Granting the high degree of success achieved by some Papal Volunteers, the rate of apparent failure (measured solely in terms of statements of dissatisfaction by both the volunteers and project directors, and by early termination) is disastrously high.

Quigley cited a dozen more glaring problems, among them the inadequate servicing of volunteers' needs, the amount of dissatisfaction among the volunteers, the lack of acceptable projects and the low number of qualified applicants, the continued inadequacy of training, financial problems at headquarters, and the extraordinarily high rate (over 50 percent) of early termination by the volunteers. "At least for the time being," Quigley concluded, "we will simply have to be most restrictive in the number and kind of volunteers to be accepted." This meant, he explained, persons of unusual maturity with specific skills, training, and experience, and with a particular interest in participating in the contemporary struggle of Latin American life, as opposed to someone looking for volunteer service in general.

> Typically, we will have to discourage applications from families (housing, health, and educational problems are still far from solved), from teachers (a general moratorium on placing teachers in middle-class schools or in positions for which nationals could be found), from recent college graduates (because of CELAM's insistence on exceptional maturity, skills, and experience), and from older people. . . .
> PAVLA is either a very special kind of program or it is one without a clear reason for existence. There are plenty of generalist volunteer programs around. The Latin Americans, for whom alone this program exists, have made it abundantly clear that they would prefer a very few but very special kind of collaborators to a large group of well-intentioned but inadequate volunteers. The question then becomes, do we have the kind of people that Latin America needs?

Quigley wrote a personal letter that same week which hinted more directly at his state of mind in regard to PAVLA and volunteerism in general:

> Because of the Peace Corps, which initially made volunteer service not

only respectable but, for a time, the thing to do, and because of groups like PAVLA, there will continue to be people like teachers, counselors, pastors, etc., promoting a form long after its content has disappeared. It's easier, after all, to recommend that someone go off and join a voluntary group than to sit down and counsel with him about what he really wants to do and is able to at this stage of his life and within the context of real needs and opportunities in his own community.

Mader, back in Newark after his brief interim administration of PAVLA, could see that the organization was about to be abandoned and made a back-to-the-wall effort to keep it going through a paper delivered in June 1970 to members of PAVLA's executive board, meeting in Washington. Reviewing Kevane's resignation the previous year, he was sympathetic to the former director:

> I feel he was ultimately just plain tired with the weariness of those who must face continual frustration with no real immediate hope of achieving a goal. At the same time, he and he alone was responsible for the fact that we [diocesan directors] continued with PAVLA ourselves over the years.

His own problems with PAVLA, Mader said, centered not on policy matters but rather on the apparent lack of communication, and crossed communication, between the national office, volunteers' dioceses, and field representatives. That problem had worsened, he continued, after Kevane left, since all but one of his staff had left with him. The "chaos" that he encountered on assuming the temporary directorship, mostly due to previous administrative shortcomings, was being eliminated, he said, with the assistance of Father Fred McGuire and others on the Latin America Division staff.

Keep PAVLA going, he pleaded: "If the Latin Americans do not want us, as some contend, then let them tell us. Let the dissolution of the program come from proof and not from lack of response to quota forms presently in the files of the Latin America Division which are outdated and obsolete." He quoted from Dom Helder Camara to indicate the desire of leading Latin American church leaders for "volunteers from wealthy countries" and warned of what would happen if PAVLA were phased out:

> It will encourage only poorer communication; misfits will be accepted by projects which should not be serviced; the laity will be patronized; the images of the church and the country will be worse than they are now. . . . If we stop now to stand back and assume a very scholarly though sincere attitude toward the poor amoeba on our classroom slides, we may never again regain the momentum built up over the years

through the dreams, sweat, and prayers of many great and sincere and generous men and women, religious and lay . . .

I entered this assignment on a temporary basis because I believed and continue to believe in the program's concepts. . . . I have no intention of attending PAVLA's wake. . . . I came here to help raise the program, not to bury it.

But burial was not far off. Despite the impassioned pleas of Mader and others who wanted to keep PAVLA going, its problems outweighed whatever promise it had left, and both Quigley and Colonnese were arranging for the last rites. The Colonnese-Kevane squabbling over PAVLA had endured even after the 1968 decision establishing the Latin America Division-PAVLA chain of command. "I knew the fight had not ended, nor had it been won," Colonnese wrote. In the interregnum under Mader, the division director did nothing to encourage anyone to start thinking about long-range plans for PAVLA. ("Colonnese thought I was a nice guy," Mader remarked, "but that I knew nothing about Latin America.")

Then Colonnese wrote to a number of bishops and other influential church people, both religious and lay, seeking their thoughts about PAVLA. Most felt, along with Colonnese, that the program had run its course, and he passed their comments along to the bishops' Latin America committee, with his own recommendation that PAVLA be discontinued. "After much dissent, fighting, and even scandal," Colonnese said, "the bishops agreed."

Quigley made the announcement in May 1971, confirming for NC News Service a report that PAVLA was being phased out of existence. Volunteers would no longer be recruited or trained, Quigley said, but those already in Latin America could be expected to finish out their terms of service. NC's story quoted a memo on the reasons behind the phaseout sent by Quigley to the diocesan directors and other interested parties, particularly the U.S. Catholic Conference's International Affairs Department. Although millions had been spent on PAVLA, the memo said, "there is little to show for this." There was "virtually nothing" in Latin America itself to give testimony to the expenditure, and "we have little evidence that former Papal Volunteers have done much to raise the North American consciousness of the Latin America reality." The memo continued:

More negatively, PAVLA has had its share of serious failures, people whose lives have become more messed up, who in effect have been at least temporarily ruined precisely because of PAVLA.

These are the people for whom the burden of trying to function in a highly unstructured situation in another country proved too much.

Some of these are casualties of the unrealistic inflated rhetoric of PAVLA, a messianic rhetoric borrowed from nineteenth century missiology, which . . . suffered a rude reversal upon contact with the Latin American reality.

Many people who were familiar with the working of PAVLA had different slants on what had gone wrong. "I think there might have been as much need for a re-entry program as there was for preparation," said Frances Neason, director of the bishops' present-day Secretariat for Latin America. Father Walter George, a Redemptorist who spent nearly twenty-five years in Brazil, and who served as regional coordinator for PAVLA, pointed to another area of weakness:

> My difficulty with PAVLA was that the program in the States was so built on motivation, and motivation alone. In other words, the volunteers felt their presence was justified by their motives alone. They didn't have the corresponding interest in programs, new or old.

Someone who was able to look at PAVLA from an especially unique vantage point said the "old-style PAVLA" created a very sophisticated dependency. "I just didn't know how to deal with that," said Barbara Webber, who had the distinction of being the last Papal Volunteer. A native Texan who was graduated from St. Mary's College at Notre Dame with a degree in Latin American affairs, she joined PAVLA in 1970 and stayed on, in a rural diocese in Northeast Brazil, until March 1975. She later recalled:

> In that '69–'70 period, when I joined PAVLA, people were having second thoughts. They no longer saw themselves as going out to save the world. The need I felt was not so much for more people to go to Latin America, but to make people at home aware of things. There should be an exchange of dialogue, much more of it, so the Americans become aware of Third World realities and answers. I see the church having a special role in this; constantly reminding the community what it's supposed to be about.

Webber's PAVLA assignment marked her second tour of duty in South America. She had spent a year in Bogota in 1968, initially through St. Louis University, but she stayed on for an unusual personal reason:

> We were living in a slum area, working in a program aimed at improving things in the *barrios*, mostly visiting people and helping however we could. We came across two small children, five and two years old, who were locked inside a room, their muscles and limbs atrophied by the confinement. They were the youngest two of eight children whose mother had to work, and so they were simply locked up. We were horrified, of course, and got them to a hospital, with the mother's permission. The doctors were surprised to see us, but not the children.

"We get cases like this all the time," they said. The doctor who headed the therapy department agreed to treat them if we would bring them in, and so I just decided to stay down. I moved in with a group of Colombian sisters and stayed for a year. This was my initiation. Most of the people with whom I was in contact were Indian; I learned through their eyes.

After spending most of 1969 in Europe, Webber joined PAVLA through the Indiana dioceses, which provided financial support. She liked her assignment to Brazil:

If we were to do anything, I felt it should be pastoral, and that tied in with the bishop's own plan. He wanted to pull the diocese closer together, paying special attention to the development of basic Christian communities. I visited people, helping with community organization work.

Did she feel as if she had accomplished anything?

Definitely, yes. This was the new PAVLA, and I was able to act as a catalyst and get things started, things you could really see working. But sooner or later, I knew it would be time to go. And then that time came. I felt I had gone as far as I could in one sense, and in another sense that I hadn't even begun to scratch the surface.

CICOP: Losing Its Way

It was early in the new decade, and PAVLA was already dead. CICOP didn't have much longer to go. The inter-American conferences that had begun with such promise and flair in 1964 were becoming increasingly political, increasingly radical. Conservatives were scandalized, moderates were annoyed, and even liberals found that in the early seventies the CICOP conferences seemed to have lost their way—and their effectiveness.

"I recall the CICOP conference in Washington in 1971," said Father William McIntire. "We were flinging marshmallows across the room as a gesture of sharing in liturgies which seemed to have become for some more symbolic than real. One of my old friends turned to me and said he had heard at the conference some of the most un-Christian things he had ever heard, and I was forced to agree with him." It was a time, McIntire said, when "church people seemed to be flailing out in some absurdly rightist or leftist directions, with all kinds of petty hangups and very little evidence of the peace of Christ."

Father Walter George:

The same small group of people, hand-picked because of their radical positions, came to the fore year after year. There was no effort to be objective. At the last CICOP meeting I attended I remember Harvey Cox starting out with a slide presentation showing tourist pictures, then, with sarcasm, the "true picture," blood-drenched generals and mud huts. There was also a dramatization of Brazilian "tortures" by a women's urban guerrilla theater. It seemed as though they were trying to outdo one another with silly caricatures. It would have been a laugh if it wasn't so pitiful.

Father Mader recalled seeing Vietcong flags displayed at the 1971 meeting in Washington, and Father Vincent Mallon, who conceded that CICOP had gotten off to a good start as a mission education vehicle, lamented the direction it had taken. "It fell into the hands of ideologues who did not represent all of the church," he said. "They were men with one drum to beat."

Tom Quigley, who had a hand in shaping the CICOP format in later years, admitted that it had undergone a significant transformation. "After 1968, the watershed year, CICOP changed," he said. "It became less a general education program and more of an advocacy forum, a place where different views were heatedly expressed."

Even Father Colonnese, CICOP's chief architect, saw its radicalization nearly get the better of him at the 1970 meeting, held in Washington. It was a meeting he referred to as crucial, since the conscientization with which delegates were so concerned seemed to be taking place within the conference itself. At one point, Dr. Julio de Santa Ana, a Protestant speaker from Uruguay, spoke so forthrightly about violence and oppression in Latin America that the CICOP participants became incensed and called for a march on the State Department. With other organizers of the meeting, Colonnese was able to calm the assembly, but it had been a close call. "I felt we were being deliberately pushed from the left," Colonnese said. "They wanted us to declare ourselves. My commitment was to radical change, but I was committed to no specific political formula, and less still to the Marxists' position—which many would have been delighted to see me adopt."

The meeting had been intended to be free of conflict; instead it turned out to be the most controversial CICOP conference up to that point. Paulo Freire, in the final major address, said the conference had "reached out effectively in a preliminary to true conscientization." That might have pleased some of the delegates, but it infuriated the bishops and embarrassed and angered many of the USCC staff people. Colonnese's position with the bishops was becoming more precarious. He recalled:

I knew by this time that there was nothing the bishops wanted more than to bring CICOP to a halt. But the only explanation I can offer for their hesitancy in doing so was the wide acceptance CICOP had earned among a large number of Latin American bishops, especially among the representatives of CELAM, who were still at the time a progressive element in the Latin American hierarchy.

When Colonnese began preparations for the 1971 conference, also to be held in Washington, he said he did so as if it would be his last—and he turned out to be right. The ungainly theme of the meeting was wide in its scope: "Freedom and Unfreedom: A Theological Reflection on the Human Situation in the Americas." Said Colonnese:

> We knew that we couldn't separate the oppression in Latin America from the oppression in the United States. It was all part of the same system and process. The stops were all pulled out. Conference speakers were among the best Latin America could send us at the time. . . . Brazilian exiles, radical revolutionaries from Latin America and the United States, grassroots people and intellectuals. They were all there to present the most controversial and probably most successful CICOP meeting we ever had.

Colonnese said a "wave of excitement" covered the conference, which featured discussions on powerlessness, dependency, oppression, violence, liberation, and commitment. But others were less impressed. "The conservatives were aghast," Colonnese said, and a State Department representative said CICOP had reached dangerous heights. Boston's Cardinal Medeiros, who had then been archbishop of Boston for only a few months, gave Colonnese "gentle but firm" warnings about CICOP's future, and Bishop Joseph Green—"who always remained a friend"—offered his own expression of concern. Some registrants wanted their money back, Colonnese said, because, as one irate participant put it, no one had realized that CICOP had become a hornet's nest of Marxists.

"I was told by Bishop [Joseph L.] Bernardin [then the NCCB-USCC general secretary] that such a conference would never, never be repeated," Colonnese recalled.

> But I was not dismayed. I really was convinced there was no further need for CICOP. . . . It was the 1971 CICOP conference's objective to discover the root causes of these problems and understand the conditions which favor their appearance. We would turn to theology to assist us in our quest for the knowledge which would lead to decisive action. And the theological answers we obtained would help determine the shape of the action to be taken by agents of social change. We were seeking totally Christian human solutions. We were not Marxists.

The CICOP conferences continued through 1973, running out their tenyear commitment period, but without Colonnese, a passive observer at the 1972 meeting on "Communications in the Americas," and an absentee from the final 1973 session in Dallas. The meetings held together, he later conceded, but the mystique, the notion of movement, the vigor and vitality of past CICOP sessions were gone. "The bishops felt that CICOP had served its purpose," said Frances Neason, "and was now mostly a case of the converted talking to the converted. It wasn't the vehicle any longer to do what had to be done."

The more conservative bishops had been disenchanted with CICOP for some time and were eager to see its demise. But others, including some in influential positions such as Cardinal Medeiros and Bishop James S. Rausch, who succeeded Bernardin as general secretary of the conference in 1972, wanted to keep it going, even if under some new kind of format. Cardinal Dearden, who headed the conference until 1972, was thought to be in favor of continuing the program, but ultimately he made the decisive move in the opposite direction. Conservatives at home and in Latin America were increasingly disillusioned with CICOP. Now that the ten-year period is up, he said in effect, let's give it a rest.

In August 1973, an NC News Service story reported an announcement of the USCC Latin America Division to the effect that the CICOP conferences would be discontinued in their "present form." Father Fred McGuire said the Latin America Division believed that CICOP "has been a success and that the U.S. church should not diminish its commitment to inter-American dialogue, cooperation, and action." Changing the format of CICOP, he said, "does not signal abandonment of that commitment."

The theme of the 1973 meeting was "Poverty, Environment, and Power: Issues of Justice in the Americas." And that was where CICOP died, in Dallas.

Bishop Bernardin had made it fairly obvious in 1971, after the Washington CICOP meeting, that Colonnese's time was growing short. But time had actually been running out on Colonnese and the Latin America Division since a meeting that took place in Caracas in 1969. The background of the meeting went back a year, to the first formal inter-American conference of bishops in Detroit in 1968. That meeting had been concerned primarily with information, but Colonnese saw the need to go far beyond that: "I felt I had been not at all effective in trying to convey to the American bishops the sense of urgency which confronted the Latin American church, the necessity of total freedom for that church." Future meetings of the bishops of the hemisphere, he believed, should be more profound, and should deal with political and theological realities such as the growing demand for liberation.

"But how could this be accomplished," he later asked, "when there was almost a terrifying reaction on the part of the North American churchmen and even Europeans to this newly-developed theology?" He went to Bogota in March 1969 to prepare, with Latin American colleagues, an agenda for a meeting that June in Caracas, the second major meeting of representatives of the hierarchies of North and South America. Colonnese said:

We devised an agenda which would hopefully force the issue. We assigned a paper to be delivered by the Latins on the pastoral lines which were indicated at Medellín for Latin American pastoral development. In this session we thought that a discussion of liberation theology would arise. The economic dependence of the Latin church on North Americans would be discussed, the question of foreign missionary assistance to Latin America, and other related topics.

The meeting which started with such lofty hopes ended in frustrations, disappointment, and recriminations, for reasons which were not totally unavoidable. According to Colonnese:

> The site of the meeting was a pleasant minor seminary building, simple in appearance, but pleasant and clean. The American bishops chose to stay at the largest and most luxurious hotel in Caracas while the Latin prelates (including the cardinals) chose to live at the seminary. This very fact was divisive. Time in the evenings which would normally be spent in pleasant interchange was lost. The Latins felt the slight because they told me so. I knew that because of this very fact, even if nothing more serious occurred, the meeting was doomed to failure.

Some U.S. bishops—including, according to Colonnese, Philadelphia's Cardinal John Krol, then vice president and later president of the conference —were unhappy over the introduction of a discussion on the nationalization by Peru of the International Petroleum Company, and the subject was dropped. The meeting's final document was a watered-down general statement that was pushed hard by the North Americans and agreed to reluctantly (except in the case of a conservative Venezuelan delegation) by most of the Latins present. The document said:

> It is recognized at this time that, when we speak of such problems [social, economic, and cultural], we frequently take differing situations as our point of departure and we find that we are speaking from different frames of reference as regards to culture and even ecclesiastical traditions, which facts make more difficult mutual understanding and the exercise of the responsibility that we have in common.

(Colonnese disagreed sharply: "What the American bishops had forgotten was that there was, in fact, a very common ground for their discussion; that both groups of bishops could begin from a common reference, that of the gospel, the encyclicals, the documents of the Vatican Council, statements of the Holy Father. The fact is, the American bishops took a totally imperialistic approach with regard to their Latin brothers. I learned later on that the bishops had consulted with a representative of the State Department prior to the meeting. They had been well prepared for their role. The meeting was sabotaged.")

There was less problem in reaching accord on the section of the document relating directly to mission work, with the North Americans accepting what their Latin brothers had to say about selection, training, and placement of U.S. personnel in Latin America. "It was easy," Colonnese noted, "because the number of Americans going to Latin America was dwindling rapidly."

Colonnese was patently unhappy with the direction the meeting had taken and with its rather abrupt termination—considerably earlier than had been planned—due, he felt, to the lack of enthusiasm on the part of the North Americans. Rarely able to submerge a complaint, he had an unexpectedly wide audience when it came time to voice his dissatisfaction. It happened because a projected (and coincidental) visit to Venezuela by President Richard Nixon was canceled due to predicted unfriendly demonstrations, and a corps of U.S. reporters in Caracas for the Nixon appearance found themselves looking for a story. They heard about the inter-American bishops' meeting and, attempting to salvage their trip with some kind of news, went to the seminary and tried to see the U.S. bishops—without success.

"Highly incensed by this," Colonnese said, "I agreed to see the reporters and I did. I spoke with total frankness about what had happened at the meeting. The stories went out over the wire and they were not flattering to the North American bishops. . . ."

Both sides agree that the Caracas meeting was a decisive factor in the eventual full deterioration of relations between Colonnese and the bishops. It was at that time, he said, that he found the bishops to be "false and shallow," and they began to find him unmanageable. McGuire recalls that it was immediately after the Caracas meeting that Cardinal Dearden, presiding for the United States delegation, decided that future inter-American bishops' meetings would be under direct control of the National Conference of Catholic Bishops, as they have remained since.

The meeting in 1970 was held in Miami, and the Latin America Division had a new representative on hand. Father McGuire's old Mission Secretariat had been abolished to make way for the new U.S. Mission Council (which would be developed more in conformity with the Vatican Council view that mission activity was the responsibility of the full church family, rather than simply its religious communities). Since the veteran missioner McGuire was unattached, Colonnese urged him to join the division, and, with Cardinal Cushing's assistance, saw that he was named associate director. It was McGuire who went to the Miami meeting, Colonnese having decided it would be "unwise" to attend himself. Later he wrote:

> The Miami meeting was taken out of my hands by the American bishops. It was told to me in a rather casual way. In a letter to me of September 26, 1969, Bishop Bernardin stated: "As you know, the meeting is now sponsored by the conference rather than the Division for Latin America." No, I didn't know it, but it didn't surprise me either. The bishops with their authoritarian manner had again destroyed what might

have been a true fellowship, a true meeting for dialogue, an attempt to bring brothers of the same church closer together.

Time of Trial for Colonnese

The Caracas encounter was not the only problem that Colonnese and the bishops had with each other; far from it. Indeed, the record makes it appear as if Colonnese's two-year administration was a period of unrelieved confrontation. To some degree, it was a reflection of the turmoil faced by the church on many fronts at that time. But more than that, it mirrored Colonnese's own views of problem areas and his manner of dealing with them. It was a result of Colonnese's impatience with the bureaucratic trappings in which he saw the conference becoming increasingly enmeshed, and his conviction that the bishops were doing nothing of substance to increase their understanding—and the understanding of the U.S. Catholic public—of Latin American realities.

There was also the matter of finances. Unlike other offices of the conference, the Latin America Division raised all of its own funds, including its operating expenses, but the conference wanted control of expenditures, particularly after institution of a centralized planning system in 1970. Colonnese, predictably, was unhappy with that suggestion: "My argument was precisely that the Latin America Division had no budget from USCC, and consequently the USCC was not responsible for what we spent or did not spend."

In a related matter, Colonnese had a problem with the 1968 USCC reorganization that left the old Latin America Bureau as the new Latin America Division, one of the several divisions within the conference's Department of International Affairs (headed by Monsignor Marvin Bordelon). It was not that the arrangement was unwelcome in itself, Colonnese said; it was simply that the chain-of-command approach made for a more bureaucratic atmosphere, when openness and flexibility were called for. A particularly rankling feature of the new system was the one that required all policy statements to be cleared at the department level.

The one great problem with the Latin America Division under this table of organization, Colonnese said, was that "it was not able to confine itself to the very narrow and very restricted area of activity which the USCC was trying to impose on it. We were not allowed flexibility. Bureaucratic requirements prevented us from responding with the vigor and timeliness of evangelical enthusiasm. Even an emotional sentiment seemed to require executive approval."

Colonnese fired off a memo to Bordelon complaining that the "no statements or declarations" rule imposed on division heads was especially difficult for the Latin America Division to observe. ("Our division was well known for its fiery statements from time to time.") The new set of regulations, Colonnese contended, had the effect of denying basic rights to people within the USCC organization, preventing them from fulfilling the obligations of their consciences. He felt the rules reflected USCC's "insecurity" and what he termed its double life: "one of political expediency (diplomacy) with the world, and the other pastoral."

He hinted at darker thoughts on the part of the USCC hierarchy: "There was little doubt in the minds of most of the personnel (those who were informed) of USCC that all of this discussion concerning public statements and declarations was due to the posture assumed by the Latin America Division in this matter."

The committee set up to approve the issuance of such statements was well-intentioned and intelligent, Colonnese said, but each new statement required a process of educating the committee, which consumed valuable time and lessened the impact of whatever statement was being made. Ultimately, Colonnese took another tack. When he felt the occasion required it, he simply issued statements on his own. Those declarations might have been timely, but they also served to widen the growing gap between him and officials of the conference.

Differences on budget and policy matters had practical effects, to be sure, but they were basically philosophical disagreements. There were disputes as well over specific actions taken by Colonnese, so many, in fact, that in retrospect they seem to have consumed almost all of the available working time, to the ultimate detriment, one imagines, of the overall Latin America program.

One such difference, with lingering international repercussions, revolved around the question of torture in Brazil. It began, innocently enough, with a papal audience arranged by Cardinal Samore for Colonnese in June 1969. In the course of the audience, Colonnese gave Pope Paul documents concerning a policy of torture allegedly being carried out in Brazil. He agreed to the pontiff's request that the documents not be made public. The following day, however, Vatican Radio did just that, at which point Colonnese, who believed that the papal restriction no longer applied, went ahead and gave a copy of the information to a wire service reporter.

When the story appeared in the *Washington Post* the day after that, Colonnese received a wire from home, directing him to "cease activities" in Rome. A memo from then-Monsignor Frank Hurley, at the time the USCC associate general secretary, said the story had given him some concern: "It does not seem appropriate to comment on a papal audience that deals with such a sensitive issue."

Scarcely less sensitive was another matter that arose during the same visit to Rome: a Colonnese press conference in which he referred critically to New York Governor Nelson A. Rockefeller's official visit to Latin America. Colonnese said that a Rockefeller staff member had asked Michael Leneghan of the Latin America Division for assistance in preparing the final draft of the official report, but Colonnese vetoed the proposal. In his press conference, he said that the section of the Rockefeller report dealing with religion "would probably be superficial," and that he wanted no part of it.

Monsignor Hurley (who went on to become bishop of Juneau, and then archbishop of Anchorage) was in quick touch with Rome again, reminding Colonnese that there was no need to publicize the fact that government officials might seek the advice of people in the church: "There are too many who seize information of this type as evidence of collusion between church and state in political affairs." Writing about the incident some years later, Colonnese referred to it as "another example" of the "diplomatic thinking" that he felt governed the conference. "The fact that Rockefeller's staff member had sought collusion seemed to be of little consequence," he noted. "And the collusion sought was to the detriment of our sister church in Latin America."

Still another incident that year which stretched the differences between Colonnese and the conference centered on Cuba. Eight Cuban Catholic bishops, quoting from *Populorum Progressio* to support their stand, attacked the United States blockade of the island, which, they said, was "contributing to unnecessary suffering and making all efforts at development more difficult." On his own initiative, Colonnese issued a statement backing the Cuban bishops, "not because of economic and political motivation, but because I agreed with their assessment that the embargo offended against the dignity of the Cuban people by imposing unnecessary suffering and deprivation."

Colonnese's action touched off more of a storm than had the original Cuban declaration. "The next day the Latin America Division offices were almost unmanageable," he said. There was a stream of telephone calls and telegrams, many from Cubans in the United States. A heavy percentage of the messages came from the Miami area, the Cuban refugee stronghold. "While there was positively favorable reaction to my statement, the majority of the calls and telegrams and letters were negative, some threatening and many obscene."

Several of the messages contained threats, and because some of them were phoned in to his unlisted apartment number, Colonnese took them seriously. (He remained security-conscious. Father George Mader recalls entering Colonnese's office when the bureau was at 14th and K Streets to come upon the director elaborately signaling for silence while he probed the walls with a sound-detecting device. He explained later that someone had told him the office was bugged.)

Some were sympathetic to Colonnese's position, and took the trouble to tell him so. Monsignor George Higgins, then director of the conference's Division for Urban Life, praised his courage and his handling of the situation, and there was a similar message of support from the Rev. William Wipfler, Colonnese's counterpart as head of the Department for Latin America of the National Council of Churches. But they and a few others were the exceptions. For many members of the hierarchy, the Cuban statement was one more indication that Colonnese was simply too reckless to operate as freely as he had in the past.

Still another Colonnese statement that touched off a furor in both the conference and the State Department was issued the following year, following the mysterious death in Uruguay, at the hands of guerrillas, of Dan Mitrione, an Agency for International Development employee. There were reports that Mitrione, a police adviser, was actually instructing secret police in torture methods, as he had been alleged to have done in Brazil as well, and Colonnese issued a statement calling for a full investigation. "I was not attacking the revered memory of a dead man," he later said. "That was an unfortunate and unavoidable byproduct of my earnest desire to criticize and expose the nefarious work of the AID public safety program in Latin America."

The statement drew a favorable reaction in some quarters. The Jesuit theologian Juan Luis Segundo wrote from Uruguay:

> Above all, I wish to congratulate you on your declaration on the notorious event which took place here. Certainly, thanks to you and your role, the image of the American bishops has changed very much, and true or not, it has become favorable even in non-Christian circles and among people radically opposed to any kind of imperialism. It is an excellent point in your favor.

But elsewhere Colonnese's stand sowed bitterness. Father Walter George, an outspoken critic of Colonnese in general, was particularly incensed with the Mitrione statement. Mitrione, George contends, was a good Catholic whose influence with the police in Brazil, where he had known him, stressed social obligations involved in their work. George said in an interview:

> Colonnese gave the coup de grace to many aspects of the Latin American program with his negative publicity. He pictured Latin America simply as a place of torture, guerrilla warfare, where the United States' presence was totally ineffective. The picture was one of a bottomless pit with insoluble problems.
>
> And that was the turning point. American missioners were demoralized because this stuff, centering on the lack of effectiveness of the Americans, kept coming out of Washington week after week. His ideas and those of his supporters were almost elevated to the level of folklore. And at the same time, the far left in Latin America was saying all the same things.

There were still more incidents involving Colonnese that alienated him further from the bishops. A minor flap arose over a rumor that a certain U.S. mission in Central America was working with the Central Intelligence Agency, and Colonnese refused to tell Bernardin the source of his information on the point. Some conservative bishops were upset when Colonnese took a leading role in blocking the bid of a leading South American churchman to have the U.S. church assist him in investing church funds from his own country within the United States, because the South American feared that a new leftist government in his homeland would suppress schools and other institutions. "Not only was I opposed to the whole thing," Colonnese said, "but it was also a hot issue. If it were ever to be discovered, there would be an embarrassing position for the U.S. Catholic church to have to explain."

One who remembers the final days of the division under Colonnese is Father Eugene Culhane, the Jesuit who moved from *America* magazine (as the publication's Latin America specialist) to the USCC in 1970. (He also recalls that little involving Colonnese proceeded along everyday lines; Colonnese was in a hospital oxygen tent, recovering from a near-fatal auto accident, when he interviewed Culhane for the job.)

In a 1976 interview Culhane said:

> More than one missioner complained to me about the division's swing to the left, and I guess there was something to it. I find myself less of a radical now. I see the problems more philosophically since I left. The people with whom we were in contact were always the same. . . . They were spokesmen for jailed Chileans, for Brazilians seeking exit visas, and so on. It did get to you. We mutually exhorted each other to a revolutionary fervor. Now I'm less doctrinaire, but also less enthused.

The constant agitation involving the Latin American Division, within the conference and, ultimately, throughout the church both in North America and Latin America, eventually became too much to contain. The division itself, rather than its activities and policies, was the focus of attention. More and more bishops, politically embarrassed by Colonnese, were calling for his scalp, and even in Latin America, where Colonnese had his strongest base of support, moderates were joining with the more conservative in expressing dissatisfaction with the direction the division was taking.

Bernardin consulted privately with some members of the Latin American hierarchy, who, he later indicated, made it clear that it would be helpful if the Latin America Division were more pastorally oriented and less given to political overtones. That concern, he said, expressed to him at his own request, was the basis for the action he finally took on September 2, 1971. That was the day he fired Mike Colonnese.

Early that afternoon, Colonnese was chairing an informal meeting at the Manger-Hamilton Hotel on 14th Street, a meeting he had called of leaders of some of the new activist groups for sisters, black Catholics, the Spanish-speaking, and others, concerned with issues of justice in the church. Colonnese had gotten them together with the idea of joining forces to form a coalition. Everything about the session was off the record, though, and when his secretary called Colonnese at the hotel to tell him that Bernardin wanted to see him at 4 o'clock, the priest had one quick thought: "Oh-oh, he's found out about this meeting."

But there was a premonition that told him it was something more serious than that, and when he walked into Bernardin's office at 4 and saw the look on his face—"he was glassy-eyed, and looked as though he were close to tears"—he realized what was happening. "This is the end, isn't it?" Colonnese asked, and Bernardin said yes. He gave Colonnese an opportunity to resign as director of the Division for Latin America, and when that was turned down informed him he was fired, effective immediately.

"Why?" was Colonnese's immediate response. Bernardin gave him a letter which listed the reasons for the action, and Colonnese left, in something of a daze, a few minutes later. He went back to the meeting at the Manger-Hamilton, told the participants what had happened, and offered to continue chairing the session. Instead, by common agreement, they adjourned to the bar.

The stories from Religious News Service and NC News Service both reported the hard truth when details of the meeting became known a few days later. Colonnese, they said, had been fired. "Father Colonnese was let go," Bernardin explained in a formal statement, "because many people in this country and Latin America, including many bishops, had lost confidence in his leadership."

Colonnese had another explanation in his own statement to the press: "My ideology was too advanced for the U.S. Catholic Conference," he said. "I have offended powerful men within the U.S. church and they have fired me."

Bernardin's remarks attempted to put the Colonnese role into perspective, from the standpoint of the conference: "In my judgment, he has a great love for Latin America and has made genuine efforts to sensitize North Americans to the conditions of their brothers to the south," he said. He noted that because U.S.-Latin American relations are complex and cause differences of opinion, the Latin America Division director should be someone able to get along with a broad range of people with divergent views.

"Increasingly, Father Colonnese has been unable to do this," Bernardin continued:

Our own observations, together with consultations with competent and responsible observers in Latin America, indicate that he found it more and more difficult to cooperate with those who did not agree with him, and indeed, at times alienated them. As a result, while the good work he has done is freely acknowledged, there has been a lessening of confidence in his leadership.

The dismissal finally took place because of "the loss of a quality which is essential for anyone who works in such an organization: mutual trust and confidence between the staff person and the administration."

Colonnese countered that he was "committed to the full spiritual and material liberation of man in Latin America and everywhere else in the world."

He said he opposed a "Band-aid" developmental approach in Latin America, which he said the U.S. bishops endorse, "because I don't believe society can be reformed at an evolutionary pace. It must be rapidly reconstructed. Therefore, according to their standards and priorities, the United States bishops were entirely correct in firing me."

He discussed the question of violence, which, he pointed out, he had never advocated:

> I have always believed that those who make peaceful revolution impossible make violent revolution inevitable. I have tried to show United States Catholics that the aid and trade policies of this country foster dependency and economic colonialism and exploitation in Latin America, and that they must be changed.

Colonnese spoke of Medellín, and how many who had attempted to implement its guidelines had been tortured, kidnapped, or unjustly imprisoned because "government, military, business, and, regrettably, some church people, seeking to preserve exploitative socio-economic structures which serve the minority at the expense of the misery of millions, consider these Catholics communists. I have attempted to make this situation known to United States Catholics," he concluded. "When I could not be silenced or co-opted, I was fired. But that is a small price to pay compared with the sacrifices being made each day in Latin America by those truly committed to implementing Christian social justice."

The experience was as unsettling for Bernardin as it had been for Colonnese. "I've just had to do one of the nastiest things I've ever done," the general secretary told McGuire immediately after the confrontation. He added that he had no choice, that Colonnese's support within the hierarchy had all but vanished in the wake of the constant turmoil in which the division found itself.

It was just before the Labor Day weekend, a weekend in which Bernardin wanted McGuire to make an important decision: whether to accept an appointment to succeed Colonnese, at least on an acting basis. Walking along the beach by his summer cottage in Delaware over the holiday, the long-time Vincentian missioner, sixty-six years old at the time, weighed the options. Bernardin said he'd probably seek a younger man for permanent appointment, but wanted the benefit of McGuire's experience to help the division recover from the period it had gone through. McGuire returned to Washington Tuesday, September 7, to announce that he would take the job on that basis, but by that time Bernardin decided he would rather go with McGuire than with some of the younger men who had already expressed some interest in the post. He gave McGuire a three-year contract, and the appointment was made public to coincide with the formal news of Colonnese's departure.

"Fred McGuire was a hard-nosed administrator," Gene Culhane said. "The staff at one time numbered in the twenties, but then it began to be reduced. It wasn't a fixation on money, or a negative political stance. . . . It was just that McGuire saw that some people had non-jobs, and he didn't want to see anything wasted."

But more than money was involved in subsequent developments. The phase-out approach that had begun with the Papal Volunteers continued with the shutdown of *Latin America Calls*, the highly-professional tabloid newspaper that reported on Latin American affairs for donors and other interested persons. The 20,000-circulation publication was canceled with half the stories for the next edition already set in type. Then it was CICOP, and finally the Latin America Division itself.

Conference administrators found plausible explanations for their decisions. Their staff was overextended, for one thing; it was time to cut back in general. Second, there was no separate division for Africa or for Asia; should there be one any longer for Latin America? Finally, the old reasoning that Rome "asked us to help" might still figure in the background. But somehow it didn't seem as cogent as it had ten years earlier.

Eventually the division became a secretariat, under the aegis of the National Conference of Catholic Bishops (where more direct control was possible) rather than the U.S. Catholic Conference. The secretariat's principal function centered around the continuation of the annual Latin America collection and its allocation; most of the other remaining staff members who had been in the division went to posts in the U.S. Catholic Conference's Justice and Peace or International Affairs departments. (In 1973, the present Department of Social Development and World Peace was formed, with the Division for International Justice and Peace reporting to it. Offices listed under that division include the one for Latin American affairs.) "Of course, it was all part of the conference restructuring," one veteran of the period recalled, "but it was generally accepted that those in charge were taking the occasion to end all the political embarrassment that the division had caused. In a way, it was like closing the barn door after the horse had left. I think they were really chasing the ghost of Colonnese."

12

Politics and the Latin American Missioner

His name was Cypher. Father Michael Jerome Cypher, a Conventual Franciscan from Medford, Wisconsin. Born 1941, ordained 1968. He took the religious name of Casimir, and people called him Father Cass. He spent a couple of years as an assistant pastor in St. Anthony's Church in Rockford, Illinois, decided he wanted to be a missionary in Latin America, and then went to Our Lady of Guadalupe parish in Hermosa Beach, California, a hilly coastal town a few miles south of Los Angeles. It was the only parish in the Conventuals' St. Bonaventure Province with a sizeable Spanish-speaking population, and he hoped to pick up something of the language that way. Father Cass acquired another nickname there because of his resemblance to Peter Falk, the actor. The people, who liked him, good-naturedly called him Father Colombo.

In 1973 Father Michael Jerome Cypher went off to the diocese of Olancha in Honduras, where another American Franciscan, Bishop Nicholas D'Antonio, was the ordinary. Father Cass's parish encompassed some five hundred square miles, with sixty villages, and he spent most of his time helping the poor *campesinos* who lived there.

On June 25, 1975, he took his truck for repairs to the town of Juticalpa, barely aware of the disturbances taking place there. Landowners in the area, enraged over burgeoning peasant unrest—and over the efforts of some clergymen to keep it stirred up—had decided on a show of force.

On that day, the peasants had massed—more than twelve thousand of them, by the best estimate—for a hunger march. That was a public embarrassment for the landowners and for the military government, which provided soldiers to stop the march. They did it by shooting at the marchers. Some of the marchers were hit, and when Father Cass came on the scene, he helped one of the wounded men into his truck and was taking him to a hospital when he himself was seized by the soldiers.

"Name?" they asked, and he told them, "Padre Casimiro." But his papers contained an old driver's license made out to Father Michael Jerome Cypher, and the soldiers, looking for an activist foreign priest named Padre Michel, were sure they had their man. They stripped Father Cass, beat him, ques-

187

tioned him, and beat him again. When he couldn't give them the answers they wanted, they gave up. They shot him, killing him, and threw his body into a deep well, and then threw dynamite into the well in an attempt to hide evidence of his death.

Another priest was killed that day, a Colombian named Ivan Betancourt. Eleven others lost their lives—two young women and nine marchers. There was no accurate count of the wounded. But the demonstration was stopped.

Father Cass was survived by his mother, eight brothers, and three sisters. The funeral was held in Honduras, and that was at his own expressed wish. No one knows if he had a premonition or not, but he had written down instructions just in case. If I die here, he had said, bury me where I'm working.

There was a price tag on Bishop D'Antonio's head—about $10,000—and he eventually had to leave his diocese. But before he did, he explained something about Father Cass's work and offered some thoughts on his death.

Priests in the area, he said, had organized radio schools, cooperatives, and farm unions, and as a result the peasant leaders learned how to talk and argue about their rights and aspirations. That was what the landowners resented most. He and his clergy, he said, had done their best to implement the directives of Vatican II and of Medellín. "We all know," he said, "this is a risky business here. The unprecedented massacre of June 25 proves this contention." But, he added, "the blood of these new martyrs . . . will some day bear fruit by changing the mentality of power groups and others in Latin America, by the power of the Holy Spirit. They think that by killing you, they will silence you and have greater riches for themselves. It is just the other way around."

Only a few might ever face the direct physical danger that he did, but what Father Cypher was doing on the last day of his life was typical of the major activity of most of his fellow North American missioners in Latin America: serving the poor. In many cases, serving the poor means assisting them when they run head on into opposition from the established order, as they often do. And when that happens, it comes up, for some, as spelling politics. "In Lima, a missionary has to be in politics," said Maryknoll Father Tom Burns. "He has to know what's going on. Here it's a culture of struggle." Lima's popular auxiliary, Bishop Germán Schmitz, understands that line of thinking. "There are oppressed people here," he said. "If they are to be helped, this is a commitment for every priest here, whether he's from Peru or somewhere else in the world."

An Approach Rooted in Scripture

Are U.S. missioners in Latin America overly "mixed up in politics"? The charge is one frequently heard from critics of the mission program, particularly conservative critics. They contend that too many U.S. missioners are involved in leftist causes, neglecting their sacramental duties in favor of social, economic, and political concerns. Statistically, there's not much to back up the contention. Yes, many missioners see the demands of their apostolate reflected in attempts to improve conditions for the people they serve. Certainly some have become radicalized, cooperating with organizations that regularly confront governments they see as unjust. But the number of missioners "involved in politics" by United States standards—running for office, supporting local candidates on partisan lines—is small.

When modern-day Latin America missioners are described as being in politics, it usually means they are attempting to translate the church's contemporary social message, enunciated in the documents of Vatican II and Medellín, into means of improving the lives of the people entrusted to their care. It is an approach rooted in the teaching of the gospel and influenced, unquestionably, by liberation theology's demand for total liberation from oppression, spiritual and material. What does that mean in practical terms?

For Father John Buckley, a young Columban priest from Boston, it means battling civic authorities to get water and sewer facilities for the 1,800 people crowded into ramshackle adobe-and-reed huts in a community that has mushroomed a scant hundred yards from the end of the main runway at Lima's Jorge Chávez International Airport. The residents are forbidden to use brick or other permanent building materials, and the government tells Buckley and his neighbors their land will be needed for a new runway. That is a pretense, they are sure, an excuse to get them out. After a protest meeting during August in 1976, government agents arrested 150 people, incuding 30 women, and kept them overnight. When Buckley went to the jail the next morning, he, too, was questioned and fingerprinted.

At another end of town, in the sprawling parish known as Ciudad de Dios, Father Tom Burns tries to apply the small-group techniques of conscientization to the needs of his flock. The Maryknoll priest from Long Island, part of a parish team that includes three priests and six sisters, recounted the parish's response to neighborhood rioting that took place in 1976, rioting which he saw as a manifestation of all the oppressive problems the people in the poor community shared.

"The rioting was a good indication that people here weren't organized properly," he said. "But it was a historical moment, and that's what liberation theology is all about—seizing the historical moment, reading the signs of the times. The moment all these people shared was the time to reflect on this." At subsequent group meetings, fostered but not dominated by the parish, neighborhood residents worked out a formal campaign to protest the injustices that had led to the rioting, held a Mass of Solidarity, and developed the framework of an organization to deal with similar problems in the future.

Burns came to Lima a few years ago from Puno, in the altiplano, where he had originally been assigned after his ordination in 1969. "This is different from Puno, where we were so isolated," he said. "It was a culture of survival in the altiplano, but here it's a culture of struggle. They fight here, because they can see the contradictions of the world."

Not all missionaries share his approach, he conceded:

> North American missioners are very much concerned with justice, but often they see things on a personal level and try to correct it that way. They're hesitant to get into politics, figuring that we're guests in this country. I respect those with different historical understandings from mine, as long as they arrive at them seriously, but I think in this case that it's a great mistake. We're preaching a historical Christianity. But the non-political approach, the catechism approach—it just takes all the vitality out of a lived faith.

Sometimes the missioner's desire to convert social teaching into practical improvement touches an open nerve, alienating the entrenched establishment—all the way up at the national level, as many deported missioners have found, or even within the narrow boundary lines of a single parish. That was how it worked with still another priest who served in Lima: Franciscan Father Joseph Nangle.

Nangle cited an especially negative reaction in his affluent parish of Santísimo Nombre when he and the other U.S. Franciscans there attempted to relate the teachings of *Populorum Progressio*, Pope Paul's encyclical on the global responsibilities of wealthy nations, to the parochial level. The well-to-do homeowners in the parish were told they represented the "rich nations," he said; the "poor nations" consisted of the servants and watchmen who held a fringe parish membership of their own. The message the priests were trying to convey, he said—perhaps too vigorously, as if to make up for lost time—was that justice demanded changes. But the parishioners were having none of it, and a group of them confronted Nangle in an angry demonstration one evening after mass:

> They felt that suddenly the priests had turned on them, that the encyclical was unfair, and that something was turning sour in a previously pleasant parish reality. . . . Perhaps the priests could have handled it better; a slower introduction to the encyclical's teachings might have saved hurt feelings and misunderstandings. In any case, the parish's honeymoon was over.

Historically there had been a time, of course, when church personnel in Latin America were not only involved in politics; they were part of the very fabric of political life. In colonial days, church and government worked hand in hand for their mutual self-interest, which, from time to time, happened to be in the people's interest as well. Libertarian protests to the contrary, that relationship became only slightly less cozy in the early years of independence. The leaders of the new Latin American nations might challenge the church's hold on the people and profess their personal divorce from church authority, yet they recognized the need for its symbolic blessing. Under the structures that were forming in the early socio-cultural development of Latin America, church and state needed each other. In elaborately formal fashion, each bolstered the other's stature in the public eye.

The marriage of convenience continued over the years; it persists, in fact, to this day—with post-Medellín exceptions, to be noted shortly. "Most of the governments, especially the national security states, place a high value on the symbol system of Christianity," Tom Quigley observed in an interview. "They like the appearance of the support of the church—the statue of the Virgin on holidays, the archbishop's prayer at the inaugural, and so forth. And in that sense, the presence of American missioners could be seen as adding to their support."

The observation was more valid in the early days of the U.S. mission program than it has been in recent years. That was a time, in the fifties and into the sixties, when U.S. missioners, just as other Americans in all walks of life, exhibited unquestioning loyalty to the United States. That was their sole political concern. They were not in mission countries to challenge the local political structures; they were there to cooperate, perhaps to maintain the status quo, and to sell, consciously or not, the advantages of the American way of life.

It was a time, for missioners, when engaging in political activities actually meant quasi-political involvement—building up cooperatives and credit unions, expanding learning opportunities. The activities were all aimed at raising standards of living. Dan McCurry's study of U.S. missioners in Peru cites the effectiveness of Maryknoll Fathers Dan McLellan and Robert Kearns in developing credit unions in the highlands of Peru and Bolivia. McCellan, who went to Peru in 1950, "represents the most successful practitioner of the socio-economic, neocapitalistic emphasis of Maryknoll during the 1950s," McCurry has written.

Gary MacEoin says the McLellan credit unions helped to reduce interest rates from 20 to 50 percent down to one percent, enabling many people to build homes or open shops. Within ten years after the first credit union opened in Puno in 1955, the town got its first bus and the number of cars doubled. "Most people were able to buy bicycles and sewing machines," MacEoin wrote, "and even refrigerators became common."

The approach was generous, well-motivated, demanding, and—in cases such as McLellan's and that of Father Harvey Steele in the Dominican Republic and Panama—markedly successful. But there were those who would criticize the approach in later years. As worthwhile as it might be, the latter-day critics said, it did not commit itself to the profound, radical changes that were needed if Latin America's masses were ever to be truly freed from oppression.

(Jesuit Father Joseph Fitzpatrick touched on the point in the 1967 *America* article in which he clarified Illich's "The Seamy Side of Charity," which had appeared several weeks earlier. There are two different approaches to the changes that all agreed were necessary in Latin America, he said: one through rapid but orderly industrial and economic development, the other through rapid and radical changes of structures. Choosing between the two, he said, divides Catholics, even outstanding Catholic churchmen. "On one side are ranged men like Father Dan McLellan, who is giving the poor a fulcrum in the economic system through the organization of cooperatives." Fitzpatrick lamented the division: "They are all dedicated, progressive men, but they perceive the nature and pace of change in very different perspectives.")

Serving Church or Country?

If there was room to argue in the mission community over the strategic value of varying approaches to address Latin America's economic woes, there was little disagreement on another point. Direct political involvement in the early mission years was strictly limited, true; but where it did exist it almost invariably was connected not with the missioner's local government, but rather with the government at home, in the United States. If his own country asked him for assistance, the missioner of the period saw no conflict of interest. After all, he concluded, one of the chief reasons we're here is to head off the advance of communism—and wasn't that the same thing we were trying to do at home? If a U.S. intelligence agency thought the missioner could provide some helpful information, it did not occur to the missioner to question the point as right or wrong. There was only one question on his mind: how could he do the best job possible for his country—and for his church?

The number involved was small. But a report issued in 1976 by the U.S. Senate Select Committee on Intelligence said the Central Intelligence Agency admitted having used United States religious personnel either for covert action projects or the clandestine collection of intelligence. There were only twenty-one people in all, the report said, involving fourteen "relationships." No names were disclosed. "In six or seven cases," the report said, "the CIA paid salaries, bonuses, or expenses to the religious personnel, or helped to fund projects run by them. . . . Several [of the people] were involved in large covert action projects of the mid-sixties which were directed at 'competing' with communism in the Third World."

Those in a position to know, or to speak responsibly for the church's official position, agree on one point. "Yes, the number of paid relationships seems to have been very small," said Tom Quigley. "Those who were involved simply went along with the old idea of cooperating with the government."

Bishop James S. Rausch, commenting on the Senate report when it was issued (and when he was general secretary of the NCCB-USCC), noted that all contract arrangements between religious personnel and the CIA had been eliminated, adding that even when the practice had been going on its scope was limited. "It was apparently occasional and extremely rare and did not, as far as we can determine, represent official policy of any church body or missionary society," he said. Nevertheless, it did go on, and those close to the Latin America scene during that period believe it safe to assume that of the twenty-one "religious personnel" who had "relationships" with the CIA, the majority had them in Latin America.

The most spectacular allegation connected with the CIA in that period, an allegation never conclusively proven, and vigorously denied by the principal, involves Father Roger Vekemans, the Belgian Jesuit social scientist. Sent from Rome to Chile in 1956 when that country's bishops requested the presence of priests skilled in the social sciences, he exerted a wide influence on theological and social thought in Latin America over a period of many years—both personally and through the Centro Bellarmino, which he founded in Santiago in 1959 along with representatives of the intellectual monthly, *Mensaje* (Message). "Bellarmino soon became the epicenter for progressive Catholic social thought and the ideological 'godfather' of programs for slum dwellers, farmers, university students, and labor unions," wrote Richard Rashke of the *National Catholic Reporter* in 1977. It was also, he implied, a home away from home for the CIA.

Reputed ties between Vekemans and the CIA had been aired—and denied—before that, but the thrust of Rashke's investigative article spelled out details of the accusation in eye-popping fashion: a CIA connection between Washington and Santiago, with Vekemans as the middle man, to win Chile's 1964 presidential election for Social Democrat Eduardo Frei.

There was an array of evidence that was at least circumstantial. Vekemans had an entree to the highest levels of the Kennedy administration in 1963, including at least one visit to the Oval Office itself. He was friendly with Robert Kennedy and with Kennedy brother-in-law Sargent Shriver, then head of the Peace Corps. Another well-known Jesuit priest, James Vizzard, said Vekemans had told him he had gotten $10 million from the United States government—$5 million covert from the CIA and $5 million overt from AID—"primarily to elect Frei president." (Vizzard subsequently went to Rome to discuss the situation with Father Pedro Arrupe, the Jesuits' general. According to Vizzard's account, Arrupe had been upset by the allegation, fearful of its effect on mission projects throughout the world, and was under pressure to make Vizzard retract the story, but at the end of the meeting said he believed the account. It should also be pointed out that Cardinal Aloisio Lorscheider of Fortaleza, Brazil, president of CELAM, told an interviewer in 1976 that he had correspondence from Arrupe which "vigorously refuted" charges of a connection between Vekemans and the CIA.)

By all accounts the church was active in the 1964 presidential campaign, which pitted Frei against Salvador Allende, the Marxist candidate. Vekemans worked closely with Jesuit Father Renato Poblete, a Fordham graduate who was a frequent CICOP speaker during the sixties, an adviser to Cardinal Raúl Silva Henríquez of Santiago, and "friend and spiritual adviser" to the Frei family.

Church leaders were careful not to endorse Frei directly, but programs emanating from the Centro Bellarmino were political in part. Father Miguel d'Escoto, Maryknoll's communications director who was working with the Bellarmino Jesuits at the time, said he doubted that the programs were founded primarily to form a political base for the Christian Democrats, as had been charged. However, he said, "I don't think it would be an exaggeration to say that one of the immediate goals of the program was to get Frei elected."

Frei was indeed elected, with nearly 56 percent of the vote, but once he took office Vekemans' influence showed signs of tailing off rapidly. The Christian Democrats denied any close alliance with the priest, one of them labeling Vekemans' alleged political clout as "mythical." Vekemans spent most of the Frei years away from the center of government, busying himself with church projects, and, according to Vizzard's account, regressed from having been a "liberal reformer" to the role of "obstructionist conservative." When Allende himself came to power in 1970, Vekemans left the country and now lives in Colombia. Rashke's *National Catholic Reporter* article notes that Vizzard has stuck by his story despite Vekemans' consistent denials and contends that a formal investigation of Vekemans' alleged misuse of funds was dropped for political reasons.

In a letter to the *NCR* editor following the Rashke story, Dana S. Green, director of the Latin American Department of the National Council of Churches of Christ, USA, from 1963 to 1969, welcomed the "exposé." As a Protestant missioner in Chile in that period, he said, he had been aware of problems connected with the Vekemans-Bellarmino "empire." He wrote: "The way in which fully-appointed chapels sprung up in the midst of construction of Centro Bellarmino projects became for us highly sensitive topics of discussion. . . . We had no documentation, but we had strong suspicions that a lot of U.S. tax dollars were building Roman Catholic chapels in Chile."

Father William Davis, former director of the Jesuits' Office of Social Ministry, told an *NCR* interviewer that the Vekemans story could be compared to that of Watergate, and Father Joe Nangle, quoted in the same issue of *NCR*, tried to look at the allegation in a historical context: "When you accept government funds, you're tying yourself in more and more with your own country and you look like a foreigner. In the 1960s I don't know how many people would have thought that way. Today, I would be totally against it."

Many other missioners in Latin America began to have second thoughts about blind allegiance to Washington's national and international policies. It was a phenomenon that spread throughout the far-flung mission community as one missioner after another—particularly those who came from non-mission backgrounds, such as dioceses and religious communities without any mission experience—came up against the hard facts of Latin American life and the big-brother image of their own country. Influenced by the challenging documents of Vatican II and the radical new theologies of Latin America, they were being conscientized in a way they found startling even to themselves. According to Father Fred McGuire:

American mission priests had a strong reaction to their first brush with the stark conditions of poverty they found in Latin America. Latin American priests didn't react that way; it wasn't as much of a staggering thing for them. Not that they were lacking in love for their people; it was just that they were used to it. But not so with the Americans; they had a tendency to be stronger in their denunciation than the local priests were. The way they denounced the flagrant injustices they saw frequently created problems with the local bishops.

Father William McIntire said that in the "rethinking" of mission roles that came about toward the end of the sixties, many missioners consciously chose to dissociate themselves from any identification with U.S. foreign policy.

"What is the missioner's role?" asked Father Fitzpatrick in his *America* article. It need not always be as extreme as it was in Panama in 1965, he said, when the Chicago priests working there openly supported the Panamanians who demonstrated violently against the United States. But that reaction, he implied, was hardly unreasonable:

If the priests and religious are genuinely with their people, they will hardly be misjudged. But it is difficult to understand how they can be genuinely with an oppressed people without understanding—even if they do not participate in—their resort to conflict in a struggle for peace.

Gary MacEoin brought the whole point home in a passage from *Revolution Next Door* in which he described the change in attitude experienced by an unidentified U.S. missioner working in Brazil. Its direct, simple eloquence spoke for untold numbers of his fellow North Americans, for the disquieting change in thinking so many had experienced. The priest told MacEoin:

I was in Brazil about four years, doing all the things I had been taught, baptizing, saying mass, preaching, signing forms, all that jazz. I was doing a good job. You couldn't knock it. I was working in a slum and it was a period of rapid inflation. The people who came to my office seemed to have only one problem: how to make ends meet. Someone suggested a protest march to dramatize the hunger of the people. It was perfectly legal, and I agreed to join. But the cops came after us and they beat up the students unmercifully. Several were hospitalized. I had never seen anything like it in my life. We fled into a school and we stayed there all night, fearing further punishment if we broke into small groups to go home. The entire night was spent in discussion of our problems and proposals for remedying them. It was then I realized that the poor have no rights, and that if my priesthood was to have any meaning, it should be devoted to changing that unjust situation.

As noted above, Chicago's archdiocesan mission of San Miguelito sided with the Panamanians it served when anti-U.S. demonstrations took place. But the Chicago priests were as tough on local leadership when they felt the needs of the people were being ignored. As Father Leo Mahon recalled in a 1977 conversation:

> We felt—to be consistent and integrated—social consciousness ought to come out of the word of God that the people have. Much of the church in Latin America advocates a strong social position but retains old theological positions. But we were concerned with the word of God as being primary, and if putting that philosophy into action meant standing up against the military government, that's what we did. Our expulsion order was signed three times, but the people protested against it. Then the government asked Cardinal Cody to remove us, but he refused. Torrijos [General Omar Torrijos, Panama's chief-of-state] said that if he lost control of the country, it would be because of the priests of San Miguelito.

Manifestations of U.S. missioners' unhappiness with their country's role and image in Latin America continued to emerge. The first major development along these lines by a mission group took place in 1969, when 160 missioners working in Peru signed a statement supporting Peru's right to expropriate properties of the International Petroleum Company, a subsidiary of Standard Oil of New Jersey. The missioners' position was that Peru had a right to control its own resources for the good of the country's poor, that private property rights were not necessarily absolute, and that a United States threat to eliminate all aid to Peru as a retaliatory measure was unjust.

One of the signers, Father Bill McIntire, then working in the town of Chimbote, later cited the passage from Maryknoll's 1966 chapter (previously referred to in Chapter 9) to illustrate the attitude of those who prepared the statement and endorsed it: "When the sign of missionary love and concern is blemished or absent in the Christian community of the homeland, it hinders and often contradicts the work of the missioners on foreign soil."

He took a slightly modified view of the incident several years later, reflecting on it in the course of a talk he gave on the "reverse mission" concept. To his knowledge, he said, it was the first statement by a United States missionary group overseas that opposed and countered official United States policy, and, as such, was well-received in Peru. However, he continued:

> In retrospect I have to say that I wish we had done some things a little differently. Among the mission ary personnel, we probably did not work hard enough to get consensus, and to reflect and pray with them on what we were doing. There were sharp divisions among the foreign missionary personnel working in Chimbote, some tendency on our part to partisan political involvement or personal attack, and at times perhaps we tended to try to dominate the Peruvians . . . instead of trying to learn more from very capable Peruvian church leaders and theologians.

A mission name that became singularly identified with anti-U.S. political activism—with negative overtones, for the most part, as far as Catholics at home were concerned—was that of Melville. Thomas Melville and his brother Arthur were Maryknoll priests who worked with Indians in the Guatemalan highland, and who developed strong feelings of empathy with them in the fifteen years they had served there. In 1968, after he and three other United States missioners, one of them his brother, had been expelled from Guatemala for aiding guerrillas, Thomas Melville explained in a newspaper interview why they had acted as they did:

> Having come to the conclusion that the actual state of violence, com-posed of the malnutrition, ignorance, sickness, and hunger of the vast majority of the Guatemalan population, is the direct result of a capitalist system that makes the defenseless Indian compete against the powerful and well-armed landowner, my brother and I decided not to be silent accomplices of the mass murder that this system generates. We began teaching the Indians that no one will defend their rights if they do not defend themselves. If the government and oligarchy are using arms to maintain them in their position of misery, then they have the obligation to take up arms and defend their God-given rights to be men.

The distressing situation, Melville said, was not accidental, but rather had been brought on by a wealthy few, backed by the army, in turn backed by the United States government and blessed by the hierarchy of the church:

> The fact that the United States is training the armies of the countries of Latin America to help maintain the state of exploitation is a further reason why we, as citizens of the United States, should struggle to correct this shocking situation.

Back in the United States, Catholics hardly knew what to make of the Melvilles and other missioners who followed their thinking, and who were receiving what seemed to be an inordinate amount of attention in the press. At best, it was an embarrassment: fine young U.S. priests and nuns going off to enrich the faith and stem the tide of communism, becoming mixed up with guns and guerrillas and attacking their own country. Some of them, in fact, seemed to be talking like communists themselves. Was that what we sent them for? If this was what happened when U.S. missionaries got involved in politics in Latin America—well, maybe it was time to reverse the tide.

That line of thinking began to develop, with various modifications, as a reaction to the strong activism of the Melvilles and others, not only at home, but in the missions themselves. One prominent missioner who felt that way, and continues to feel that way now, is Carmelite Bishop Nevin Hayes, auxiliary of Chicago and head of the bishops' Latin America committee. He was bishop of Sicuani, Peru, in the sixties. In a 1977 interview he said:

> Your foreign missionary should never be the one who executes political changes in a country. He should talk to people on both sides, explain the principles of the gospel, animate them. . . . He should give help to them so they can start something positive. Then the missionary should follow them. If he tries to effect changes himself, the first thing anyone would ask is: What does he know about this?

Bishop Hayes spoke critically of U.S. missioners who travel to Latin America and become associated with local radical leaders and then present solutions to long-standing social problems. He likened the practice to a hypothetical instance in which a European comes to America, teams up with a political activist here, and offers a remedy for—in the example he used—the problem of the American Indian.

"What's the first thing you're going to ask?" he said. "'What does he know? Who made him an expert?' It's the same thing with an American priest who gets involved in Latin American politics. The people there will want to know the same thing: Who made him an expert?"

Another Carmelite priest, Father Michael La Fay, voiced similar sentiments. A native of Chelsea, Massachusetts, he has been in Peru since 1964, four years after his ordination. He is pastor of a Carmelite parish in an upper-class section of Lima (the parish conducts an extensive education program for the 2,000 or so members who are servants for the remaining 10,000 parishioners). He is also superior for Peru's Carmelite community. "I don't see a political role for United States priests," he said flatly, reflecting an attitude he has held since the question arose in the sixties:

> More and more are getting involved, though. They're trying to solve things without a faith response. People admit a problem, but resent foreign priests coming in and telling them what to do. We don't see liberation theology as liberating at all—or as theology.

Boston's Cardinal Medeiros was bishop of Brownsville when the political controversy flared in the sixties, serving also as a member of the bishops' Latin America committee. His views today are similar to those he maintained at the time. He said in an interview:

Some of the poorest of God's people have a high degree of understanding of life and their faith. A missionary must be open to this. But if he goes in with the whole idea of changing everything—well, that's wrong. It's also wrong to go in with the idea of overthrowing the oppressors. I can understand a missionary's frustration with civil authorities in the face of extreme social problems, but this is not the way of the gospel. We are told to love not only the oppressed but the oppressors as well.

The Melvilles' political activism failed to impress another key figure of the period, for reasons entirely different from the others cited. "Dilettantes! Ingenues!" said Ivan Illich, when he was asked for a comment on the Melvilles. "One does not take short cuts."

As the best-known radical voice of the day on U.S.-Latin American relationships, Illich might logically have been expected to support mission priests whose activism led them to criticize their country's policies, but on this point, as on so many others, his position was not always that predictable. Not only did he fail to support Latin America missioners who spoke out on social and political questions; he chided them for not remembering that they were always considered a voice of the church. The church, he said, should condemn evil but not support or take stands on specific issues. "A priest should not identify with any political or social question," he said. "It is impossible to do this without either confirming the status quo or supporting certain social directions." Priests, he said, should renounce political alliances or resign.

In her book *Divine Disobedience*, Francine du Plessix Gray tells of two Los Angeles priests who visited Illich at Cuernavaca and complained, in the course of their conversation, that Cardinal McIntyre had refused to let them march in a demonstration for civil rights legislation. "If I were your cardinal," Illich replied, "I would not let you march either. If you want to parade against discrimination in general, okay, but not for the passage of another lousy stopgap law."

(Gray saw Illich's apparent stand on an apolitical church as, in fact, highly political, tied to a series of violently anti-U.S. statements. He sarcastically compared the U.S. peace movement's techniques to "cough syrup given to nineteenth-century syphilitics" because of its failure to protest United States intervention in Latin America in the same way it protested intervention in Vietnam. In 1967 he wrote that the violence in Watts, in Guatemala, and in Vietnam all had the same root cause: "United States messianism." "It is not the American way of life lived by a handful of millions that sickens the billions," he said, "but rather the growing awareness that those who live the American way of life will not tire until the superiority of their quasi-religious persuasions is accepted by the underdog." Illich also compared the Alliance for Progress to the War on Poverty: "Both programs were designed to have the poor join in the American dream. Both programs failed. The poor refused to dream on command.")

A Need to Speak Out

Reaction might have been setting in to the extreme position taken by the Melvilles, but not all U.S. missioners shared the negative feeling of Hayes and La Fay (and fewer still would go along with Illich). In fact, there was a growing sentiment that U.S. missioners had to speak out against injustice, especially if it affected the people they served. If that meant, as it did to some, that they were getting involved in politics, so be it.

That was the way Father Daniel Panchot felt about it, and a position paper he delivered to the 1976 Bicentennial Convocation on Justice and Peace at Maryknoll provides an eloquent account of the development of his thinking on the subject. Panchot, the U.S. Holy Cross priest who was in Chile during the historic Frei-Allende presidential campaign, as a theology student at the University of Santiago, recalls it as an exciting time to be involved in church affairs there:

> The awakening of the Chilean church to the social problems and the social doctrine of the church was led by Bishop Manuel Larraín of Talca and the Centro Bellarmino of Santiago. This also influenced the faculty of theology, especially since all of this indicated that theology must be dynamic and open to the needs of real people, and not just something abstract or static.

The years that followed brought greater challenge and, at times, greater tension. Deeply affected by a far-reaching diocesan synod in 1967 and 1968 and then by Medellín, some in the Chilean church wanted to move faster and some slower, he said; some to the right and some to the left. "What was certain was that the church and the message of Christ were important for the new society Latin Americans were trying to construct."

Assigned to parish duties in Santiago throughout the late sixties, Panchot felt some apprehension, as did many of his companions, about the 1970 presidential election, and what seemed sure to be an Allende victory. When that did, in fact, take place, the newly-elected Marxist leader took pains to assure the bishops of Chile that they would have no problems with him. A small but vocal element wanted the church to be a closed bastion of opposition to the regime, Panchot said, but others took a different stand. The church might have some misgivings, but it wanted to be in on the social changes

Allende had promised, and, for the most part, it worked with the new administration. According to Panchot:

> Many of the church's members felt that the action would be in the political arena. There men's lives and the future of society would be decided. The church ran the danger of being left out—irrelevant, useless. . . . The bishops of Cuba told their brothers in the Chilean episcopacy: "You are lucky. We did not have the insight of the Second Vatican Council to orientate us to live and work in a revolutionary process."

There was a period of friction in the church, Panchot continued, accusations of infiltration by Marxists, but in general the administration and the church got along reasonably well. Then in 1973 the revolution ended with the takeover by the military that continues today. The church was challenged again to defend individual rights, Panchot said, and he, along with many others, became active in organizations designed to defend the persecuted and to do everything possible to restore a peace based on justice in Chile.

In November 1975 Father Panchot was arrested and held for two weeks and then was expelled from the country he had come to know as his second home. His testimony at Maryknoll described his steadily maturing view about missions, about Latin America's poor, about his own country, about the missioner's role. Countless other North Americans who were formed by events in the same period can relate to what he said:

> If you have worked in Latin America and especially if you have worked in Chile, you do not see yourself as a missionary. You have worked with a well-organized church which has a strong sense of renovation. You *do* feel that you are a part of that church.
>
> You become aware of something else, too. Since childhood you have been taught that the United States was founded on high ideals and that it defends the values of human life. All of this is included in the vague term "American system." People—inside and outside of the United States—just presume that you accept and will defend the system. You have to distinguish, however, between the ideal of democracy and freedom, and the economic system that historically has gone along with it, the so-called free enterprise system. One is not necessarily the other.
>
> Meanwhile, something else has happened. Your work and commitment to the church, the working class of Chile and Latin America, has made you absorb many of their values, prejudices, and insights. And you see again and again that the "American economic system" is not interested in people; it is interested in making a profit for its stockholders. If that can be done while still maintaining a nice image of promoting progress and prosperity, fine. But the system can as easily

furnish arms and counter-insurgency training. It can and will de-stabilize or bolster a government according to whether that government is considered "friendly" or not.

Governments that challenge points of international justice, Panchot said, and that challenge the power and practices of multinational corporations, are not considered friendly. And the system is reinforced by the State Department, despite the good intentions of some of its people. He continued:

> Meantime, from your contacts with the people of Latin America and especially of Chile, by working with them, by listening to them, by following their line of thought, you conclude that there are oppressor and oppressed. This does not necessarily mean that the oppressors are acting out of bad will. Many times the people are not even aware that they are oppressors.
>
> You, however, as a person living with and working with the people of Latin America and Chile, have learned. . . . You have to make an option for them. You have to be loyal to your people.

Not all saw the picture drawn quite that clearly. Many did not see even the Chilean picture that clearly, as Father McIntire has noted:

> We had some Maryknollers working in Chile then (and now) who were very radicalized, completely opposed to Pinochet and his group. But I have to be honest and say that other Maryknollers in Chile were in favor of the coup, thinking that it had saved Chile from communism and that the number of deaths and excesses by the Pinochet junta were moderate and even necessary to save Chile from a bloody civil war. Even now a couple of our men would still be pro-Pinochet. Others would say that the Pinochet regime is the lesser of two evils, a lesser evil in their mind than the Allende years or the way the Allende regime was heading.

There was tension in the mission communities when political differences of that nature arose in the late sixties—crippling tension, at times, which all but destroyed the effectiveness of some mission houses. But in recent years, there has been more of a tendency toward accommodation, toward concentrating on points of Christian agreement rather than on those of political division. McIntire referred to that in a 1976 interview, citing changes in his own outlook:

> I think I'm a pretty radicalized person, but I'm less confident about the use of political means by religious. We're getting more and more back to the old idea of preaching the gospel, and preaching it from the side of the poor. I hope this attitude will bridge the gap between the old and new approaches.

Father Mike Colonnese made a related point in a letter written in 1977:

> In the whole process of trying to radically change our mission effort, we accomplished change, but not to the core. One problem is that many United States missionaries in Latin America have tried to make the revolution their own, and this cannot be done. You can assist, yes. But you can't do it yourself.

Father Dunstan "Tex" Dooling, a plain-talking Franciscan who has spent more than twenty-five years in Latin America—from 1950 to 1962 in Brazil, and from 1962 to the present in Bolivia—pointed to another pitfall of political involvement in the missions:

> Latin American politics are so damn byzantine that you have to be very careful about where you tie your star. In a situation like Chile's, the church should take a stand, okay, . . . but it should come from the organized church, or a leader of the hierarchy, not from anyone else. When you take on a government regime, you've got to have an alternate in mind. And down here the alternates often turn out to be worse than what you've got right now.

Finally, Father Walter George, the Redemptorist veteran of mission work in Brazil, took the position that both sides in some of the confrontations between state and church had "heroes and villains," and, citing the advice of Dom Helder Camara, added that political involvement simply isn't for everyone:

> The most dangerous people—both priests and laymen—are those with a little taste of adventure who want a confrontation. It was Helder who made the distinction between prophet and model. He said he had been given the prophet's role, had access to publicity, and so forth, and had the ability to bear the brunt of criticism for the statements that he made. But he said he didn't want everyone to try to do the same things that he was doing. The church couldn't survive if everybody became a martyr.

By the mid-seventies, political involvement among Latin American missioners was following a more predictable pattern. For one thing, the old CIA technique of using U.S. missioners to help in garnering information overseas was—officially speaking, at any rate—a thing of the past. William Colby, the former CIA director, had defended the use of church people as operatives and sources; he felt a missionary could work for the CIA without betraying his religious commitment. But his successor, George Bush, was in office only a short time before announcing a prohibition of future CIA use of religious personnel (and, parenthetically, of journalists as well). That policy was in line with the report of Senator Frank Church's Select Committee on Intelligence, which said: "Making operational use of United States religious groups for national purposes both violates their nature and undermines their bonds with kindred groups around the world."

However, the new regulations still allowed for the CIA to be able to seek information from missioners returning here from abroad, which led to criticism from the USCC. Father Bryan Hehir, associate secretary for international justice and peace, said the provision was "not acceptable." "The function of mission organizations and the institutional church should be precisely to instruct people not to cooperate," he said.

Bishop Rausch wrote directly to Bush. "We hope that the logical extension of the regulations, namely eschewing a policy of seeking out returned missionaries, will also be considered," the general secretary said. "We believe that United States missionaries in today's world cannot knowingly serve the goals of the CIA or other governmental intelligence agencies and maintain intact the integrity of their mission."

The new ground rules for missioners and politics were taking on something of a more ordered quality, by implied mutual consent of the missioners and local bishops. Increasingly aware of their role in the "Medellín spirit," the bishops found themselves more and more at loggerheads with their own governments on human rights issues. They realized that in many of their North American mission priests, they had reliable allies.

Lima's Auxiliary Bishop Schmitz stressed two points in an interview on the subject: the integration of the mission priest in the local church, and the necessity of dialogue and consensus as a prelude to political action. "First of all, what is a foreign priest?" he asked.

We try to avoid the term, and not simply to be amiable about it. It's such a relative term. I'm as foreign to Juli as a priest from New York or New Jersey is to Lima. In each case, the cultures are different.

Second, when we speak of political involvement, it has to be considered at the level of the pastoral agent—the priests, nuns, and lay people acting as representatives of ecclesiastical authority. Our pastoral plan sets firm conditions in which pastoral agents are supposed to take concrete commitments. But before making these commitments to action in the political or economic areas, the agent should have the consensus of the community and the approval of the hierarchy.

It is important, too, that if I ask for justice in regard to a certain point, it should not be within a partisan format, but because of the call of Christ, considering all children of God and brothers in Christ, working from the deepest possible motive.

As regards those from outside the country, they should abide by whatever is said for priests in general, on rights and their limits. But they especially should watch that they don't offend by injecting something that doesn't belong. The hierarchy will back every pastoral agent who—accepting all the conditions mentioned above—takes a stand or an action and gets involved in trouble as a result, because of his commitment or his nationality. He is simply fulfilling his prophetic ministry in announcing the evangelical truth.

The Church Finds Its Voice

As the seventies progressed, more and more Latin American bishops saw the need to announce those evangelical truths, and found the voice, with their brothers in the hierarchy, to do it. Democratic governments had tumbled in many countries, to be replaced by military governments—which managed to remain in power year after year despite hints of a return to policies of free and open elections. Murders, unwarranted arrests, accounts of torture, the disappearance of political activists who spoke up in opposition—these and other human rights violations became increasingly obvious, and the new Latin American church, the church of Vatican II and Medellín, refused to take it quietly.

Conferences of bishops formally denounced government policies in many countries: Argentina, Bolivia, Brazil, Chile, El Salvador, Paraguay. Other church protests took place in countries such as Ecuador, Honduras, Nicaragua, and Guatemala, where rights violations were clearly documented.

The church received support from U.S. missioners in many forms, including a formal statement signed by three hundred United States missionaries in March 1977, calling on religious leaders at home to support President Carter's stand on human rights.

The signers—Catholic priests and nuns, Protestant ministers, Jewish rabbis—listed a few names as representative of

> thousands of people who have been killed or have disappeared . . . because they were peacefully working to change the oppressive social structures in their countries. . . . We mention these events to you, fellow Americans, because all these victims have suffered under military governments which receive U.S. military and financial aid paid for by your tax dollars.

Some missioners paid the full price for "political involvement" on behalf of their people, such as Father Cypher in Honduras. Dozens of others have been jailed or expelled, or both, because of violations, real or imagined, of repressive laws and policies aimed at maintaining the inhuman status quo for peasants in their adopted mission lands.

Oblate Father Lawrence Rosebaugh of Milwaukee, for example, was arrested in 1977 with his lay helper, Thomas Capuano of New York, a Catholic working for a Mennonite mission, and held for three days in a packed cell.

They had been arrested while pushing a cart laden with vegetables, the daily ration they distributed to beggars, prostitutes, and other indigents in downtown Recife. Their case leaped into world prominence in June, a month after their arrest, because they were able to meet Rosalynn Carter on her Latin America trip and tell her of the unspeakably harsh treatment they had received. "Now I know the value of a piece of bread," Rosebaugh said.

The list of U.S. missioner victims goes on; this one is far from complete. Father Evarist Bertrand, a Capuchin from Antigo, Wisconsin, was denied re-entry into Nicaragua in 1976, after thirteen years of mission service there. He and thirty-two other missioners had denounced mass killings of *campesinos* by Nicaragua's national guard. He spent the next year in the Honduras village of Danli, near the Nicaraguan border, and was ordered expelled from that country as well, for allegedly aiding guerrilla training. But the Tegucigalpa archdiocese intervened. A chancery official said the Somoza government in Nicaragua had pressured Honduras to get Bertrand out. "Far from serving the guerrilla cause," the spokesman said, "Father Bertrand is achieving social and economic improvements for the rural people." Ultimately, though, the Honduran government had its way, expelling the priest in 1978.

Father Daniel Driscoll, a Maryknoller from Louisville, who went to Venezuela shortly after his ordination in 1966, was arrested and beaten by national police in November 1976 as he led a demonstration protesting conditions in the slum town of Tacagua, near Caracas. He was supported by the local church, with Auxiliary Bishop Alfredo Rodríguez Figueroa of Caracas securing his release and filing a protest with President Carlos Andrés Pérez. Father Driscoll's protest was more than justified, the bishop said, since the town, with a population of 3,300, lacks schools, health clinics, adequate streets or transportation.

Father James M. Weeks, a La Salette priest from Clinton, Massachusetts, was a missioner in Argentina for twelve years when he was arrested in August 1976 as part of a government drive against political activists. Four native seminarians and one from Chile were arrested with him; Weeks was held incommunicado for a week and detained in jail for a week more. Ultimately he was expelled from the country. Those who arrested him said they had found subversive literature and recordings in his quarters. The literature turned out to be a critical book on communism written by Bishop Alfonso López Trujillo, CELAM's secretary general, and the record was a collection of folk songs by Joan Baez, a gift from a friend. "Our ministry involved working with the poor in the formation of Christian grassroots communities to help them improve their lives," Weeks said when he had returned to the United States. "Our arrest and mistreatment were just part of a larger pattern of repression occurring now in a large number of Latin American countries."

Father John Kevin Murphy, Benedictine of Wilmette, Illinois, and Father Lawrence McCulloch, Maryknoller of Waterford, Michigan, were both expelled from El Salvador early in 1977. McCulloch was told he had been "mingling with local factional politics," and Murphy was accused of telling his parishioners not to vote, or to vote for the opposition candidate, in the February 20 general election. "That is absolutely false," he said:

> What I did, as many priests did, was to remind them of their civic obligation to go to the polls and vote for whomever their consciences dictated. But I was never engaged in any activity resembling politics. My role was simply preaching social justice for the needy, calling on those better off to do what is right. But apparently they do not want us in the way.

Certainly there have been U.S. mission priests in Latin America over the last twenty-five years who have mingled unwisely in local political concerns, but their number, by the best estimates of those in a position to know, is minuscule. Many, many more accused of political meddling have simply been attempting to help their people toward better lives in accordance with church teaching—the old teaching of the gospel, the new teaching of twentieth-century popes and bishops.

One of them was Father Bernard Survil, the Greenburg diocesan priest and Maryknoll associate who spent two years working in El Salvador before his expulsion from that country, along with Murphy and McCulloch, in 1977. A few months earlier he had written to a friend, explaining what his day-to-day work was all about:

> I believe that liberation theology on the parish level is in the making in our own tired section of San Salvador, when our group leaders meet in my living room every Thursday: two nuns, a street peddler, a store clerk, a construction worker or two, a housewife or two, a gas station attendant, a day laborer often without work, my landlady. We pray, we sing, we study, we plan, we evaluate, we laugh, and we read Revelation to maintain hope. Outside the door there might be a street fight, since we live in one of the skid rows of the city; around the corner people live in cardboard shacks. The "ears" of the security forces are everywhere, as are the unemployed, the shoeless kids. And the shoeless adults.

When he was arrested, a young officer told him that his work on behalf of grassroots movements was behind his ouster. "Why is it that you priests are preaching hatred?" the young officer asked. "Why aren't you preaching love?"

13

U.S. Missioners in Latin America Today

"Where to begin? Where? Everywhere. It's overwhelming," Father Bernard Survil wrote to a friend in the United States.

How remarkable it is to be considered a wonder-worker just for inviting people to join the Fellowship, and have them accept. That, basically, is what we're doing. . . . We are consciously "church" in our barrio of Lourdes.

Before, the people of our little group say, their idea of church was a weekly or monthly or festive visit to the parish or to a shrine church downtown. Now, because they study the Bible they are called "Protestants," because they assume responsibility they are considered "fanatics," because the men desire to be married sacramentally they are considered over the hill, and because we read church documents about the national socio-economic reality, they are called "communists."

For sure, with this kind of reputation and with Mass or a popular devotion just blocks away in properly "Catholic" churches, we don't expect to have people knocking down our door to attend our Thursday evening meeting.

That was in 1976, a few months before the El Salvador government forced Father Survil out of his slum parish in San Salvador and expelled him from the country, leaving him to take up a new assignment, working with the same kind of poor people, first in Guatemala, then in Nicaragua.

About the same time, a U.S. priest almost thirty years his senior was explaining something about his own work in Nicaragua. "My personal mission assignment for thirty years has been among the Miskito Indians," wrote Father Philip Casper, "living in fifty villages along the Rio Coco in northern Nicaragua. I learned their language and taught them in their own tongue. We gave them a popular translation of the Bible."

It was 1976, thirty-two years after Father Casper, a Franciscan Capuchin from Pewoukee, Wisconsin, had gone to the missions because of "a desire to

208

help the people know Christ better, and thereby help them love God more so that God will receive greater glory." He was pleased with the results he had achieved, but declined to comment on U.S. mission efforts anywhere outside that narrow strip of civilized land along the Rio Coco. "I know nothing of other places," he said.

At first glance, the two U.S. mission priests appear to be far, far apart—in age, in the nature of their work, in the way they have been taught about missions and the church. But in addition to their other training, they have been formed by Vatican II, by Medellín, and by the realities of Latin American life, and in many respects, despite surface differences, they have much in common. Father Survil wrote:

Our role in Latin America is indeed changing. It seems to be more of an auxiliary service to the local church, rather than that of holding front-line responsibilities such as pastorates.

Father Casper, who began his mission career among the Nicaraguan Miskitos in 1944, when Survil was four years old, speaks along remarkably similar lines. U.S. missioners must prepare, encourage, never dominate, he said. They must place the highest priorities on the training of lay leaders and catechists and deacons, all chosen by the community. And they must remember the sacred tradition of what they find: "Too many are still guilty of paternalism," he said. "We must respect the people we serve—their culture, customs, language, and all they hold on to that is good."

Bernard Survil and Philip Casper are two of the 2,300 U.S. Catholic missioners still in Latin America—priests, sisters, and laypeople who have achieved a kind of unified approach to their work, in marked contrast to the polarization that characterized the late sixties and early seventies. There is less attention now to "liberal-conservative" divisions that were typical of the years immediately after Vatican II, and more agreement that service—under, perhaps, a myriad of forms—is the key to contemporary success in the missions.

"In the earlier years," commented Holy Cross Father Philip Devlin, a fifteen-year veteran of mission service in Chile, "it was extremely difficult to maintain a stable staff. Those presently in the work seem much better suited to the situation and committed to the people. . . . There are more attempts now to identify with the masses of poor and persecuted and to serve them well."

As will be noted in a later chapter, some critics of the present United States mission effort believe that no matter how well-motivated today's corps of missioners might be, many are still out of touch with Latin American realities, even those who might voice the "correct" catch-phrases used to describe techniques in dealing with contemporary problems. But others, particularly those on the day-to-day scene, object vigorously to that criticism, contending that the missioners remaining in Latin America today are those whose commitment has been fully tested. "Yes, we've lost a lot of people," noted Father Gerard McCrane, until recently the Maryknoll regional superior in Peru. "But now, the one who has stayed is the one who has thought this through. He knows he wants to spend the rest of his life with those who need him most."

The Numbers Decline

In round numbers, the United States Catholic mission presence in Latin American has dwindled by about one-third since the peak year, the watershed year of 1968. At that time, the United States had 3,391 missioners—priests, sisters, brothers, seminarians, and laypeople—in Latin America, according to figures in the Mission Handbook of the United States Catholic Mission Council. By 1977, the number had fallen off to 2,293, continuing a downward trend that had gone on unchecked for eight years. Admittedly, the loss mirrored the overall drop in U.S. religious personnel during that period and paralleled to some degree the general decline in U.S. missionary personnel overseas—from 9,655 in 1968 to 6,760 in 1977.

But the figures show just as clearly that it was the Latin American involvement that caused the greatest fluctuations. It was Latin America that pushed the nation's mission commitment up so dramatically from 1960 (a total of 6,782 overseas missioners) to 1968. The overall gain of some 2,800 throughout the world included nearly 2,000 in Central and South America. And similarly, the decline in mission presence from 1968 to 1977 was heavily weighted in the direction of Latin America. While that figure decreased by roughly one-third, the number of U.S. missioners in Africa was relatively constant—1,157 in 1968, and 1,003 in 1977. Taking into consideration the general decline in religious personnel during that period, that number reflects a significant percentage gain. Not so with Latin America, where the numbers soared upward from 1960 to 1968—more than two-and-a-half times the mission personnel—but have spiraled down ever since.

Brazil and Peru continued to be the Latin American countries with the greatest numbers of U.S. mission personnel in 1977: 468 in Brazil, and 448 in Peru. In other parts of the world, only the Philippine Islands had more United States mission personnel, a total of 472. Other Latin American countries with more than 100 U.S. Catholic missioners were Bolivia, 279; Mexico, 190; Chile, 189; and Guatemala, 186.

The largest U.S. Catholic mission-sending organization, the Jesuits, had a total of 647 priests and brothers throughout the world, including 35 in Belize, 23 in Honduras, and 20 each in Brazil and Peru, as well as smaller numbers in Argentina, Chile, Colombia, Ecuador, and Mexico. Maryknoll, with a total of 607 priests and brothers, was heavily represented in Bolivia (51), Peru (45), Guatemala (44), and Chile (40), with representation in Brazil, Colombia, El Salvador, Mexico, Nicaragua, and Venezuela. Other organizations with more than 100 missioners in Latin America included the Franciscans, with concentrations in Brazil and Bolivia; the Oblates of Mary Immaculate, and the Redemptorists, both with greatest numbers in Brazil.

The Maryknoll Sisters' worldwide total of 1,020 missionaries (508 working overseas) included large groups in Bolivia, Chile, Guatemala, and Peru. Other U.S. sisters' communities maintaining significant numbers of Latin American missioners included the Dominicans, Franciscans, Felicians, Servants of the Immaculate Heart of Mary, Sisters of Notre Dame de Namur and the School Sisters of Notre Dame, Sisters of the Most Precious Blood, Sisters of St. Joseph of Carondelet, Benedictines, and Sisters and Daughters of Charity.

Almost without exception, and some of those exceptions will be discussed later in this chapter, the 1977 figures for the religious communities, both men and women, showed sharp losses from comparable totals in the late sixties.

There was an even more noticeable drop in the totals for diocesan priests and lay missioners, particularly the latter, reflecting, for the most part, the absence of a PAVLA-type organization. Most of the organizations of lay volunteers today—such as the Lay Mission Helpers of Los Angeles, the Jesuit Volunteer Corps, and the Catholic Medical Mission Board—concentrate their work in other areas of the world. Exceptions are the Maryknoll Lay Missioners, twenty-eight of whose fifty-one members were working in Latin America in 1978, and the Milwaukee Latin American Office, with eight members.

The direct involvement of dioceses in Latin American missions, for both priests and lay people, is down by 50 percent from its peak years of 1969 and 1970. In 1970 there were 373 diocesan priests in overseas missions, about 90 percent of them in Latin America; today the number is down to 182 (165 in Latin America).

(A bishop whose diocese remains in the forefront of Latin American mission work finds that drop regrettable. Asked if he would recommend mission undertakings to his fellow U.S. bishops, Bishop Michael F. McAuliffe of Jefferson City replied with an emphatic yes. "If they really want their people to be mission-minded," he said, "this is the way to turn them on.")

Jefferson City is represented not only by seven priests in Latin America, but by six lay missioners as well. Only one U.S. diocese—Erie, Pennsylvania—has more than two lay missioners overseas under diocesan auspices, and the Erie involvement has a unique quality. The diocese maintains a two-way relationship with a Yucatan diocese, which had begun as part of the PAVLA enterprise. When PAVLA was disbanded, the dioceses decided to keep the program going. Not only do people from Erie go to Mexico, but those from the Yucatan diocese were invited to Erie to help with projects involving the Spanish-speaking. ("The Erie program's goal is not to absorb, but to be mutually understanding," said Father Walter George, who has followed its progress closely. "Maybe this is one of the directions to come. Maybe we should think more of being ourselves, as these people from Erie are.")

Boston remains the diocese with the largest number of overseas priest-missioners—twenty-seven, all but three of them in Bolivia, Ecuador, and Peru with the St. James Society. As noted earlier, Cardinal Humberto Medeiros wants to keep the program as strong as possible, but finds himself unable to encourage new volunteers because of the archdiocese's needs at home.

In St. Louis, in 1976, Cardinal John Carberry marked the twentieth an-niversary of his archdiocese's pioneering mission effort with gratitude to all the priests who had served in Latin America, but less than a year later he was forced to announce the closing of its thirteen-year-old mission at Arica, Chile, because of insufficient volunteers. Monsignor Bernard H. Sandheinrich, di-rector of the archdiocese's Latin America Apostolate, explained that the cutback was due to problems in recruiting younger priests. Arica, a small seacoast city in northern Chile, had offered an "altitude leave" post for other St. Louis missioners serving in La Paz as well as Bolivia's altiplano. "It seems better to us to have all our missionaries in one country," Sandheinrich said.

The eleven St. Louis priests staffing four Bolivian parishes made the archdiocese the second leading United States diocese in terms of clergy serving in Latin America, and the cardinal wants a vigorous kind of commitment to continue in the future. "We are firmly committed to the continuation of the Latin America Apostolate," he wrote in a letter to his priests. "We hope and pray with you that more of our younger priests may, with God's grace, respond to the mission call." There were hopeful signs in regard to native vocations, and Sandheinrich pointed out that four Bolivians ordained in 1976 chose to serve at parishes staffed by St. Louis priests, "indicating the kind of support our priests are giving the development of local clergy."

Father Robert Leibrecht, a St. Louis priest interviewed in La Paz in 1976, pointed to the change in attitude he and his fellow missioners had undergone. "Now there's an overrriding rejection of paternalism," he said. "We've gained a lot of knowledge. Instead of ramrodding, we're trying to serve the people better." But, he added significantly: "Most of our people have been here about ten years or more."

Said Monsignor David Ratermann, one of the three original St. Louis volunteers:

Cardinal Ritter said from the beginning that we would benefit from this more than we would give, and he was right. I have been enriched tremendously from having been given the challenge, the privilege, to serve in another part of the world. This is not to criticize my classmates who have not gone, but their life is not as enriched as mine is. That's certainly nothing I can take credit for; it is a gift from God, and that's all.

Father Chuck Tobin, the Kansas City priest who is not only a fellow Missourian but a La Paz neighbor as well, remains sold on the idea of diocesan missions. In 1976 he said:

The way things are, a lot of people I know feel they have a personal interest in La Paz, Bolivia, because of what I'm doing here. Six people from my old parish at home have already come down here. But none of the younger priests has done that, which is too bad. I'd like to have them come down so they can get an idea of what's needed, to see what's what.

The diocese still doesn't have the best idea of what we're really doing. It's more the old idea of "those guys down there are really sacrificing," not the new idea that it's the missioner's role to raise his voice against oppression.

Only a handful of U.S. dioceses had four or more priest-representatives in Latin America in 1977. Others—in addition to Boston, St. Louis, and Kansas City—include Cleveland, Camden, La Crosse (Wisconsin), Ogdensburg (New York), Pittsburgh, St. Paul-Minneapolis, and, as mentioned earlier, Jefferson City.

"I indicated in my first address to the people that I certainly wanted us to continue our mission work in Peru," said Bishop McAuliffe, who succeeded Bishop Marling in 1969, "But they had to show me that they wanted it too, by their interest and their support." Financial problems were severe, and Bishop McAuliffe named former missioners—first Father Larry Stockman, and then Father Donald Greene—to direct local fund-raising efforts. "It was a massive educational effort," the bishop said, "but it didn't take long until we had the support of almost everyone in the diocese—pastors, associates, the religious, our lay people, and our seminarians. They all seem to feel it is their mission as well as ours. The fact that we relate very closely to the two dioceses in Peru solidifies and maintains this support."

As noted previously, Bishop McAuliffe maintains close personal contact with the seven Jefferson City priests in Peru, but also with the local ordinaries: "A spirit of collegiality exists, with due respect for the local bishop and his authority." That kind of relationship benefits both dioceses, Bishop McAuliffe believes. "Bishop Calderon of Puno feels it has had profound effects for the good of his diocese and I feel it explains at least to a certain degree the support and concern of our diocese and their great interest in the people of Peru," the bishop said. "Overall it explains why our priests wish to spend at least part of their lives in missionary service." (Its mission-mindedness also helps to explain Jefferson City's response to an appeal for aid following the disastrous 1976 earthquake in Guatemala, Bishop McAuliffe believes. Within the diocese, the average contribution was $4 per household, the best response, on the average, of any U.S. diocese.)

There are no signs at present that Jefferson City will be forced to reduce its mission commitment sharply, as many other dioceses have had to, but Bishop McAuliffe concedes that it is difficult to maintain a high number of priests in Peru. There are 115 diocesan priests to care for over 90 parishes at home, for one thing. Another factor is that many who volunteer do so without too many years of experience in the priesthood and cannot be selected for that reason.

"It will be interesting to see how or whether the interest of our younger priests will be maintained," Bishop McAuliffe said, "so that when they have obtained the necessary experience, they will still want to go. . . . It's been a real pleasure working with our missionaries now more than ever," Bishop McAuliffe concluded. "With the very difficult political situation, the work becomes even more difficult, but we hope to be able to continue."

For the most part, religious communities shared the same downward direction taken by the Latin American mission rolls of dioceses and lay organizations, but the dropoff was not quite as precipitous. Many of the organizations, for one thing, were mission-oriented to begin with and were less likely to suffer wholesale mission losses than those who only entered the mission apostolate in the big push of the early sixties. Too, a number of them were engaged in developing "native vocations," a phrase with a lingering aura of colonialism about it, but one that nevertheless described the process through which the communities have helped to maintain the strength of their mission presence. But even allowing for those variables, religious communities—men and women—have far fewer people in Latin America today than ten years ago.

"At the peak period, we probably had twenty-six or twenty-seven men down here," said Father Elias Manning of his Conventual Franciscan community in Brazil. "Now there are fourteen of us. I feel satisfied and happy here, and I think that most of those who are still here feel the same way. The average age is going up all the time. I'm thirty-eight and I'm the third youngest. The average age is probably around forty-five."

In Lima, Maryknoll Sister Bernadette Desmond painted a similar picture:

Maryknoll has half the number in Peru it did ten years ago. We're trying to reassess things. The focus used to be on the emphasis of change; most people now are focusing instead on the quality of life. It's in keeping with the great re-evaluation of our whole mission that's going on. Do we want more nuns here? We ask ourselves if we want to be more selective. The median age of the community as a whole is fifty-six; here in the Peru region it's forty-six. There were fifty-four in my class and sixty in the class of 1960. In recent years the number has been down as low as two or three. A few sisters are beginning to question our overall presence.

Redemptorist Father Joseph R. May, in Brazil since 1954, has been a pastor and seminary director. Now superior of his vice province, he sees some signs of hope.

In spite of passing frustrations, in general our mission effort here has all been worthwhile. Our main difficulty is the shortage of personnel, but with thirty clerical students at the level of philosophy and theology we hope to improve this situation in a few years.

A few communities serve as the exceptions to prove the rule of declining mission interest; they are the ones whose current mission enrollment is at its peak, or was, at any rate, in 1976, when they answered questions about their mission involvement. The Jesuits of Oak Park, Illinois, for example, had eighteen priests at work in Peru and Venezuela, where they had been serving since 1960, and Father Edward F. Mann attributed their relative success to two factors: "An open stance to select ministries most useful in each area; an increase of vocations in Peru itself."

Father James Zelinski, O.F.M. Cap., reported a similar situation for the Detroit Capuchins, who have been in Nicaragua since 1939 and opened a Honduras mission in 1975: forty-two men in mission assignments in 1975 and 1976, an all-time high. He cited several reasons for the missions' healthy status: the pastoral approach of the missioners themselves, which attracts those still in training; the missioners' continued attempts to move as a group to update themselves, and "the presence of a very pastoral, people-oriented bishop."

Another group that has not sustained mission losses is the community of Dominican Sisters of Adrian, Michigan, which has thirty-three women assigned to missions in the Dominican Republic (opened in 1945), Puerto Rico (1946), and Peru (1963). Many sisters from overseas areas have returned to their home lands to help account for the relative constancy of the apostolate, a spokeswoman wrote.

Still another group of Dominican Sisters, those from Sinsinawa, Wisconsin, at work in Bolivia and Paraguay since 1960, had an encouraging report in 1976: The ten sisters in the two missions at that point represented the highest figure ever for the community. They listed six reasons for their apparent success: careful determination of the kind of apostolic work needed, especially as it was changing; planning and provision for needed personnel for a given ministry; careful determination of a sister's qualifications ("both the professional competence and the ability to handle the entire South American experience"); constant theological updating in South America; a healthy and stable community life; and a vital interest and support from the congregation.

Their greatest area of satisfaction, the sisters wrote, has been "in our positive relationships with the Bolivian and Paraguayan people and in the areas of ministry where we have been able to educate the people to assume their own responsibility for the particular apostolic work—to help the local church become more responsive and alive, to help the people to *be* church." The most difficult aspect of their mission endeavor: "Knowing how to cope with the changing concept of mission in a changing church."

Most of the U.S. missioners still at work in Latin America would know what the Dominican Sisters from Wisconsin meant, because they have been through it themselves. They have been through it as individual missioners, as members of congregations or communities, as North Americans. U.S. men and women who went off to Latin America found a world they had never seen, one that some had never even imagined. In the changing church—and the changing world—of the late sixties and the seventies, they discovered new ways to deal with it, and had their religious, social, and political convictions altered dramatically as a result.

"I've become aware of the evils of the individualistic, capitalistic free enterprise system," said Dominican Father Mathias Mueller, a missioner in Bolivia for nearly twenty years. "I favor a Christian socialism, pacifism, and have become bitterly opposed to most United States foreign policy, political and economic."

Another Dominican in Bolivia, Father John Risley, expressed similar thoughts: "I have a greater sensitivity and awareness of the whole area of social justice, of the need for radical changes in the international economic-political order and of United States 'imperialism' in Latin America."

Father May, superior of his Redemptorist vice-province, said:

I came to Brazil in the pre-Vatican II days with very little knowledge of sociology and vague concepts of Latin American and North American politics. The experience of these years has undoubtedly awakened me to the problems of poverty, to a certain mistrust of the intentions of politicians in general, both North and South American, to a recognition of the need of building Latin American society from the base with education, formation of principles for thinking, community consciousness.

Oblate Father Michael Pfeifer wrote from Mexico that his views, too, had changed:

I now realize that our labor must in some way always be connected with social justice and that the gospel must in some way communicate hope to people who may be in a hopeless socio-political structure. . . . My experience has made me grow. . . . It taught me to come out of the clouds and find God right here on earth with his people.

Father John Clermont, a Capuchin, went to Honduras in 1972 armed with a Ph.D. in economics and said his socio-political views had not changed substantially. However, he added:

If anything, Honduras has taught me "socially" that the United States might learn something about lowering its sights concerning its pursuit of worldly goods, etc. Obviously, the majority of people there live poorly, many in misery. But their attitutdes, sometimes fatalistic, offer much to us concerning life and death. They need better health care, more expansive educational facilities, more intensive agriculture, peace, and much more, but a word of caution seems in order: all within the context of the culture of that society.

"I feel much more a part of the Latin American scene than the American scene, which I see as provincial and closed," wrote Father Justinian Liebl, a Capuchin who worked twenty-one years in Nicaragua, studied nine months in Ecuador, and visited at least ten different Latin American countries. "Through my mission experience—covering twenty-one years of my priestly life—the Vatican II documents, ecclesial efforts, and the Medellín documents, my faith today is much more biblical, realistic, and compassionate than it was twenty-five years ago."

Complex Changes

The changes in Latin American mission life in the seventies affected all the United States missioners, diocesan and religious. But diocesan personnel were affected mainly in terms of numbers; the problems affecting religious order priests were more numerous, and more complex.

For example, there was a growing isolation—not all bad, at that—noted by Father Manning in Brazil:

Years ago we used to have steady contact with other United States missionaries in Brazil, a steady flow. But we don't have it anymore, probably due to two reasons: first, there have been big drops in manpower, and as a result people are more tied down. There's not as much time as there used to be.

But secondly, and this is probably a more significant reason, the people who have stayed here, in general, are the ones who are set. They don't feel as ill at ease in a foreign country; they don't feel the need to visit with other American priests the way they used to. You get more international in your outlook. We used to feel that anything from the United States was the best, anything from Brazil was secondary. That all contributed to building up the wall.

Both Fathers McCrane and Survil (a Maryknoll associate) pointed to the changing nature of Maryknoll's work in Latin America. According to McCrane:

Our smaller number today hasn't left us weaker in terms of effectiveness. It's forced us to rethink the nature of our missionary presence. We're being forced to look for pastoral leaders among the people themselves. Maybe the Holy Spirit got tired of waiting after these 400 years and decided that these people themselves should take responsibility. . . .

The diminution of mission personnel has sharpened us. The emphasis now is much more along the lines of developing Christian communities. Missionary work used to be seen more in terms of starting pastoral activities; what we're seeing now, with the urgent problems we have and fewer hands to deal with them, is a move to a more active role. It's like St. Paul's style of missionary activity. He stayed in one place just long enough to get things started.

"We're less tied down to daily pastoral responsibilities," Survil said, " which is not to say that our contribution is not crucial." He cited the efforts of Maryknoll priests in many fields—catechetical centers, the Latin American press, CELAM—adding: "The emerging role of Maryknoll in Latin America may be just that—providing communication between the Latin American churches on the level of middle management operating out of the United States. A benign multinational, in other words."

Oblate Father James Sullivan is doing something along those lines in Rio. He is the director of a renewal course in the Theological Center of Studies and Spirituality for Religious Life, operated by the National Conference of Religious for Brazil. Attended by fifty religious, representing thirty-nine different congregations from twelve states of Brazil, the course is aimed at training leaders and animators for renewal in religious life, as well as deepening the personal religious life of those who are enrolled.

Sullivan, a friendly and gregarious New Yorker, prepared for his role by studying in St. Louis after winding up a term as provincial in Brazil. "After I finished the job," he commented drily, "somebody said, 'Let's teach him about reality and leadership,' so at fifty I began a whole new career—after being here twenty-three years."

The Oblates' drop in Brazil is slight compared to some others, Sullivan agreed, down from twenty-five at its peak in the sixties (the mission began in 1945) to twenty-two in 1976. The particular closeness of the group, he believes, is the responsible factor:

We pushed for community. The more we're together, the better things are. I'm very sensitive to it, trying to see who's happy and who's not. I got a call one night a few months ago. It was in May, and all the guys were together for an ordination anniversary party. Just about every priest from the São Paulo province was there that night, and they were calling those of us who couldn't be with them—just to let us know they were thinking of us.

Father Vincent Dougherty, a Philadelphian, has spent fifteen of his twenty years as a Franciscan priest in South America, six years in Brazil and nine more in Bolivia, where he works out of the Alto parish near the La Paz airport. One of six children, he has two brothers who also became priests and two sisters who became nuns, and the closeness of his family life carries over into his concept of religious orders and mission work. In an interview he said:

In the long run, for the stability of a mission, I feel that religious order priests are best. The majority of diocesan priests here probably felt a commitment for a fixed term, five years or so. That's fine, but their vocation is not to be a missionary all their lives, as ours is.

The whole idea of the Franciscans is to live the gospel. I've seen changes in the men who came down here first. As friars, our apostolate is the fraternal life. I feel a minimum of three Franciscans is needed in a community. We're not committed so strongly any more to a single parish, but more to a community. This is the biggest change that's taken place.

Of course, there's been a drop in religious priests coming to the missions too. Younger priests in religious communities today have too many options. In the old days, it was teach, parish work, or missions. Today you do your own thing; that's part of it. I've always felt we should have more missionaries.

I've seen good changes in our own mission. We're making theology down here while they're studying it up home in the States. Teamwork in parishes began here a long time ago; it was a natural development for the good of the people. We've come a long way pastorally, without studying how to do it.

Here in Bolivia we used to have sacramental priests, but none of us is just that any more; we're involved in the social aims of the people. This means working with the poor. You're never going to change the rich down here except for one or two; you have to start at the bases.

I suppose we haven't been forerunners in speaking out forcefully on matters of social justice, but we've done it effectively, in a quiet way, by working with the poor. What kind of a revolutionary was Francis? He didn't accomplish an awful lot, but he changed the world by his example. That's what we're trying to do.

The U.S. missioner's spiritual life in Latin America is different from what it was a decade ago, reflecting new lifestyles and changing apostolates. There is less emphasis on external devotions and sacramental activity, greater concern for living the gospel and influencing others to do the same. Three missioners in present or recent leadership positions—Fathers Sullivan and Manning in Brazil, and McCrane in Peru—considered the new expression of personal religious activity with varying reactions. According to Sullivan:

We went through an activist period, and the work was so tremendous that many got away from their own prayer life, and their community prayer life. But a couple of years ago, we came back to the fact that prayer and spiritual life were needed. If we think back to the reason we got together in the first place, the rest follows.

Manning conceded that spiritual life in Latin American missions today is less external and more personal, in marked contrast to the old regimented style of reading at meals, daily rosary, and other devotions:

> We've drifted from that, although we're getting back in that direction a little. Is it better or worse now? I really don't know; you can't compare it. We can't live what we lived a few years ago. In general, the men—myself included—used to feel the need for that kind of regimented life. I do miss aspects of it, getting together for prayer, the benefits that can come from that.
>
> If you can drop some of the barriers that set you apart, and get a little more human, operate from confidence instead of from fear, that will get you close to the people. That's the way that this greater freedom has had most of its impact. For me it's been a tremendous help, and I'm sure it has been that to others too. Because of it, many are leading a more profound personal life.

McCrane, who has been in Peru since 1966, spending five years in the altiplano before being elected Maryknoll's regional superior in 1971, considered the question thoughtfully, and provided a lengthy reply. It is a deeply-felt, moving, and highly accurate reading of the spiritual mood of today's Latin American missioner, trying to reconcile traditional practices with the demanding new insights of his work:

> The former old style of "spiritual life" does not exist as it did before, that is true. And yet, I would say that the average missionary here feels as deep a need for something along these lines as ever before. He would not stick around if he did not do something about it. Good will alone will not get one very far.
>
> As far as the individual goes, he moves as he can, through his work, reading, private prayer, and religious activities. Most often today it takes the form of a reflection on what his daily life consists of and how it shapes up each day, and lining that up according to the gospel and what it demands of him. The younger men feel that very much—a reflection on life and their own life and work, and the gospel criteria.
>
> Community? While a missioner is generally rather an independent person and somewhat of an individualist, I think today he feels the need for community support more than ever. . . . In the different areas I see developing, especially in the more remote areas, more and more spontaneous group activity like discussions and reflection groups, prayer groups, social opportunities, often with a good liturgy or biblical discus-

sion. While we as superiors promote these, they are handled locally and run by the men themselves.

Summing things up, McCrane said, missioners today feel a need for spirituality, both as individuals and as members of a community, but it is taking a different form from that of former times. He went on to evaluate the change:

> Not to canonize the present, but I sense something pretty healthy and authentic about it, too. It is more human. It is more authentic in the sense that it responds more to the living situation of a missioner. It is more integrated in the sense that it is not just a head trip, but other human dimensions figure in—the emotions, for example—and it is more frank, too.
>
> I see it, for example, in the deepening commitment made by the liberation theologians—a commitment to Christ, to the Scriptures, to the church. Now, the church may not always coincide with the "official" church, but these men do all they can to inform and keep themselves linked with the local church, often at difficult sacrifices. Poverty, chastity, and obedience are often more seen in terms of service to the poor, to the oppressed, to the marginated, to the need for a change in structures.
>
> *Bueno*, I do not want to paint only a rosy picture, as there are problems for sure. But this is how it is shaping up as I see it.

The "colonial-power lackey chaplains" Ivan Illich complained about more than a decade ago are difficult to find in the seventies, if, indeed, they ever existed in force at all when he was writing about them. As wrapped up in the American way of life as they might have been in the sixties, missioners of that era were hardly insensitive to the needs of the poor; today, the commitment to that apostolate is quite overwhelming. Conducting an orphanage in Mexico, as Father William Wasson does; ministering to the homeless boys of Ecuador, as does Jesuit Father Jack Halligan, "the Shoeshine Priest"; encouraging slum-dwellers from Rio to San Salvador to get together to reflect on their station in life, U.S. missionaries in Latin America are almost totally dedicated to the cause of the poor.

"It's called an orphanage, because there is no other word in English for it, but this is not a simple sheltering effort," Sister Mary Jean Dorcy wrote of Father Wasson's project in Mexico. A Dominican Sister of the Congregation of the Holy Cross who worked at the orphanage for several years, Sister Mary Jean said:

> Father Wasson plans to put all the children through school, to the point (1) where they can earn a decent living so that they can raise a family in decent circumstances, and (2) where they can do something to help their disadvantaged neighbor. . . . They are being taught a richly workable

sort of religion, being trained to go immediately to help wherever help is needed.

Father Halligan's "shoeshine project" in Quito, the Working Boys Center, serves more than three hundred children as combination second home, school, and dining hall. He hopes to break the kind of life pattern he described to an interviewer in 1977, talking about a typical youngster in his care:

> The kid's mother isn't a prostitute. She's probably lived with a man in common law marriage until the kids piled up and the man took off. So, as soon as the boy is able, he goes out, shines shoes until he's about fifteen. Then he gets himself a girl, produces his own children, and the cycle of poverty continues.

In La Paz, a plumber named Miguel welcomed a visitor who accompanied Father Chuck Tobin, ushering him into a meeting room he had provided for the *comunidad de base* which meets there. The furnishings are spare: a few benches, a battered desk, bare electric light bulbs hanging from the ceiling. There is room for perhaps twenty-five or thirty people, who meet there, with Tobin's fond encouragement, to consider their life, their faith, and their method of dealing with both. The plumber, Miguel, shows the meeting room proudly, as proudly as if it were a cathedral, which, if today's U.S. missioners are to be believed, it just might be. Someday.

Said Father Survil:

> The majority of priests, simply because they have such a heavy burden just to maintain a sacramental church, will not be the agents to usher in the servant-model of the church, or indeed, to save the Latin American church from this inhibiting form of self-concept. Father José Marins, the noted Brazilian pastoral theologian, believes that only those free to pioneer new ministries—namely nuns, laypeople, and missionaries—are in a position to recreate the church from the bottom up. I agree with his assessment.

U.S. missioners are looking more and more for pastoral leaders among the people. Father Elias Manning said in Rio:

> There are fifty or sixty thousand people in our parish in Rio Comprido, and if we get a total of a thousand of them at mass on weekends we're doing well. Obviously, we're not touching nearly enough people. We're trying to do that now through small groups, Bible discussions, and the like. They're all exclusively lay-oriented, in keeping with the approach of the archdiocese here.

Among the Miskito tribe in Nicaragua, Father Casper has nine Indian deacons helping him to put into practice his thesis that local cultures must not only be preserved, but encouraged as well:

We have placed the highest priorities on the training of lay leaders and catechists and deacons. All must be chosen by their own community. We try to get two or three catechists in each village, and one or two young ladies to teach the children. The catechists instruct parents who wish to have their children baptized, also those who wish to marry. They conduct religious services and teach the Bible.

Father Jim Madden, the Maryknoller in Peru, carried the approach to its fullest extreme, immersing himself, and the three sisters who joined him in his experiment, into the culture of the altiplano Indians in the Juli prelature. The program began to develop after the eight bishops of southern Peru formed the South Andean Region in 1968 and decided that each would establish one experimental community to search out new approaches in apostolates. "It looked ready-made for me," Madden said, "but it took me more than two years to sell my idea."

He started out with a hypothesis that included three principal points. First, he said, the people he would serve must be considered as Catholic Christians and that, therefore, "the church exists here in the people of God." Second, one must assume that there are two churches (as noted earlier): the "official" church and that of the People of God. Third: the "official church" must be recognized as being marginated from the People of God, or, as he put it, "the real church." He continued:

My approach was that I had to get in contact with this real church by getting in contact with the *campesinos*. This church is almost all rural, and my idea is that that's where reality is down here. So, the first step was to get out of town. The second was to speak the language. The third was to live a simple lifestyle, and the fourth was to make a minimum commitment of five years.

Three U.S. sisters, all from different communities, joined Madden in the five-year experiment. They lived in adobe huts, without running water or any other amenities that most North Americans take for granted, and had the most general of objectives: to establish dialogue, to personalize, to form basic Christian communities, to reach the confidence of the people to lead them to form local missioners. "We hoped," Madden said, "that the local church, the People of God, would indicate to us how to contribute, invite us to help, become committed to social issues. And we made friends out there. There were no locks, no walls. And I think we got through to them."

One of the three sisters who took part in the experiment was Sister Bernadette Desmond, the Maryknoll superior in Peru, who described the project as her "greatest experience." During that period, she said, "we were able to move from a paternalistic image to a role of service." She questions the program's practicality for large groups of missioners, and concedes that without other obligations, those in the experiment were able to concentrate in one small area. "We adjusted to the confinement," she said, but noted an interesting paradox: "One of the most challenging things was that we were called to be a presence, rather than simply becoming involved in projects. But this caused frustration in our experiment. Most of us were underemployed."

Madden said that a study of the experiment will be distributed for discussion and possible future guidelines. "I'm sure that some will agree with what we were doing," he said, "and some will challenge it. But a lot of people will begin to think it through and search for their own answers."

New Directions

The overwhelming emphasis placed by today's U.S. missioners on the laity, especially the laity in the local church, is strong, almost intense. In San Salvador, before his expulsion, Father Survil wrote of pastoral week programs with heavy representations of lay people, intent on building basic Christian communities. "The idea is not new," he wrote:

> Church history will surely give credit to the Chicago priests who first implemented the San Miguelito plan in Panama. Since then the Latin American bishops (CELAM) and now Pope Paul, in *Evangelii Nuntiandi*, have recognized the necessity to renew or even altogether restructure the Latin American church by means of these small groups.

Father Philip Catanzaro, a New Jersey priest of the Oblates of St. Francis de Sales, in Brazil since 1964, wrote several years ago of the "new direction" of Brazil's bishops away from traditional lines:

> This type of leadership gives heart to the many local religious and lay leaders to continue their efforts to provide hope for the suffering rural peasants, urban workers, academic classes, and the far too many unemployed who seek liberation, not to join ranks with either the right or the left, as identified by present-day capitalist and communist powers, but rather to find a new way, free of all built-in and extracted injustices, free to form new men sensitive to the human values of Christian fraternal love, justice, freedom, and equality.

Monsignor David Ratermann of St. Louis also referred to Latin America's "Third Church," adding:

It seems quite obvious that our top priority task is to accompany, support, foment, and serve the birth and growth of this Third Church which is springing up all around us, so that with the light and grace of the Lord, it may become stronger, be purified of its defects, and become more authentically what it should be.

Capuchin Father Joseph Walsh, who spent the years from 1940 to 1968 in Nicaragua, and the time since then in Honduras, sums up an older missioner's viewpoint in eloquent terms:

The fact that I've lasted this long in Central America would seem to indicate that I'm satisfied and happy in the work. There have been ups and downs, misjudgments, re-evaluations, and changes, but in general my attitude is that I'm here to help the people to solve their problems, and not to give them imported solutions. It's a slow, grueling process.

I believe the church must be on the side of the poor in helping them to get organized and reclaim by peaceful means their rights. The church must also stand up to the rich and the government to help farm reform, better education, health and living condition programs, even though it brings down the wrath and persecution of those in power. Unfortunately, Latin American priests tend to side with the powers that be and it is the foreign priests who plead for social justice, and hence are persecuted and expelled.

The people have a great faith in God, great patience and long-suffering, bordering, it might seem, on the fringe of fatalism, but with great confidence in the Lord. Their spirit of hospitality and charity and also endurance for their religious convictions and commitments is bound to rub off on anyone who is open to the Spirit of the Lord. Their example, friendship, and faith have been a source of encouragement to me in my work. They're worth all I can give—and more.

How do today's U.S. missioners feel about their work, about their effectiveness? A mood of guarded optimism seems to prevail, but there is also a great deal of impatience. Despite the fact that many of them perceive themselves as having made necessarily radical changes in their mission roles as individuals, they are dissatisfied with the overall approach of the U.S. church in confronting Latin America's problems.

"Mission efforts from the States have largely been an importation obstructing the growth of a real Latin American church responding to the needs of its people," said Dominican Father Risley in Bolivia. Said fellow Dominican Father Mueller:

I would distinguish between the Americans who come on a short-term basis and those who remain indefinitely. The former fill temporarily what most bishops think is a need, being responsible for a certain area known as a parish, frequently building a church with outside funds, and providing the sacraments. The latter group of missioners can also be divided: those who continue to do as the former, only for a longer period, and others who finally see the real needs: helping the people to be aware of social injustice and recognizing their Christian obligation to do something about it, and helping them to form a local autonomous church. . . . Unfortunately, most U.S. mission effort in Bolivia has been short-term stopgapping, and has enabled the bishops to avoid facing the real problems and seeking more permanent solutions.

"The danger to religious missionaries," Brother Thomas More Page had written some years earlier, "lies in the fact that they think they are solving the problems of the church by sending personnel who will perpetuate the status quo of endemic misery." By the latter part of the seventies, most if not all U.S. missioners were acutely aware of that danger and tailored their roles as best they could to avoid its consequences.

In Lima, the politically-active Father Tom Burns put it this way: "We've got to stop thinking 'mission' in terms of going from one place to another. It's a matter of going from one time to another. The church has to recognize this—these 'signs of the times'—and play its role. We missioners have to see these things, and then act."

Monsignor Ratermann, home in St. Louis on vacation, spoke to his diocesan newspaper about the missioner's role as catalyst, of working with small groups to aid, support, and guide, but always in the context of what the local group has set up:

The greatest satisfaction I can possibly get is to see people grow in their faith. I've seen this on an intimate, individual basis within a limited circle of a few people that I know well, and also in the ministry of the sacrament of penance. I listen to these people in confession and I am ashamed because I realize that they have a lot more faith than I do. So the people save the priest, me, as much as the priest helps the people. But really, God does it all.

To see people grow as individuals and to see a community of people grow in maturity, grow in awareness of what it means to be God's people, to see them grow in awareness of what the challenges are, to see them face up to injustice and the desire to reach out to people who are getting the short end of the stick, and the desire to serve them in any way at all—this really turns me on.

More than one hundred missioners in Latin America today were interviewed personally or through correspondence in connection with work on this book. In assessing the effectiveness of their performance, there was a remarkable incidence of agreement on several key factors. Successes were largely attributed to programs in which missioners incorporated local customs and culture, efforts which took into consideration the Latin mentality, and those in which there was a conscious avoidance of attempts to impose U.S. solutions on Latin problems.

Respondents emphasized the need to avoid any effort at Americanizing the Latin church, to improve screening and training methods for prospective United States missioners, and to work wherever possible within the Latin American culture and mentality. In short, they indicated a genuine awareness, a painful awareness, at times, of the record of mistakes made by an earlier wave of U.S. missioners and a pervasive intent to avoid them in the future.

Father Philip Devlin, the Holy Cross priest exiled from Chile, could complain about an overall record no better than mixed, in which U.S. missioners might still be engaged in "very dubious alliances" with "oppressive regimes." But he had positive words as well for all the gains that had been made—the conscious identification with the masses of poor and persecuted, the desire to serve them well.

Perhaps the most objective summary of the current state of United States mission efforts in Latin America, one which saw its strengths and weaknesses with an expert eye, came from an old Latin America hand. Early in 1977, shortly before he returned to his home diocese of Davenport after six years of self-imposed exile—three years in Mexico, three years in El Salvador—Father Mike Colonnese reflected on the contemporary condition of the U.S. mission presence:

> I don't think there is any one "direction" of the U.S. mission effort in Latin America today. Possibly that accounts for a limitation to generalized error and also for the presence of some very positive programing. Within the same community, you will find highly divergent opinions about what is to be done, and so forth.
>
> I know there are some very solid, dedicated, and committed U.S. missionaries in Latin America. They don't make waves, don't get into the newspapers, but they are providing an indispensable ministry and giving good witness to the Truth. They live very modest lives, make no unreasonable demands, and are motivated by a love for the people whom they serve. They do provide positive accomplishments for the U.S. mission effort.
>
> But I do firmly believe that as long as the United States church retains its highly institutionalized structure, it can never be a truly "missionary" church. Oh, there will be efforts like those we know today and have known in the past, but that there will be a true outpouring of love in the missionary context is highly doubtful.
>
> Our U.S. church is too self-protective, too involved in things not-

gospel, too bureaucratic, and too top-heavy to ever hope to produce a strong mission arm for its catholicity—unless it undergoes some very radical (and difficult) internal changes. The U.S. church indulges in too many 'campaign-type' activities instead of activities of real love. It launches great movements (such as PAVLA, or even the Campaign for Human Development) without really being totally committed to their objectives . . . and not totally committed, not disposed to make the sacrifices really required.

But even these campaigns and "movements" have their positive results, and it is my belief—because I believe in the presence of the Spirit in the American church—that some day it will all happen. Just as Jesus planned it.

14

U.S. Mission to
Latin America: An Assessment

The American church—the bishops—felt it was a question of doing a big job in a hurry. They shouldn't be overly criticized for all the things that went wrong; the Latin American church has to shoulder some of the blame, too. The local bishops didn't want to make things sound too bad, and so they told us the job could be done, and done quickly. And once we were involved, we saw how wrong everybody was.

Maryknoll Father Vincent Mallon was expressing one aspect of a fairly common point of view about the Latin American mission endeavor of the North American church: that it was an enterprise for which we were not adequately prepared, and, therefore, one doomed to failure from the outset.

A few might argue the point, but in the long run its logic seems inescapable. The United States church just did not know enough about the job it was called on to do. Bishop John Fitzpatrick summed it up in an earlier chapter, in more colorful but no less accurate terms: we should have cased the joint before opening up a franchise.

As one missioner after another has explained, the training offered was simply not equal to the task at hand. Few were sufficiently versed in the language to allow their labors to be effective; fewer still had an accurate reading of the culture and tradition in which they were asked to live and work. Not nearly enough saw their role as one that might last a lifetime; they felt, as Mallon notes above, that the job to be done was one that American know-how could handle with dispatch. There was a "can-do" attitude about the adventure that was unable to see it any other way.

If problems developed early enough in the mission grassroots, they multiplied even more rapidly for the North Americans at the national level. It was not simply the lack of coordination of tactical mission efforts that stalled the overall enterprise (although that in itself was a serious problem). More important, a split developed over the long-range strategies to be employed. Two planes of thinking emerged, planes whose trajectories veered ever further apart, with disastrous results for the Latin America program. On one plane, one level, were most of the bishops and religious superiors, people whose mission philosophy followed traditional lines; on the other were Colonnese and those who shared his increasingly radical approach to meeting Latin America's problems. It was a classic matchup of command versus staff, and, predictably, when pushed far enough, it was command that would have the final say.

That ever-widening rift foreshadowed an even more ominous break that loomed ahead: the confrontation between a U.S. mission program still operating mostly along traditional, sacramental lines, and a bold new church of liberation that would shoot up from the soil of oppression and flower in the field of Medellín. The fact that U.S. mission efforts had, in one sense, spurred the growth of the new Latin American church made it no less impatient with U.S. shortcomings and no less vocal in its demand to control its own destiny.

The "big job that could be done in a hurry" turned out to be, of course, anything but that, leading some critics to declare, years later, that we never should have gotten involved at all. Few share that extreme view. But Sister Marlene De Nardo probably spoke for many others when she considered an interviewer's question: Was it all a bad idea? "Historically, it was an inevitable idea," she replied. "But that doesn't mean we should repeat it."

United States mission involvement in Latin America, infinitesimally small before the forties, began its growth period in the late 1950s, boomed in the early sixties, faded toward the end of that decade, and continues today, on a reduced scale, with a different set of values behind it. Only a few of its harshest critics would contend that it has been an unrelieved disaster, utterly without redeeming values. And even fewer see it in a totally positive light. Most observers—missioners themselves, and those in a position to evaluate the effectiveness of their work—give it mixed grades, with the poorest marks reserved for the early years. According to Father Frederick McGuire:

> Many of the things that did go wrong with the mission endeavor are directly traceable to the lack of properly-trained personnel, especially in the early part of the sixties. Too many people were trying to implant U.S.-style options. They were well-meaning, but what they did was a terrible mistake.
>
> We had our bad points, true, but the missioners earned the respect of the church. There wasn't much of that anti-Americanism as far as the missioners were concerned; they liked us, and not just for our money— although maybe it would have been better if we hadn't had so much of that. Also, there was good dialogue created through meetings of religious, and that's still going on today.

Anyone attempting to assess the U.S. mission program along simple lines of success or failure faces a number of difficulties, not the least of which is that of determining the criterion to be used. If it were simply a matter of measuring U.S. religious participation against the initial goal of 10 percent, there would be no problem. The numbers fell far short of that mark, as, indeed, even Father John Considine, who developed the 10 percent plan and convinced the Vatican of its potential, must have known they would.

But it was not the percentage, of course, that was the major concern; it was what that number of U.S. missioners might accomplish. Here, again, the results, with curiously interesting overtones, are mixed. The mission drive had negative results or only partial success in meeting its stated goals: evangelizing the people, fostering native vocations, stemming the communist threat. It scored its greatest successes in areas that were not part of the original mission plan: assisting at the birth of a dynamic new Latin American church, a church of the people, and internationalizing the thinking of a large and influential segment of the church in the United States. There will be more assessments to make in the future, because the mission program continues to this day. But the odds seem to be that success will outweigh failure in the years to come as far as the Latin American program is concerned. If any endeavor of the modern U.S. church has benefited from the mistakes it made in the past, it surely must be this one.

No Shortage of Critics

And mistakes there were. There has been no shortage of critics to point them out over the years, and there were even a few prophets to warn—unsuccessfully—against them.

Ivan Illich was one of them from the start, telling even his earliest classes at Cuernavaca that half of the students never should have come in the first place. His friend, Father Fitzpatrick of Fordham, tried to make the same point in more palatable terms. Writing in *America* in 1962, he said that Illich's training center was trying to overcome the idea that North Americans had to get to Latin America on the next airplane to bolster the Latins' faltering faith:

> This emphasis on urgency and haste can easily create the impression that any Catholic of good will can find a rich harvest waiting to be gathered in Latin America, and that painstaking preparation is not needed. What is more serious, it could encourage, especially among Catholics in the United States, a typical American reaction: "Let's show them how to do it." Obviously, it is a religious imperialism of a damaging kind that says, "When we have made the Church in Latin America like the Church in the United States, things will be much better."

Individual missioners were all too aware of that problem. Chicago Augustinian Father Gerard Theis, who arrived in Peru in 1964, lamented the lack of spiritual formation in U.S. missionary preparation. "Too many come with a messiah complex," he wrote, "not to share the kingdom of God on earth, but rather to impose their hopes and images on what to them is a foreign land."

Theis and many others pointed to another problem missioner, a prototype of many who went to Latin America in the big mission push of the sixties:

> Problems are created by missioners who volunteer because they are dissatisfied at home. If such missionaries came humbly to a mission to truly "find themselves" (as it were: to begin a renewed religious and pastoral life), they might become a positive factor. But too many of this type are volunteers or "sent to do their thing" away from the controls found back home.

"What we failed to do," observed Bishop Fitzpatrick, "is to continue to be aware of Pope John's plea to help Latin America. There was a great number of priests who discovered they were in the wrong place, at the wrong time, with the wrong vocation."

Colonnese, writing in 1976, saw in our failures not only a lack of preparation, but an outright refusal to prepare ourselves. "The absolutely impenetrable nationalistic mentality of many United States bishops made the task all but impossible," he said. He referred to the "cultural arrogance" of U.S. bishops and accused them of an inability to recognize competence, particularly in theological and sociological fields, in their Latin American counterparts.

The greatest problems? They were too numerous to cite, Colonnese complained: selection of candidates ("I found a lot of psychological problems, especially among the lay volunteers"); preparation and training ("the lack of humility required to enter and live in another culture made it difficult to persuade superiors, bishops, etc., of the need for expensive, lengthy preparations"); coordination ("all but impossible; every diocese had to establish its own little mission in Latin America"). There was "foolish" construction, initiation of programs that had not been well thought-out, lack of direction from the local church, all compounded beyond redemption, Colonnese said, by the "obsession with power" of the U.S. bishops. "I honestly believe," he said, "that the United States could have launched one of the most enthusiastic, dynamic, and successful mission efforts in the church's history. We had the manpower, the money, the mobility, the communications. We failed because we refused to serve."

There were other serious problem areas, pointed out by missioners and commentators alike. One of them was self-interest, noted Holy Cross Father Claude Pomerleau. "Even where we made generous contributions, we tended to expect a payoff of some kind," said Pomerleau, who was active in his community's Chile mission program. "If the Marxists weren't voted out, for example, we looked on whatever we had done as a bad investment."

Tom Quigley had a close-up view of the slapdash approach to coordination coming out of Washington. "There were so many differences on how to do things," he said. "In all, we ran a seat-of-the-pants operation."

Father Harvey Steele pointed to the failure of many missioners to free themselves from the sacramental mentality, even in the face of overwhelming poverty and injustice:

> We continue to see ourselves as fulfilling our total commitment by saving an abstraction which we call the soul, rather than a living person composed of body and soul. We think we can fulfill this function by conferring the sacraments on people who have no understanding of the true spiritual significance of the actions we perform for them. We are content to exhort to virtue in circumstances which call for action to change structures that prevent man from being either virtuous or vicious, because they maintain him in a subhuman condition.

Father George Dudak, who opened the Paterson diocesan mission in Ica, Peru, recalled a persistent U.S. reluctance to entrust projects such as catechist training to the local people. "Maryknoll had a catechist program," he said, "and so did we—helping us to get people ready for communion, for confirmation, and so on. If we put it into their hands, it worked out. But when we did it ourselves, it was a guarantee of failure."

Latin American criticism of U.S. mission failures was slow to build —except for those in the radical wing of the church, who had been skeptical from the outset. But most bishops welcomed U.S. personnel and financial aid initially and were reluctant to call undue attention to problem areas. Even years later, the criticism tends to be moderate. "When working in small groups," Brazil's Cardinal Aloisio Lorscheider, the president of CELAM, said in 1976, "American missionaries have been excellent. But when working in large groups, especially in a limited area, it's as if the church itself there is a foreign one. Maintaining their own style of living and relating to the local people is very difficult."

Interviewed in the same year, Lima's Auxiliary Bishop Germán Schmitz said that cultural differences between U.S. missioners and Peruvian priests seemed to be no problem at first: "At the beginning, United States missioners were moved by a blind mission zeal (and not too negatively). They wanted to help the church in Latin America, in Peru. We ourselves didn't see this as negative. We accepted them coming with their ideas, and we were happy to have them. It wasn't their fault or ours that problems developed." Arguments over cultural differences resulted in a lack of integration, he said—some "foreign islands" with their own types of parishes. Most of the missioners came with religious communities, Bishop Schmitz said, and took their direction from them. "But more and more," he added, "they have started to accept local criteria."

Criticism was more pointed when it was expressed in forums designed to improve the United States mission effort. One such assembly was the first Inter-American Conference of Major Superiors in Mexico City in February 1971, the results of which stand even today as a fair appraisal of the U.S. endeavor. (Specifically, the findings and recommendations of the conference dealt with religious personnel only, but for the most part they applied as well to diocesan and lay missioners.)

A lengthy evaluation of the previous decade's mission effort from North America was delivered by the Chilean Jesuit sociologist, Renato Poblete, whose critique, while couched in respectful terms, nonetheless read like a compendium of errors. Few complained that his judgments were inaccurate.

The presence of so many foreign missioners, Poblete said, had led some Latin American bishops to neglect the area of local vocations. Another problem dealt with the missioners themselves and their "inadequate preparation." The Chilean repeated the frequently-heard complaint about a lack of proper language training and acculturation, with a slightly different twist: U.S. superiors make the mistake of sending English-speaking missioners because they think the work will be simple and they can get by easily enough. "Alas," he said, "in that way totally North American customs are transplanted. This may flatter the upper-class groups—people who are delighted to have their children acquire the social veneer of North American ways, but who are also totally uninterested in the service the religious could bring to the society where they live."

Poblete called attention to a "special problem" in adapting to the mentality of slum-dwellers clamoring for rights to liberation:

Either the [North American] religious is tempted to look skeptically at every demand they make, suspecting them to be communist-inspired and subconsciously interpreting them as criticisms of his own country's way of life; or else he falls into the opposite temptation and becomes a revolutionary, a promoter of struggles that, because of their political nature and the intimate knowledge of the country they require, are more properly the business of laymen and natives.

Poblete's check-list continued: foreign missioners should have not only the obvious formal preparation in regard to language and culture, but should live for a while in their newly-adopted lands, before beginning their labors: "not among their own kind, but in native communities, in order to grasp faster and better the mentality of the local church." They should avoid the formation of foreign ghettos, and not be concerned only with "their own little projects." They should not "repeat unimaginatively the methods they knew in parishes back home"; they should overcome their psychological blocks against starting projects that offer less than 100 percent chance of success. And money? There was simply too much of it, Poblete implied. "Some, too, import luxury items as part of their baggage, oblivious of the impression such items give in a relatively poor country. Odious comparisons are bound to be made, which further impede the integration of the newcomers."

They were the operational shortcomings. Some who heard Poblete might challenge the extent of the problems he cited, but none could deny that they existed. Others attempted to analyze their meaning in relation to the missioners' overall effectiveness: in the long run, despite their weaknesses, did the U.S. missioners succeed or fail? What happened to Latin America, its church, and its people as a result of the U.S. presence?

Phillip Berryman took a gloomy view. "The noble experiment which sought to bail out the Latin American church perhaps distracted attention from more substantial issues by delaying the inevitable moment of truth," he wrote in 1971. "It is by now clear that the church cannot expect much help in personnel from other lands, including Spain, which over the centuries has been the traditional source."

Augustinian Father John J. Burkhart, who worked in Peru from 1963 to 1971, agreed on that point: "South America today has the nucleus of a great growing church—small but truly apostolic. The majority of the 'Catholics' have not been affected. The source of vocations is still there, but it has not been tapped. With the assured influx of missionaries there was no need to tap it, and develop programs."

Franciscan Father Gratian Buttarazzi saw the same thing in Honduras: "The lifestyle of religious isn't evangelical, economically; there's been limited promotion of native vocations." So did Dominican Father John Risley in Bolivia, who felt the mission effort had a negative effect on more than vocations. "The results are very limited, and even obstructive to real needed renovation or change in many cases," he said.

Father Fidelis Michael Travaglione, a Franciscan who has worked in El Salvador, Honduras, and Guatemala, lamented the continued lack of success in another area: "I guess our greatest sadness has occurred because of our lack of ability to induce the governments in these parts to increase their efforts in the field of justice and better living conditions."

The reality behind Father Fidelis's observation is beyond challenge; many Latin American governments clearly are unjust, and unconcerned about the poor. Some critics of the U.S. mission program, in fact, will find that his sentiments border on the naive. They are those who contend that the program's pervasive western-capitalistic flavor—particularly, again, in the early years—not only permitted but actually encouraged those rightist, repressive, militaristic regimes to exist. It is true, they concede, that one of the goals of the early mission drive was the containment of communism, and that to outward appearances, the goal has been met—but at the staggering cost of allowing corrupt dictatorships to remain in power, all in the name of staving off the red menace.

One former missioner who has written and lectured extensively on this topic is Sister Marlene De Nardo, who focused attention on it at the Maryknoll Justice and Peace Convocation in 1976. She takes the position that in time of war, the state becomes the source and dispenser of rights because of the need for national security, and that what United States policy has done in Latin America since the end of World War II is to export an ideology that has kept most Latin American countries in a state of war against communism for all that time:

> This has allowed for inestimable atrocities and total deprivation of human rights in the name of "national security." How is it possible to assure human rights and to declare the value of sovereignty of individual rights while accepting all the practical, everyday circumstances imposed by the western world's ideology of war?

Because of its identification with U.S. national policies, she says, the problem is one that must be of overriding concern to the U.S. mission church.

> Can the church at the same time proclaim basic human rights for all people and identify itself with the capitalistic goals of the western world, which include this ideology of war? Furthermore, to what extent is the combating of alien ideologies only a pretext for the excesses of economic dictatorships and the exportation of the western-style production system?
> From a Latin American perspective, the real war that is being fought is not the war against communism. It is the war against the poor, the war of the developed north against the underdeveloped south. It is the war of the rich in the northern hemisphere allied with the rich in the southern hemisphere against the poor.

De Nardo admits total incompatibility between the doctrines of Christianity and communism, but maintains that the present social situation is not a doctrinal question. Rather, she says, it is a "calculated war of the international economic powers" against the underdeveloped, seeking to control their lands, minerals, and energy resources. How can the church, she asks, justify "this interminable war against the defenseless?"

Quoting Dom Helder Camara, she wonders if the dread of communism has not blinded the people of the western world to the horrors of their own social system, which "enshrines profit as the all-powerful engine of economic progress; competition as the supreme law of economics, and private ownership of the means of production as an absolute right, without limits or corresponding social obligations."

Operating on Different Planes

In Washington during the 1960s, that particular danger of the U.S. mission program was not apparent to a great number of people. But those who were aware of the problem, and of related hazards, bore influence beyond their numbers. They represented much of the leadership of the program, and their very immersion in it carried them even further away from the mainstream of traditional U.S. mission philosophy—represented, still, by the bishops who maintained the final word on the conduct of mission operations.

"We really were operating on different planes," Colonnese recalled in an interview in 1977:

It was a case of "we" and "they." "They" were the establishment, everybody tied in with the 10 percent plan—the bishops, the superiors, and so on. And "we?" You'd have to include people like Joe Gremillion, Leo Mahon, Bill Quinn, Illich—at least at first. We were operating on a different wave length. We were exposed to so much more in the way of Latin thinking, in the dangers that the wrong kind of mission approach could bring about.

We weren't opposed to the mission program as such, although if I knew then what I know now, I think I would have been. Our concern was quality, form, style, preparation, the meaning of mission. We were listening to lay people as it had never been done before, and this alienated many bishops at the time. That was because we realized the new Latin American church had to be a lay-led church. Only the laity were in a position to do this. We wanted a more flexible church. The Latin America Bureau, CICOP, our publications—all these were working toward this end.

John Considine was in an anomalous position. By temperament he was more with the official, the traditional group, but by title he was at the head of the other group—ours. It was a period of great conflict in his life. He wound up by moving into the background, trying to maintain peace with the bishops.

At that point, we went further along on our own plane, and they went down—pulling out missioners, ending commitments. I had said that within twenty years the American mission presence in Latin America would be insignificant, and it came true sooner than I thought, in terms of numbers, in terms of priority—it's not seen as a great priority any more, either with the U.S. or the Latin American bishops—and in terms of contact. For most people there, the only contact they have with the United States now is money.

One running battle that typified the struggles involved in the "we-they" confrontation was the one that resulted, at last, in the dismantling of PAVLA.

The official church was committed to the operation, but its staff people, in the Latin America Division, were doing all they could to put it out to pasture.

There is some irony now in rereading the impassioned plea of Father George Mader in 1969—when he was PAVLA's interim director—for more recognition for the organization:

> PAVLA should be a central point of concern in the Latin America office in Washington, and funds should be channeled to it. There should be greater identity of the PAVLA program with CICOP meetings. I feel it should receive greater consideration than at present. I further feel that much is taken for granted. In effect, the dioceses are supplying Latin American bishops with needed personnel. Why, then, must the additional factor of paying all the way down the line be considered the dioceses' role? It has been a one-way street, and I think this may eventually lead to its downfall.

The downfall would not be far off, as recorded in an earlier chapter, and the problems cited by Mader surely had something to do with it. But PAVLA's track record had failed to impress those on the "Colonnese plane," and the organization's problems of survival centered not in the field but in Washington. As far as the Latin America Division was concerned, PAVLA had been a dead letter for some time.

As the Colonnese group drew further away from the official line, more and more of the U.S. church's Latin America programs showed the effects of the division at home. Almost in defiance of what would be sure criticism, the programs—CICOP, for example—became increasingly provocative in their content. Not only were they upsetting U.S. Catholics, who bristled when they heard "their" Latin American mission operation labeled an act of imperialism, but they caused serious morale problems among some of the missioners themselves. If their own home church failed to back up their work, they wondered—with perfect reason, it now seems—why on earth they should keep it going.

The treatment might have been harsh, but the results were precisely what the Colonnese group hoped to achieve: a thorough reappraisal of the style and content of the U.S. mission program. CICOP, he believes now, was especially important in that regard:

> Out of CICOP came a profound re-examination of United States involvement in Latin America, especially as regards religious personnel. A number of programs were closed down when religious superiors realized that along with some good that was being accomplished, the traditional and enslaving structures were being maintained by their presence. Other programs changed their format radically. CICOP had a most definite and lasting impact on the part of United States religious working in Latin America.

CICOP's education program, one of the services that paralleled the widely-publicized national meetings, didn't have that significant an impact, Colonnese said, primarily because of the lack of cooperation on the part of diocesan educational officials. But it did produce coordinating services for priests, brothers, and sisters—out of which came a closer liaison with CELAM and various national conferences of bishops—and developed close ties with Latin American intellectuals who proved to be valuable resource persons. It also produced a Latin American Cooperation Week, from which the national collection for Latin America evolved. "There is little question," Colonnese concluded, "that the CICOP program produced a 'pattern for progress' for the North American church in its relationship to the churches of Latin America."

The U.S. mission effort influenced the growth of the "new" Latin American church, to be sure. But there is some disagreement as to whether the influence was positive or negative in nature. Some U.S. missioners feel their presence hindered the development of the new church, their numbers serving to defer necessary reforms or experimentation. "We arrived equating Christianity with North American Catholicism and culture," said Jesuit Father James B. Malley, who spent 1965 through 1971 in Brazil. "The foreign presence—just by being there and letting the old structures survive—was holding back the painful birth of a bright new Brazilian Christian expression." Berryman and others, as noted earlier in this chapter, also saw the U.S. presence choking off the growth of the new church, forcing the postponement of decisions that would have to be made sooner or later. Father John Risley added: "The mission effort from the States has largely been an importation obstructing the growth of a real Latin American church responding to the needs of its people."

Others who were there disagree. Augustinian Father Theis, who gave the U.S. program mixed grades overall, said its encouragement of local lay leadership did much to assist Latin Americans to "rediscover a church, built on prayer and the Scriptures, that is not dependent on either the political situation or on the 'number' of clerical-religious pastoral agents available."

Bishop Fitzpatrick, in a talk to the Society for the Propagation of the Faith in 1976, said that U.S. missioners "have made and are making a major contribution" in Latin America, especially in regard to the new church there, and in their generous response to the proddings of Latin America's post-Medellín hierarchy. "The Latin American bishops didn't want 'more of the same,' " he said. "They did not say that things had been done badly, but that it was time for a new thrust, new structures, and a new, broader vision of what the church's role should be in Latin America."

U.S. missioners, he said, can take pride in having shared in the process:

One thing appears certain to me: Despite the turmoil the church is experiencing these days in almost every country and every diocese in Latin America, we can look south for the brightest spot on our church horizon. The faith of our people is strong; the courage of so many bishops, priests, religious, and dedicated laypeople is worthy of our esteem and praise; the blood of martyrs is still able to plant the seed of faith and nourish it to maturity. It could well be one of the stars in the crown of the American Catholic church that we were part of this century's struggle for Christ.

Even so consistent a critic as Colonnese sees this field—the growth of the new Latin American church—as one in which the United States mission effort played a positive role. It would not be that way in regard to vocations, he wrote; the idea that the example of foreign priests could foster a growth in the priestly ranks was one of "fantasy." But the North Americans would affect the Latin American church in another way, he said:

> I think it was the heavy presence and leadership of United States personnel in Latin America which resulted in the awakening of the more radical Latin Americans. They were forced to face the issue of their own inadequacy and to prepare themselves. Many have done that. Even though they became critical of the gringos, it was precisely the presence of the gringos which was a sign for them.
> I think that some of these radicals in Latin America were unfair and even too harsh in their criticism of North American efforts in Latin America, . . . but that having been said, they came alive. Many of them came alive only with words, but enough followed through with action, too, to create a new, a reborn church. This awakening wasn't only due to the presence of the gringos, but our presence stimulated, aided, and abetted it. I think in God's providence, the Spirit was stirring the church in Latin America. Also, their reality became so harsh that the well-educated, the reflective ones had no alternative.

The relationship between Latin America's new church and the North American mission program was one, of course, that worked both ways. And however much the new church of Latin America owed the missioners from the north, the reverse influence—that of the Latin American church on the U.S. mission program—ended up as a much stronger force.

In the early 1960s, two great movements were at work that would profoundly affect both church and state throughout the western hemisphere, particularly in Latin America. The first stirrings of a new church were beginning to be felt throughout the southern continent, as the challenges raised by Comblin, by Freire and Gutiérrez, found increasingly receptive audiences, first in the academic community, then in a steadily-conscientized general population. The charismatic figures of Larraín and Camara, among others, helped to inspire more and more church people to follow the new direction—an irony, since the church, traditionally identified as it was with Latin America's elite power structure, was a target of those who were calling for change.

Many messages were incorporated into the new movement. One of them said, in effect, that the church should go public—take a stand on behalf of the oppressed, risking material and even physical danger, if necessary—if it wanted to have any meaning for the multitudes of Latin America's poor. The new school of thought also demanded more of a "Latin-Americanization" of the church, an acknowledgment of its solidarity with the Latin American masses in their struggle, an end to cooperation with all those forms of outside influence that contributed to the discredited neocolonial pattern of the past. Specifically, the church was called on to rethink the wisdom of accepting aid from wealthy nations. As Gutiérrez wrote (and as was cited earlier), such aid is self-defeating if it conditions the Latin American church to accept only reformist solutions and superficial social changes, when more radical steps are required.

At the same time that the precedent-shattering movement was gathering strength and influence in Latin America, an army was massing up north—an army of missioners, prepared to respond to the call of its leader to aid the Latin American church. Instead of responding in a way that would nurture the infant new church of liberation, however, the North American army was operating along old, established lines, totally out of contact with the emerging new Latin American thought. Not only was the army bearing the burden of an outdated mission approach—for a continent that was already steeped in its own style of Catholicism—but it staggered under the added impedimentum of a superior U.S. attitude that said, in effect, that it knew best what to do for the Latin American church. What that meant, one missioner said disparagingly, was the "Yank-ification" of the Latins' church; another described it in later years as the "red, white, and blue-ing of Latin America." It added up to superimposing North American structures on a Latin American church ill-prepared to cope with them.

When the two forces met head on—the emerging new church, the crusading army from the north—explosive results were bound to occur. For the Latin Americans, that meant impatience and even hostility, often masked behind a friendly attitude that assured the North Americans that they were doing just fine. For the missioners, it manifested itself in frustration, an inability to understand the slow progress, the failure to advance, the retreats.

As if those immense forces were not enough to thwart the U.S. mission program, a third was at work in Rome: the Second Vatican Council, the aftermath of which would produce shock waves in the church throughout the world. For all the long-range good it would accomplish, for all it still promises to bring about in the future, the Council left a legacy of turmoil in the years immediately following its conclusion. And the U.S. Latin America mission program would feel its impact as much as—perhaps, given its relatively free-wheeling operation to begin with, more than—any other segment of the church in the world.

Those three factors—the self-awareness of a new Latin American church, an outdated missiology with colonialist overtones, the confusing commotion of the postconciliar years—made it certain that the U.S. mission to Latin America would fail, at least to some degree. Given that series of circumstances to contend with, it is remarkable that the program scored any successes at all.

Positive Accomplishments

When he spoke of the U.S. contribution to the growth of the new Latin American church, Colonnese said it was something positive, even though it might have come about in a negative way:

You cannot wipe away with a herculean blow the great good undoubtedly accomplished by numerous American missionaries over the years in Latin America. God still watches over us and blesses our efforts no matter how feeble they be. Yes, I definitely think there have been positive accomplishments.

And many share his view. "Perhaps our biggest contribution was the way we conducted our priesthood," said Franciscan Father Joseph Nangle.

It was catching for all the other priests down there. And there was the humility of American missioners in taking leadership from someone else. Both the ones who stayed and the ones who left were humble enough in the best sense of the word to accept leadership from those who knew better—local people. They were finally grateful for our presence. In my last sermon I apologized for the mistakes I had made, and said I had probably made them because I was a foreigner. Afterward, one woman in the parish came up to me and said that she had never thought of me as a foreigner. In that one instance, at least, I felt I had accomplished something very positive.

Bishop Fitzpatrick expressed a similar view:

In the old days the priests went down with the ideas they were brought up with, not wanting to impose themselves but hardly being able to help it. Now they're much more sophisticated. What's happened is that American missionaries are looking now to the local bishop for direction, rather than looking back to the U.S. The bishops down there are much happier with this arrangement, working arm-in-arm with our people.

One of the most frequently-cited contributions of the U.S. mission program, especially in recent years, is its record of training local lay leadership. "We succeeded in developing lay leaders in all aspects of the life of the church," Father Buttarazzi wrote from Honduras, "and in promoting the dignity of the poor who consequently organized themselves in social pressure groups."

Father James Zelinski, mission secretary for the Detroit Capuchins, cited three key contributions of North Americans in Latin America:

> Renewal at the roots through interest in basic Christian communities and biblically-oriented pastoral plans and catechetics; promotion of the local church membership into roles of church responsibility; bringing organizational abilities in areas of human promotion, human development.

Sister Phyllis Morris of the Sisters of St. Francis, Clinton, Iowa, spent a dozen years in Peru, where, she concluded:

> Generally, the caliber of United States missionaries whom I encountered was very high, truly Christian, and, therefore, very well received by the Peruvian people. Also, they have been resoundingly rejected by anti-Christian interests such as the unjust rich and the atheistic revolutionary types, which, in my judgment, is a great endorsement in itself.

Beyond the direct contributions the missioners made by their presence in Latin America, there were longer-range results of the U.S. mission program that would leave an imprint on the universal church. Monsignor Joseph Gremillion, as noted earlier, said the opening toward Latin America was the most significant growth toward collegiality expressed by the U.S. bishops and began a conscientization of the U.S. church of its ecclesial universality. That development, he said, was the most significant effect of the Latin American apostolate on the North American church, one which in itself had justified the effort. In a 1976 interview, he expanded on that theme:

> All of this was occurring just as the Vatican Council began, and the Council reinforced the idea. It gave us the occasion to see, to be with Latin American bishops. It helped us to develop a sense of rapport and Christian community.
>
> Through this and through the visits which followed, the North American bishops and religious orders were exposed to the Third World and awakened to its realities. It gave them an opportunity to realize what poverty was like, to see the way so many people live in misery, to understand the frustrations of political instability. How many bishops have visited Latin America? I'd guess over a hundred. It's opened their eyes to the reality of human misery. It's helped to prepare them to understand phenomena like the War on Poverty, black power, the Chavez movement, the Campaign for Human Development. They've seen that they can take stands on these things. They've said to themselves, "Look how the Latin American bishops stick *their* necks out."

And another thing: until Vatican II our bishops attempted no role in relation to the foreign policy of the United States government. They supported the country without question; it was part of their assimilation into the U.S. mainstream. They regarded anything having to do with overseas matters as an affair of the Vatican, period. But then the Latin American experience—and especially the accusations that came about through CICOP, which was very significant—began to awaken the American church. We were awakened to the relationships between American multinational corporations, U.S. embassies, the United States Information Service, and military power in Latin America. We became aware of the fact that we had to exercise some influence on U.S. policy in these matters.

Archbishop Bernardin, interviewed in 1976 when he still served as president of the National Conference of Catholic Bishops, saw benefits to both the North American and Latin American churches as a result of the mission endeavor:

One of the points we've constantly made is that the church is a community, a communion. We all need each other, whatever we do. We were not the only givers. They gave, too. They have enriched us with the insights which flow from their own faith-filled heritage; they have helped us to broaden our own vision of the church.

Archbishop Bernardin said the inter-American bishops' meetings that began in 1968 constituted one of the most tangible benefits of the mission to Latin America.

These meetings began for the express purpose of arriving at a better understanding of how our money should be used, and also how our personnel might be used more effectively. For the first few years, that was where the emphasis was placed. Then, at a given point, it was agreed that there was more to talk about, that there were other ideas on church life to be exchanged. Then the meetings were expanded. These meetings had as much influence as anything else on the developments in Latin American-U.S. church relationships in recent years.

Did the meetings actually change things? "Certainly as far as distribution of funds was concerned," the archbishop said. "And with personnel formation, too—perhaps in a more subtle way."

The church in the United States is still committed to the Latin America mission, Archbishop Bernardin said, and if the statistics appear to deny that, it is principally because of the overall decline in vocations. But even if the mission commitment is smaller in number, it is more attuned to the needs at hand:

We've become much more sensitive to the needs of the church in Latin America. As a conference we've concerned ourselves with not doing anything without the endorsement of the bishops of Latin America. We understand better now that what they don't need are little enclaves of the U.S. church. Whatever we do must be part of their plan.

Bishop James S. Rausch of Phoenix—interviewed at the same time in 1976, when he was the NCCB's general secretary—said that U.S. Catholics' awareness of the desperate situation of their brothers and sisters in Latin America continues to rise. Nationally, he said, the collection for Latin America goes up each year, as does the number of dioceses participating in it. Funds are distributed in accordance with guidelines developed by the Latin Americans, he said: "The influence we have in the conference is all in that direction." He also noted that "contacts with Latin America have increased enormously; hardly a week goes by that someone from Latin America doesn't stop in."

North Americans are no longer unaware of the dangers involved in mission programs to another land, Bishop Rausch added. "A point I would emphasize," he said, "is our increased sensitivity to the culture of these people and a realization on the part of many North Americans that some of the things we do, no matter how good our intentions might be, can still be destructive."

What Gremillion, Bernardin, and Rausch were saying in their analyses was—at the lofty level of intercontinental relationships—the same thing that many individual missioners were saying from a personal standpoint: that the primary beneficiary of the Latin American mission apostolate was, paradoxically, the sending church in North America. The U.S. church was much better off for its experience, said Gremillion and the two bishops. And because of that, perhaps, the universal church was better off, too—even the church in Latin America. Individual missioners were more inclined to view the experience on a personal basis, and the great majority believed they had gained something as a result.

For some, the perceived benefits seem shallow, based on little more than the adventure involved, the satisfaction of having taken part in something that was clearly the thing to do at the time. As Tom Quigley has observed, "It was their Camelot, a good time." But the experience was much more profound for others, he was quick to point out. As noted earlier, he said that one of the most positive things to come out of the Latin American experience, especially in regard to the clergy, is that it was a turning point in their lives. "There was a new realization of what it meant to be a priest, and also of what it meant to be an American," he said. "They saw the United States in a new light. They had a renewed concept of mission in that sense."

Today's missioners—as well as those who are now home, looking back on their mission years—identify easily with Quigley's observation. Father Theis's comment in that regard is fairly typical: His Peruvian brothers, he said, had taught him how to be human—open, warm, trusting, and self-giving. And now he wants to carry that learned experience forward. His mission experience, he says, and that of other returned U.S. priests, provides an opportunity to "help in a dynamic renewal of the church here in the United States."

That relates to a further observation of Quigley's:

What I see as a major development has been in effect since Maryknoll's general chapter of 1973, when they discussed what missions should be saying to the U.S. Since then there has been a lot more discussion among missionaries about their responsibilities for U.S. policies that affect the Third World—policies which they have seen in their effect. They want to insure that their work will be, in a sense, validated by making an impact back here in the States.

(Others have explored this "reverse mission" approach in detail, among them Father William McIntire, whose suggestions will be treated in the concluding chapter.)

More Gain Than Gift

The conclusion from these observations—a frustrating one, it would seem, for many Latin Americans—is that the North American church has enriched itself, Christianized itself, through its Latin America apostolate. What has it done for the Latin American church in that period? It registered limited successes in evangelization and social services, provided encouragement and some degree of inspiration for the growth of a new church of the people, and contributed massive funding for a variety of projects, good and bad. The degrees of success or failure in each area of accomplishment are open to debate, based on varying interpretations.

What seems less arguable is that the North American church gained more than it gave. At least one leading Latin American spokesman believes that not all the fault for that lies with the North Americans. Cardinal Eduardo Pironio, speaking in 1971, when he was still a bishop and president of CELAM, said that necessary foreign aid at times seems futile or even counterproductive because of human shortcomings, but that that does not make the aid any less justified. "Poor churches would be less poor," he said, "in resources and personnel, if they were more detached and more ready to give of the little they already have." The receiving churches must have an effective pastoral plan, he said:

> Can we be surprised if the [foreign] personnel are let down by makeshift procedures, that they feel frustrated, uselessly wearied, thoughtlessly assigned? No priests—or sisters or laymen either—should be sent till we have decided precisely what work they will take up. Neither should they be called if the local clergy are not ready to welcome and integrate them.

No matter how extensive have been the problems of the past, or where most of the blame is placed for them, some, Bishop Rausch among them, decline to be pessimistic about the future. According to Bishop Rausch:

> The last ten or fifteen years are a learning experience, a period of sowing seeds rather than reaping a harvest. What Pope Paul called for in *Populorum Progressio* has value here: a call for radical transformation that will turn the corner toward full human dignity in these poor countries. Teaching people to be followers of Christ must include more than baptism; it must include giving them a sense of their own worth. That can't happen until structures reform themselves to address basic questions of human rights. Consciousness of that has grown in the church in Latin America, and that is a sign of hope. We've learned. We've taken the first steps.

Today, the evaluation, the questioning, goes on, as the U.S. mission presence continues. How do today's missioners stack up compared to those who have gone before? A commonly accepted appraisal has optimistic overtones. Yes, it concedes, the early mistakes were plentiful, and they were damaging. But we have learned. We are taking our signs from the new Latin American church; we are doing the things that have to be done. Our commitment has been tried, and we have passed the test. And yet . . .

And yet, it is not that simple. True, there are those missioners, many of them, who have gotten the message of Medellín and of the Council, and who work at it and live at it day after day. Also true, sadly, there are those who are still conducting business as usual. "Everyone who has stayed in Latin America is not necessarily the best suited to be there," says Father Joseph Nangle. "The fact that some have survived doesn't mean they have survived for the right reasons."

Another Franciscan, Father Fidelis McKee, superior of the Franciscan community in Bolivia, has similar reservations. "We're still very much North Americans in Latin America," he said, "tied into the parochial structure which is really foreign here. We have much more influence than we really should."

Frances Neason, the executive director of the U.S. bishops' Latin America

Secretariat, believes that the majority of U.S. mission priests now in Latin America are well-prepared, aware of the problems that should concern them:

> But there are still others who are obsessed with the need to send numbers to fulfill a commitment. In theory, there are great statements to the effect that we are there as servants to the local church. But that's only good if the local church is determining the priorities. There's a growing tendency to feel that they are drawing away from the force of the statements made at Medellín.

What is the legacy of our long record of service in Latin America? How many of today's missioners are doing the job they should? What percentage has an accurate reading of the signs of the times? Again, there is no foolproof litmus test, no examinations on which to give out grades. Most of the people in the field who were interviewed for this book believe that their work is the kind that is demanded by the times; that they are, indeed, serving the new servant church.

Some observers disagree, including one as knowledgeable as Gary Mac-Eoin. He is one of the handful of recognized authorities in North America on the Latin American church, and his words bear a thoughtful listening —even if the message is discouraging to hear. In a letter dated early 1977 he wrote:

> Some U.S. missionaries (a minority, I believe) have got the message. Unfortunately, many of these leave the structures because they cannot square their conscience with the institutional tasks they have to perform. Others have learned to talk the new language without a change of soul. And still others are still the centurions of the empire, as a bishop [from the United States] I visited a few years ago in Brazil's wild west. He runs a Mafia operation where the need is for prophets.

15

A Course for the Future

Anyone who comes to Latin America should arrive aware that God has special designs for this continent, which must be discovered and carried out. He should know that the church of Latin America . . . mirrors the face of the Savior in a particular way. He should be convinced that it is a church of hope. . . .

Cardinal Eduardo Pironio's advice still stands as a watchword for anyone who would take up a mission assignment in Latin America today. So does an observation written even earlier, by another great figure of the modern Latin American church. Yes, said the late Bishop Larraín to a U.S. audience, our churches need priests, religious and lay apostles, material help. "But above all these problems our greatest need is for your understanding." In exchange, he said—and a deeper exchange is what he hoped for—Latin America had much to offer: "What Latin America wishes to give is the testimony of a faith which conquers difficulties, a hope which does not falter before problems, and above all a charity which makes all men equal in the love of Christ."

Once North Americans are able to understand Pironio's church of hope, to identify with it, how can they best serve it? How can they reach out to accept the generous gifts so lovingly offered by Larraín? How can the U.S. church best serve its sister church in Latin America, and, through the graces gained by both, serve the universal church as well?

Some would end the U.S. mission presence altogether, contending that it is only restraining the full development of a new Latin American church. Others would pump new life into the North American mission movement, under the impression that an enlightened, postconciliar, post-Medellín missionary campaign would speed the flowering of that same new Latin church, a church attuned to the needs of the impoverished masses who see in it their only hope for a change in the realities of day-to-day living. Still others would concentrate all effort into the "reverse mission" approach, in which the church would attempt to effect changes in U.S. policies designed to promote justice and peace in Latin America.

There is, obviously, no one answer. A careful consideration of the experience of the last twenty years, a reading of the judgments of some of Latin America's church leaders, and an evaluation of the reflections of scores of returned U.S. missioners, suggest the following three-point plan:

1. Continuation of the placement of North American missioners in Latin America, with an awareness that the intense demands of the assignment can be met by only a small number of superior personnel.

2. Vigorous North American support—material and spiritual—for the Latin American church, with special attention given to its theological, political, and social role.

3. A concentrated effort to educate the U.S. public about Latin American realities and about North American policies that have helped to bring them about, and, where necessary, attempts to effect changes in those policies deemed to be harmful.

It is not a simple blueprint, but neither is it impossible to follow. Nor is it unreasonable to expect its fulfillment. The U.S. mission experience in Latin America has been one of constant learning, and even if the course has been difficult, there is no reason to believe that the lessons have not been well absorbed.

"The church of Latin America will need help for a long time," Cardinal Avelar Brandão Vilela of São Salvador, Brazil, said in 1976. Cardinal Humberto Medeiros of Boston told an interviewer that on his trip to Brazil in that same year, as on earlier visits, he was "besieged" for missioners. "Would I still want American missionaries if I had my own diocese?" Auxiliary Bishop Gennaro Prata of La Paz answered the question without hesitation: "Yes, of course."

U.S. priests are still needed in Latin America. So are sisters, brothers, lay people, anyone willing to put a career—or a life—on the line in the cause of justice and peace. They should be there, for one thing, because Vatican II made it clear that that is part of their job. "If the church is not missionary, it is not the church," Bishop John Fitzpatrick told an audience of Propagation of the Faith directors in 1976.

There will never be a time when each nation will be able to provide sufficient personnel for its own apostolic work. And whenever we become so self-sufficient that we don't need the influence of other nations, there is something wrong with us altogether. So, we cannot be the church if we stay at home, nor can an area that lacks sufficient personnel continue to be the church if it refuses the apostolic thrusts, the missionary thrusts of other nations.

Franciscan Father Joseph Nangle considered the question from a basic level. "Christ's command to 'go and preach the Good News to all nations' has not been carried out," he said. "Our Christian communities understand ever more clearly that they exist not for themselves but in function of the world around them."

Father Colonnese made the same point, with a qualifying reservation:

> If the U.S. church does not continue to send missionaries, it fails to be Catholic. But the real question is whether the U.S. church is ready, able, and willing to accept the consequences of that mission. There is a real difference between what the good missionary is doing in Latin America—his or her testimony—and the testimony given by the hierarchy to the same issues in the U.S.A. The hierarchy wants the church to "be on top," and to "look good." It can't be so if the church is to faithfully perform its mission. Jesus knew it, and told us so. "Men," he said, "will persecute you. . . ."

But if there is widespread agreement that continued U.S. mission presence is desirable in Latin America—and only a relative handful suggest its cessation or even an interruption through some kind of moratorium—there is less of a consensus in regard to the numbers of people to be used. Some still long for the days of the early sixties, when the U.S. church gave Pope John a record-setting response to his call for assistance to the Latin American church. Most observers of the mission picture take a more sanguine view now. "It's better not to mobilize a new 'army' of missioners," Colonnese said. "We simply don't have the cultural preparation."

Pironio, too, advised caution. He stopped short of saying that fewer North Americans should be sent to Latin America, but said that if the selection process were properly handled only a few would qualify. The qualities needed—psychological and spiritual maturity and a capacity for integrating into the Latin American culture—are those "that by no means everyone possesses," Pironio said diplomatically. Not only that, he added, but prospective missioners also need a solid theological formation, "so that from the depths of their faith they can interpret history, understand man, and transform this world."

There were other problems, he pointed out: adaptation, for one. It presupposes a "perfect mastery" of language, assimilation of culture, a discovery of the values of the people with whom the missioner will work, and a respect for their mentality and the qualities of their religious life. Pironio warned that acquiring these traits is extremely difficult:

> What principally keeps apostolic personnel from fitting effectively into the Latin American church is a certain ingrained theological formation they bring along with them—a formation structured and received amid conditions totally alien to those of Latin America. That is what fundamentally prevents them from getting to know the true face of our church.

Although the requirements of the job might sharply restrict the number of qualified personnel, Pironio said, those few people were needed—desperately needed—to assist in the development of the Latin American church. "In order that this hour of the Spirit may be more than just a promise and a hope," he said, "the Latin American church appeals to the fraternal generosity of other churches, whose aid it considers indispensable more than ever before, and it is grateful to them in the Lord." (Tom Quigley's interpretation of Pironio's comment about still wanting "the right kind of missioner" was slightly caustic: "I interpret this to mean something like 'The great invasion of the sixties is over, thank God. We don't want that whole presence again. We want a more selective kind of missioner, and we want more of a say in determining who he is and what he is going to do.'")

Another commentator took a stand that was even more restrictive in tone. Father José Alemán, director of the Jesuit Research and Social Action Center (CIAS) in Santo Domingo, delivered a talk in 1972 which, for many, stands as the definitive statement on the subject. Although specifically directed to U.S. Jesuits and their mission role in Latin America, it is applicable, for the most part, to all potential North American missioners.

The question of sending manpower at all, Alemán believes, is somewhat debatable. If missioners do continue to go to Latin America, he said, it must be with an understanding that they have to start from the Latin American reality as it exists and participate in the training of people for liberation. It will not be easy, he warns:

> We must forget the dream that we can speak directly to the plain people, the masses. It is impossible. The cultural difference is so vast that we cannot bridge it. We can perhaps understand them, but we cannot become one of them. We can speak with the natural leaders, and indirectly speak to the people and understand them, but if you try to speak to them directly, they will say yes to everything you suggest, but they will not internalize it and make it part of their value system. Your suggestion will not become a factor in their future self-improvement. If in every case the priest or the social promoter is on hand to solve the problem—that's not promoting; that's not liberating.
>
> The task [of understanding the complicated social reality] is so difficult that I would say only very young Jesuits, perhaps only novices, who start out their religious lives down here, could hope to be of use in this situation.

The men who come, he said, will always be foreigners—something akin to technicians—and they must always remember that. "The only effective way to work," he said (emphasizing that the Jesuits would have to be working within the structure of local Jesuit provinces, rather than those at home in the United States), "is to convince people that they are participating with you in the making of the decision."

The Church's Mission

There is, in general, an acceptance of the fact that the number of U.S. missioners to Latin America will continue to decline, and an understanding of the reasons that is taking place—along with a belief that the mission movement cannot be allowed to die out. "I would never deny the idea of sending people," Colonnese said. "That's the mission of the church. But remember what the Bible said—that many people wanted to go out to preach, and that only a few were called. It's the same idea today. They may not be all that numerous, but there are Americans who were born to be prophets for Latin America."

North American mission ranks in Latin America have been thinning on several counts: disappointment with mission experiences and the overall vocation decline, in addition to the more restrictive criteria that have emerged in recent years. But still another factor looms in the future: a conscious decision on the part of mission-sending organizations to seek other areas of the world for evangelization. As of now, there is no widespread move in that direction, and in some quarters it has met with stiff opposition. But if for no other reason than that it is making inroads in the mission thinking of Maryknoll, traditionally the pace-setter among mission organizations, it could have far-ranging effects in the future.

"We're moving in the direction of de-emphasizing Latin America," Father William McIntire conceded. "We opted to do so at our last two inter-chapter assemblies." McIntire said Maryknoll is especially anxious to work with poor and oppressed peoples in non-Christian settings. A main area of emphasis in Latin America now is the development of a sense of mission responsibility within the local church, particularly in Peru and Brazil (although Maryknollers have continued, and will continue, to concentrate efforts in two directions: development of lay leadership, and working with the marginated peoples of the barriadas and the altiplano). "Yes, we regard our Latin American mission as important, but there is more emphasis developing in places like Bangladesh and the Sudan," he said. "They better meet our present criteria."

In an address to a mission institute in Chicago in 1976, McIntire explained the concept further, stressing the idea of interdependence that lies behind it.

> In choosing our new commitments for mission, we have sought especially locations where direct witness to and/or evangelization of non-Christian peoples is possible, in some of the poorest and most needy areas of the world. Our new mission of five men in Bangladesh is of particular interest to me. . . . We hope soon to expand our commitments in that part of the world, where "classical" mission work with an updated approach and attitude on our part seems possible.

The Maryknoll official explained that the mission in Bangladesh includes two men who had worked in the Bolivian altiplano, and that on a trip to Bolivia he asked if their former "parishioners"—Aymara Indians—felt abandoned:

I was told that the Aymaras do not feel that way at all, and instead include the intentions of "their" missioners in Bangladesh in every prayer of the faithful in the liturgies being celebrated in the altiplano. The Aymara Catholic pastors and local religious leaders would like to send a group from their own number to serve as missioners in Bangladesh. It would be a wonderful thing if it were possible to realize such a dream: to have Aymara missioners living and sharing their faith alongside our men in Bangladesh.

But to others, such as Bishop Fitzpatrick, the former chairman of the U.S. bishops' Latin America committee, that kind of dream is unsettling. Bishop Fitzpatrick is critical of missionaries who "leave Latin America and go off to pagan lands, on the assumption that our Latin American people are at least culturally Catholic." He said, in his talk to Propagation of the Faith officials in 1976: "We should say very bluntly that we are scarcely missionary when we pick out our own mission work and area of activity, rather than listen to the call of our Holy Father—and he asks us to go to Latin America."

How widely the Maryknoll approach will be followed in the future is impossible to forecast; for the time being it does not seem to signal a trend. Most mission societies involved in Latin America, and most individual missioners, as well, are more concerned with the style of their work and its application to the people whom they serve. What changes should they make in their pattern of operation? If their numbers are to be smaller, can they still be as effective? How will their work be most beneficial to the Latin American church?

The experience of the years to date, the emergence of new directions within the Latin American church, and the recommendations of the Latin Americans themselves suggest a program with several readily identifiable facets:

1. A period of preparation infinitely more thorough—including spiritual formation—that will result in the missionary's immersion (to the extent that is possible) in Latin America's culture and the Latin American church.

2. A longer period of commitment—where possible, for life.

3. A willingness to work in the Latin American church, and to serve it, not simply from a structural standpoint, but in the sense of absorbing its changes and its overriding commitment to liberation.

Pironio's thoughts in this regard still constitute a valid blueprint to follow, although it was several years ago that they were spelled out:

The essential point in asking for foreign personnel is that they should help the church of Latin America to find itself and become capable of fulfilling its unique vocation. Their task is not to "preserve" the faith or keep the church from "disappearing." Nor are they to increase quantitatively the statistics of Christian communicants, or have more sacraments administered, or see that the Eucharist is more fittingly celebrated. They must help to make the church in our continent truly a "sign and instrument"—a sacrament—of the full salvation that Christ the Lord brought us.

The careful selection of personnel is all-important, Pironio said, and it is not simply a matter of choosing those with psychological and spiritual maturity and the ability to integrate: "They need a solid theological formation, so that from the depths of their faith they can interpret history, understand man, and transform the world."

U.S. missioners have made the same point themselves. Said Augustinian Father Gerard Theis:

> Too many missionaries arrive, perhaps well-prepared in the language and in knowledge of the cultural reality of the people they are to serve. But too many are not prepared spiritually and evangelically. . . . To be a good missionary, anywhere, one must be able to empty oneself, expose oneself to a challenging purification of values. I would suggest that no missionary begin his or her work until after having undergone, willingly, a long period of renewal including something similar to the Jesuit thirty-day retreat, during which one's motives and ways of evaluating life and people might be purified with the two-edge sword of Christ's Word. . . . My life in the missions was one of continual conversion-purification; I would have been of greater service to God in Peru if that process had been begun on firm ground even before I left the United States.

The proper kind of preparation will lead missioners almost automatically to the next step, Colonnese has said: the discovery of the authentic values (moral, religious, and especially cultural) of the people they have come to serve. But he warned:

> It is impossible to achieve this without truly entering into the culture of the people as a participant rather than as an aloof observer. . . . The missionary must obtain a change of heart, attitude, and mind if he is to function as a servant to foreign cultures. Cultural imperialism in any degree is intolerable, counter productive, and the antithesis of the servant role in a servant church.

(There is still no single office, incidentally, formally charged with coordinating all U.S. mission activities in Latin America. When the structure of the old Division for Latin America was scrapped in 1974, some personnel went to the Justice and Peace section of the Social Development and World Peace department, U.S. Catholic Conference, others to the new Secretariat for Latin America of the National Conference of Catholic Bishops. Frances L. Neason is executive director of the secretariat, which is principally concerned with fund-raising activities, including the annual collection for Latin America, and the allocation and distribution of grants to aid specific projects. The secretariat, which operates directly under the NCCB's Committee for the Church in Latin America, headed by Bishop Nevin Hayes, also serves as a clearinghouse for exchanges of information about Latin America and advises personnel on the prospects for service in Latin America. The secretariat also contracts with the Mexican-American Cultural Center (MACC) for the training of North American personnel assigned to Spanish-speaking Latin America. This center was opened in 1969 in Mexico City under the direction of Divine Word Father Wilbert Wagner. Several years later it was shifted to San Antonio, although the program it offers still includes six weeks of field work in Mexico. Since 1974, some thirty-five prospective missioners have participated in its courses.)

How long should a U.S. missioner plan to stay in Latin America? Mission thinking has undergone a full turn on that point since the early sixties, when any U.S. presence, no matter how short-term, was thought to be worthwhile. Today the emphasis is on long-range service, even for life. Where shorter commitments are suggested at all, they are seen almost exclusively in terms of benefits to the missioner.

Father Theodore Hesburgh, for example, advocates what amounts to a clerical equivalent of universal military training, under which every newly-ordained priest would spend five years in mission work of one kind or another, preferably overseas, but if not, in a home mission setting. "It would be a guarantee of his priesthood," said the Notre Dame president. "Why not go somewhere like that when you're young, when you feel the need of priestly ministry, when you can get a sense of the meaning of being Christ to a people without him? It would give a priest a real sense of his priesthood."

But going off as a missioner for only a few years with the idea of making a significant contribution to Latin America is unrealistic, in the eyes of observers such as Bishop Fitzpatrick. "It seems to me," he said, "that it is part and parcel of a missionary's commitment that he is willing and really wants to stay where he is going forever—and not for a time."

Archbishop Mark McGrath agrees, and once told an audience that his suggestion along those lines might have been misinterpreted on at least one occasion:

We always tell American priests, sisters, and brothers going to Latin America that they should plan on staying for life. I told some new sisters who had just arrived, as replacements for other sisters being rotated home, that we hoped to bury them in Latin America. I don't know how they took it. I tried to explain later on what I meant: that for a deep effect on the religious and social area, a great ability for communication is required.

That ability, he suggested, doesn't come overnight, or, perhaps, even in five or ten years.

In Bolivia, Father Fidelis McKee uses a fixed-term concept as a reference point for the eventual conversion of his area of responsibility into a non-mission church community.

We should plan in terms of ten years, with a strong evaluation in five years, especially in terms of native vocations and preparation of the people, so that we're not a foreign church. Their idea of church will be different from ours as it grows stronger. We should continue here only to this extent, with native Franciscans taking over, and any of us who want to remain would do so as a member of this native province. I still feel we should be working to put ourselves out of business.

Most U.S. mission people share that kind of thinking to one degree or another. Asked what direction the North American mission program should be taking today—and tomorrow—they emphasize service and training, particularly, in the latter case, that of lay leadership. As it was expressed by Father Eugene Catanzaro, a New Jersey member of the Oblates of St. Francis de Sales who has been in Brazil since 1964:

The foreign missionary effort will have to become a true sign of poverty and, second, gradually be confined to specialized areas of work that have a direct relationship with the long-range goal of developing Christian leadership, first among the laity and springing from there among the clergy.

"The thrust has changed in the last ten years," said Bishop Fitzpatrick.

There were great efforts that took place to build seminaries, but when no seminarians came the bishops saw the handwriting on the wall and began developing laymen as leaders, especially in remote areas. Many of the projects funded by the Latin America Committee of the American bishops are for just that purpose.

What other tasks should be entrusted to U.S. missioners? Father Renato Poblete provided some suggestions: They might staff research centers, form model parishes, educate those who will devote themselves to the marginalized, preach the need for structural reforms in Latin American society, staff parishes without priests, participate seriously in social education.

Father Alemán, the Jesuit, had some specific ideas of his own, and warned of the psychological and practical problems missioners would find in the anti-Americanism they would encounter.

> Even the poor are likely to be anti-American. But if you go to them, and do not try to push them but try to understand and inspire them, they will probably respond. In the long run, the simple people will accept you, whatever your nationality. My experience has been that the most difficult to deal with will be the students, the priests, and the bishops.

Alemán advised missioners above all to learn the people's problems. The first priority, he said, should be to identify the problems of the people; the second is to determine how a Christian answer to those problems can be provided. It is practically impossible, he cautioned, for people formed in the old mission style to work in this newer atmosphere: "The moment we leave our institutions and try to understand the real problems of the people, we are lost, because we don't really have any idea of how people are living."

Missioners, then, difficulties notwithstanding, must continue to be sent, and although their number will continue to decline, their training should equip them for genuine service to the people and church of Latin America.

Education at Home

The second leg of the three-point plan for future mission activity in Latin America involves something closer to home. North Americans must support the Latin American church and its efforts on behalf of justice and peace, as they have never done before. The support required is not just material and not just spiritual, but a combination of both. It must be informed; it must be genuinely felt; it must be freely given.

Colonnese emphasizes the financial support needed in Latin America, and contends that the U.S. church can effect widespread economies to find the funds it will require. He questions the massive investments made in Catholic education, for example, claiming that much of the money spent in that field could be put to better use in Latin America. He suggests the training of catechists as a likely area for support. The Latin American bishops, he says, have people who could serve in that capacity if they were trained, but their talents go to waste because of a lack of money to feed them, to house them, to care for their families while they are being trained. "Why all the expenses here?" he asked. "Why do we have to have cocktail rooms at all our meetings? It's wrong. Not at the expense of a man dying of starvation. We haven't learned how yet, but we can still do it."

Moral support is only slightly less important to people who risk their lives in the cause of justice and peace, asserts Father Bernard Survil, who discussed its value in a 1977 newspaper column. The Maryknoll associate cited the immeasurable benefit of support from people and groups in the United States for beleaguered Salvadoreans, who had been wondering if anyone else in the world knew about their struggles. He quoted from a message sent by Archbishop Bernardin, then the NCCB president, who said:

> In few other countries today has the church's pastoral ministry met with such intense and organized opposition. . . . The tiny majority of the rich and powerful, the zealous guardians of a sterile and unjust status quo, has not hesitated to employ every means at their disposal to obstruct the preaching of the Gospel.

There were "hundreds" of messages of hope from U.S. church organizations, Survil said, such as one sent by officers of the Priests' Council of Des Moines: "We pledge to remind ourselves and our people of our bonds of unity with you who are suffering for our faith; it is the faith of the suffering church which offsets our guilt." Concluded Survil:

> The impact of these messages is indescribable for shoring up the morale of those many sideline Catholics in Latin America who find it easier to believe when they see miracles. International public support from average people *is* a miracle for those who live in Third World countries who believe that the only way to merit attention or win sympathy is to suffer some enormous natural disaster such as an earthquake or hurricane.

Whether U.S. service to the Latin American church is direct, in the form of mission personnel, or indirect, as expressed through financial and/or moral support, it must be provided with the understanding that the new church, the church of the people, holds the key to liberation in Latin America. It is a church building from the roots, finding itself, serving all the people of Latin America rather than a liberal constituency or a conservative power base. The priests building this new church, writes Gary MacEoin, "see themselves as not even starting from scratch, but rather forced to tear away a mass of superstitions and distortions in order to begin. The new church they envision would be strikingly different—one which would assert its dissimilarities honestly, and would be in the hands of its own popular leaders."

Meanwhile, the leaders of Latin America's institutional church—its bishops—struggled to develop a stronger sense of identity during the seventies. One positive note was a continuous sense of healing of the often bitter liberal-conservative divisions of the post-Vatican II, Medellín years.

Redemptorist Father Walter George recalled a story to illustrate a point in that regard. A concelebrated Mass was taking place in Brazil, he said, at which

Archbishop Helder Camara and another bishop, known for his conservatism as much as Dom Helder is for his outspoken progressivism, were among the concelebrants. It was time to exchange the kiss of peace, and the two prelates whose views were so dissimilar performed that ritual rite. The other bishop paused, looked at Camara, and said, "Now, let's do it again. This time, on our own."

The reasons that kind of healing process was taking place throughout Latin America—away from the demands of liturgical renewal, closer to the heart—were varied: the natural restorative effect of time, the unity required to confront jointly-perceived problems of poverty and injustice, the common front formed to take on repressive governments. Whatever the most significant reason, the rapprochement was genuine.

The attitude of the bishops of Brazil typified the spirit of reconciliation, Father Catanzaro wrote four years ago:

> The bishops of Brazil, both nationally and regionally, in the past few months, have documented their strong and courageous public denunciations of unbending government suppression of human and civil rights. This type of leadership gives heart to the many local religious and lay leaders to continue their efforts to provide hope for the suffering rural peasants, urban workers, academic classes, and the far too many unemployed who seek liberation, not to join ranks with either the right or the left, as identified by present-day capitalist and communist powers, but rather to find a new way, free of all built-in and extracted injustices, free to form new men sensitive to the human values of Christian fraternal love, justice, freedom, and equality.

At the same time that liberal-conservative lines were blurring, however, a new area of conflict was developing. It finally took as its focus the third major meeting of Latin American bishops—being held in Puebla, Mexico, in January 1979 as a followup to the meetings at Rio in 1955 and Medellín in 1968. Those who were pushing for revolutionary change, the Marxist-oriented radicals within the church community, found themselves doing battle with a new element—not the voices of old-style conservatism, which was largely submerged and ineffective, but those labeled as moderates or even as liberals, frequently identified with the Christian Democrats. The radicals were concerned because they saw the liberal-moderates co-opting their language and their programs, watering down both in the process.

Their protests found a specific target in the 214-page working document for the Puebla meeting, preparations for which were being carried out under the firm direction of Bishop López Trujillo (elevated, in May of 1978, to the rank of coadjutor archbishop of Medellín). The working paper, prepared in secret and devoid of contributions from radical theologians, drew a strong series of complaints from the left. The document, its critics said, indicated that

CELAM was about to turn its back on all that Medellín had endorsed. They said the preparatory paper treated the problem of poverty too lightly, was flavored throughout with an outdated, paternalistic attitude, and fostered the old idea of a modern Christendom as the answer to Latin America's oppressive social ills.

There was tangible evidence to substantiate another complaint, that preparations for the Puebla conference were leaning strongly in the direction of the Vatican. One of the three Puebla copresidents (along with Cardinal Lorscheider and Archbishop Corripio Ahumada of Mexico City) was Cardinal Sebastiano Baggio, prefect of the Congregation of Bishops (and former nuncio both in Chile and Brazil). Others who figured in the inner circle of those providing the backdrop of Puebla were Father Vekemans—a resident of Bogotá since he fled Chile following the Allende election in 1970—and Bishop Franz Hengsbach, head of the German church aid agency, Adveniat. The radical critics saw all of them, along with López Trujillo, as unswerving enemies of liberation theology, which they believed would be a major target at Puebla.

Gary MacEoin wrote that the Puebla planners envisioned the new Christendom, and not liberation theology, as the church's response to the continuing crisis brought on by Latin America's move from a pastoral to an urban-industrial society. The Puebla mindset, he said, "requires the Christian religiosity of the people to be safeguarded during the transition so that the new society will be defined by the Christian religion."

He continued:

Instead of following Medellín in its challenge to internal and external neo-colonialism, it looks to "a new civilization of love animated by the church" to achieve a unity of goals and motivations among all Latin Americans, the exploiters and the exploited, that will resolve the social, economic, and political problems.

López Trujillo had been trying to shake the conservative label for some time. In 1976, he told the Italian journal *Avvenire* that he had many areas of agreement with Gustavo Gutiérrez, the liberation theologian:

I share his concern for the poor, the situation of underdevelopment and injustice in Latin America, for the immense chasm between the wealthy few and the multitude of poor. I condemn international injustice and the dominating roles played by economically developed countries, whether they're called the United States or whether they're called the Soviet Union.

But his protestations left many critics unsatisfied. He figured in an intercontinental tiff in 1977 when a number of German theologians, among them Karl

Rahner, complained about Adveniat's behind-the-scenes role in preparations for Puebla, which, they said, were beginning to amount to an organized campaign to repudiate liberation theology. Not so, López replied: "What I am trying to do is work toward a deepened understanding of what authentic liberation is."

Both López and Lorscheider attempted to keep the pre-Puebla debate at a moderate level, promising a fair discussion of all issues once the meeting began. Lorscheider said he expected two trends to develop at Puebla: one spiritual, the other social. López, whom Pope Paul appointed as secretary of the meeting, vowed its openness and said it would take place "in full consistency with the Medellín conference and not with distorted interpretations of it."

López, continuing as CELAM secretary general in addition to his new assignment, expanded on that theme in a lengthy interview with John Muthig, the Rome bureau chief for NC News Service, referring to a "deep accord" growing among Latin American theologians. "The third conference will not create opposition or useless divisions," he said, and concluded:

The Medellín conference will be the greatest foundation for Puebla, along with the last world bishops' synods. With the spirit of Medellín we will work to take a pastoral look at the new situations in our churches. All of us in CELAM believe in Medellín. We worked for it before and after. We have great hope for the possibilities opening up to the church in Latin America.

Fears of the radicals notwithstanding, there seemed little that Puebla might do that would turn back the clock on liberation theology, the emphasis on lay leadership, the mushrooming growth of basic Christian communities. "No matter what the bishops may decide at Puebla," MacEoin wrote some months before the meeting, "the march of events will not be significantly affected." Indeed, the intensity of the debate over the future of liberation theology provided dramatic evidence that far from having had its day—as some commentators had written—it was alive and well. Father Ernest Ranly was one who had made that point some time earlier, even though he conceded that the unbounded enthusiasm which initially greeted liberation theology is pretty well played out:

What is needed now for those caught up in the theory of liberation theology is the daily hard work of making a practice out of a theory and of defending and extending its basic principles. . . .

Liberation theology correctly sees that the role of the church, its leaders and its rank and file, is to come to grips with economic and political realities, to speak out clearly against institutional injustices and to lead in the movements of social and economic changes at the local, national, and international level.

He laments earlier failures of liberation theologians, who, he says, in their zeal to base their teachings solidly on scripture and the person of Christ, played down the importance of folk religion. Recently, however, those who leaned in that direction are having second thoughts and are stressing their Latin American roots and the values found in communal and festive aspects of their customs. (Bishop Roger Aubry, Swiss-born president of CELAM's mission department, has stressed the same theme in pointing to the value of the roots of Latin American ethnic groups, based on both Indian and African heritages: "Evangelization is not a transplanting of one church diagram within another culture. No roots grow this way.")

Within the U.S. church structure, no less a figure than Bishop Rausch, at the time the general secretary of the bishops' conference, gave the liberation theology concept his strong endorsement, only loosely qualified. Catholics have an obligation to study liberation theology and evaluate it in the light of faith, he said at a Serra symposium in St. Paul in 1976:

Correctly understood, I believe, it is one of the greatest blessings of our time. Unfortunately, many who claim to be spokesmen for the school or who mouth the language of the theologians are naive, ill-informed attention-seekers, concerned with what appears to be something spectacular. . . . We must be champions of people's freedom from sin, from enslavement by governments that are totalitarian, from institutions that are cruel and do not recognize the dignity of the human people. This kind of liberator the Christian must be in today's world.

As intimately bound up in the future of the Latin American church as the concept of liberation theology is the continued growth of the small Christian community approach, the *comunidades de base* that are revolutionizing the relationship of impoverished peasants, in the country and in the city, to their church. Foreign priests as well as those from Latin America must recognize its potential and draw on its resources if they are to make their modern mission meaningful.

Father José Marins, who has pointed out that basic Christian communities are growing because they are building a living church, rather than building structures, and that they are concerned with the formation of leaders for new and functional ministries, stressed their importance for the future, for foreign and native priest alike:

The future will expect the church to be more effectively, more evangelically present in the world. It must be present, not as a powerful society, but as a network of communities of people who love one another in Christ, as sons and daughters of the same Father God, who speaks eagerly but modestly with all men, conscientizing them to build a world that will care for everyone.

Monsignor David Ratermann, the St. Louis veteran of service in Bolivia, has some thoughts about the future of U.S. missioners in Latin America that take into account the strength of the *comunidad de base* movement, and go beyond it as well. Future U.S. missionaries should consider his advice carefully. Decentralization is necessary to escape an outmoded parish structure, he says:

> Instead of trying to organize church life and pastoral services to God's people around the traditional parish structures (parish church in a central town, rectory, meeting rooms, parish organizations, etc.), we should think of these small groups of believers *(comunidades de base)* as the more authentic "micro-structure" of the church.

After insuring the authenticity of these communities, Ratermann said, missioners should plan functions around them. "All of this," he says, "implies on our part a much less pretentious attitude, an attitude that is simpler and more humble."

He calls for mandatory team ministries, to overcome the genuine problems brought on by loneliness and isolation, and urges economic sacrifices, concentrated training of catechists, evaluation of pastoral planning, and a redesign of "our whole style of presence." The mentality persists, he says, that U.S. missioners are indispensable to whole communities; the reality is that they establish close relationships with only a few.

> We should leave aside once and for all the idea that we are so terribly important (almost irreplaceable) for the salvation of so many people who live within our ecclesiastical jurisdictions. The truth is that Jesus' Paschal Mystery and the salvation won for all by him are a reality. What's important is that the few people with whom we can arrive at a certain depth of friendship on the personal level come to know and believe, come to let themselves be guided by this Paschal Mystery and by the Good News that the Risen Lord is constantly working through his Holy Spirit. In this way it becomes possible that at least a few people grow to a certain maturity of faith, and also be inspired to want to share that faith with others.

Service, limited goals, humility, identification with the people—these are the signs of the times for the missioners of the future, and, in many cases, the missioners of today. They will be working closely with—and for—local pastoral ministers. And, as with many other features of life in the Latin American church, the ministers of tomorrow may be radically different from those at work today.

For one thing, they will certainly emerge more regularly from the people of Latin America rather than coming from overseas, although their training might not always be along the traditional seminary lines with which we are familiar. There is a mixed reading on the "native vocations" picture. Bishop Fitzpatrick finds it a discouraging one, and says the past failure to develop a native clergy has been a "disastrous mistake." Hesburgh struck a similar note: "The great indictment of colonialism is that there are so few Latin vocations."

But others on the scene have taken different soundings. In Brazil, both Oblate Father James Sullivan and Father Elias Manning, the Conventual Franciscan, see encouraging signs. According to Sullivan:

The vocations picture is very hopeful. We have eleven philosophers, two professed theologians, one priest—all Brazilian. Fourteen other young people are interested. There is a whole youth mystique movement in the church in Brazil. People are seeing a new slant on popular religion; they're seeing its basic faith values instead of superstition. The question is: what can we do to deepen it? I would recommend more American missioners, but not the way it was done in the past.

Manning was also enthused:

We've been here for thirty years, and never before have we had eight young Brazilians professed and en route to the priesthood. That's a good sign, for us as Americans and as Franciscans. We'd like to see our order established here. If we did have to leave, it would hurt to see things simply fold up. But if we left a Brazilian province of Conventual Franciscans, we will have left something worthwhile. And who's going to continue our work if not the Brazilians?

Franciscan Father Fidelis McKee and Bishop Gennaro Prata, the La Paz auxiliary, saw hopeful signs in Bolivia as well. "We should have eight or ten native priests in three or four years," McKee said. "At that rate, we could get up to forty priests in ten years." Prata said that with five ordinations for the La Paz archdiocese in 1976 and ten throughout the country, and with seventy studying in the major national seminary, the vocation situation was "definitely improving."

Improving or not, the numbers of "native priests" being ordained through the traditional seminary route will never be sufficient to provide spiritual care for Latin America's millions. And, with the continued decrease in missioners from overseas, neither will the ranks of foreign priests. Yet there is a full-blown optimism that the people's socio-religious needs will be met, and met well—by a new breed of minister who may hold the key to the future of the faith in Latin America. It is too early to refer to this ministry accurately as a married clergy, and yet it has gone far beyond a simple "lay leadership" program. It is an emerging, developing phenomenon in which sincere and dedicated people—natural leaders, good Christians, usually but not exclusively from simple backgrounds—are assuming the responsibility for providing sacramental services and the spiritual direction of their own communities.

Many projects being funded by the North American church are for the training of such lay persons, Bishop Fitzpatrick has pointed out. "Right now, these leaders do almost everything except offer Mass and hear confessions," he said. "And it would seem to me that this may be some kind of wedge for bringing about a married clergy."

A married clergy looms with ever-increasing probability as an answer to the overwhelming spiritual needs of the Latin American people, and more and more influential church members recognize its potential. "Our main concern should be to get Latin Americans in the priesthood," said Father Hesburgh. "I don't care if they have married priests there. . . . There are a lot of places where a married priesthood would be good." U.S. missioners in the future will have to be attuned to the movement. The evidence indicates that those who have already been there not only recognize it, but urge that it develop more rapidly.

"There are never going to be enough priests," said Conventual Franciscan Father Conall McHugh, who spent eleven years in Costa Rica, "so maybe they have to come up with a married clergy. The Latin America value for the family militates against celibacy. I think we have to decide between the preaching of the gospel and administering the sacraments, and an unmarried clergy."

Augustinian Father John Burkhart: "The sending of missionaries will continue to decrease. The mission churches need and deserve a married clergy. It will provide the only solution."

Father George Dudak, of the Paterson Diocese:

> I see a celibate clergy as never working out there. There's a big attrition rate, with the loneliness of the job as a primary factor. I can see a married couple able to survive much better. In fact, I think that without optional celibacy, the church in Latin America is doomed. We need a new style of priesthood—with more informal training, something similar to the training we give deacons here. Ordain them, and let them bring the church to the people. That's the direction we should go in.

Gary MacEoin described the work of a team of U.S. priests in a poor urban setting: training a few heads of families to become deacons in the hope that after a further interval of experimentation and preparation, they might be ordained to the priesthood. MacEoin explained:

The current discipline in the Roman Catholic church permits the ordination to the diaconate of married men, and there are strong pressures for extension of this provision so that mature married men can become priests. Those who are working to create a revolutionary mentality among the peasants and slum dwellers regard this as absolutely necessary. The present system of preparation of celibate priests in seminaries effects a total emotional estrangement from the people, even in the rare cases in which the candidate is one of them.

The role of these "priests-to-be" was further outlined by Father Alemán in his message to U.S. Jesuits, as he described their functions of distributing communion, preaching, and celebrating the liturgy in small villages of the Dominican Republic:

The bishops seem to prefer this kind of new priest. They will want to ordain them even if they are married. These men will not be seminarians who are ordained and after that marry. They will be ordinary people, married, who are religious leaders of their communities. Such a man will not be a priest for the general service of the church, but for his own community only.

Learn the problems of the people first, Alemán had advised, then provide a Christian answer. The need is for a community leader to keep his people in touch with God. New ministers appear to be doing that, in rural villages, in big-city slums. The "Christian answer" is indeed being provided, with outside help, to be sure, but mostly from the people themselves.

"Reverse Mission"

The third element of a U.S. mission program for Latin America—along with the continued sending of carefully selected, properly trained personnel, and material and spiritual support for the Latin American church—is known, somewhat clumsily, as "reverse mission." The designation might be unwieldy, but reverse mission offers an opportunity for all concerned North Americans, eventually, to take a direct role in working to improve conditions for their brothers and sisters in Latin America.

Exactly what is it? Father William McIntire's definition covers the major points succinctly:

For us, for me, reverse mission is our effort to communicate back here in the United States what we have learned from our missionary experiences and contacts overseas, with a particular interest in communicating and sharing ideas with those who support and sponsor our work, the U.S.

sending church from which we ourselves come, and the whole body of Christians in the United States. This includes insights we have learned on matters of a pastoral, religious, social, cultural, political, and economic nature. We also want to reach U.S. opinion leaders and policy makers.

Father Joseph Nangle described reverse mission in more informal terms:

This happens when persons who have followed the call to transcultural ministry return to work in their home country and church. The possibilities for this new phenomenon in missionary activity have yet to be appreciated, but they are incalculable. From personal experience I know that the years overseas make such an impact on the missionary that he or she comes back more a citizen of the world than of their particular nation-state and greatly sympathetic to the insights and aspirations of "foreigners." Once back, they can speak to the homeland in a very objective, even prophetic way.

How well will the homeland listen? If the homeland is the United States and the mission area is Latin America, not well at all. For a variety of reasons that trace their roots to colonial times, U.S. intellectual, cultural, commercial, and spiritual ties have been overwhelmingly directed to Europe. Its attention span in regard to Latin America has been brief indeed, a phenomenon which persists to this day. What little average North Americans think they know about Latin America is laced with Hollywood clichés of the forties, leaving them with a pop-culture montage: sleepy, unshaven bandits; steamy banana ports; mustachioed dictators; and dark-eyed senoritas on the beach at Copacabana—all of it accompanied by a thirty-year-old rhumba beat.

Worse, there seems to be little inclination to improve that discouraging situation, even among those who might be expected to do so. The editor of a leading American diocesan weekly, participating in the yearly critique of the output of NC News Service, had this recent comment: "Many stories from Latin America may be of some significance to a magazine, but in space-conscious Catholic papers which accent hard news, most of these sleep-producers go right into the wastebasket." Among Father John Reedy's recollections of his years as editor of the highly-respected *Ave Maria* magazine: "The easiest way to guarantee a few cancellations was to run another piece on Latin America."

Commonweal led off an editorial in 1977: "Someone once wrote that the American people would do anything for Latin America except read about it. That pretty much matches our experience here; when you talk about Latin America, you are talking into a dead mike." That particular editorial went on to make the point that the Panama Canal issue was a notable exception to the rule, the reason being—the editorial concluded—that it had a nostalgic appeal for those who wanted to recall fondly the days when the United States could do just about anything it pleased in Latin America.

Colonnese had another slant on the question, one with depressing overtones for what it says of our national state of mind. "We can get so exercised over the Panama Canal," he said. "Why can't the Catholic church muster that kind of interest in human rights? The problem is that we're so concerned with property here, and the Canal is an issue that involves property. Material things. What we need is a spirit of poverty."

It will be up to returning missioners to help to develop that spirit, to tell North Americans about the realities of Latin America, to let them know how they can work to improve the situation. Some observers see it, in fact, as the most significant aspect of the U.S. missionary presence in Latin America today. "Unless this can be understood," said Sister Marlene De Nardo, "I wouldn't favor us going on and on." She envisioned the long-range result of effective work in the reverse-mission field:

What might it mean to the Latin American church, to the poor and to the rest of the world, if, in our time, the Catholic church in North America began to say and to do things differently from the dominant American culture? What if it happened that all over the globe, people began to learn that within North America . . . a people existed, albeit a minority, who in words and action resisted all this in the name of Jesus Christ? What if Catholics in the United States threw off all symbols of neutrality and refused to celebrate or bless their own political economy which—in Camara's words—"holds in bondage and in hunger millions of children of God, both in poor countries and in the poverty pockets of their own country"?

Father Daniel Panchot, the exile from Chile, spoke along more specific lines, contending that the U.S. bishops must demonstrate the incompatibility between the Gospel message and the U.S. economic system—"with its competitiveness, individualism, materialism at home, and the constant support of repressive regimes abroad." More than making statements, Panchot continued, the bishops must take action; they must demonstrate their sincerity in the entire way they focus the church's apostolic work. "The bishops cannot remain silent while the rich become richer and the poor poorer. They have to feel the anguish of people who are so frustrated that they sometimes turn to terrorism . . . which in turn is self-defeating. But you cannot condemn this unless you do something to effectively change abusive social structures which give rise to terrorism in the first place."

Panchot wondered aloud how limited the church's prophetic vision might be when Catholic institutions have on their boards the same people who are on the boards of multinational corporations that have had such a repressive effect on Third World countries. North Americans must be jarred into realizing that

Christians should not accept this society's definition of success, he concluded, and a start would be for the hierarchy and clergy of this country to lower their own standards of living.

MacEoin wrote in 1977:

I now believe that the primary benefit [of the U.S. mission experience in Latin America] is to the missionary who—if he or she is sensitive—gets a new understanding of what it means to be a Christian; and his/her major mission is to make fellow Americans aware of our part in destroying the world.

Father McIntire recalled that the Conference of Major Superiors of Men's presentation, entitled "Awareness," at the Second Inter-American Conference of Religious at Bogotá in 1974, indicated that religious community missioners have a particular obligation in the area of reverse mission:

The meaning of the vows of poverty, chastity, and obedience is gutted unless they are lived in a community which corporately seeks to challenge the dehumanizing elements of our United States society and other societies—and which at the same time reinforces and supports the positive values which are still very much present in the United States people. . . . The way we live and work and pray should help us to speak out frankly, boldly, and prophetically in our own communities and in the public forum.

"Our wish in our reverse mission effort is also to evangelize and educate, and not just antagonize," McIntire said in another talk on the subject.

Finally, two respected Jesuits—Renato Poblete and José Alemán—have spoken in eloquent and specific terms of the need for the U.S. reverse mission from a Latin American viewpoint. Poblete referred to it as "a precious task." He said:

Not that those religious should merely describe mission work and solicit funds, but rather that they should make people see the reasons for our countries' helplessness, which to a large degree is often the result of unjust treatment given them by developed countries. The prosperity of many of the developed nations has been built on the exploitation of underdeveloped countries.

Alemán urged his Jesuit audience—and, by extension, other United States mission personnel—to wield what influence they could in a variety of fields, not only political, but also, for example, cultural, as he cited "the really unpleasant quality of some sick films, of commentators, of newspapers, of a magazine such as *Time*, which depict the United States as the summit of historical experience, with the implication that every other country in the world is underdeveloped." Economic influence is of major importance, Alemán continued. He contended that the United States has "reasonable" policies in its commercial dealings with Europe and Japan, in its support system for domestic fair prices. "But when it comes to the problem of the underdeveloped world, you forget this humane point of view of the economy, and you want to hear only about supply and demand." This hurts especially smaller, one-crop nations, he said, adding: "There is something you can do for Latin America in the United States. You can work for a just price for our goods."

Alemán suggested other fertile areas in which a returned missioner's testimony might be heard: on the questions of international credit and international development assistance, and, finally, in helping to reshape traditional U.S. attitudes toward the revolutionary movement.

Let a poor man say something against the government, and perhaps the next day he is killed. There is no justice in our countries. In the countries where I have lived there is no justice, absolutely no justice, and everyone knows it. You support this injustice by continuing to support the training of military people who, although they may be poor men themselves, continue to serve the interests of the worst elements of our society.

There are many things you can do in North America to help Latin America. If you could but study concretely, and not just in the general way in which I have outlined them to you, the mechanisms of oppression or injustice that exist in your relations with us in economics, politics, and the influence of your film industry and mass media on our culture! . . . And you see that all of these problems—economic, political, and social—reflect something in the North American culture that is, in the last analysis, basically un-Christian.

Much of the U.S. mission experience in Latin America over the past few decades has been negative, producing results that were negative as well—often disastrously so. But a great deal has been beneficial, particularly in the last few years, as much of the U.S. mission movement reset its attitudes and its methods in accordance with the teachings of the Second Vatican Council and the challenging documents of Medellín.

The new direction of the movement came about the hard way. It was earned only after sacrifice—in lost personnel, in frustration, in overwhelming efforts that often yielded little or nothing in the way of results. It continued, and it continues today, because there are enough North Americans who have learned to share and appreciate that compellingly beautiful observation of Cardinal Pironio: "God has special designs for Latin America. . . . It mirrors the face of the Savior in a particular way."

And so it will continue, with personnel, with financial help, with understanding, with efforts to proclaim the harsh truths about Latin American life here in the United States, so that some North Americans will do what they can to change policies for the better, to right wrongs. All of these efforts must be harmonized with—must take their direction from—those of the new Latin American church, that church of the people, still growing, still evolving, which promises so much not only for Latin America but for the rest of the world.

All of that bright promise, and all of the U.S. mission effort as well, is tragically darkened by today's political realities, by policies of oppression and torture and other injustices—sins, as we learned in catechisms long ago, that cry to heaven for vengeance. But the new church of Latin America has not buckled under for a moment; its eloquence on behalf of freedom and justice has given hope to Latin America's masses and inspiration to the rest of the world.

The U.S. church can be no less courageous in its response. "The question," said Maryknoll Father Thomas Peyton, director of peace and justice ministries for the National Federation of Priests' Councils, "becomes not just the survival of the persecuted churches in Latin America, but also the moral survival of the U.S. church as well."

How, finally, should the U.S. movement go forward? Here are three thoughts from Latin America that, with prayer, might provide the ultimate answers.

Father Alemán told his Jesuits:

If you want to change your society, the only way to do so is to forget yourselves a little and to work for others, either in the United States or in Latin America. That is the old Christian formula, is it not? To set out to help others, and then find that you have been changed, you have been converted.

Said Father Poblete:

Down through history God has proposed various forms of service to one's fellow man. . . . There isn't just one way, but God indicates how we should do it, speaking through external circumstances. It is not easy to foretell what new forms our service of man will take. But we may be sure that in Latin America, it will be especially along the line of his spiritual and material liberation—and this latter goal requires us to take a firm stand for justice.

And, at the funeral of Father Rutilio Grande, the Jesuit murdered in El Salvador in 1977, there were these words from the eulogy:

It is dangerous to be a true Catholic at this moment. By merely preaching the gospel, one becomes a subversive in the view of some groups. That is the way it should be.

Appendix I

Appeal of the Pontifical Commission to North American Superiors

Address of Monsignor Agostino Casaroli
August 17, 1961

It is indeed an honor and a privilege for me to bring you, distinguished members of this great assembly,[1] the cordial greetings, the thanks, and the good wishes of the Pontifical Commission for Latin America.

When the Holy See was informed that the Congress of the Major Religious Superiors of the United States was to consider the problems confronting the Church in Latin America as part of its program of studies and deliberations, Archbishop Samore, Vice-President of the Pontifical Commission and Secretary of the Sacred Congregation for Extraordinary Ecclesiastical Affairs, was designated to represent the Commission at this gathering and to speak to you of the struggles, of the desires, and of the hopes of the Church in those countries.

Undoubtedly Archbishop Samore was the person most qualified to accomplish this mandate, not only because of the prestige of his office in the Church, but particularly because of the deep knowledge he has of questions concerning all the facets and perspectives of the situation in Latin America where he spent three years as apostolic nuncio to Colombia. Moreover, Archbishop Samore also knows the great generosity and the resources of the Church in the United States where he spent some years at the apostolic delegation in Washington. But above all, his passionate and unstinting dedication to the cause of the Church in Latin America, which for many years has been one of the main concerns of his life, would have made him, perhaps, the best informed and most authoritative speaker at this convention on that subject.

Unfortunately, recent sorrowful events[2] have prevented him from being present here for a task that he considered as a mission to be accomplished for the Church itself.

Since I am not in a position to speak with his eloquence and his personal authority, I shall limit myself to submitting briefly for your consideration some objective facts and remarks. Their compelling eloquence together with the heart-rending appeals of the Popes in favor of Latin America will, I am confident, lead you to adopt positive resolutions such as the Holy See eagerly expects from this assembly and from the magnificent group of thousands of men and women religious you represent.

I. — OBJECTIVE FACTS

A. No one can remain indifferent

The appeal of the Holy See in favor of Latin America is fundamentally based on two considerations to which no true son of the Church, much less religious men and women, can remain indifferent.

First, that duty of *charity* by which the family, the Body, which constitutes the Catholic Church, feels as its own the problems and needs of each of its parts; all the more so when such needs and problems are more serious and the part of the Church affected by them is more important.

Second, the *interest*—in the highest and noblest sense of the word—of the entire Catholic Church, since weakness of or dangers to the Christian life in such an important sector of the Church, as undoubtedly Latin America is, represents for it a serious menace, while progress there represents a bright promise.

B. Concerning Latin America

Here are a few facts to support these two propositions:

1. Importance of Latin America

a) Numerical importance

The importance of Latin America to the Church; first of all, its numerical importance, since, with about one hundred and eighty million inhabitants, the overwhelming majority of them Catholic, Latin America represents about a third of world Catholicism in numbers. Moreover, the demographic increase of Latin America—noted, not always without alarm, by sociologists, economists, and political experts—together with the fact that children are traditionally baptized in the Church of their parents even if the latter are not practical churchgoers, would seem to indicate that such increase will augment proportionally in the future.

b) International influence

Secondly, an importance arising from the fact that the twenty nations of Latin America, frequently acting *en bloc*, exercise in international assemblies—which often treat of principles and questions of vital interest to the Church—a very considerable influence.

c) Richness of Catholicism

A third motive of importance is the richness of Latin-American Catholicism —although still rather potential than actual—both in quantity and quality, with the consequences deriving therefrom for the future development of Catholicism and its spread throughout the world.

2. Perilous elemental weaknesses

This sector of Catholicism—imposing as it is both in numbers and unity, in sincerity and solidity of sentiment, so heroic in times of persecution, so strongly resisting internal insufficiencies and dangers from without—yet suffers from perilous elemental weaknesses of structure.

Characteristically, these weaknesses are manifested and in a way summarized by the well-known lack of clergy, and indeed of all apostolic workers, in Latin America; a lack which is at the same time the cause and the result of the dangerous situation there, aggravated by the greater menace of the enemies of Catholicism in those countries. Such enemies and such menaces are particularly—as Pope Pius XII declared to the Second World Congress of the Apostolate of the Laity in October, 1957—"the inroads of Protestant sects; the secularization of the whole way of life; Marxism, the influence of which is felt in the universities and is very active, even dominant, in almost all labor organizations; and finally a disquieting practice of spiritism." This list, we might add, is only indicative.

3. Possible loss for the Church

Faced with this situation, and foreseeing its future developments, some people, pessimists who lack confidence in Divine Providence and the Church's supernatural resources and who very often are not objective in observing and judging things as they are in reality, even wonder whether in a few decades Latin America will still be a Catholic continent or if it will not rather be completely lost to the Church. The Holy See does not at all share such pessimistic views. On the other hand, the Holy See does not ignore the danger there might be, if opportune measures are not taken or if they are not taken sufficiently urgently.

The mere possibility that even part of a continent holding such an important place in the Church could be lost to her is more than enough motive to excite in her children, and particularly in you religious, that feeling of dutiful charity and interest mentioned above.

4. Luminous prospects

In contrast with these deprecable and deprecated possibilities, there shine forth the luminous prospects emphasized with such eloquence and paternal satisfaction by the Sovereign Pontiffs when speaking of Latin America; but always on condition that the necessary efforts and sacrifices be made now, with wise generosity and without delay.

a) Pope John XXIII

His Holiness Pope John XXIII, speaking on March 25, 1960, to the Fathers and Mothers General of institutes of perfection, asserted:

The future of the Church in the vast territories of Latin America appears rich in ineffable promise; and We nourish the firm conviction that Catholic spirit and life in those regions have in themselves sufficient strength to encourage the most optimistic hopes for the future. Those treasures of spiritual wealth so profusely bestowed there in the past, and yet more those which will be given with full hands in the future, will surely give rise to rich fruits of holiness and grace, to the greater joy of the Church of God.

b) Pope Pius XII

Earlier still, Pope Pius XII had affirmed with prophetic confidence:

We are confident that the benefits now received will later be rendered back a thousandfold. There will come the day when Latin America will be able to give back to the entire Church of Christ all that it has received; when, as We hope, it shall have put to use those ample and powerful energies which seem only to await the hands of the priest, that they may at once be employed for the honor and worship of God and the spread of Christ's kingdom on earth.[3]

C. Duties of the Church

Hence, the conclusions to be drawn from these considerations, which could and should be developed at greater length, are the following: first, the Church—that is, all of us who, with the Pope, the bishops and our brothers in the faith, constitute the Church—has the duty of collaboration so that not even a small part of that precious heritage of the Catholic religion which is Latin America should be lost; second, that the Church has the sacred duty of aiding those apostolic forces, mostly still latent in Latin-American Catholicism, to activate themselves, so that their strong support may be relied upon to engage with high hopes of success in the great adventure of the conquest of the world to the truth of the faith and to the beauties of Christian living.

II. — PRESENT CATHOLIC ACTION

What is the Church doing, what is the Holy See doing, in regard to the religious problem of Latin America? It would take too long to answer exhaustively or even summarily; a few indications are all we can give.

A. Insufficient means of Latin American Catholicism

First of all, it must be said that Latin-American Catholicism—bishops, clergy, religious and faithful—is resolutely working to break the vicious circle in which it seems to be imprisoned. Good results have been and are being obtained, admirable, praiseworthy, full of promise for the future.

We must also, with all fraternal charity, but also with necessary objectivity, add that the disproportion between the available means, especially of personnel, and the ever-growing gravity of the tasks to accomplish and the perils to avert is so great, that humanly speaking it would seem impossible, or at least extremely difficult, for Latin-American Catholicism to be able, unaided, to overcome this critical situation in time.

B. Twofold effort of the Holy See

The work of the Holy See then, especially in most recent times, has been exercised in a twofold effort: that of encouraging, aiding and promoting the initiative of the Latin-American hierarchy, clergy, religious institutes, and laity; and that of encouraging, requesting and discovering collaboration therein from other parts of the great Catholic family.

1. In Latin America

Regarding the first point, and apart from what concerns the single dioceses or nations, I shall only recall the convocation of a General Conference of the Latin-American Episcopate in Rio de Janeiro in the year 1955 in order to study the problem together and lay the bases for a vigorous collective effort; then the constitution in 1956 of a permanent office for contact and collaboration between the hierarchies of the various Latin-American countries, called the Latin-American Episcopal Council (CELAM), with its General Secretariat located in Bogota; and consequently the establishment of the Latin-American Religious Conference (CLAR) in 1958.

2. In other countries

Passing to the second point, and omitting for brevity's sake any reference to the collaboration furnished by Spain, Belgium, and other European countries, I shall recall only the meeting held in Washington, D.C. in November, 1959, between representatives of the hierarchies of the United States of America and Canada, and of Latin America, which prepared the foundations of a more intense and more closely organized apostolic co-operation of the two great North American nations in favor of those nations situated south of the Rio Grande.

C. Resources of North American Catholicism

As a matter of fact, the Holy See has very great confidence, as regards a concerted "Catholic action" in favor of Latin America, in the resources and the generosity of the Catholics of the United States and of Canada, that is to say, concretely, of the bishops, priests, and men and women religious. It is clear that, first of all and above all, this refers to resources of personnel, of men and women.

1. Special confidence in North American religious

In fact, this is the whole purpose of the presence among you of the Pontifical Commission for Latin America in my humble person; namely, to tell you how greatly the Holy See and the Pontifical Commission count upon the understanding and generosity of your religious institutes to aid Latin America; to urge you to respond heartily to its pressing appeal for this work, which the Holy See considers essential for the general interests of the Church; and, if necessary, to work together with you to prepare a plan of assistance according to the desires expressed by the Holy See.

Of course, the Holy See is quite well aware of all that American religious communities—with their approximately 2,700 members who are now in Latin America—are already doing in this sense. Their spirit of helpfulness and collaboration has been admirably proven, and the Holy See is sincerely and deeply grateful. But the need is felt to request yet more from your generosity, just as more is being asked also from the generosity of other parts of the Church in favor of Latin America.

2. Objections answered

Among the papers which Archbishop Samore had prepared for this meeting, I have found a reference to some possible objections, and I quote his own words in this regard:

a) Needs of one's own country

It may be objected: First, that just as numerous needs require your presence here in your own country. And I reply: This is true. You do great good here, and yet, in spite of your great numbers, there are not enough of you to meet the evergrowing exigencies of the modern apostolate. But it is also true that in comparison you are much more numerous in proportion to total Catholic population than your confreres in Latin America.

In the United States, for a total Catholic population of about 41,000,000 souls, you had in 1960 more than 21,000 religious priests, 10,000 religious brothers and 170,000 religious sisters.

Certainly, for the more or less 180 million of Catholics of Latin America—a total more than four times greater than yours—we are very far from your total number of more than 200,000 members of religious communities and institutes of perfection. You can see how great is the disproportion.

You, then, are rich, rich in personnel. And it is from you that personnel is sought, in the confidence that the Lord will reward you for the generosity with which you give, by sending you ever more numerous vocations. Indeed, I know of particular cases in which, after the acceptance by a particular congregation, for a supernatural motive and at the cost of no little sacrifice, of new fields of apostolic endeavor, their vocations were actually multiplied in a geometrical progression. Thus once more the word of the Gospel was verified: Give and it will be given to you, good measure, pressed down, shaken together and flowing over. . . . [4]

b) The call of other continents

Second, it may be objected that you are already answering the appeal made in favor of other continents. This too is true. And here too you deserve the highest admiration for what you are doing. Be sure I shall never say: Go to Latin America rather than to other countries; I should be guilty of a serious fault and would feel remorse for it. But I do venture to say: Go, even more than you do now, in even greater numbers, to Latin America, without diminishing your efforts and your contribution in favor of other parts of the earth.

These are the words of Archbishop Samore; and I believe they remain valid and convincing. And thus we may pass on to the third and last point to consider; namely, what aid does the Holy See expect for Latin America from the religious communities of men and women of the United States, over and above that assistance already being given.

III. — FUTURE PLANS

I spoke earlier of a "plan"—a popular word nowadays, but truly appropriate in our case. That which the Church feels it necessary to do for Latin America cannot be done through isolated and unco-ordinated efforts, no matter how numerous or immediately efficacious they might be. The field is so vast, the urgency so great, and the danger of being circumvented by enemy forces so real, that all such efforts must be added together, properly channeled, opportunely co-ordinated, and organically promoted. We could even speak of a real apostolic strategy, to assemble every possible means (which result always in less than those needed), so that none is lost, none underutilized; to determine the fundamental points of attack and defense; and to concentrate there a common effort so that, by God's grace, action may be prompt, timely, and effective.

We all recall that His Holiness Pope John XXIII, in his discourse to those attending the third meeting of the CELAM in Rome, spoke of the opportuneness of setting up a double program for Latin America: a long-term program to solve the basic problems; and an immediate short-term one. The basic solution would be that Latin America succeed in being self-sufficient for its own needs and, we may add, capable also of giving a full and valuable contribution towards the progress of the universal Church. The collaboration of outside forces should also be aimed towards this end; although immediate needs and exigencies must not be forgotten or neglected, nor yet be given precedence over the long-term basic solution.

A. Co-ordinating Offices

On its side, the Holy See saw to the establishment in 1958 of a "high command" for this effort; namely, the Pontifical Commission for Latin America, which has the duty of "studying in a unified way the fundamental problems of Catholic life in Latin America, and to promote the closest collaboration between the various Sacred Congregations and Offices interested in their solution."

1. Endeavors of the hierarchy

In their own respective spheres and ranks, the CELAM and CLAR have analogous purposes and aims. On its part, the hierarchy of the United States of America has set up in the National Catholic Welfare Conference a Latin America Bureau (LAB), with a dynamic and experienced director in the person of Father John J. Considine, M.M.

In order the better to co-ordinate the collaboration requested of your communities, it might appear opportune to instruct the Secretariats of your two Conferences [of major superiors] to act directly or in co-operation with this Latin America Bureau as the circumstances dictate.

In any case, the offices already set up—together with the Pontifical Representatives in the various countries—can doubtless favor the study and effective realization of an opportune plan. In particular, it becomes possible to co-ordinate the requests of the ordinaries of each single country, so that the Pontifical Commission for Latin America can consider and evaluate their priority of importance and urgency, and recommend them to those organizations or religious communities best able to cope with them.

2. Function of the major superiors' assembly

In order that such a plan be realistic, it is of course necessary to know and study, not only the requests presented, but also the means available to meet them. For this reason, the Pontifical Commission would be most grateful to this assembly if, on its part, it were to prepare at least the fundamental lines of a plan of its own. Such a plan should manifest approximately what means and personnel it will place at the disposal of the Holy See and the Pontifical Commission from the men and women religious of the United States of America.

B. Archbishop Samore's Ten-Year Plan

Archbishop Samore, in the name of the Pontifical Commission, intended to propose to you a great Ten-Year Plan of aid to Latin America, by means of personnel and of foundations, thus corresponding to the needs and requests already received and listed by the Latin America Bureau, and to those which will arrive later. The Archbishop's personal knowledge of the generosity of American religious communities, confirmed by their actual contribution in so many diverse fields, encouraged him to make this proposal, which I now submit to you in the name of the Pontifical Commission:

A Ten-Year Plan: for the decade of the 1960's, which may be decisive for the destiny of Latin America even in religious matters, with all the consequences for the Church either for good or evil. If an extraordinarily generous and wise effort is made within those ten years, we have every reason to expect that, with God's help, the battle will be won.

A Great Plan: great on the part of the Holy See, of Latin America, and of the Church in general. Great, so the Holy See hopes, in the contribution of the North American nations, so closely linked to those of Latin America. And great also on your part.

This, then, is an appeal to the magnanimity of your communities, and presupposes generosity, self-sacrifice, lofty ideas and great love, love for the Church of Christ, love for God.

The concrete content and scope of a plan is something you must be so kind as to study together among yourselves.

Certainly, immense progress would already be made if every community represented here were formally to undertake to make, especially during the next ten years, a truly generous contribution of personnel and foundations in favor of the Church in Latin America. Naturally this should be a contribution within the limits of each community's abilities, but also to the extent of your possibilities, measured in a great spirit of generosity, sacrifice, and love for the Church, and also measured against the requests presented in a plan organized and co-ordinated by the competent offices.

1. Requests presented

A plan such as this would comprise several divisions, just a few of which we may briefly review:

a) direct pastoral ministry, either in parishes, or in groups of parishes such as a deanery, or occasionally in entire ecclesiastical jurisdictions such as prelatures *nullius*, vicariates, and prefectures apostolic;

b) seminaries;

c) educational activities, particularly the foundation of American schools, which are so necessary and so strongly desired in Latin America, in a special manner in order to combat the perilous propaganda spread by such schools directed by Protestant sects;

d) catechetical activities;

e) charitable activities, health programs, social service.

This list is merely partial and indicative; but I feel that each of the communities represented here today can already see the part it could play therein, either to begin its apostolate in Latin America or to enlarge and intensify those works that several have already undertaken there.

2. Ten per cent of present membership

Is it worthwhile making more precise engagements? Is it opportune for each community to determine now a certain percentage of its personnel which will be set aside for the service of the Church in Latin America?

The judgment and the decision is left to you. However, interpreting the mind of the Pontifical Commission, I offer you an ideal toward which we request every religious province to strive. This ideal is the following, namely, that each religious province aim to contribute to Latin America in the next ten years a tithe—ten per cent—of its present membership as of this current year. For example, if the present membership is 500, the ideal would be to contribute by the end of this decade fifty members for Latin America.

Naturally, all will not be able to achieve this ideal. But it may be possible to reach at least ninety or eighty per cent of it.

3. Your best and most qualified vocations

For myself, I should like to add one further consideration: in no case, should personnel of what might be called inferior quality be set aside for this work. The Church's cause in Latin America requires that your communities make the sacrifice and have the generosity to devote to it some of the best and most qualified of the vocations sent to them by the Lord.

To you, and to the committee you will elect to consider and study this point of your program, let us leave the task of moving forward.

The saintly and fatherly Pastor, whom God has set over His Church in our day, when speaking to the superiors general of the institutes of perfection on March 25, 1960, said, "It is necessary that all those who wish to share in the apostolic anxiety of Our heart, should make every effort and every sacrifice to meet the expectations of that great continent, Latin America".

With that prayer, the Holy Father includes his gratitude and his benediction upon all those of his children who give a generous response.

Msgr. Agostino Casaroli

NOTES

1. This is the text of a speech delivered, August 17, 1961, by Msgr. Agostino Casaroli, at the Second Religious Congress of the United States, held at the University of Notre Dame, Indiana, August 16–19, 1961.

Msgr. Casaroli is *Minutante* of the Sacred Congregation for Extraordinary Ecclesiastical Affairs and substitute of His Excellency Archbishop Antonio Samore as representative of the Pontifical Commission for Latin America.

2. The death of His Eminence Domenico Cardinal Tardini, Secretary of State and Prefect of the Sacred Congregation for Extraordinary Ecclesiastical Affairs.

3. Pius XII, Apostolic Letter *Ad Ecclesiam Christi*, 1955.

4. See Luke 6, 38.

—

Appendix II

The Seamy Side of Charity

by Ivan Illich

(This article first appeared in America *magazine of January 21, 1967. It is reprinted here with permission of* America.*)*

Five years ago, U.S. Catholics undertook a peculiar alliance for the progress of the Latin American Church. By 1970, ten per cent of the more than 225,000 priests, brothers and sisters would volunteer to be shipped south of the border. In the meantime, the combined U.S. male and female "clergy" in South America has increased by only 1,622. Halfway is a good time to examine whether a program launched is still sailing on course and, more importantly, if its destination still seems worthwhile. Numerically, the program was certainly a flop. Should this be a source of disappointment or of relief?

The project relied on an impulse supported by uncritical imagination and sentimental judgment. A pointed finger and a "call for 20,000" convinced many that "Latin America needs YOU." Nobody dared state clearly why, though the first published propaganda included several references to the "Red danger" in four pages of text. The Latin America Bureau of the NCWC attached the word "papal" to the program, the volunteers and the call itself.

A campaign for more funds is now being proposed. This is the moment, therefore, at which the call for 20,000 persons and the need for millions of dollars should be re-examined. Both appeals must be submitted to a public debate among U.S. Catholics, from bishop to widow, since they are the ones asked to supply the personnel and pay the bill. Critical thinking must prevail. Fancy and colorful campaign slogans for another collection, with their appeal to emotion, will only cloud the real issues. Let us coldly examine the American Church's outburst of charitable frenzy which resulted in the creation of "papal" volunteers, student "mission crusades," the annual CICOP mass assemblies, numerous diocesan missions and new religious communities.

I will not focus on details. The above programs themselves continually study and revise minutiae. Rather, I dare to point out some fundamental facts and implications of the so-called papal plan—part of the many-faceted effort to keep Latin America within the ideologies of the West. Church policy makers in the United States must face up to the socio-political consequences involved in their well-intentioned missionary ventures. They must review their vocation as Christian theologians and their actions as Western politicians.

Men and money sent with missionary motivation carry a foreign Christian image, a foreign pastoral approach and a foreign political message. They also bear the mark of North American capitalism of the 1950's. Why not, for once, consider the shady side of charity: weigh the inevitable burdens foreign help imposes on the South American Church; taste the bitterness of the damage done by our sacrifices? If, for example, U.S. Catholics would simply turn from the dream of "ten per cent," and do some honest thinking about the implications of their help, the awakened awareness of intrinsic fallacies could lead to sober, meaningful generosity.

But let me be more precise. The unquestionable joys of giving and the fruits of receiving should be treated as two distinctly separate chapters. I propose to delineate *only the negative* results that foreign money, men and ideas produce in the South American Church, in order that the future U.S. program may be tailored accordingly.

During the past five years, the cost of operating the Church in Latin America has multiplied many times. There is no precedent for a similar rate of increase in Church expenses on a continental scale. Today, one Catholic university, mission society or radio chain may cost more to operate than the whole country's Church a decade ago. Most of the funds for this kind of growth came from outside and flowed from two types of sources. The first is the Church itself, which raised its income in three ways:

1. Dollar by dollar, appealing to the generosity of the faithful, as was done in Germany and the Low Countries by Adveniat, Misereor and Oostpriesterhulp. These contributions reach more than $25 million a year.

2. Through lump sums, made by individual churchmen—such as Cardinal Cushing, the outstanding example; or by institutions—such as the NCWC, transferring $1 million from the home missions to the Latin America Bureau.

3. By assigning priests, religious and laymen, all trained at considerable cost and often backed financially in their apostolic undertakings.

This kind of foreign generosity has enticed the Latin American Church into becoming a satellite to North Atlantic cultural phenomena and policy. Increased apostolic resources intensified the need for their continued flow and created islands of apostolic well-being, each day farther beyond the capacity of local support. The Latin American Church flowers anew by returning to what the Conquest stamped her: a colonial plant that blooms because of foreign cultivation. Instead of learning either how to get along with less money or close up shop, bishops are being trapped into needing more money now and bequeathing an institution impossible to run in the future. Education, the one type of investment that could give long-range returns, is conceived mostly as training for bureaucrats who will maintain the existing apparatus.

Recently, I saw an example of this in a large group of Latin American priests who had been sent to Europe for advanced degrees. In order to relate the Church to the world, nine-tenths of these men were studying teaching methods—catechetics, pastoral theology or canon law—and thereby not directly advancing their knowledge of either the Church or the world. Only a very few studied the Church in its history and sources, or the world as it is.

It is easy to come by big sums to build a new church in a jungle or a high school in a suburb, and then to staff the plants with new missioners. A patently irrelevant pastoral system is artificially and expensively sustained, while basic research for a new and vital one is considered an extravagant luxury. Scholarships for non-ecclesiastical humanist studies, seed money for imaginative pastoral experimentation, grants for documentation and research to make specific constructive criticism—all run the frightening risk of threatening our temporal structures, clerical plants and "good business" methods.

Even more surprising than churchly generosity for churchly concern is a second source of money. A decade ago, the Church was like an impoverished *grande dame* trying to keep up an imperial tradition of almsgiving from her reduced income. In the more than a century since Spain lost Latin America, the Church has steadily lost government grants, patron's gifts and, finally, the revenue from its former lands. According to the colonial concept of charity, the Church lost its power to help the poor. It came to be considered a historical relic, inevitably the ally of conservative politicians.

By 1966, almost the contrary seems true—at least, at first sight. The Church has become an agent trusted to run programs aimed at social change. It is committed enough to produce some results. But when it is threatened by real change, it withdraws rather than permit social awareness to spread like wildfire. The smothering of the Brazilian radio schools by a high Church authority is a good example.

Thus Church discipline assures the donor that his money does twice the job in the hands of a priest. It will not evaporate, nor will it be accepted for what it is: publicity for private enterprise and indoctrination to a way of life that the rich have chosen as suitable for the poor. The receiver inevitably gets the message: the "padre" stands on the side of W. R. Grace and Co., Esso, the Alliance for Progress, democratic government, the AFL-CIO and whatever is holy in the Western pantheon.

Opinion is divided, of course, on whether the Church went heavily into social projects because it could thus obtain funds "for the poor," or whether it went after the funds because it could thus contain Castroism and assure its institutional respectability. By becoming an "official" agency of one kind of progress, the Church ceases to speak for the underdog who is outside all agencies but who is in an ever-growing majority. By accepting the power to help, the Church necessarily must denounce a Camilo Torres, who symbolizes the power of renunciation. Money thus builds the Church a "pastoral" structure beyond its means and makes it a political power.

Superficial emotional involvement obscures rational thinking about American international "assistance." Healthy guilt feelings are repressed by a strangely motivated desire to "help" in Vietnam. Finally, our generation begins to cut through the rhetoric of patriotic "loyalty." We stumblingly recognize the perversity of our power politics and the destructive direction of our warped efforts to impose unilaterally "our way of life" on all. We have not yet begun to face the seamy side of clerical manpower involvement and the Church's complicity in stifling universal awakening too revolutionary to lie quietly within the "Great Society."

I know that there is no foreign priest or nun so shoddy in his work that through his stay in Latin America he has not enriched some life; and that there is no missioner so incompetent that through him Latin America has not made some small contribution to Europe and North America. But neither our admiration for conspicuous generosity, nor our fear of making bitter enemies out of lukewarm friends, must stop us from facing the facts. Missioners sent to Latin America can make 1) an alien Church more foreign, 2) an over-staffed Church priest-ridden and 3) bishops into abject beggars. Recent public discord has shattered the unanimity of the national consensus on Vietnam. I hope that public awareness of the repressive and corruptive elements contained in "official" ecclesiastical assistance programs will give rise to a real sense of guilt: guilt for having wasted the lives of young men and women dedicated to the task of evangelization in Latin America.

Massive, indiscriminate importation of clergy helps the ecclesiastical bureaucracy survive in its own colony, which every day becomes more foreign and comfortable. This immigration helps to transform the old-style hacienda of God (on which the people were only squatters) into the Lord's supermarket, with catechisms, liturgy and other means of grace heavily in stock. It makes contented consumers out of vegetating peasants, demanding clients out of former devotees. It lines the sacred pockets, providing refuge for men who are frightened by secular responsibility.

Churchgoers, accustomed to priests, novenas, books and culture from Spain (quite possibly to Franco's picture in the rectory), now meet a new type of executive, administrative and financial talent promoting a certain type of democracy as the Christian ideal. The people soon see that the Church is distant, alienated from them—an imported, specialized operation, financed from abroad, which speaks with a holy, because foreign, accent.

This foreign transfusion—and the hope for more—gave ecclesiastical pusillanimity a new lease on life, another chance to make the archaic and colonial system work. If North America and Europe send enough priests to fill the vacant parishes, there is no need to consider laymen—unpaid for part-time work—to fulfill most evangelical tasks; no need to re-examine the structure of the parish, the function of the priest, the Sunday obligation and clerical sermon; no need for exploring the use of the married diaconate, new forms of celebration of the Word and Eucharist and intimate familial celebrations of conversion to the gospel in the milieu of the home. The promise of more clergy is like a bewitching siren. It makes the chronic surplus of clergy in Latin America invisible and it makes it impossible to diagnose this surplus as the gravest illness of the Church. Today, this pessimistic evaluation is slightly altered by a courageous and imaginative few—non-Latins among them—who see, study and strive for true reform.

A large proportion of Latin American Church personnel are presently employed in private institutions that serve the middle and upper classes and frequently produce highly respectable profits; this on a continent where there is a desperate need for teachers, nurses and social workers in public institutions that serve the poor. A large part of the clergy are engaged in bureaucratic functions, usually related to peddling sacraments, sacramentals and superstitious "blessings." Most of them live in squalor. The Church, unable to use its personnel in pastorally meaningful tasks, cannot even support its priests and the 670 bishops who govern them. Theology is used to justify this system, canon law to administer it and foreign clergy to create a world-wide consensus on the necessity of its continuation.

A healthy sense of values empties the seminaries and the ranks of the clergy much more effectively than a lack of discipline and generosity. In fact, the new mood of well-being makes the ecclesiastical career more attractive to the self-seeker. Bishops then turn servile beggars, become tempted to organize safaris, and hunt out foreign priests and funds for constructing such anomalies as minor seminaries. As long as such expeditions succeed, it will be difficult, if not impossible, to take the emotionally harder road: to ask ourselves honestly if we need such game.

Exporting Church employees to Latin America masks a universal and unconscious fear of a new Church. North and South American authorities, differently motivated but equally fearful, become accomplices in maintaining a clerical and irrelevant

Church. Sacralizing employees and property, this Church becomes progressively more blind to the possibilities of sacralizing person and community.

It is hard to help by refusing to give alms. I remember once having stopped food distribution from sacristies in an area where there was great hunger. I still feel the sting of an accusing voice saying: "Sleep well for the rest of your life with dozens of children's deaths on your conscience." Even some doctors prefer aspirins to radical surgery. They feel no guilt having the patient die of cancer, but fear the risk of applying the knife. The courage needed today is that expressed by Daniel Berrigan, S.J., writing of Latin America: "I suggest we stop sending anyone or anything for three years and dig in and face our mistakes and find out how not to canonize them."

From six years' experience in training hundreds of foreign missioners assigned to Latin America, I know that real volunteers increasingly want to face the truth that puts their faith to the test. Superiors, who shift personnel by their administrative decisions but do not have to live with the ensuing deceptions, are emotionally handicapped facing these realities.

The U.S. Church must face the painful side of generosity: the burden that a life gratuitously offered imposes on the recipient. The men who go to Latin America must humbly accept the possibility that they are useless or even harmful, although they give all they have. They must accept the fact that a limping ecclesiastical assistance program uses them as palliatives to ease the pain of a cancerous structure, the only hope that the prescription will give the organism enough time and rest to initiate a spontaneous healing. Much more probably, the pharmacist's pill will both stop the patient from seeking a surgeon's advice and addict him to the drug.

Foreign missioners increasingly realize that they heeded a call to plug the holes in a sinking ship because the officers did not dare launch the life rafts. Unless this is clearly seen, men who obediently offer the best years of their lives will find themselves tricked into a useless struggle to keep a doomed liner afloat as it limps through uncharted seas.

We must acknowledge that missioners can be pawns in a world ideological struggle and that it is blasphemous to use the gospel to prop up any social or political system. When men and money are sent into a society within the framework of a program, they bring ideas that live after them. It has been pointed out, in the case of the Peace Corps, that the cultural mutation catalyzed by a small foreign group might be more effective than all the immediate services it renders. The same can be true of the North American missioner—close to home, having great means at his disposal, frequently on a short-term assignment—who moves into an area of intense U.S. cultural and economic colonization. He is part of this sphere of influence and, at times, intrigue. Through the U.S. missioner, the United States shadows and colors the public image of the Church. The influx of U.S. missioners coincides with the Alliance for Progress, Camelot and CIA projects and looks like a baptism of these! The Alliance appears directed by Christian justice and is not seen for what it is: a deception designed to maintain the status quo, albeit variously motivated. During the program's first five years, the net capital leaving Latin America has tripled. The program is too small to permit even the achievement of a threshold of sustained growth. It is a bone thrown to the dog, that he remain quiet in the backyard of the Americas.

Within these realities, the U.S. missioner tends to fulfill the traditional role of a colonial power's lackey chaplain. The dangers implicit in Church use of foreign money assume the proportion of caricature when this aid is administered by a "gringo" to keep the "underdeveloped" quiet. It is, of course, too much to ask of most Americans that they make sound, clear and outspoken criticisms of U.S. socio-political aggression in Latin America; even more difficult that they do so without the bitterness of the expatriate or the opportunism of the turncoat.

Groups of U.S. missioners cannot avoid projecting the image of "U.S. outposts." Only individual Americans mixed in with local men could avoid this distortion. The U.S. missioner of necessity is an "undercover" agent—albeit unconscious—for U.S. social and political consensus. But, consciously and purposely, he wishes to bring the values of his Church to South America; adaptation and selection seldom reach the level of questioning the values themselves.

The situation was not so ambiguous ten years ago, when in good conscience mission societies were channels for the flow of traditional U.S. Church hardware to Latin America. Everything from the Roman collar to parochial schools, from the CCD to Catholic universities, was considered salable merchandise in the new Latin American market. Not much salesmanship was needed to convince the Latin bishops to give the "Made in U.S.A." label a try.

In the meantime, however, the situation has changed considerably. The U.S. Church is shaking from the first findings of a scientific and massive self-evaluation. Not only methods and institutions, but also the ideologies that they imply, are subject to examination and attack. The self-confidence of the American ecclesiastical salesman is therefore shaky. We see the strange paradox of a man attempting to implant, in a really different culture, structures and programs that are now rejected in the country of their origin. (I recently heard of a Catholic grammar school being planned by U.S. personnel in a Central American city parish where there are already a dozen public schools.)

There is an opposite danger, too. Latin America can no longer tolerate being a haven for U.S. liberals who cannot make their point at home, an outlet for apostles too "apostolic" to find their vocation as competent professionals within their own community. The hardware salesman threatens to dump second-rate imitations of parishes, schools and catechisms—outmoded even in the United States—all around the continent. The traveling escapist threatens to further confuse a foreign world with his superficial protests, which were not viable even at home.

The American Church of the Vietnam generation finds it difficult to engage in foreign aid without exporting either its solutions or its problems. Both are prohibitive luxuries for developing nations. Mexicans, to avoid offending the sender, pay high duties for useless or unasked-for gifts sent them by well-meaning American friends. Gift-givers must think not of this moment and of this need, but in terms of a full generation, of the future effects. Gift-planners must ask if the global value of the gift in men, money and ideas is worth the price the recipient will ultimately have to pay for it. As Fr. Berrigan suggests, the rich and powerful can decide not to give; the poor can hardly refuse to accept. Since almsgiving conditions the beggar's mind, the Latin American bishops are not entirely at fault in asking for misdirected and harmful foreign aid. A large measure of the blame lies with the underdeveloped ecclesiology of U.S. clerics who direct the "sale" of American good intentions.

The U.S. Catholic wants to be involved in an ecclesiologically valid program, not in subsidiary political and social programs designed to influence the growth of developing nations according to anybody's social doctrine, be it even described as the Pope's. The heart of the discussion is therefore not *how* to send more men and money, but rather *why* they should be sent at all. The Church, in the meantime, is in no critical danger. We are tempted to shore up and salvage structures rather than question their purpose and truth. Hoping to glory in the works of our hands, we feel guilty, frustrated and angry when part of the building starts to crumble. Instead of believing in the Church, we frantically attempt to construct it according to our own cloudy cultural image. We want to build community, relying on techniques, and are blind to the latent desire for unity that is striving to express itself among men. In fear, we plan *our* Church with statistics, rather than trustingly search for it.

[MSGR. IVAN ILLICH is director of the Center of Inter-cultural Documentation (CIDOC), in Cuernavaca, Mexico, which for many years has been preparing missioners for work in Latin America.]

Chronology

Significant dates associated with the North American mission effort in Latin America.

1899	Convocation of Latin American bishops in Rome by Pope Leo XIII
1945	Meeting in Havana; delegates chosen by bishops of Pan-American nations
1953	First international Rural Life Conference, Manizales, Colombia
1955	First general conference of Latin American bishops, Rio de Janeiro
1956	Formal establishment of CELAM, the Latin American bishops' council
1956	Establishment of Bolivian mission by St. Louis archdiocese; first U.S. diocesan mission in Latin America
1957	Issuance of *Fidei Donum*, encyclical on missions, by Pope Pius XII
1957	Establishment of Society of St. James the Apostle by Cardinal Richard Cushing
1958	Establishment of Latin American Religious Conference (CLAR)
1958	Foundation by Pope Pius XII of Pontifical Commission for Latin America (CAL)
1958	Death of Pope Pius XII; election of Pope John XXIII
1959	Meeting at Georgetown University, Washington, D.C., of delegates from Latin America, Canada, and U.S. to formulate inter-American church program
1960	Establishment of Latin America Bureau, National Catholic Welfare Conference (NCWC); appointment of Father John Considine, M.M., as first director
1960	Formation of Papal Volunteers for Latin America (PAVLA)
1960	Election of John F. Kennedy as 35th U.S. president
1961	Incorporation of Center of Intercultural Formation (CIF); foundation of Center of Intercultural Documentation (CIDOC), training course for U.S. missioners to Latin America, at Cuernavaca, Mexico; Monsignor Ivan Illich named director
1961	Issuance of *Mater et Magistra*, encyclical on Christianity and social progress, by Pope John XXIII

1961	Address by Monsignor Agostino Casaroli to U.S. religious superiors at University of Notre Dame, asking that 10 percent of personnel be sent as missioners to Latin America
1961	Formation of Peace Corps by U.S. government
1962	Opening session of Second Vatican Council
1963	Issuance of *Pacem in Terris*, encyclical on peace, by Pope John XXIII
1963	Death of Pope John XXIII; election of Pope Paul VI
1963	Assassination of President Kennedy
1964	CICOP I (first meeting of Catholic Inter-American Cooperation Program, sponsored by Latin America Bureau, NCWC), Chicago; topic: "The Church in the New Latin America"
1964	Appointment of Father Raymond Kevane as director of PAVLA
1965	CICOP II, Chicago; topic: "The Church and Social Revolution in Latin America"
1965	Final session of Second Vatican Council; approval of major documents including *Gaudium et Spes* (Pastoral Constitution on the Church in the Modern World) and *Ad Gentes* (Decree on the Church's Missionary Activity)
1966	CICOP III, Chicago; topic: "Religious Values in a Changing Latin America"
1966	First official "Latin American Cooperation Week" in U.S. church, including national collection for Latin America
1967	CICOP IV, Boston; topic: "The Integration of Man and Society in Latin America: A Christian View"
1967	Publication in *America* magazine of "The Seamy Side of Charity," article by Monsignor Illich attacking U.S. mission program in Latin America
1967	Issuance of *Populorum Progressio*, encyclical on the development of peoples, by Pope Paul VI
1968	Presence in Latin America of 3,391 U.S. missioners (priests, sisters, brothers, lay men and women), representing peak figure of U.S. personnel
1968	CICOP V, St. Louis; topic: "Cultural Factors in Inter-American Relationships: Bond or Barrier?"
1968	Redesignation of Latin America Bureau as Division for Latin America, Department of International Affairs, U.S. Catholic Conference; consolidation of activities in Washington; retirement of Father Considine and appointment of Father Louis M. Colonese as successor
1968	Foundation of ONIS (National Office of Social Information) by priests in Peru; issuance of declaration against social injustice

1968   First plenary meeting of inter-American bishops, Detroit

1968   Second general conference of Latin American bishops, Medellín, Colombia; convocation by Pope Paul VI; adoption of conclusions stressing radical Christian approaches to problems of poverty and injustice; endorsement of techniques of conscientization, basic Christian communities, and liberation theology

1969   CICOP VI, New York; topic: "Human Rights and the Liberation of Man in the Americas"

1969   Resignation of Father Kevane as director of PAVLA

1970   CICOP VII, Washington; topic: "New Dimensions in Hemispheric Realities"

1971   CICOP VIII, Washington; topic: "Freedom and Unfreedom: A Theological Reflection on the Human Situation in the Americas"

1971   Inter-American meeting on mission program sponsored by Confederation of Latin American Religious, Mexico City

1971   Dissolution of PAVLA

1971   Dismissal of Father Colonnese as director, Division for Latin America; appointment of Father Frederick McGuire, C.M., as successor

1972   CICOP IX, Washington; topic: "Communications in the Americas"

1973   CICOP X, Dallas; topic: "Poverty, Environment, and Power: Issues of Justice in the Americas"

1973   Discontinuance of CICOP conferences

1974   Resignation of Father McGuire as director, Division for Latin America; creation of new Secretariat for Latin America, National Conference of Catholic Bishops, under USCC-NCCB reorganization; appointment of Frances L. Neason as executive director

1978   Deaths of Pope Paul VI and Pope John Paul I; election of Pope John Paul II

1979   Third general conference of Latin American bishops; Puebla, Mexico

Select Bibliography

Bigo, Pierre, S.J., *The Church and Third World Revolution*, Orbis, 1977
Bühlmann, Walbert, *The Coming of the Third Church*, Orbis, 1977
Colonnese, Louis M. (editor), *Conscientization for Liberation*, Division for Latin America, U.S. Catholic Conference, 1971
Comblin, José, *The Meaning of Mission*, Orbis, 1977
Considine, John J., M.M. (editor), *The Church in the New Latin America*, Fides, 1964
———, *The Religious Dimension in the New Latin America*, Fides, 1966
Cutler, John Henry, *Cardinal Cushing of Boston*, Hawthorn, 1970
De Broucker, José, *Dom Helder Camara*, Orbis, 1970
Dussel, Enrique, *History and the Theology of Liberation*, Orbis, 1976
Gray, Francine du Plessix, *Divine Disobedience*, Random, 1971
Gremillion, Joseph, *The Gospel of Peace and Justice*, Orbis, 1976
Gutiérrez, Gustavo, *A Theology of Liberation*, Orbis, 1973
MacEoin, Gary, *Agent for Change*, Orbis, 1973
———, *Latin America, The Eleventh Hour*, Kenedy, 1962
———, *Revolution Next Door*, Holt Rinehart Winston, 1971
Pironio, Eduardo, "Foreign Priests in Latin America," in *Between Honesty and Hope: Documents from and about the Church in Latin America*, Maryknoll Publications, 1970
Second General Conference of Latin American Bishops, *The Church in the Present-Day Transformation of Latin America in the Light of the Council* (The Medellín Conclusions), Division for Latin America, U.S. Catholic Conference, 1973
Segundo, Juan Luis, *The Hidden Motives of Pastoral Action: Latin American Reflections*, Orbis, 1978
Shapiro, Samuel (editor), *Integration of Man and Society in Latin America*, Notre Dame, 1967
Swomley, John M., Jr., *Liberation Ethics*, Macmillan, 1972
Yzermans, Vincent A., *The People I Love*, Liturgical Press, 1976

Index

297

Rowe, Sister Kathleen, S.C., 12
Ruiz García, Bishop Samuel, 159
Rural life conferences, 28

Sacred Congregation for Extraordinary Ecclesiastical Affairs, 44
Sacred Heart Seminary (Detroit, Mich.), 131
Saint Cloud (Minn.), diocese of, 73
Saint James Society, see Missionary Society of St. James the Apostle
Saint Joseph's College (Philadelphia, Pa.), 131
Saint Louis, archdiocese of, 74-76, 80, 132, 138, 212-213, 226, 264
    Latin America Apostolate of, 212
Saint Louis Review (newspaper), 74
Saint Louis University, 172
Saint Mary's College (Notre Dame, Ind.), 172
Saint Paul-Minneapolis, archdiocese of, 213
Samore, Cardinal Antonio, 1, 29, 33-35, 41-42, 44, 45-46, 47, 48, 52, 56, 104, 180
Samperio, Rev. Hector, 114
San Antonio (Tex.), archdiocese of, 81-82, 256
San Miguelito parish (Panama), 81, 155, 196, 224
San Salvador (El Salvador), 207, 208, 224
Sandheinrich, Msgr. Bernard H., 212
Sanschagrin, Bishop Albert, 70
Santa Ana, Dr. Julio de, 174
Santiago (Chile), 31, 113, 194
Santo Domingo (Dominican Republic), 252
Schierhoff, Bishop Andrew B., 74
Schlarman, Bishop Joseph, 28
Schmitz, Bishop Germán, 50, 55, 188, 204-205, 233
School Sisters of Notre Dame, 211
School Sisters of St. Francis, 57
Secretariat for Latin America (of National Conference of Catholic Bishops), 94, 172, 186, 247-248, 256
Segundo, Rev. Juan Luis, S.J., 145, 182
Select Committee on Intelligence (of U.S. Senate), 192-193, 203-204
Seper, Cardinal Franjo, 130
Serra International, 124, 145, 263
Servants of the Immaculate Heart of Mary, 29, 62-63, 211
Seton Hall University (South Orange, N.J.), 93
Shannon, James P., 112, 115
Sheen, Archbishop Fulton J., 6
"Shoeshine Priest, the," see Rev. John Halligan, S.J.
Shriver, Sargent, 94, 193
Sicuani (Peru), 198
"Signs of the Times," 148-149
Silva Henríquez, Cardinal Raúl, 115, 131, 194
Sioux City, diocese of, 91, 140
Sisters of Charity, 211

Sisters of Charity of St. Elizabeth, 7, 8-9, 12, 13, 16-17
Sisters of Mercy, 62
Sisters of Notre Dame, 66-67, 211
Sisters of Notre Dame de Namur, 211
Sisters of St. Francis, 243
Sisters of St. Joseph of Carondelet, 54, 61, 62, 72, 211
Sisters of the Holy Cross, 57
Sisters of the Most Precious Blood, 62, 211
Sisters of the Third Order of St. Dominic, 64, 211, 215
Smrekar, Janice, 101-102
Social Development and World Peace Department (of U.S. Catholic Conference), 256
Society of Jesus, 20, 29, 50, 65, 66, 127, 194, 210, 215, 252, 255, 267, 271, 272
Society of Mary, 29, 68
Society of St. James the Apostle, see Missionary Society of St. James the Apostle
Society for the Propagation of the Faith, 56, 77, 239, 250, 254
Spain, 19, 20, 21, 23, 235
Spellman, Cardinal Francis J., 28, 35, 51, 82, 105-106, 130
Spokane, diocese of, 79
Standard Oil of N.J., 196
Steed, Rev. Donald, M.M., 30-31
Steele, Rev. Harvey, 32, 191, 233
Stockman, Rev. Lawrence, 213
Stritch, Cardinal Samuel, 28
Sudan, 253
Suenens, Cardinal Leon-Joseph, 136
Sullivan, Rev. James, O.M.I., 65-66, 218, 219-220, 265
Survil, Rev. Bernard, 141, 207, 208-209, 217-218, 222, 224, 259
Sweeney, Msgr. Edward, 37-38, 77

Tanner, Bishop Paul F., 35, 42, 104, 106
Tardini, Cardinal Domenico, 34, 44
Theis, Rev. Gerard, O.S.A., 68, 71, 231-232, 239, 246, 255
Theology, 103, 117, 144-145, 150, 262
Theology of Liberation, 16, 143, 144-145, 149-150, 151-153, 161, 164, 177, 189, 207, 261-263
"The Seamy Side of Charity," 69, 122, 124-129, 192
Thorman, Donald J., 124
Tobin, Rev. Charles, 80, 163, 212-213, 222
Tobin, Sister Mary Luke, 114
Topel, Bishop Bernard, 79
Torrijos, Gen. Omar, 196
Travaglione, Rev. Fidelis Michael, O.F.M., 235
Treacy, Bishop John P., 79

Abbreviations

AID	Association for International Development (U.S. church)
	Agency for International Development (U.S. gov't.)
CAL	Pontifical Commission for Latin America (Vatican)
CARA	Center for Applied Research in the Apostolate (U.S.)
CCD	Confraternity of Christian Doctrine
CELAM	Consejo Episcopal Latinoamericano (Latin American Bishops' Council)
CFM	Christian Family Movement
CIA	Central Intelligence Agency (U.S.)
CICOP	Catholic Inter-American Cooperation Program
CIDOC	Center of Intercultural Documentation
CIF	Center of Intercultural Formation
CLAR	Confederation of Latin American Religious
CMSM	Conference of Major Superiors of Men (U.S.)
CMSW	Conference of Major Superiors of Women (changed in 1971 to Leadership Conference of Women Religious) (LCWR) (U.S.)
CODEL	Coordination in Development (U.S.)
LADOC	Latin America Documentation (of U.S. Catholic Conference)
MACC	Mexican-American Cultural Center (San Antonio, Tex.)
MEB	Movimento de Educação de Base (Basic Education Movement) (Brazil)
NC	National Catholic News Service (U.S. Catholic Conference)
NCCB	National Conference of Catholic Bishops (U.S.)
NCR	National Catholic Reporter
NCWC	National Catholic Welfare Conference (U.S.) (divided in 1966 into U.S. Catholic Conference and National Conference of Catholic Bishops)
ONIS	National Office of Social Information (Peru)
PAVLA	Papal Volunteers for Latin America (U.S.)
RNS	Religious News Service (of the U.S. National Conference of Christians and Jews)
USCC	United States Catholic Conference
YCS	Young Christian Students
YCW	Young Catholic Workers